MAUI REVEALED
The Ultimate Guidebook

4th Edition

Andrew Doughty

WIZARD
PUBLICATIONS
INC

MAUI REVEALED
The Ultimate Guidebook; 4th Edition

Published by Wizard Publications, Inc.
Post Office Box 991
Lihu'e, Hawai'i 96766–0991

ISBN 13: 978–0–9717279–9–1
ISBN 10: 0–9717279–9–6   4028
Library of Congress Control Number 2007928487
Printed in China

Cataloging–in–Publication Data

Doughty, Andrew
    Maui revealed : the ultimate guidebook / Andrew Doughty – 4th ed.
Lihue, HI : Wizard Publications, Inc., 2008.
    312 p. : col. illus., col. photos, col. maps ; 21 cm.
    Includes index.
    Summary : a complete traveler's reference to the Hawaiian island of Maui with full-color illustrations, maps, directions and candid advice by an author who resides in Hawaii.
    ISBN 13: 978-0-9717279-9-1
    ISBN 10: 0-9717279-9-6
    LCCN 2007928487
    1. Maui (Hawaii) – Guidebooks. 2. Maui (Hawaii) – Description and travel.
    I. Title.

DU 628   919.6921__dc21

All photographs (except the cover) taken by Andrew Doughty and Leona Boyd.
Cartography by Andrew Doughty and Margaret Goode.
All artwork and illustrations by Andrew Doughty and Lisa Pollak.

Cover imagery courtesy of NASA. The image has been enhanced and is copyrighted.

Pages 2–3: Honolua Bay, right side, taken from the cliffs above.

We welcome any comments, questions, criticisms or contributions you may have, and have incorporated some of your suggestions into this edition. Please send to the address above or e-mail us at **aloha@wizardpub.com**.

Check out our website at **www.wizardpub.com** for up-to-the-minute changes.

Dedicated to Leo Doughty, whose love of flight and adventure has left its mark, and who has always paid his dues in silence.

CONTENTS

CONTENTS

8

Maui is the undisputed playground of Hawai'i. No other island has the range of activities and scenery available to you here. There's almost nothing you can't do on Maui: hike in pristine rain forests, snorkel in an extinct crater, coast a bicycle 10,000 feet down a volcano, walk along miles of beaches, frolic under a waterfall, dive into a natural freshwater pool, lie on a black or even red sand beach, or sip a drink as the sun sets over nearby islands. Whatever fantasy you have, Maui is bound to deliver.

Most travel publishers send a writer or writers to a given location for a few weeks to become "experts" and to compile information for guidebooks. To our knowledge, we at Wizard Publications are the only ones who actually *live* our books.

We hike the trails, ride the boats, eat in the restaurants, explore the reefs and do the things we write about. It takes us one to two *years*, full time, to do a first edition book, and we visit places *anonymously*. We marvel at writers who can do it all in a couple weeks staying in a hotel. Wow, they must be *really* fast. Our method, though it takes much longer, gives us the ability to tell it like it is in a way no one else can. We put in many long hours, and doing all these activities is a burdensome grind. But we do it all for you—only for you. (Feel free to gag at this point.)

We have found many special places that people born and raised here didn't even know about because that's *all we do*—explore the island. Visitors will find the book as valuable as having a friend living on the island.

We recognize the effort people go through to visit Maui, and our goal is to expose you to as many options as possible so you can decide what you want to see and do. We took great pains to structure this book in such a way that it will

be fun, easy reading and loaded with useful information. This book is not a bland regurgitation of the facts arranged in textbook fashion. We feel strongly that guidebooks should present their information so that you don't have to look through every single page every time you want to find something.

If you are here on vacation, your time is extremely precious. You don't want to spend all your time flipping through a book looking for what you want. You need to be able to locate *what* you want, *when* you want it. You want to be able to access a comprehensive index, a thorough table of contents and refer to high-quality maps that were designed with you in mind. You want to know which helicopter, SCUBA, boat tour or lu'au is the best on the island. You want to find special hidden gems most people overlook. You want to be shown those things that will make this vacation the best of your life.

A quick look at this book will reveal features never before used in other guidebooks. Let's start with the maps. They are more detailed than any other maps you will find, and yet they omit extraneous information that can sometimes make a chore out of reading a map. We know that people in unfamiliar territory sometimes have a hard time determining where they are on a map, so we include landmarks. Most notable among these are mile markers. At every mile on main roads, the government has erected numbered markers to tell you where you are. We are the first to put these markers on a map so you can use them as reference points. In addition, we repeatedly drove or walked every inch of every road on the maps. This is important because many of the roads represented on existing maps have been shifted, moved or eliminated, making "current" maps obsolete. Where needed, we've drawn legal public beach access in yellow, so you'll *know* when you're legally entitled to cross someone's land. Most guidebooks have the infuriating habit of mentioning a particular place or sight but then fail to mention how to get there! You won't find that in our book. We tell you exactly how to find the hidden gems and use our own special maps to guide you.

One of the things unique to this book is the acceptance of change. We produce brand new editions of our books every two years, but during that time we are constantly incorporating changes into the text nearly every time we do a new printing. We also post many of these changes on our website. This allows us to make some modifications throughout the life of each edition. We don't have the luxury of making *every* change that happens on a weekly basis, but it does give us more flexibility than if we only acknowledged changes every two years.

As you read this book, you will also notice that we are very candid in assessing businesses. Unlike some other guidebooks that send out questionnaires asking a business if they are any good (gee, they *all* say they're good), we've had personal contact with the businesses listed in this book. One of the dirty little secrets about guidebook writers is that they sometimes make cozy little deals for good reviews. Well, you won't find that here. We accept no payment for our reviews, we make no deals with businesses for saying nice things, and there are no advertisements in our book. What we've seen and experienced is what you get. If we gush over a certain company, it comes from personal experience. If we rail against a business, it is for the same reason. All businesses mentioned in this book are here by *our* choosing. None have had any input into

what we say, and we have not received *a single cent* from any of them for their inclusion. (In fact, there are some that would probably pay to be left out, given our comments.) We always review businesses as anonymous visitors and only later as guidebook writers if we need more information. This ensures that we are treated the same as you. (Amazingly, most travel writers *announce* themselves.) What you get is our opinion on how they operate. Nothing more, nothing less.

Sometimes our candor gets us into trouble. More than once we've had our books pulled from shelves because our comments hit a little too close to home. And powerful local businesses that don't like our reviews and their friends in the media have stirred up lots of trouble for us on Maui. That's OK, because we don't work for the people who *sell* the book; we work for the people who *read* the book. It's also true that a handful of local residents have become upset because we've told readers about places that they'd rather keep for themselves. Ironically, it's usually not people born and raised here who have this selfish attitude, but rather the newcomers who have read about these places in our book, then adopted the *I'm here now— close the door* mentality.

Maui Revealed is intended to bring you independence in exploring Maui. We don't want to waste any of your precious time by giving you bad advice or bad directions. We want you to experience the best that the island has to offer. Our objective in writing this book is to give you the tools and information necessary to have the greatest Hawaiian experience possible.

We hope we succeeded.

Andrew Doughty

From the bottom of the ocean to their summits above the clouds, the Hawaiian Islands owe their existence to enormous volcanic and seismic pressures.

HOW IT BEGAN

Sometime around 70 million years ago an event of unimaginable violence occurred in the Earth's mantle, deep below the ocean floor. A hot spot of liquid rock blasted through the Pacific plate like a giant cutting torch, forcing liquid rock to the surface off the coast of Russia, forming the Emperor Seamounts. As the tectonic plate moved slowly over the hot spot, this torch cut a long scar along the plate, piling up mountains of rock, producing island after island. The oldest of these islands to have survived is Kure. Once a massive island with its own unique ecosystem, only its ghost remains in the form of a fringing coral reef, called an atoll.

As soon as the islands were born, a conspiracy of elements proceeded to dismantle them. Ocean waves unmercifully battered the fragile and fractured rock. Abundant rain, especially on the northeastern sides of the mountains, easily carved up the rock surface, seeking faults in the rock and forming rivers and streams. In forming these channels, the water carried away the rock and soil, robbing the islands of their very essence. Additionally, the weight of the islands ensured their doom. Lava flows on top of other lava, and the union of these flows is always weak. This lava also contains countless air pockets and is crisscrossed with hollow lava tubes, making it inherently unstable. As these massive amounts of rock accumulated, their bases were crushed under the weight of subsequent

After their long journey across the sea, the island's first life-forms found nothing but stark rock to greet them.

lava flows, causing their summits to sink back into the sea.

What we call the Hawaiian Islands are simply the latest creation from this island-making machine. Kauaʻi and Niʻihau are the oldest of the eight major islands. Lush and deeply eroded, the last of Kauaʻi's fires died with its volcano a million years ago. Oʻahu, Molokaʻi, Lanaʻi, Kahoʻolawe—their growing days are over as well. Maui is in its twilight days as a growing island. After growing vigorously, Hawaiian volcanoes usually go to sleep for a million years or so before sputtering back to life for one last fling. Maui's volcano, Haleakala, awakened from its long sleep and is in its final eruptive stage. It *probably* last erupted around 1790 (see box on page 135 for an explanation) and will continue with sporadic eruptions for a (geologically) short time before drifting into eternal sleep.

The latest and newest star in this chain is the Big Island of Hawaiʻi. Born less than a million years ago, this youngster is still vigorously growing. Though none of its five volcano mountains is considered truly dead, these days Mauna Loa and Kilauea are doing most of the work of making the Big Island bigger. Mauna Loa, the most massive mountain on Earth, consists of 10,000 *cubic miles* of rock. Quieter of the two active volcanoes, it last erupted in 1984. Kilauea is the most boisterous of the volcanoes and is the most active volcano on the planet. Kilauea's most recent eruption began in 1983 and was still going strong as we went to press. Up and coming onto the world stage is Loʻihi. This new volcano is still 3,200 feet below the ocean's surface, 20 miles off the southeastern coast of the island. Yet in a geologic heartbeat, the Hawaiian islands will be richer with its ascension, sometime in the next 100,000 years.

These virgin islands were barren at birth. Consisting only of volcanic rock, the first life forms to appreciate these new islands were marine creatures. Fish, mammals and microscopic animals discovered this new underwater haven and made homes for themselves. Coral polyps attached themselves to the lava and succeeding generations built upon these, creating what would become coral reefs.

Meanwhile, on land, seeds carried by the winds were struggling to colonize the rocky land, eking out a living and breaking down the lava rock. Storms brought the occasional bird, hopelessly blown off course. The lucky ones found the islands. The even luckier ones arrived with mates or were pregnant when they got here. Other animals, stranded on pieces of floating debris, washed ashore against all odds and went on to colonize the islands. These introductions of new species were rare events. It took an extraordinary set of circumstances for a new species to actually make it to the islands. Single specimens were destined to live out their lives in lonely solitude. On average, a new species was successfully deposited here only once every 20,000 years.

As with people, islands have a life cycle. After their violent birth, islands grow to their maximum size, get carved up by the elements, collapse in parts, and finally sink back into the sea. Someday, all the Hawaiian islands will be nothing more than geologic footnotes in the Earth's turbulent history. When a volcanic island is old, it is a sandy sliver called an atoll, devoid of mountains, merely a shadow of its former glory. When it's middle-aged, it can be a lush wonderland, a haven for anything green, like Kaua'i. And when it's young, it is dynamic and unpredictable, like the Big Island of Hawai'i, but lacking the scars of experience from its short battle with the elements. Maui is unique among the Hawaiian islands because it's in its prime—young enough to show the dynamism of its volcanic heritage, yet old enough for the elements to have carved lovely lines of character onto its face. The first people to occupy the island were blessed with riches beyond their wildest dreams.

Water and plants take turns converting lava into paradise.

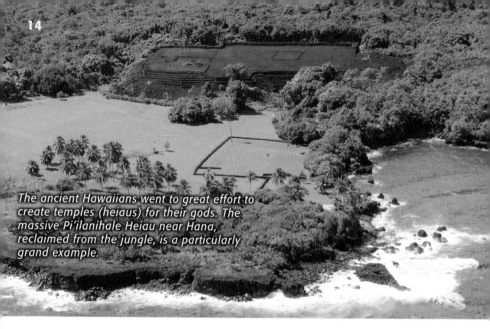

The ancient Hawaiians went to great effort to create temples (heiaus) for their gods. The massive Pi'ilanihale Heiau near Hana, reclaimed from the jungle, is a particularly grand example.

THE FIRST SETTLERS

Sometime around the fourth or fifth century A.D. a large, double-hulled voyaging canoe, held together with flexible sennit lashings and propelled by sails made of woven pandanus, slid onto the sand on the Big Island of Hawai'i. These first intrepid adventurers, only a few dozen or so, encountered an island chain of unimaginable beauty.

They had left their home in the Marquesas Islands, 2,500 miles away, for reasons we will never know. Some say it was because of war, overpopulation, drought or just a sense of adventure. Whatever their reasons, these initial settlers took a big chance and surely must have been highly motivated. They left their homes and searched for a new world to colonize. Doubtless most of the first groups perished at sea. The Hawaiian Islands are the most isolated island chain in the world, and there was no way for them to know that there were islands in these waters. (Though some speculate that they were led here by the golden plover—see facing page.)

Those settlers who did arrive brought with them food staples from home: taro, breadfruit, pigs, dogs and several types of fowl. This was a pivotal decision. These first settlers found a land that contained almost no edible plants. With no land mammals other than the Hawaiian bat, the first settlers subsisted on fish until their crops matured. From then on, they lived on fish and taro. Although we associate throw-net fishing with Hawai'i, this practice was introduced by Japanese immigrants much later. The ancient Hawaiians used fishhooks and spears, for the most part, or drove fish into a net already placed in the water. They also had domesticated animals, which were used as ritual foods or reserved for chiefs.

Little is known about the initial culture. Archeologists speculate that a second wave of colonists, probably from Tahiti, may have subdued these initial inhabitants around 1000 A.D. Some may have resisted and fled into the forest, creating the legend of the Menehune.

Today Menehune are always thought of as being small in stature. Initially referring to their social stature, the legend evolved to mean that they were physically short and lived in the woods away from the Hawaiians. (The Hawaiians avoided the woods when possible, fearing that they held evil spirits, and instead stayed on the coastal plains.) The Menehune were purported to build fabulous structures, always in one night. Their numbers were said to be vast, as many as 500,000. It is interesting to note that in a census taken of Kaua'i around 1800, some 65 people from a remote valley identified themselves as Menehune.

The second wave probably swept over the island from the south, pushing the first inhabitants ever north. On a tiny island north of Kaua'i archeologists have found carvings, clearly not Hawaiian, that closely resemble Marquesan carvings, probably left by the doomed exiles.

This second culture was far more aggressive and developed into a highly class-conscious culture. The society was governed by chiefs, called Ali'i, who established a long list of taboos called kapu. These kapu were designed to keep order, and the penalty for breaking one was usually death by strangulation, club or fire. If the violation was serious enough, the guilty party's family might also be killed. It was kapu, for instance, for your shadow to fall across the shadow of the Ali'i. It was kapu to interrupt the chief if he was speaking. It was kapu to prepare men's food in the same container used for women's food. It was kapu for women to eat pork or bananas. It was kapu for men and women to eat together. It was kapu not to observe the days designated for the gods. Certain areas were kapu for fishing if they became depleted, allowing the area to replenish itself.

While harsh by our standards today, this system kept the order. Most Ali'i were sensitive to the disturbance their

Hawai'i's First Tour Guide?

Given the remoteness of the Hawaiian Islands relative to the rest of Polynesia (or anywhere else for that matter), you'll be forgiven for wondering how the first set-

tlers found these islands in the first place. Many scientists think it might have been this little guy here. Called the kolea, or golden plover, this tiny bird flies over 2,500 miles nonstop to Alaska every year for the summer, returning to Hawai'i after mating. Some of these birds continue past Hawai'i and fly another 2,500 miles to Samoa and other South Pacific islands. The early Polynesians surely must have noticed this commute and concluded that there must be land in the

direction that the bird was heading. They never would have dreamed that the birds leaving the South Pacific were heading to a land 5,000 miles away and that Hawai'i was merely a stop in between, where the lazier birds wintered.

INTRODUCTION

Kalolopahu—Olowalu's Day of Infamy

There were numerous incidents in the first 20 years of western contact of Hawaiians killing westerners for weapons, and westerners killing Hawaiians for revenge or to demonstrate superiority. But no skirmish between Hawaiians and westerners compares to the massacre of Kalolopahu.

A dozen years after Captain Cook was killed on the Big Island, a trading ship run by a vicious, contemptible captain named Simon Metcalf stopped at the Big Island to trade goods. His ship was followed by a small six-man sloop carrying the captain's son. A chief tried to climb on board Metcalf's ship, and a crewman smacked him with a rope to prevent it. The chief was humiliated and vowed to take revenge on the next foreign vessel that came by. It was a vow that would change the destiny of the islands.

Metcalf then went to Maui and began trading. One night, north of Lahaina, a Hawaiian sneaked over to the ship, cut loose the ship's cutter, killed the guard in the boat, then dragged the small boat to shore to break it up. (The Hawaiians didn't care about the boat; they wanted the iron.) When Metcalf found out what happened, he fired his cannons into the village in rage, then kidnapped some Hawaiians who told him that people from Olowalu did it (which was true). Metcalf then moved his ship to Olowalu.

At this time, a high chieftess had declared the bay around Olowalu off limits. She was celebrating a family function, and the penalty for a commoner going into the water was to be burned alive. (Naturally, none violated the kapu.) When she finally lifted the order three days later, commoners rushed in their canoes to begin trading with the foreign ship (Metcalf's). Metcalf told all the Hawaiians to line their canoes up on one side of the ship. When they were crowded around, Metcalf unleashed his revenge. He opened fire with all his cannons (loaded with small shot) and muskets. More than 100 innocent Hawaiians were slaughtered (but not the one who had stolen the boat; he wasn't even there). The screaming and wailing went on for hours, and the natives named the place, Kalolopahu, meaning the place of spilt brains.

But remember the man who Metcalf's crew had smacked with a rope? He got his revenge, too, beyond his wildest dreams. He didn't know about the Olowalu massacre, but as fate would have it, that first foreign vessel he found was the one with Metcalf's son. The chief and some warriors went on board on the pretense of trade, then seized the sloop, killed young Metcalf and all but one of his crew, then stripped the boat of its weapons, including a cannon. And the one person from the sloop he let live, along with a man from the senior Metcalf's ship who King Kamehameha had captured earlier, soon became Kamehameha's trusted advisers. They helped Kamehameha defeat his island neighbors using the stolen cannon and guns, starting with the battle at 'Iao Valley described on page 65. Kamehameha eventually became king of all the islands.

As for Simon Metcalf, he was unable to find his son and eventually went back to the U.S. mainland. He had no idea that his presence had forever changed the politics of the islands.

presence caused and often ventured outside only at night, or a scout was sent ahead to warn people that an Ali'i was on his way. All commoners were required to pay tribute to the Ali'i in the form of food and other items. Human sacrifices were common and war among rival chiefs the norm.

By the 1700s, the Hawaiians had lost all contact with Tahiti, and the Tahitians had lost all memory of Hawai'i. Hawaiian canoes had evolved into fishing and inter-island canoes and were no longer capable of long ocean voyages. The Hawaiians had forgotten how to explore the world.

OUTSIDE WORLD DISCOVERS HAWAI'I

In January 1778 an event occurred that would forever change Hawai'i. Captain James Cook, who usually had a genius for predicting where to find islands, stumbled upon Hawai'i. He had not expected the islands to be here. He was on his way to Alaska on his third great voyage of discovery, this time to search for the Northwest Passage linking the Atlantic and Pacific oceans. Cook approached the shores of Waimea, Kaua'i, at night on January 19, 1778.

The next morning Kaua'i's inhabitants awoke to a wondrous sight and thought they were being visited by gods. Rushing aboard to greet their visitors, the Kauaians were fascinated by what they saw: pointy-headed beings (the British wore tricornered hats) breathing fire (smoking pipes) and possessing a death-dealing instrument identified as a water squirter (guns). The amount of iron on the ship was incredible. (They had seen iron before in the form of nails on driftwood but never knew where it originated.)

Cook left Kaua'i and briefly explored Ni'ihau before heading north for his mission on February 2, 1778. When Cook returned to the islands in November after failing to find the Northwest Passage, he visited the Big Island of Hawai'i.

The Hawaiians had probably seen white men before. Local legend indicates that strange white people washed ashore on the Big Island sometime around the 1520s and integrated into society. This coincides with Spanish records of two ships lost in this part of the world in 1528. But a few weird-looking stragglers couldn't compare to the arrival of Cook's great ships and instruments.

Despite some recent rewriting of history, all evidence indicates that Cook, unlike some other exploring sea captains of his era, was a thoroughly decent man. Individuals need to be evaluated in the context of their time. Cook knew that his mere presence would have a profound impact on the cultures he encountered, but he also knew that change for these cultures was inevitable, with or without him. He tried, unsuccessfully, to keep the men known to be infected with venereal diseases from mixing with local women, and he frequently flogged infected men who tried to sneak ashore at night. He was greatly distressed when a party he sent to Ni'ihau was forced to stay overnight due to high surf, knowing that his men might transmit diseases to the women (which they did).

Cook arrived on the Big Island at a time of much upheaval. The mo'i, or king, of the Big Island had been militarily spanked during an earlier attempt to invade Maui and was now looting and raising hell throughout the islands as retribution. Cook's arrival and his physical appearance (at 6-foot-4 he couldn't even stand up straight in his own quarters) almost guaranteed that the Hawaiians would think he was the god Lono. Lono was responsible for land fertility. Every year the ruling chiefs and their war god Ku went into abeyance, removing their power so that Lono could return to the land and make it fertile again, bringing back the spring rains. During this time all public works stopped, and the land was left alone. At the end of this *makahiki,* man would again seize the land from Lono so he could grow crops and otherwise make a living upon it. Cook arrived at the beginning of the makahiki, and the Hawaiians naturally thought *he* was the god Lono coming to make the land fertile. Cook even sailed into the exact bay where the legend predicted Lono would arrive.

The Hawaiians went to great lengths to please their "god." All manner of supplies were made available. Eventually they became suspicious of the visitors. If they were gods, why did they accept the Hawaiian women? And if they were gods, why did one of them die?

Cook left at the right time. The British had used up the Hawaiians' hospitality (not to mention their supplies). But shortly after leaving the Big Island, the ship broke a mast, making it necessary to return to Kealakekua Bay for repairs. As they sailed back into the bay, the Hawaiians were nowhere to be seen. A chief had declared the area kapu to help replenish it. When Cook finally found the Hawaiians, they were polite but wary. Why are you back? Didn't we please you enough already? What do you want now?

As repair of the mast went along, things began to get tense. Eventually the Hawaiians stole a British rowboat (for the nails), and the normally calm Cook blew his cork. On the morning of February 14, 1779, he went ashore to trick the chief into coming aboard his ship where he would detain him until the rowboat was returned. As Cook and the chief were heading to the water, the chief's wife begged the chief not to go.

By now tens of thousands of Hawaiians were crowding around Cook, and he ordered a retreat. A shot was heard from the other side of the bay, and someone shouted that the Englishmen had killed an important chief. A shielded warrior with a dagger came at Cook, who fired his pistol (loaded with small shot). The shield stopped the small shot, and the Hawaiians were emboldened. Other shots were fired. Standing in knee-deep water, Cook turned to call for a ceasefire and was struck in the head from behind with a club, then stabbed. Dozens of other Hawaiians pounced on him, stabbing his body repeatedly. The greatest explorer the world had ever known was dead at age 50 in a petty skirmish over a stolen rowboat.

KAMEHAMEHA THE GREAT

The most powerful and influential king in Hawaiian history lived during the time of Captain Cook and was born on the Big Island around 1758. Until his rule, the Hawaiian chain had never been ruled by a single person. He was the first to "unite" (i.e. conquer) all the islands.

Kamehameha was an extraordinary man by any standard. He possessed herculean strength, a brilliant mind and boundless ambition. He was marked for death before he was even born. When Kamehameha's mother was pregnant with him, she developed a strange and overpowering craving—she wanted to *eat* the eyeball of a chief. The king of the Big Island, mindful of the rumor that the unborn child's real father was his bitter enemy, the king of Maui, asked his advisers to interpret. Their conclusion was unanimous: The child would grow to be a

What rice is to Asians, taro is to Hawaiians—their most important food.

rebel, a killer of chiefs. The king decided that the child must die as soon as he was born, but the baby was instead whisked away to a remote valley to be raised.

In Hawaiian society, your role in life was governed by what class you were born into. The Hawaiians believed that breeding among family members produced superior offspring (except for the genetic misfortunes who were killed at birth), and the highest chiefs came from brother/sister combinations. Kamehameha was not of the highest class (his parents were merely cousins), so his future as a chief would not come easily.

As a young man Kamehameha was impressed by his experience with Captain Cook. He was among the small group that stayed overnight on Cook's ship during Cook's first pass of Maui. (Kamehameha was on Maui valiantly fighting a battle in which his side was getting badly whupped.) Kamehameha recognized that his world had forever changed, and he shrewdly used the knowledge and technology of westerners to his advantage.

Kamehameha participated in numerous battles. His side lost many of the early ones, but he learned from his mistakes and developed into a cunning tactician. When he finally consolidated his rule over the Big Island (by luring his enemy to be the inaugural sacrifice of a new temple), he fixed his sights on the entire chain. In the 1790s his large company of troops, armed with some western armaments and advisers, swept across Maui, Moloka'i, Lana'i and O'ahu. After some delays with the last of the holdouts, Kaua'i, their king finally acquiesced to the inevitable, and Kamehameha became the first ruler of all the islands. He spent his final years governing the islands peacefully from his Big Island capital and died in 1819.

MODERN HAWAI'I

During the 19th century, Hawai'i's character changed dramatically. Businessmen from all over the world came here to exploit Hawai'i's sandalwood, whales, land and people. Hawai'i's leaders, for their part, actively participated in these ventures and took a piece of much of the action for themselves. Workers were brought from many parts of the world, changing the racial makeup of the islands. Government corruption became the order of the day, and everyone seemed to be profiting, except the Hawaiian commoner. By the time Queen Lili'uokalani lost her throne to a group of American businessmen in 1893, Hawai'i had become direction-less. It barely resembled the Hawai'i Captain Cook had encountered the previous century. The kapu system had been abolished by the Hawaiians short-ly after the death of Kamehameha the Great. The "Great Mahele," begun in 1848, had changed the relationship Hawaiians had with the land. Large tracts of land were sold by the Hawaiian government to royalty, government officials, commoners and foreigners, effectively stripping many Hawaiians of land they had lived on for generations.

The United States recognized the Republic of Hawai'i in 1894 with Sanford Dole as its president. It was annexed in 1898 and became an official territory in 1900. During the 19th and 20th centuries, sugar established itself as king. Pineapple was also heavily grown in the islands, with the island of Lana'i purchased in its entirety for the purpose of growing pineapple.

As the 20th century rolled on, Hawaiian sugar and pineapple workers found themselves in a lofty position—they became the highest paid workers for these crops in the world. As land prices rose and competition from other parts of the world increased, sugar and pineapple became less and less profitable. Today, these crops no longer hold the position they once had. The "pineapple island" of Lana'i has shifted away from pineapple growing and is focused on tourism. The sugar industry is now dead on the Big Island and O'ahu, leaving only Maui and Kaua'i to grow it commercially.

The story of Hawai'i is not a story of good versus evil. Nearly everyone shares in the blame for what happened to the Hawaiian people and their culture. Westerners certainly saw Hawai'i as a potential bonanza and easily exploitable. They knew what buttons to push and pushed them well. But the Hawaiians, for their part, were in a state of flux. The mere existence of westerners seemed to bring to the surface a discontent, or at least a weakness, with their system that had been lingering just below the surface.

In fact, in 1794, a mere 16 years after first encountering westerners and under no military duress from the West, Kamehameha the Great volunteered to cede his island over to Great Britain. He was hungry for western arms so he could defeat his neighbor island opponents. He even declared that as of that day, they were no longer people of Hawai'i, but rather people of Britain. (Britain declined the offer.) And in 1819, immediately after the death of the strong-willed Kamehameha, the Hawaiians, on their own accord, overthrew their own religion, dumped the kapu system and denied their gods. This was before any western missionaries ever came to Hawai'i.

Nonetheless, Hawai'i today is once again seeking guidance from her heritage. The echoes of the past seem to be getting louder with time, rather than diminishing. Interest in the Hawaiian language and culture is at a level not seen in many decades. All of us who live here are very aware of the issues and the complexities involved, but there is little agreement about where it will lead. As a result, you will be exposed to a more "Hawaiian" Hawai'i than those who might have visited the state a decade ago. This is an interesting time in Hawai'i. Enjoy it as observers, and savor the flavor of the islands.

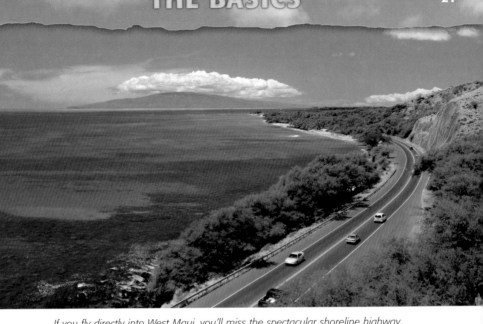

If you fly directly into West Maui, you'll miss the spectacular shoreline highway.

GETTING HERE

When planning your trip, a travel agent can be helpful. Their commission has been paid directly by the travel industry, though that may change in the future. The Internet has dot.com sites such as Orbitz, Expedia, Cheaptickets, Cheapair, Panda-online, Priceline, Travelocity, etc. If you don't want to or can't go through these sources, there are large wholesalers that can get you airfare, hotel and a rental car, often cheaper than you can get airfare on your own. The biggest one is **Pleasant Holidays** (800–742–9244), which provides complete package tours.

If you arrange airline tickets and hotel reservations yourself, you can often count on paying top dollar for each facet of your trip. The prices listed in the WHERE TO STAY chapter reflect the RACK rates, meaning the published rates before any discounts. Rates can be significantly lower if you go through a travel company.

When you pick your travel source, shop around—the differences can be dramatic. A diligent agent can make the difference between affording a *one-week* vacation and a *two-week* vacation. They don't all check the same sources for bargains; there is an art to it. Look in the Sunday travel section of your local newspaper—the bigger the paper, the better, or check online versions of major papers.

Though most visitors fly into Honolulu before arriving, there are some direct flights to Kahului. Not having to cool your heels while changing planes on O'ahu is a *big* plus since interisland flights aren't quite as convenient as they used to be. If you fly to Maui from Honolulu, the best views are *usually* on the left side (seats with an "A") coming in, and also the left side departing (for most routes). When flying to O'ahu from the mainland, sit on the left side coming in, the right going home.

Interisland flights are done by **Hawaiian** (800–367–5320 from the mainland; 800–882–8811 from the islands), **go!** (888–435–9462) and **Island Air** (800–652–6541). Flight attendants zip up and down the aisle hurling juice at you for the short interisland flights.

If you're staying in West Maui, it's tempting to look at a map and decide to fly into **Kapalua West Maui Airport** for the sake of convenience. Though it *is* nearby, we still recommend flying into Kahului. That's because the drive around the coastline into Lahaina during the day is dramatic and worth the extra time. It's during your drive along the coastline to either west or south Maui that you realize that this island, more than any other Hawaiian island, has an extremely intimate relationship with the water. No other Ha-waiian island has highways that embrace the ocean so much.

If you're staying in Hana, **Pacific Wings** (888–575–4546) has pricey flights to Hana Airport from Honolulu and Kahului.

WHAT TO BRING

This list may assist you in planning what to bring. Obviously you won't need everything on the list, but it might make you think of a few things you may otherwise overlook:

- Waterproof sunblock (SPF 15 or higher)
- Two bathing suits
- Shoes—flip-flops, trashable sneakers, reef shoes, hiking shoes
- Mask, snorkel and fins
- Camera with lots of film or a digital
- Warm clothes (for Haleakala trips) and junk clothes for bikes, etc.
- Light rain jacket
- Small flashlight for Haleakala sunrise
- Mosquito repellent for some hikes (*L otions*—not liquids—with DEET seem to work the longest)
- Large insulated water jug; keep in car
- Shorts and other cool cotton clothing
- Fanny pack—also called waist pack, to carry all your various vacation accouterments; waterproof ones are convenient for snorkeling
- Cheap, simple backpack—you don't need to go backpacking to use one; a 10-minute trek to a secluded waterfall is much easier if you bring a pack
- Hat or cap for sun protection

GETTING AROUND
Rental Cars

Rental car prices in Hawai'i *can be* (but aren't always) cheaper than almost anywhere else in the country, and the competition is ferocious. Nearly every visitor to Maui gets around in a rental car, and for good reason. Many of the island's best sights can only be reached if you have independent transportation.

At Kahului Airport, rental cars can be obtained from the booths to the right (as you look out) of baggage claim. It's a good idea to reserve your car in advance since companies can run out of cars during peak times. Cars are also available at the Kapalua and Hana airports.

On the Hana Highway, a roadside shrine, ensconced in a natural lava cave, utilizes flowers from nearby.

Many hotels, condos and rental agents offer excellent room/car packages. Find out from your hotel or travel agent if one is available.

Here's a list of rental car companies. The local area code is 808. Some have desks at various hotels.

The Big Guys

Alamo	(800) 327–9633
	Kahului: 871–6235
Avis	(800) 321–3712
	Kahului: 871–7575
	Kihei: 874–4077
	Kapalua: 661–4588
Budget	(800) 527–0700
	Locally: 871–8811
Dollar	(800) 800–4000
	Lahaina/Kahului/Hana:
	(866) 434–2226
Enterprise	(800) 736–8222
	Kahului: 871–1511
	Ka'anapali: 661–8804
Hertz	(800) 654–3131
	Kahului: 877–5167
	Lahaina: 661–7735
National	(800) 227–7368
	Kahului: 871–8851
	Ka'anapali: 667–9737
Thrifty	(800) 367–5238

The Little Guys

Kihei	(800) 251–5288
	Kihei: 879–7257
Maui Cruisers	(877) 749–7889
	Wailuku: 249–2319
Word of Mouth	(800) 533–5929
	Kahului: 877–2436
Bio-Beetle	(877) 873–6121
	Kahului: 873–6121
	(Rents bio-diesel cars)

4-Wheel Drive

On Kaua'i and especially the Big Island we've strongly recommended getting a 4WD vehicle, but it isn't as important on Maui. There aren't many off-road opportunities, and there are few places where access will require one. The drive past Hana doesn't require one, despite what you may read elsewhere. A few places in remote parts of West Maui will allow 4WDs to get *slightly* closer, but it's hard to justify the increased price here. Skip the 4WD. If you want to splurge, spring for a convertible instead. They can be fun, especially on the Hana drive.

Motorcycles & Scooters

If you think riding a HOG is something you do at a lu'au, you may want to skip this section. There's something about Harleys. Maybe it's the sound, or maybe the looks. But riding a Harley-Davidson around Maui is a blast. If you want to rent one to experience things on your own (freedom, after all, is what HOGs are all about), you can get them from Aloha Toy Store (662–0888) and Maui Harley-Davidson Rentals (667–2800) in Lahaina. Kanaka Metal Horse (875–4800) in Kihei rents custom bikes that appeared to be in fantastic shape. Expect to pay *(gulp!)* $130–$200 for 24 hours, about $100–$155 for 5–6 hours.

If you want to rent a scooter, try Aloha Toy Store (662–0888) in Lahaina and Island Riders (874–0311) in Kihei. Scooter rentals start at around $45 and you need a driver's license.

Exotic Cars

Maui has lots of opportunities to rent a flashy ride. Cars such as Vipers, 'Vettes, Porsches and other sexy autos can be had—for the right price. You're looking at $330–$1,500. That's *per day!* Half-day rates are available on some. Bear in mind that there are no opportunities to open them up—we have no wide open highway straightaways—but if you just want to experience the thrill of driving a

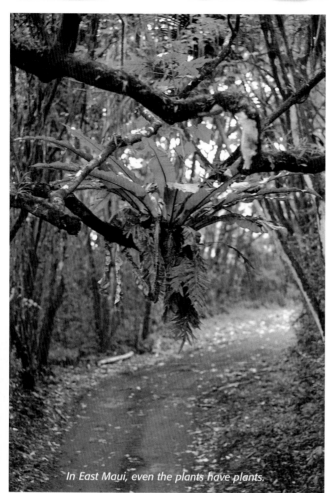

In East Maui, even the plants have plants.

mon police tactic on Maui.

It's best not to leave anything valuable in your car. There are teenagers here who pass the time by breaking into cars. It's not a *huge* problem, but it does happen. Thieving scum will work an area until the heat gets too hot, then move on to another area. When we park at a beach, waterfall or any other place frequented by visitors, we take all valuables with us, leave the windows up, and leave the doors unlocked. (Just in case someone is curious enough about the inside to smash a window.) There are plenty of stories about people walking 100 feet to a waterfall, coming back to their car and finding that their brand new video camera has walked away. And don't be gullible enough to think that trunks are safe. Someone who sees you put something in your trunk can probably get at it faster than you can with your key.

If you are between the ages of 21 and 25, **Maui Cruisers** and **Word of Mouth** don't charge you extra for the crime of being young and reckless. Enterprise charges $10 more per day, others tack on $25 and up. If you're under 21—rent a bicycle or scooter or take the bus.

fantasy car and you have a wad burning a hole in your pocket, give it a shot.

Aloha Toy Store (662–0888) in Lahaina lives up to its name with lots of grown-up car toys to rent.

A Few Driving Tips

Seat belt and **child restraint** use is required by law, and the police will pull you over for this alone. Open roads and frequently changing speed limits make it easy to accidentally speed here. Sobriety checkpoints are not an uncom-

Buses

Maui doesn't have a typical public bus system. Our version is called the **Maui**

Bus (871–4838), mainly used for shopping. Fare is $1–$3; call for schedules and routes.

GETTING MARRIED ON MAUI

Maui is a wildly popular place to get married. Every romantic setting from a beach at sunset, a tropical garden or a waterfall is here for you to use as a background for your important day.

Finding a good person or company to help you isn't easy and in this particular section, we can't review the companies the way we normally would. (After all, it's not exactly practical to get married 25 times and rate the performance of a company.) That said, we *can* say that one particularly reputable source for your wedding planning is **Pacific Island Weddings** at (888) 824–4134 or (808) 874–9899.

Other full-service wedding coordinators that are available to contact for their wedding packages are listed below. Discuss your arrangements in detail with the coordinator to avoid misunderstandings over what your ceremony will be like and what it will cost.

A Dream Wedding Maui Style
(800) 743–2777 or (808) 661–1777
Romantic Maui Weddings
(800) 808–4144 or (808) 249–8484
A Paradise Dream Wedding
(888) 304–7750 or (808) 875–9503

Almost all the large resorts on Maui have wedding coordinators to help you arrange your wedding at their hotels. Be aware that site fees can be pretty high. Some of the more popular resorts for weddings are the **Maui Prince**, the **Grand Wailea**, the **Hyatt**, the **Westin**, the **Hotel Hana Maui**, and the **Ritz-Carlton**.

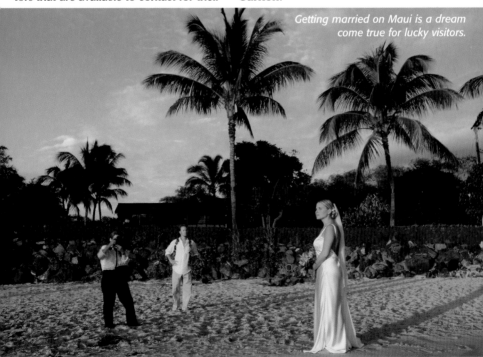

Getting married on Maui is a dream come true for lucky visitors.

Obtaining a License

Contact the State Department of Health (808) 984–8210 on Maui to obtain an application or to get the names of license agents on Maui. Both the bride and groom must be at least 18. No residency or blood tests are required. The fee is $60 in cash and it's good for 30 days. Both the bride and groom must be present with a photo ID at the time of the appointment with the marriage license agent.

WEATHER

How's the weather on Maui? A picture speaks a thousand words. The photo on the cover is very typical of the cloud and rain coverage on Maui and, to a practiced eye, tells you exactly what to expect around the island. You can see how the windward areas (meaning areas exposed to the trade winds out of the northeast) get most of the clouds and how Hana is dry, but farther uphill it's cloudy, feeding the waterfalls. Kihei and Lahaina (called *leeward* areas) are warmer, drier and sunnier than the rest of the island because they are shielded from the northeast trade winds. Notice how the clouds don't go all the way to the top of Haleakala except where they are squeezed into the Ko'olau Gap; it's because of a temperature inversion at the 6,000 foot level. (The air actually gets warmer above that for a few thousand feet, causing the temperature-sensitive clouds to dissipate.) The top of West Maui Mountain is cloudy, as usual. And you can see how the northeast trade winds build up along the bottom of Haleakala, heading southwest along the flank, and are directed off into the sea near La Pérouse Bay, leaving Kihei and Wailea calmer. You can see that because the line of demarcation between calm and choppy water makes the transition almost instant, and the line heads all the way to the island of Kaho'olawe and beyond. This photo is quintessential Maui trade wind weather until about 1 p.m. Then more clouds will build as the island heats up, causing the air to rise, cool and condense into clouds. The summit of Haleakala may cloud up. Winds will increase all around the island as ocean air rushes in to replace the rising air.

To get current weather forecasts, call 877–5111. Call 877–3611 for a surf forecast.

The Different Weather Regions

What does all this mean? It means the weather is radically different around the island. Many times we've been at the airport in Kahului and seen people coming off the plane looking gloomy and worried. "It's so windy and rainy here," they often say. Sometimes we wish the county would erect a sign at the airport saying, *"Don't worry, da weather mo betta in Kihei and Lahaina."*

In the leeward area of South Maui, Kihei and Wailea will be warmer and drier. Winds that have just been squished between the two mountains will travel south along the Kihei coast, veering slightly offshore, so winds will be lighter the farther you go down the Kihei coast until you get to La Pérouse Bay. There the fierce wind from the bottom of the island meets calm air, creating a distinct wind line over the span of about 100 feet. That means mornings are usually calm from Makena to south Kihei. In the afternoon, however, onshore breezes will form to fill the void from the heated rising air, and the trade winds that have been absent along the coast at Makena and Wailea will start wrapping around the island parallel to the coast here. This means strong afternoon winds. Winters are less windy. The sunnier and hotter it is, the stronger the afternoon winds will be. If there's heavy cloud cover over much of Haleakala, the afternoon winds will diminish. (We're trying to avoid

Rainfall Map

Arrows represent normal trade wind direction

Windward

Kapalua •

Ka'anapali •

haina •

Kahului •

Olowalu •

Ma'alaea •

360
320
280
240
200
160
120
100
80
60
40
30
20
16 Inches per year

Kihei •

Kula •

Hana •

Wailea •

Leeward

sounding like weather geeks, but if you understand the weather processes here, it helps you to plan your day.) High temperatures will average 80° in the winter, 86° in the summer. South Maui nights can be cooler than in Lahaina because the air that has built up atop Haleakala during the day will tumble down to the bottom. If your condo has a skylight, you may notice puffs of cool air coming down at night.

Rainfall in leeward areas is small and variable. For instance, one year there were only seven days with rain in Kihei. It was going to total 4¾ inches for the year until New Years Eve brought *another* 4¾ inches, doubling the year's rainfall tally. Other years have seen 20 or more inches of rain.

In **Lahaina**, **Ka'anapali** and **Kapalua**, the exact direction of the trade wind is crucial. Lahaina is usually protected from the trades. There are fewer afternoon breezes in Lahaina than Kihei, making it warmer. High temperatures are

82° in January and 88° in August and September. As you head toward Ka'anapali, at some point the trade winds that you've been protected from in Lahaina will complete their wrap-around from the other side, making wind a semi-constant companion. That's good if you like cool breezes, bad if you are trying to get a golf ball from Point A to Point B. It also means that the ocean is more susceptible to whitecaps and poor visibility north of Lahaina. **Kapalua**, farther north, is even windier, more drizzly and has the worst weather of any of the resort areas.

Just south of Lahaina, **Olowalu** would normally be protected from the trade winds except for one slight detail. Its large, rain-cut valley leading to the center of West Maui Mountain connects with rain-cut 'Iao Valley on the windward side, cracking the mountain in two and making a natural diversion ditch for the wind to rip through, leaving Olowalu windy.

Kahului gets a concentration of winds deflected along the northern part of Haleakala that slither around the island here and are squeezed between the two mountains. So it's *almost always* windy in Kahului. This has made Kahului one of the greatest places on the planet for windsurfing and kiteboarding. Big-time riders from all over the world make pilgrimages here.

Ma'alaea at the south end of the valley gets a concentration of wind and dust that has been squeezed between the mountains, making it one of the windiest places on the island.

Hana is sunnier than most people think since the clouds usually form farther uphill, but it is more vulnerable to whatever the trade winds bring to the island. Most of the time Hana has beautiful weather, but sometimes systems can bring rain that can last for days, especially in the winter. The temperature is incredibly equitable. Average high in February is 78°, and the average high in September is only 84°. How's *that* for a change of season?

The summit of **Haleakala** has an average high of around 50° and low of 32° in February and reaches a scorching 58° and a low of 38° in August. It's *usually* not as windy *after sunrise*, but any wind on a cold morning can cut right through you.

Upcountry areas, such as **Kula** and **Pukalani**, are cooler due to their elevation and less windy.

Maui is the only place we've ever seen where you can get waterfall fatigue. There are so many beautiful ones, like Wailua Falls here, that you start to take them for granted.

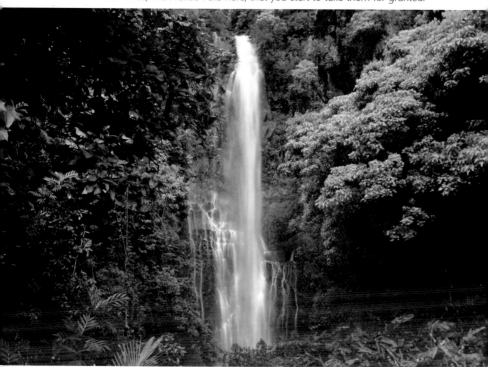

Average humidity around the island ranges from 65%–75%.

In general, windward areas like Hana and Kahului get most of their rain at night and in the early morning. Leeward areas like Kihei and Lahaina get their more sporadic rain in the late afternoon and early evening.

Ocean temperatures average 75° in February, 80° in September.

GEOGRAPHY

The island of Maui is made up of two large volcanoes called...well, that's a little confusing. The largest mountain, on the east side, is commonly referred to as Haleakala, meaning *house of the sun*. To the ancient Hawaiians, Haleakala referred only to a portion of the summit of the mountain, not the whole mountain. In fact, as far as we know, they had no name for either of the two large mountains that make up Maui. But the word Haleakala has been used so often in recent years to describe the entire mountain that it's now generally accepted. The other great mountain is topped by a small peak called Pu'u Kukui, or *hill of the candlenut tree*. A bit duller, huh? That name has never been used to describe the entire mountain, so it's commonly referred to by its less-than-exotic name, West Maui Mountain. Even scholarly geology books refer to them as Haleakala and West Maui Mountain. Annoyed at the western name, visitor bureaucrats are now pushing to refer to West Maui Mountain as Mauna Kahalawai, but that name was never accepted by Hawaiian linguists. We've also heard tour guides, such as boat captains, refer to West Maui as Halemahina, or *house of the moon*. Sounds so symmetric next to the *house of the sun*, but it's bogus.

West Maui is the oldest of the two. Streams have cut deeply into its slopes, and the results are lovely. Though you'd expect more erosion on the wet side, an accident of geology capped the wet side with more erosion-resistant lava, so big valleys aren't as prevalent as they normally would be.

Haleakala is the younger, still-active mountain. It's just over 10,000 feet high, but it wasn't always so. At one time it rose to 15,000 feet, making it the tallest mountain in the world at over 32,000 feet high (when measured from its base at the bottom of the ocean). But Haleakala is crushing itself under its own weight. Someday it will sink back into the sea. (But probably not before your trip here.) Its smoother slopes and 10,000-foot height hide an enormous volume of rock. The Hana side is a lush wonderland whose beauty is legendary. Kihei is in the dry rain shadow of the mountain, so there are few streams or eroded areas. The summit features the awesome Haleakala Crater. (Actually it's an erosion crater; see page 123.)

At one time, all the islands surrounding Maui formed one big island, which geologists called Maui Nui. (Meaning *Big Maui*—darned clever, those geologists.) In fact, if you'd visited here just 18,000 years ago, during a mini ice age that drastically lowered the sea level, you could have driven from Maui to Lana'i and on to Moloka'i. (Of course, finding a rental car might have been an issue.) As the volcanoes sank and the seas rose, the mountains separated, forming today's configuration. They continue to sink, and in about 15,000 years Maui will be two separate islands. We live in an era when Maui is perfectly arranged to easily explore the two sides. Enjoy our fortunate timing.

WHERE TO STAY

The vast majority of visitors to Maui stay on the leeward side of the island—

Lahaina to the Kapalua area in the west, or Kihei–Wailea in the south. This is the exact opposite of how things were 50 years ago. Back then all the major towns were on the windward side, where rain was abundant and crops grew vigorously. Few lived on the leeward side because it was harder to grow things there. (Lahaina has been around longer than most Hawaiian leeward towns because it was a good whaling port.) But the rain that makes everything so beautiful and lush also makes short-time visitors leery. So with the advent of jets and mass travel, the heretofore sparsely populated leeward sides of the islands became a magnet for travelers. Sure, the rain on the windward side makes things green, but it also means the ocean will have more runoff, the surf will be higher and clouds will obscure the sun. On the leeward side you don't have the tropical lushness you may associate with Hawai'i, but you usually have clear weather, calm oceans, sparkling water and lots of sunshine. (And, after all, you can always *drive* to the lush areas.)

It's hard to decide *which* leeward side of the island to stay on, West or South. West Maui has more activities because it has a working harbor, and it doesn't get as windy off Lahaina in the afternoon as it does off South Maui, though they get plenty of wind north of Lahaina. Activities such as submarine rides, Jet Skis and dinner cruises are common there, but helicopter flights are more convenient from South Maui. West Maui is more remote, making drives to Hana, Haleakala or Kahului much longer. Parking in Lahaina is a mess. Also, it's hotter in Lahaina than in Kihei or Wailea, though northwest Maui (i.e. Ka'anapali and Kapalua) gets lots of cooling wind. West Maui (Lahaina) has more nightlife. South Maui has better access to Molokini, and South Maui reefs

are better. West Maui has easier access to Lana'i and Moloka'i. Beaches are less crowded in South Maui, and its beach accesses don't fill up as often. Shopping is better in West Maui. West Maui's backdrop is more scenic, but it is also more densely developed. Food is better and more varied in West Maui, but South Maui has some of the most kickin' resorts. Golf is better in South Maui, and so is the diving and snorkeling. If you're traveling with kids, West Maui is more popular with families, though South Maui has two parks that are very kid-friendly. West Maui has more cheap condos, but gas and grocery prices seem higher in West Maui. Both sides are hugely popular, but West Maui has a busier and more crowded feel.

So which is better? After living here and spending countless hours exploring and experiencing both sides, in our professional opinion, we'd have to say…we don't know. Each has advantages and disadvantages that sway us back and forth. Consider the pros and cons listed above, and the answer may become obvious to you.

IS MAUI TOO EXPENSIVE?

Maui has a reputation of being pricey. That's because…well, it *is* pricey. The truth is restaurants cost more here than on the other islands. So do groceries and almost everything we can think of. Anyone who says otherwise hasn't lived on the different islands. Also, many of the activities available involve giving a company money to show you something, such as boat trips, SCUBA, aerial tours, lu'aus and more. So spending time on Maui is synonymous with spending money. Some activities, like helicopters, cost more here than on other Hawaiian islands, while others, like SCUBA diving, cost less.

This doesn't mean that Maui has to put you in hock for the next decade. There are *lots* of things to do that don't involve spending a fortune, and there are some tremendous values in restaurants—if you know where to look. Some of our favorite restaurants are some of the cheapest, and we point them out in DINING. The ACTIVITIES and ADVENTURES chapters have some delightful things that won't cost you a cent. Also, if you have a Costco membership or want to sign up for one, the Costco in Kahului near the airport is where most of us here buy lots of our groceries and other items. If you're here for a week or more, a Costco run can save you a bundle. Also consider the Wal-Mart and Kmart in Kahului, both on the map on page 66.

That said, count on spending some dollars on this trip. Some of the paid activities are definitely worth the splurge. Others are a rip-off, and we'll try to point them out.

HAZARDS
The Sun

The hazard that by far affects the most people (excluding the accommodations tax) is the sun. Maui, at 20° latitude, receives sunlight more directly than anywhere on the mainland. (The more overhead the sunlight is, the less atmosphere it filters through.) If you want to enjoy your *entire* vacation, make sure that you wear a strong sunblock. We recommend a waterproof sunblock with at least an SPF of 15. We use lotions when hiking, and the gel types like Bullfrog when going in the water (because they stay on better). Many visitors who get burned do so while snorkeling. You won't feel it coming because of the water. We *strongly* suggest you wear a T-shirt while snorkeling, or you may get a nasty surprise.

Try to avoid the sun between 11 a.m. and 2 p.m. when the sun's rays are particularly strong. If you are fair-skinned or unaccustomed to the sun and want to

soak up some rays, 15–20 minutes per side is all you should consider the first day. You can increase it a bit each day. *Beware of the fact that our breezes will hide the symptoms of a burn until it's too late.* You might find that trying to get your tan as golden as possible isn't worth it. Tropical suntans are notoriously short-lived, whereas you are sure to remember a bad burn far longer. If, after all our warnings, you *still* get burned, aloe vera gel works well to relieve the pain. Some come with lidocaine in them. Ask your hotel front desk if they have any aloe plants on the grounds. Peel the skin off a section and make several crisscross cuts in the meat, then rub the plant on your skin. *Oooo,* it'll feel so good!

Water Hazards

The most serious water hazard is the surf. Though more calm in the summer and on the leeward side, high surf can be found anywhere on the island at any time of the year. The sad fact is that more people drown in Hawai'i each year than anywhere else in the country. This isn't said to keep you from enjoying the ocean, but rather to instill in you a healthy respect for Hawaiian waters. See BEACHES for more information on this.

Ocean Critters

Hawaiian marine life, for the most part, is quite friendly. There are, however, a few notable exceptions. Below is a list of some critters that you should be aware of. This is not mentioned to frighten you out of the water. The odds are overwhelming that you won't have any trouble with any of the beasties listed below. But should you encounter one, this information should be of some help.

Sharks—Hawai'i does have sharks. Most are the essentially harmless white-tipped reef sharks, plus the occasional hammerhead or tiger shark. Contrary to what most people think, sharks are in every ocean and don't pose the level of danger people attribute to them. In the past 25 years there have been a few documented shark attacks off Maui, mostly tigers attacking surfers. But considering the number of people who swam in our waters during that time, you are statistically more likely to get mauled by a hungry timeshare salesman than be bitten by a shark. If you do happen to come upon a shark, however, swim away slowly. This kind of movement doesn't interest them. *Don't* splash about rapidly. By doing this you are imitating a fish in distress, and you don't want to do that. The one kind of water you want to avoid is murky water, such as that found in river mouths. Most shark attacks occur in murky water at dawn or dusk since sharks are basically cowards who like to sneak up on their prey. In general, don't go around worrying about sharks. *Any* animal can be threatening. (Even President Carter was once attacked by a wild rabbit.)

Portuguese Man-of-War—These are related to jellyfish but are unable to swim.

They are instead propelled by a small sail and are at the mercy of the wind. Though small, they are capable of inflicting a painful sting. This occurs when the long, trailing tentacles are touched, triggering hundreds of thousands of spring-loaded stingers, called nematocysts, which inject venom. The resulting burning sensation is usually very unpleasant but not fatal.

Fortunately, the Portuguese Man-of-War is not a common visitor to Maui. When they *do* come ashore, however, they usually do so in great numbers, jostled by a strong storm offshore, and usually land on north-facing beaches. If you see them on the beach, don't go in the water. If you do get stung, immediately remove the tentacles with a gloved hand, stick or whatever is handy. Rinse thoroughly with salt or fresh water to remove any adhering nematocysts. Then apply ice for pain control. If the condition worsens, see a doctor. The old treatments of vinegar or baking soda are no longer recommended. The folk cure is urine, but you might look pretty silly applying it.

Sea Urchins—These are like living pin cushions. If you step on one or accidentally grab one, remove as much of the spine as possible with tweezers. See a physician if necessary.

Coral—Coral skeletons are very sharp and, since the skeleton is overlaid by millions of living coral polyps, a scrape can leave proteinaceous matter in the wound, causing infection. This is why coral cuts are frustratingly slow to heal. Immediate cleaning and disinfecting of coral cuts should speed up healing time. We don't have fire coral around Maui.

Sea Anemones—Related to the jellyfish, these also have stingers and are usually found attached to rocks or coral. It's best not to touch them with your bare hands. Treatment for a sting is similar to that of a Portuguese Man-of-War.

Bugs

Though we're devoid of the myriad hideous buggies found in other parts of the world, there are a few evil critters brought here from elsewhere that you should know about. The worst are **centipedes**. They can get to be six or more inches long and are aggressive predators.

They shouldn't be messed with. You'll probably never see one, but if you get stung, even by a baby, the pain can range from a bad bee sting to a moderate gunshot blast. Some local doctors say the only cure is to stay drunk for three days. Others say to use meat tenderizer.

Cane spiders are big, dark and fast and they *look* horrifying, but they're not poisonous. (But they seem to *think* they are. I've had *them* chase *me* across the room when *I* had the broom in my hand.) We *don't* have no-see-ums, those irritating sand fleas common in the South Pacific and Caribbean.

Mosquitoes were unknown in the islands until the first stowaways arrived on Maui on the *Wellington* in 1826. Since then they have thrived. A good mosquito repellent containing DEET will come in handy, especially if you plan to go hiking. *Lotions* (not thin liquids) with DEET seem to work and stick best. Forget the guidebooks that tell you to take vitamin B12 to keep mosquitoes away; it just gives the little critters a healthier diet. If you find one dive-bombing you at night in your room, turn on your overhead fan to help keep them away. Local residents and resorts often rely on genetically engineered plants such as Citrosa, which irritate mosquitoes as much as they irritate us.

Bees and wasps are more common on the drier leeward sides of the island and in Haleakala Crater. Usually, the only way you'll get stung is if you run into one. If you rent a scooter, beware; I received my first bee sting while singing *Come Sail Away* on a motorcycle. A bee sting in the mouth can definitely ruin one of your precious vacation days.

Regarding cockroaches, there's good news and bad news. The bad news is that here, some are bigger than your thumb and can fly. The good news is that you probably won't see one. One of their predators is the gecko. This small, lizard-like creature makes a surprisingly loud chirp at night. They are cute and considered good luck in the Islands (probably 'cause they eat mosquitoes and roaches).

There are no snakes in Hawai'i (other than some reporters). There is concern that the brown tree snake *might* have made its way onto the islands from Guam. Although mostly harmless to humans, these snakes can spell extinction for native birds. Government officials aren't allowed to tell you this, but we will: If you ever see one anywhere in Hawai'i, please *kill it* and contact the Pest Hotline at 643–7378. At the very least, call them immediately. The entire bird population of Hawai'i will be grateful.

Swimming in Streams

Maui offers lots of opportunities to swim in streams and under waterfalls. It's the fulfillment of a fantasy for many people. But there are several hazards you need to know about.

Leptospirosis is a bacteria that is found in some of Hawai'i's fresh water. It is transmitted from animal urine and can enter the body through open cuts, eyes and by drinking. Around 100 people a year in Hawai'i are diagnosed with the bacteria, which is treated with antibiotics if caught relatively early. You should avoid swimming in streams if you have open cuts, and treat all water found in nature with treatment pills before drinking. (Many filters are ineffective for lepto.)

While swimming in freshwater streams, try to use your arms as much as possible. Kicking an unseen rock is easier than you think. Also, consider wearing reef shoes or, better yet, tabis, while in streams. (Tabis are a sort of fuzzy mitten for your feet that grab slippery rocks quite effectively. You can get them at Kmart in Kahului or any Longs Drugs.)

Though rare, **flash floods** can occur in any freshwater stream anywhere in the world, and it can happen when it's sunny where you are but raining up the mountain. Be alert for them.

Lastly, remember while lingering under waterfalls that not everything that comes over the top will be as soft as water. Rocks coming down from above could definitely shatter the moment—among other things.

Dehydration

Bring and drink lots of water when you are out and about, especially when you are hiking. Dehydration sneaks up on people. By the time you are thirsty, you're already dehydrated. It's a good idea to take an insulated water jug with you in the car or one of those 1½ liter bottles of water. Our weather is almost certainly different than what you left behind, and you will probably find yourself thirstier than usual. Just fill it before you leave in the morning and *suck 'em up* (as we say here) all day.

Sugar Harvesting

When a cane field is ready to harvest, they cut off water for several weeks, then set the whole field on fire. A mushroom cloud of smoke and ash rises into the air, then travels downwind to harass South Maui. Once the cane has been gathered, machines plow the fields along central Maui, where trade winds are strongest, and huge clouds of dust can fill the air, looking more like Los Angeles than Hawai'i. The result for South Maui visitors (and residents) can be poor quality air when certain fields end their two-year growing cycle. We don't want to overstate it. During the winter, harvesting is suspended, and during the rest of the year you may have days with no harvesting, but you can't *count* on it. The only remaining Maui sugar company,

HC&S, has 37,000 acres of sugar under cultivation, nearly all in the windswept valley between the two great mountains that make up Maui. Ironically, the same conglomerate that owns the sugar company (and the main shipping company to Hawai'i) also owns many of the resorts around the island. The resorts generate *far* more profit than sugar operations, but they still insist on burning the cane and filling the air with thousands of tons of smoke and dust. By the way, in case you're wondering where the county government is in all this, it's simple. They're in Wailuku—which is upwind of all the cane fires and dust storms. So as far as they're concerned, there's no problem.

Frogs

There are some irritating visitors that first arrived on Maui in the late '90s and won't leave. (Well, besides the in-laws.) They're small coqui tree frogs that emit a whistle all night long. Cute at first, like a bird. But incessant and ultimately irritating. Most of the resorts do their best to deal with them, but there's a chance that some errant froggies may occasionally give you a long night. West Maui seems to be slightly froggier (I *swear* that's a real word) than South Maui.

Traffic

Traffic can be a problem here. West Maui traffic between Lahaina and Kapalua is notoriously bad, especially at pau hana (quittin' time). Allow extra time during that part of the day. Road work also slows things down a great deal, and on Maui, road projects seem to be measured in decades rather than months or years. In South Maui, both South Kihei Road and Hwy 31 can be terrible during commute hours (and other times as well).

Grocery Stores

A decided hazard. Restaurants are expensive, but don't think you'll get off cheap in grocery stores. Though you'll certainly save money cooking your own food, a trip to the store here can be startling. Phrases like *they charge how much for milk?* echo throughout the stores. Even items such as pineapple—*grown a mile from the store!*—may cost more here than the ones jetted to you on the mainland. Go figure. West Maui stores seem to be the worst, but Kihei stores aren't much better. If you're stocking up, consider buying groceries at Kahului stores and at the Costco, Kmart and Wal-Mart there.

TRAVELING WITH CHILDREN (KEIKI)

Should we have put this under HAZARDS? It's been our observation that visitors with kids are far more numerous in West Maui than South Maui, perhaps because most of the Ka'anapali resorts have such good keiki infrastructure. If you want to stay in the south, the Grand Wailea seems the most keiki-friendly.

Baby's Away (875–9030) has the usual assortment of keiki paraphernalia for rent, such as car seats, strollers, cribs, bathtubs, etc. Wild Wheels Wentals (800–339–4743) has similar services (and a much cuter name).

Kalama Park in Kihei between Welakahao and Auhana on South Kihei Road has lots of lawn, a playground, a skateboard park, inline skating park, playground and a ball field. But stay out of the nasty water here. (See BEACHES on page 158.) The Fourth Marine Division Memorial Park has a vast playground that'll keep the kiddies entertained for hours. See Upcountry map on page 115.

Maui Golf and Sports Park (242–7818) has mini golf, bumper boats climbing wall and a trampoline. A bit packed but a worthwhile keiki diversion. In Ma'alaea next to Maui Ocean Center on Hwy 330 near Hwy 310.

The accommodation reviews describe the resorts with good keiki programs. By the way, if your objective was to get *away*

When the sugar's ready to harvest, they set gigantic fields of it ablaze. The smoke and dust wafting from sugar operations help keep Maui cleaning people happy and employed.

from the kids, then maybe these resorts won't be at the top of *your* list.

Hawai'i Nature Center (244–6500) has an interactive science arcade with lots of stuff to touch, wiggle and pull. Good for kids 3–8. Entrance is $6 for adults, $4 for kids. They also have a 2-hour rain forest walk for $30 ($20 for kids.)

Surfing Goat Dairy (878–2870) is a goat dairy farm where your kids will be able to milk other kids (the four-legged kind) for $12. See Upcountry map on page 115.

Kids who want to try something more involved than snorkeling may want to try SNUBA. See page 226.

Lastly, you should know that it's a big fine plus a mandatory safety class if your keiki isn't buckled up. And booster seats are required for kids under 8.

THE PEOPLE

There's no doubt about it—people really *are* friendlier in Hawai'i. You will notice that people are quick to smile and wave at you here. (Those of us who live in Hawai'i have to remember to pack our "mainland face" when we journey there. Otherwise, we get undesired responses when we smile or wave at complete strangers.) It probably comes down to a matter of happiness. People are happy here, and happy people are friendly people. Some people compare a trip to an outer island in Hawai'i to a trip back in time, when smiles weren't rare, and politeness was the order of the day. Maui has dominated the Condé Nast's Reader's Choice poll most years as the "Best Island In the World." The people are one reason.

Some Terms

A person of Hawaiian blood is Hawaiian. Only people of this race are called by this term. They are also called Kanaka Maoli, but only another Hawaiian can use this term. Anybody who was born here, regardless of race (except whites), is called a local. If you were born elsewhere but have lived here a while, you are called a kama'aina. If you are white, you are a haole. It doesn't matter if you have been here a day or your family has been here for over a century, you will always be a haole. The term comes from the time when westerners first encountered these islands. Its precise meaning has been lost, but it is thought to refer to people with no background (since westerners could not chant kanaenae—praise—of their ancestors).

The continental United States is called the Mainland. If you are here and are returning, you are not "going back to the states" (we *are* a state). When somebody leaves the island, they are off-island.

Hawaiian Time

One aspect of Hawaiian culture you may have heard of is Hawaiian Time. The stereotype is that everyone in Hawai'i moves just a little bit slower than on the mainland. Supposedly we are more laid-back and don't let things get to us as easily as people on the mainland. This is the stereotype...OK, it's *not* a stereotype. It's real. Hopefully, during your visit, you will notice that this feeling infects *you* as well. You may find yourself letting another driver cut in front of you in circumstances that would incur your wrath back home. You may find yourself willing to wait at a red light without feeling like you're going to explode. The whole reason for coming to Hawai'i is to experience beauty and a sense of peace, so let it happen. If someone else is moving a bit slower than you want, just go with it.

Shaka

One gesture you will see often and should not be offended by is the *shaka* sign. This is done by extending the pinkie and thumb while curling up the three middle fingers. Sometimes visitors think it is some kind of local gesture indicating *up yours* or some similarly unfriendly message. Actually it is a friendly act used as a sign of greeting, thanks or just to say, *Hey*. Its origin is thought to date back to the 1930s. A guard at the Kahuku Sugar Plantation on O'ahu used to patrol the plantation railroad to keep local kids from stealing cane from the slow-moving trains. This guard had lost his middle fingers in an accident and his manner of waving off the youths became well known. Kids began to warn other kids that he was around by waving their hands in a way that looked like the guard's, and the custom took off.

THE HAWAIIAN LANGUAGE

The Hawaiian language is a beautiful, gentle and melodic language that flows smoothly off the tongue. Just the sounds of the words conjure up trees gently blowing in the breeze and the sound of the surf. Most Polynesian languages share the same roots, and many have common words. Today, Hawaiian is spoken *as an everyday language* only on the privately-owned island of Ni'ihau. Visitors are often intimidated by Hawaiian. With a few ground rules you will come to realize that pronunciation is not as hard as you might think.

When missionaries discovered that the Hawaiians had no written language, they sat down and created an alphabet. This Hawaiian alphabet has only 12 letters. Five vowels: A, E, I, O and U, as well as seven consonants, H, K, L, M, N, P and W. The consonants are pronounced just as they are in English, with the exception of W. It is often pronounced as a V if it is in the middle of a word and comes after an E or I. Vowels are pronounced as follows:

A—pronounced as in *Ah* if stressed, or *above* if not stressed.

Maui Ocean Center's aquarium in Ma'alaea is a hit with kids—and us not-so-kids.

Ahh, August in the tropics. These poor slobs nearly froze to death watching the sunrise from atop Haleakala. Make sure you are prepared, or you won't thaw out for a week.

E—pronounced as in *say* if stressed, or *dent* if not stressed.
I—pronounced as in *bee.*
O—pronounced as in *no.*
U—pronounced as in *boo.*

If you examine long Hawaiian words, you will see that most have repeating syllables, making them easier to remember and pronounce.

One thing you will notice in this book are glottal stops. These are represented by an upside-down apostrophe ' and are meant to convey a hard stop in the pronunciation. So if we are talking about the type of lava called a'a, it is pronounced as two separate As—ah-ah.

Another feature you will encounter are diphthongs, where two letters glide together. They are ae, ai, ao, au, ei, eu, oi and ou. Unlike many English diphthongs, the second vowel is always pronounced. One word you will read in this book, referring to Hawaiian temples, is *heiau* (hey-ee-ow). The e and i flow together as a single sound, then the a and u flow together as a single sound. The ee sound binds the two sounds, making the whole word flow together.

Let's take a word that might seem impossible to pronounce. When you see how easy this word is, the rest will seem like a snap. The Hawai'i state fish is the humuhumunukunukuapua'a. At first glance it seems like a nightmare. But if you read the word slowly, it is pronounced just like it looks and isn't nearly as horrifying as it appears. Try it. Humu (hoo-moo) is pronounced twice. Nuku (noo-koo) is pronounced twice. A (ah) is pronounced once. Pu is pronounced once. A'a (ah-ah) is the ah sound pronounced twice, the glottal stop indicating a hard stop between sounds. Now, you can try to pronounce it again. Humuhumunukunukuapua'a. Now, wasn't that easy? OK, so it's not easy, but it's not impossible either.

Below are some words that you might hear during your visit:

'Aina (EYE-nah)—Land.

Akamai (ah-kah-MY)—Wise or shrewd.

Ali'i (ah-LEE-ee)—A Hawaiian chief; a member of the chiefly class.

Aloha (ah-LOW-ha)—Hello, goodbye, or a feeling or the spirit of love, affection or kindness.

Hala (hah-la)—Pandanus tree.

Hale (hah-leh)—House or building.

Hana (ha-nah)—Work.

Hana hou (ha-nah-HO)—To do again.

Haole (how-leh)—Originally foreigner, now means Caucasian.

Heiau (hey-ee-ow)—Hawaiian temple.

Hula (hoo-lah)—The story-telling dance of Hawai'i.

Imu (ee-moo)—An underground oven.

'Iniki (ee-nee-key)—Sharp and piercing wind (as in Hurricane 'Iniki).

Kahuna (kah-HOO-na)—A priest or minister; an expert in a profession.

Kai (kigh)—The sea.

Kalua (KAH-loo-ah)—Cooking food underground.

Kama'aina (kah-ma-EYE-na)—Long-time Hawai'i resident.

Kane (KAH-neh)—Boy or man.

Kapu (kah-poo)—Forbidden, taboo; keep out.

Keiki (kay-key)—Child or children.

Kokua (KOH-koo-ah)—Help.

Kona (koh-nah)—Leeward side of the island; wind blowing from the south, southwest direction.

Kuleana (koo-leh-ah-nah)—Concern, responsibility or jurisdiction.

Lanai (LAH-nigh)—Porch, veranda, patio.

Lani (lah-nee)—Sky or heaven.

Lei (lay)—Necklace of flowers, shells or feathers. The lokelani lei is the lei of Maui.

Liliko'i (lee-lee-koy)—Passion fruit.

Limu (lee-moo)—Edible seaweed.

Lomi (low-mee)—To rub or massage; lomi salmon is raw salmon rubbed with salt and spices.

Lu'au (LOO-ow)—Hawaiian feast; literally means taro leaves.

Mahalo (mah-hah-low)—Thank you.

Makai (mah-kigh)—Toward the sea.

Malihini (mah-lee-hee-nee)—A newcomer, visitor or guest.

Mauka (mow-ka)—Toward the mountain.

Moana (moh-ah-nah)—Ocean.

Mo'o (moh-oh)—Lizard.

Nani (nah-nee)—Beautiful, pretty.

Nui (new-ee)—Big, important, great.

'Ohana (oh-hah-nah)—Family.

'Okole (OH-koh-leh)—Derrière.

'Ono (oh-no)—Delicious, the best.

Pakalolo (pah-kah-low-low)—Marijuana.

Pali (pah-lee)—A cliff.

Paniolo (pah-nee-oh-low)—Hawaiian cowboy.

Pau (pow)—Finish, end; i.e. pau hana means quitting time from work.

Poi (poy)—Pounded kalo (taro) root that forms a paste.

Pono (poh-no)—Goodness, excellence, correct, proper.

Pua (poo-ah)—Flower.

Puka (poo-ka)—Hole.

Pupu (poo-poo)—Appetizer, snacks or finger food.

Wahine (vah-hee-neh)—Woman.

Wai (why)—Fresh water.

Wikiwiki (wee-kee-wee-kee)—To hurry up; very quick.

Quick Pidgin Lesson

Hawaiian pidgin is fun to listen to. It's like ear candy. It's colorful, rhythmic and sways in the wind. Below is a list of some of the words and phrases you might hear on your visit. It's tempting to read some of these and try to use them. If you do, the odds are you will simply look foolish. These words and phrases are used in certain ways and with certain inflections. People who have spent years living in the islands still feel uncomfortable using them.

Thick pidgin can be incomprehensible to the untrained ear (that's the idea). If you are someplace and hear two people engaged in a discussion in pidgin, stop and eavesdrop a bit. You won't forget it.

Pidgin Words & Phrases

An' den—And then? So?
Any kine—Anything; any kind.
Ass right—That's right.
Ass wy—That's why.
Beef—Fight.
Brah—Bruddah; friend; brother.
Brok' da mouf—Delicious.
Buggah—That's the one; it is difficult.
Bus laugh—To laugh out loud.
Bus nose—How one reacts to bad smell.
Chicken skin kine—Something that gives you goosebumps.
Choke—Plenty; lots.
Cockaroach—Steal; rip off.
Da kine—A noun or verb used in place of whatever the speaker wishes. Heard constantly.
Fo Days—Plenty; "He got hair fo days."
Geevum—Go for it! Give 'em hell!
Grind—To eat.
Grinds—Food.
Hold ass—A close call when driving your new car.
How you figga?—How do you figure that? It makes no sense.
Howzit?—How is it going? How are you? Also, Howzit o wot?
I owe you money or wot?—What to say when someone is staring at you.
Make house—Make yourself at home.
Make plate—Grab some food.
Mek ass—Make a fool of yourself.
Mo' bettah—This is better.
Moke—A large, tough local male. (Don't say it unless you *like beef*.)
No can—Cannot; I cannot do it.
No make li dat—Stop doing that.
No, yeah?—No, or is "no" correct?

'Okole squeezer—Something that suddenly frightens you ('okole means derrière).
O wot?—Or what?
Pau hana—Quit work. (A time of daily, intense celebration in the islands.)
Poi dog—A mutt.
Shahkbait—Shark bait, meaning pale untanned people.
Shaka—Great! All right!
Shredding—Riding a gnarly wave.
Sleepahs—Flip flops, thongs, zoris.
Stink eye—Dirty looks; facial expression denoting displeasure.
Suck rocks—Buzz off or pound sand.
Talk stink—Speak bad about somebody.
Talk story—Shooting the breeze; to rap.
Tanks eh?—Thank you.
Tita—A female moke. Same *beef* results.
Yeah?—Used at the end of sentences.

MUSIC

Hawaiian music is far more diverse than most people think. Many people picture Hawaiian music as someone twanging away on an 'ukulele with their voice slipping and sliding all over the place like they have an ice cube down their back. In reality, the music here can be outstanding. There is the melodic sound of the more traditional music. There are young local bands putting out modern music with a Hawaiian beat. There is even Hawaiian reggae. Hawaiian Style Band, the late Israel Kamakawiwo'ole (known locally as Bruddah Iz) and Willie K are excellent examples of the local sound. Even if you don't always agree with the all the messages in the songs, there's no denying the talent of these entertainers. If you get a chance, stop by **Borders Books** (877–6160) at the Maui Marketplace in Kahului. They have a good selection. **Request** (244–9315) in Wailuku on Market St. is a local music store with *pleny kine* music, new and used.

THE HULA

The hula evolved as a means of worship, later becoming a forum for telling a story with chants (called mele), hands and body movement. It can be fascinating to watch. When most people think of the hula, they picture a woman in a grass skirt swinging her hips to the beat of an 'ukulele. But in reality there are two types of hula. The modern hula, or hula 'auana, uses musical instruments and vocals to augment the dancer. It came about after westerners first encountered the Islands. Missionaries found the hula distasteful, and the old style was driven underground. The modern type came about as a form of entertainment and was practiced in places where missionaries had no influence. Ancient Hawaiians didn't even use grass skirts. They were brought later by Gilbert Islanders.

The old style of hula is called hula 'olapa or hula kahiko. It consists of chants and is accompanied only by percussion and takes years of training. It can be exciting to watch as performers work together in a synchronous harmony. Both men and women participate, with women's hula being softer (though no less disciplined) and men's hula being more active. This type of hula is physically demanding, requiring strong concentration. Keiki (children's) hula can be charming to watch, as well.

FARMERS' MARKETS

Maui isn't the best island for farmers' markets. In fact, you'll probably pass a few roadside fruit stands on your way to the market with deals just as good. We suggest shopping at the Central Maui markets for their abundant selection and convenient locations.

West Maui—In the Farmers' Market parking lot across from Honokowai Beach Park, Mon., Wed. and Fri. from 7 a.m. to 11 a.m.

Central Maui—Inside both the Queen Ka'ahumanu Shopping Center and the Maui Mall on Tues., Wed. and Fri. from 7 a.m. to 4 p.m.

Upcountry—At the Eddie Tam Center in Makawao on Makawao Ave. Saturday mornings from 6 a.m. to noon.

South Maui—In the ABC parking lot at the corner of Uwapo and South Kihei Rd. Mon.–Fri. 8 a.m. to 4 p.m.

BOOKS

There is an astonishing variety of books available about Hawai'i and Maui. Everything from history, legends, geology, children's stories and just plain ol' novels. **Borders Books** (877–6160) at the Maui Marketplace in Kahului has a dazzling selection. **Barnes & Noble** across from the Cannery Mall in Lahaina was under construction at press time. Walk in these stores and lose yourself in Hawai'i's richness.

THE INTERNET

Our website, **www.wizardpub.com** has recent changes, links to cool sites, the latest satellite weather shots, calendar of events and more. We also show our own aerial photos of most places to stay on Maui, so you'll know if oceanfront *really* means oceanfront. It has links to *every* company listed in the book that has a site—both those we like and those we don't recommend. For the record we don't charge a cent for links (it would be a conflict of interest), and there are *no advertisements* on the site. (Well...except for our own books, of course.) We've been asked why we don't list websites and e-mail addresses in the book. Linking from the site makes more sense. Nothing is more mind-numbing than seeing URL addresses in print.

If you're on-island and need Web access (to check your mail, etc.), most of the big resorts have business services available for around $20 an hour. **Blue Moon** (874–8600) in South Maui has free Wi-Fi, if you order food. **Livewire Café** in West Maui (661–4213) and **Morning Glories** in Pa'ia (579–3336) offer Internet services.

If you brought your own computer—then shame on you, you're on vacation. Nonetheless, **MauiNet** (875–2535) has dial-up service for visitors for $20/mo. with unlimited access; call them for details. **Lava.net** (888–545–5282) can arrange unlimited local Web access for $32 for a month. We also have a link to them on our website.

A NOTE ON PERSONAL RESPONSIBILITY

In past editions we've had the sad task of removing places that you can no longer visit. The reason, universally cited, is *liability*. Although Hawai'i has a statute indemnifying landowners, the mere threat is often enough to get something closed. Because we, more than any other publication, have exposed heretofore unknown attractions, we feel the need to pass this along.

You need to assess what kind of traveler you are. We've been accused of leaning a bit toward the adventurous side, so you should take that into account when deciding if something's right for you. To paraphrase from the movie *Top Gun*, "Don't let your ego write checks your body can't cash."

Please remember that this isn't Disneyland—it's nature. Mother Nature is hard, slippery, sharp and unpredictable. If you go exploring and get into trouble, whether it's your ego that's bruised or something more tangible, please remember that neither the state, the private land owner nor this publication *told* you to go.

You *chose* to explore, which is what life, and this book, are all about. And if you complain to or threaten someone controlling land, they'll rarely fix the problem you identified. They'll simply close it… and it will be gone for good.

Sometimes even good intentions can lead to disaster. At one adventure, a trailhead led hikers to the base of a wonderful waterfall. There was only *one* trail, to the left at the parking lot, that a person could take. Neither we, other guides nor websites ever said, "stay on the trail to the left" because at the time there was only one trail to take. The state (in their zeal to protect themselves from liability at an unmaintained trail) came along and put up a DANGER KEEP OUT sign at the trailhead. Travelers encountering the sign assumed they were on the wrong trail and started to beat a path to the right instead. But that direction started sloping downward and ended abruptly at a 150-foot-high cliff. Hikers retreated and in a short time a previously non-existent trail to the right became as prominent as the correct (and heretofore *only*) path to the left. Not long after the state's well-intentioned sign went up, an unwitting pair of hikers took the new incorrect trail to the right and fell to their deaths. They probably died because they had been dissuaded from taking the correct trail by a state sign theoretically erected to keep people safe.

Our point is that nothing is static and nothing can take the place of your own observations and good judgment. If you're doing one of the activities you read about in our book or someplace else and your instinct tells you something is wrong, *trust your judgment* and go do another activity. There are lots of wonderful things to do on the island, and we want to keep you safe and happy.

MISCELLANEOUS INFORMATION

Travelers' checks are usually accepted, but you should be aware that some merchants might look at you like you just tried to offer them Mongolian money. You should also know that Discover Cards seem to be less welcome here than other destinations. *Many* places will not accept them.

It is customary here for *everyone* to remove their shoes upon entering someone's house (sometimes their office).

If you are going to spend any time at the beach, woven bamboo beach mats can be found all over the island for about $2. Some roll up; some can be folded. The sand comes off these easier than it comes off towels.

If you're looking for a church to attend, the Saturday *Maui News* has complete listings and times.

Around the island you'll see signs saying VISITOR INFORMATION or something similar. Allow me to translate. That's usually code for WE WANT TO SELL YOU SOMETHING.

If you want to arrange a lei greeting for you or your honey when you disembark at Kahului Airport, **Ali'i Leis** (800) 575–4443 and **Greeters of Hawai'i** (800) 366–8559 can make the arrangements for around $20. Nice way to kick off a romantic trip, huh?

A WORD ABOUT DRIVING TOURS

Maui is split into geographic regions. We are well aware that for some regions, our chapter names such as SOUTH MAUI SIGHTS, aren't geographically accurate. Hey, don't blame us; we didn't invent these names. Other regions, like the "North Shore" are also strangely worded, since it's not where you'd think. It refers to the Hana Highway coastline, not the real north shore of the island. But this is how people here refer to the areas, so who are we to argue? The inside *front* cover shows how the tours are labeled.

Most main roads have mile markers erected every mile. Since Hawai'i is mostly devoid of other identification signs, these little green signs can be a big help in knowing where you are at a given time. Therefore, we have placed them on the maps represented as a number inside a small box 🔢. We will often describe a certain feature or unmarked road as being "⁴⁄₁₀ miles past the 22 mile mark." We hope this helps.

For directions, locals usually describe things as being on the **mauka** (MOW-kah) side of the road—toward the mountains—or **makai** (mah-KIGH)—toward the ocean.

Beaches, activities and adventures are mentioned briefly but are described in detail in their own chapters.

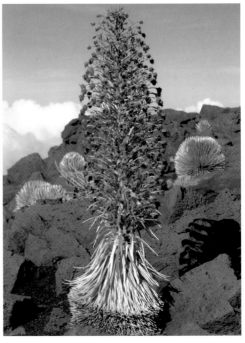

Found nowhere else in the world...Maui is home to many endemic species, such as this silversword.

Little known Olivine Pools are proof that there is still much to discover in West Maui.

West Maui—playground of the rich and famous? Those are the words that could have described this area hundreds of years ago, when Hawaiian royalty spent considerable time frolicking in West Maui waters and sampling its delights. Today, West Maui serves as a playground for the rest of us. Calm waters, some great beaches, limitless activities and an exciting, dynamic town: West Maui delivers on its legacy of fun.

Whether you're staying in West Maui or just passing through, there's only one road in and out—Hwy 30, which changes its name to Hwy 340 once you get past the populated areas. We'll describe it as most see it, coming from Central or South Maui going clockwise.

MA'ALAEA TO LAHAINA

Between the 7 and 8 mile markers you'll see a road on the left leading to Mc-Gregor Point and Lighthouse (actually a beacon). This is a good place to watch a sunset or look at whales during the season (mid-December through mid-May). Past the 8 mile marker is the more popular scenic lookout. In addition to a beautiful view of South Maui, it's a well-known whale-spotting place. In fact, there must be an underwater sign for the whales, because they seem to approach this area a lot. Maybe it's a scenic lookout for them, too, where they can come and observe us humans in our natural habitat. Morning and early afternoon bring more spottings, since the light winds produce less

West Maui

45

Slaughterhouse Beach
(Moluleʻia Bay)

Two-tiered
Tide-pools

Punalau
Beach

Light
Beacon

D.T. Fleming
Beach Park

Honolua
Bay

Pools

Nakalele
Blowhole

Makalua-puna Point
(Dragon's Teeth)

Oneloa Beach

Olivine
Pools

Short, paved, very
narrow one-lane section

Kapalua

Honokohau

37 38

33 34 35 36

39

40

41

42 16

14

Kahakuloa

Kapalua Beach
Napili Beach

32

31

Short, paved
narrowish
one-lane
section

Detail map
on page 53

30

Napili

15

13

12

Detail map
on page 51

29

Kahana

11 10

Kekaʻa
(North Beach)

28

Mahinahina

9

Kahekili
Beach Park

27

Honokowai

8 7

E. Poelua Rd

Waikalai Rd

Kahekili Hwy

6

Honokohau Stream

Black Rock
(Puʻu Kekaʻa)

26

25

30

5

Waiheʻe Valley

340

Kaʻanapali
Beach

24

Kaʻanapali

West Maui Mountains

330

Hanakaʻoʻo/
Canoe Beach

23

Puʻu Kukui
Summit
(5,788')

Honokohau Valley

1

Wahikuli
Wayside Park

22

2

Wailuku

Puʻunoa Beach
(Baby Beach)

21

Front St.

Lahaina

20

ʻIao
Valley

ʻIao
Needle

1

Puamana Park

19

2

Maui Tropical
Plantation

30

Carthaginian Shipwreck
20°50.931
156°40.210

18

Honoapiilani Hwy

Launiupoko
Park

Petroglyphs
20°49.163
156°37.092

Olowalu Valley

Ukumehame Valley

Kahili Golf
Course

3

16

15

14

Olowalu

4

380

13

12

Lahaina Pali Trail

5

Maʻalaea

310

Ukumehame
Park

11

Papalaua
Wayside Park

10

Pali

9 8

6

McGregor Pt.
& Light Beacon

Tunnel

Scenic
Lookout

0   5 MILES

N
W   E
S

11 Roadside mile markers
Unpaved Roads
Foot Trails

Central Maui / Wailuku & Kahului map on page 66

Kihei map on page 129

From the shoreline highway, it's easy to pull off the road and lose yourself in an idyllic setting.

still visible in places, such as near the tunnel. It's possible to awkwardly scramble up to the old road and walk along it (if you're so inclined). You get an idea of how something as "permanent" as a road can be quickly consumed by nature, even on this dry side of the island. This part of West Maui is called the **Pali** (cliffs) and soon gives way to a shoreline highway.

In ancient times there was a legendary female robber named Kaiaupe. She would lure men to get friendly with her at the edge of the pali, then kick them over the cliff and rifle their body for valuables (a practice that was named Ka-ai-a-Kaiaupe in her honor). So if you see a woman hitchhiker with a big *K* embroidered on her clothes...you might want to pass.

Descending to sea level, you'll find yourself constantly stealing glances toward the water. Views up the mountain are also

choppy seas, making the behemoths easier to spot.

Less known is the good snorkeling and diving below the lookout. See BEACHES on page 157 for more.

Highway 30 is a modern, two-lane highway. In the old days (which anthropologists define as any time before TVs had remote controls) there was a narrow, winding road along West Maui. Parts are

scrumptious, and you'll probably want to pull over around the 13 mile marker and take them in.

At the 14 mile marker you'll see lots of cars. This area is listed in virtually all visitor information as having some of the best snorkeling on the island. Don't waste your time. That's *way* out of date. Runoff (perhaps from the old sugar operations) has created cloudy water with terrible visibility. Farther offshore it's good, but the shoreline snorkeling usually stinks. See BEACHES for more.

At the 15 mile marker is the pea-sized town of Olowalu, the site of the massacre described on page 16. It's also here that you'll find Maui's best petroglyphs. (See map on page 45.) In an era before pen and paper, the best way to record your thoughts was to scratch them on lava rock. At this site, pre- and post-contact Hawaiians left their artistic impressions in the smooth lava. (These have been augmented recently by mindless mutts leaving behind their more modern thoughts.) To get there, enter at the 15 mile marker, drive past the Olowalu General Store, then right, left and right. The latter is marked by a water tank. There is a gate there granting access to this private land, though they may prefer walkers to drivers. The sign says it's a ¼ mile walk. Actually, it's ½ mile *each way*. Be careful walking around the petroglyphs as the platform is an OSHA nightmare.

Back on the highway, more ribbons of beach come and go. Parks like Launiupoko dot the shoreline. Though the valleys up mauka are beautiful, there are no roads to the center of West Maui, and only a few private subdivision roads penetrate a short distance. The farthest inland you can go up is on Lahainaluna Road in Lahaina. From there the view of Lahaina is peaceful and broad.

LAHAINA TOWN

Lahaina is the only town in all of leeward Maui with a *real* downtown. If someone told you to meet them in downtown Kihei, you wouldn't have any idea where they meant. Same goes for Wailea, Kapalua, Kaʻanapali or Napili. Though it's only 1½

NOT TO BE MISSED!

© 2008 Wizard Publications, Inc.

miles long, downtown Lahaina is well-defined and bursting with things to see and do.

The biggest problem with Lahaina is that it's crowded. And even when it's not crowded...*it's crowded*. A secluded stroll along Front Street is about as likely as a snowy day in Miami. But Front Street has an electricity that defies explanation. No matter how much you curse its popularity, you can't deny Lahaina's charm. It's busy, tacky, weird and wonderful. It's full of old world character and new world annoyances. It manages to energize and relax at the same time. If you visit West Maui without strolling along Front Street (abiding by that old Yogi Berra axiom, "*Nobody* goes there anymore; it's too crowded"), then you missed out on more than you think. Because for all its faults, Lahaina works.

Lahaina should be viewed as an event, not a place. You *do* Lahaina. You go there to eat, shop, walk and gawk. Lots of activities, especially boating-related, are centered around Lahaina. (This was, after all, an old whaling port.)

Ironically, as a place to stay, Lahaina lacks many of the things that make West Maui special. Namely good, clean beaches, cool breezes and a slow pace. Plus, there are relatively few places to stay in town. (Nearly all West Maui accommodations are north of Lahaina, in Ka'anapali, Honokowai, Kahana, Napili and Kapalua.) Of course, what it lacks in some areas, it makes up for by having a better nightlife, tons of restaurants and a more happenin' feel.

Lahaina means *cruel sun*. According to one legend there was a chief named Hua many generations ago who, in a huff, killed all his priests. Drought soon followed, and villagers referred to the area as the land of the cruel sun. Today, that ever-present sun is the very thing that attracts people from all over the world, though it can get pretty hot in the summer.

Parking in Lahaina is a *bugga!* If anything can bring on that old-fashioned

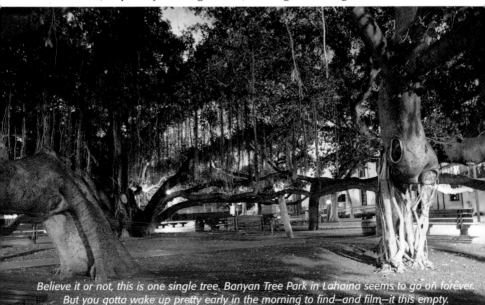

Believe it or not, this is one single tree. Banyan Tree Park in Lahaina seems to go on forever. But you gotta wake up pretty early in the morning to find—and film—it this empty.

mainland road rage, this is it. Lahaina is woefully under-equipped in the parking department (though fully staffed in the *enforcement* department). The county makes a tidy sum from unsuspecting visitor naïveté, and parking fees have created a cash bonanza for the ever-hungry county coffers. Even at night, big brother is watching. An example: There's a three-hour lot near the harbor, but if you park there at 5 p.m. for a sunset cruise and return at 8:10, you may find that the ever-efficient parking paratroopers have targeted you for a fee. Be very careful or you'll end up paying for some new carpet at City Hall. Here are a few tips.

Parking is free on Front Street for three hours if you can get a stall, and yes, they *do* keep an eye on your car. There are several pay lots marked on the map. If you're having a hard time finding *any* spots in Lahaina, the pay lot on Dickenson near Wainee seems to fill up later than other lots. Don't forget to try the free lots shown on the map. They're usually full, but you may get lucky. (I don't mean it *that* way.) If you're doing an early morning boat trip, look at the free Luakini Street lot first.

Your best parking opportunities are in the morning. Arrive in Lahaina between 9 and 10 a.m., and you stand a reasonable chance of getting a street-side stall. You'll also find the shops and street much less crowded.

There is a huge four-hour lot at Lahaina Center. It's free if you buy something at the center. We guess that technically means that you could park there and walk the town, picking up a bottle of water at ABC before you leave. But we *know* you'd never do anything so sneaky.

While strolling around town, your personal tastes will dictate which shops and attractions work for you. Additional attractions, all labeled on the map, include the old courthouse (where they have a detailed brochure describing all historic sites in town), Banyan Tree Park (an incredible must-see tree that encompasses an entire park), Baldwin House (the oldest house on the island) and the old prison (called Hale Pa'ahao, or "stuck in irons house"). It's kind of interesting to visit this last site, made with coral walls, to get an idea of the kind of crimes that people were imprisoned for in the 1850s. They include "profanity, furious riding, adultery and fornication (the second most common offense), refusing to work on the road, giving birth to bastard children, lewd conversation, and affray." (We had to look up that last one; it basically means disturbing the peace.)

Offshore of the Lahaina Marketplace you *may* (if it's still there) see a 22-ton steel hull sailboat named the *Dolfijn* washed up on the reef. How it got there is fairly boring. (An unexpected swell shook it from its sand anchor.) Personally, we like asking locals such as waiters how it got there. Stories range from renegade fugitives running from the law in South Africa to a local hiding from a $100,000 per day fine.

While strolling Front Street, you'll notice that activity salesmen are unusually aggressive. Lines like, *You folks have any questions? Ya need some coupons? Want to make a free phone call?* or *Interested in any activities?* are sales speak for *I want to sell you something* or *Want to see a timeshare presentation?* See ACTIVITIES on page 171 for more on activity brokers.

You'll also find the Lahaina Ka'anapali Railroad. *(Yawn to all but very young keiki.)* See page 206 for more on that thrilling *(not)* trip of a lifetime.

And the best show we've ever seen in Hawai'i, Warren and Annabelle's (see Nightlife on page 285) is on Front Street near Papalaua.

KA'ANAPALI TO KAPALUA

Ka'anapali was part of a large sugar plantation when the sugar company's board met in 1956 and hatched a plan that would soon be repeated around the globe—the master planned destination resort, the first in Hawai'i. The large land owners had their pick of where to put the resort, and they chose the fantastic Ka'anapali Beach here as their showcase to the world. (If *you'd* owned the **A REAL GEM** entire island back then, you too, probably would have chosen this beach.) It opened in 1962 and has been admired ever since.

Half a dozen fancy resorts line the beach. There's a wonderful paved beachside path that runs along all the resorts. It's an excellent place to stroll at sunset and can take an hour or more. Beach accesses are shown on the map. You can also park at the Whalers Village Shopping Center. Any shop will validate if you spend around $20. (Heck, you can practically knock that out with a scoop from Häagen-Daz.)

Separating the two halves of the great beach is Black Rock. As mentioned earlier, Hawaiian volcanoes fall asleep for up to a million years before awakening for a **A REAL GEM** last series of eruptions. West Maui had only four small eruptions during its final days. Black Rock was one. (Another is the rock where the Olowalu petroglyphs are located.)

The ancient Hawaiians believed Black Rock, which they called Pu'u Keka'a, was the jumping off point for their spirits or souls, called 'uhane, leaving this world. Each island had such a point. When Hawaiians died, it was here that their souls would leave this life and join their ancestors forever. If there were no 'aumakua, or family spirits, to receive them, they would wander around the area, attaching themselves to rocks and

The sunset torch lighting ceremony at Black Rock is followed by a plunge into the ocean.

Kahana to Ka'anapali

Map continued on page 53

Kahana Gateway

Kahana Beach

KAHANA

Pohaku Park
(S-Turns)

Mahinahina

Akahele

Kapalua/
West Maui
Airport

*Honokowai
Beach Park*

Honokowai

*Keka'a
(North Beach,
Airport Beach)*

Honokowai Marketplace
(Grocery Store)

Halawai Dr

Lower Honoapi'ilani Rd

Honoapi'ilani Hwy

Kai Ala Dr/Puukolii St

*Kahekili
Beach Park*

Ka'anapali North
Golf Course

Ka'anapali

*Black Rock
(Pu'u Keka'a)*

Fairway
Plaza

Dig Me Beach

20 parking spaces
50 parking spaces

Ka'anapali South
Golf Course

Kekaa Dr

Ka'anapali Pkwy

Whalers Village
Shopping Center

11 parking spaces

20 parking spaces
20 parking spaces

Nohea Kai Dr

Halelo St

Beach Path

Ka'anapali Beach

Honoapi'ilani Hwy
(traffic sometimes
heavy)

Hanaka'o'o / Canoe Beach

Lahaina map on page 47

© 2006 Wizard Publications, Inc.

Resorts from Mahinahina to Ka'anapali

1. Noelani
2. Mahina Surf
3. Polynesian Shores
4. Kuleana
5. Hoyochi Nikko
6. Hale Mahina Beach Resort
7. Lokelani
8. Hale Ono Loa
9. Kaleialoha
10. Makani Sands
11. Kulakane
12. Nohonani
13. Hale Maui
14. Pikake
15. Hale Kai
16. Paki Maui
17. Maui Sands
18. Papakea Resort
19. Ka'anapali Shores
20. Ka'anapali Beach Vacation Resort
21. Maui Kai
22. Mahana at Ka'anapali
23. Maui Ka'anapali Villas
24. Royal Lahaina Resort
25. Maui Eldorado
26. Sheraton Maui
27. Ka'anapali Beach Hotel
28. Ka'anapali Royal
29. The Whaler
30. Westin Maui
31. Ka'anapali Ali'i
32. Hyatt Regency Maui

0   1 MILE

[11] Roadside mile markers
Public Beach Access
Public Beach Parking
Beachside Path
Good Snorkel Areas

generally causing mischief. That's why it's considered unwise to take any rocks from this area. You may bring back a spirit itching to get back home.

The snorkeling around Black Rock is excellent. See page 154 for more.

Kahekili was the last king of Maui. He was utterly fearsome looking, with tattoos almost blackening one side of his body from head to foot, but completely clean on the other. He loved the sport of lele kawa (cliff diving), and legend states that he had once jumped from as high as 350 feet. Though terrifying to look at (even Captain Cook made reference to his scary appearance in his logs), he had a tiny, weak voice (sort of an ancient version of boxer Mike Tyson). This is the man that Kamehameha fought so hard to defeat when he conquered all the islands. It was only years later that Kamehameha learned Kahekili was actually his father. Kahekili Beach Park, a great beach north of the 25 mile marker, is one way islanders remember him.

We should alert you that grocery stores in West Maui are renowned for their *hurt me* prices. Prepare for the stomping of your life the first time you go in for some milk here (which they may have run out of!).

Also, allow for traffic when driving to Lahaina in the afternoon from Ka'anapali or Kapalua. Pau hana (end of work) traffic can be a problem, at its worst between Ka'anapali and Lahaina.

There are dozens of condos north of Ka'anapali. This is where the more reasonably priced West Maui accommodations are found. Unfortunately, a few of the beaches north of Ka'anapali are unpleasant for the same reasons listed for north Kihei on page 158. The first great beach after Kahekili Beach is Napili Bay, described under BEACHES on page 152. (Ah, and what a wonderful beach it is…)

Sugar has been the symbol of West Maui since before the American Civil War. All who grew up here lived their lives in its shadow. A single company dominated all commerce here. Ironically, it was a German company that ran the sugar operations until WWI, when

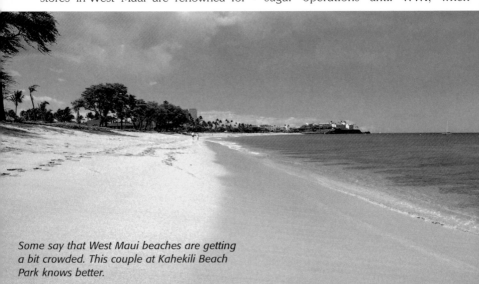

Some say that West Maui beaches are getting a bit crowded. This couple at Kahekili Beach Park knows better.

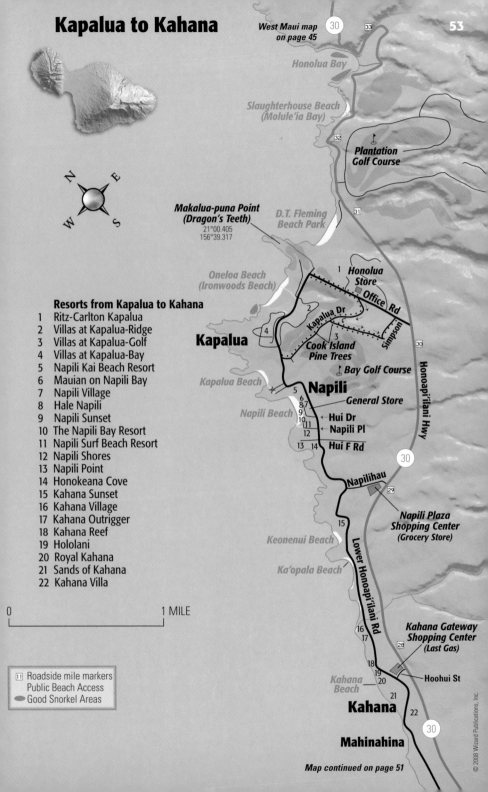

Kapalua to Kahana

West Maui map
on page 45

Honolua Bay

Slaughterhouse Beach
(Molule'ia Bay)

Plantation
Golf Course

Makalua-puna Point
(Dragon's Teeth)
21°00.405
156°39.317

D.T. Fleming
Beach Park

Oneloa Beach
(Ironwoods Beach)

1 Honolua
Store

Office Rd

Kapalua Dr

Simpson

Resorts from Kapalua to Kahana

1   Ritz-Carlton Kapalua
2   Villas at Kapalua-Ridge
3   Villas at Kapalua-Golf
4   Villas at Kapalua-Bay
5   Napili Kai Beach Resort
6   Mauian on Napili Bay
7   Napili Village
8   Hale Napili
9   Napili Sunset
10 The Napili Bay Resort
11 Napili Surf Beach Resort
12 Napili Shores
13 Napili Point
14 Honokeana Cove
15 Kahana Sunset
16 Kahana Village
17 Kahana Outrigger
18 Kahana Reef
19 Hololani
20 Royal Kahana
21 Sands of Kahana
22 Kahana Villa

Kapalua

Cook Island
Pine Trees

Bay Golf Course

Kapalua Beach

Napili

General Store

Napili Beach

Hui Dr

Napili Pl

Hui F Rd

Napilihau

Napili Plaza
Shopping Center
(Grocery Store)

Keonenui Beach

Ka'opala Beach

Lower Honoapi'ilani Rd

Honoapi'ilani Hwy

Kahana Gateway
Shopping Center
(Last Gas)

Hoohui St

Kahana
Beach

Kahana

Mahinahina

0   1 MILE

[11] Roadside mile markers
      Public Beach Access
●   Good Snorkel Areas

Map continued on page 51

© 2008 Wizard Publications, Inc.

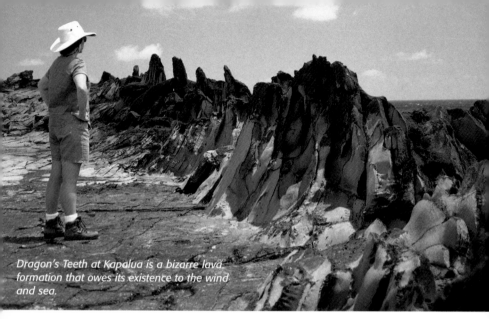

Dragon's Teeth at Kapalua is a bizarre lava formation that owes its existence to the wind and sea.

an irritated U.S. government seized the company and sold it to Americans. (In an *eat this* gesture to the Germans, they named it American Factors, and their retail stores were named Liberty House.)

The waning days of the 20th century brought an end to sugar here. Even after a decade, nobody still really knows how the previously sugar-laced slopes will look in the years to come. Longtime sugar workers have moved on to other industries, sometimes pineapple. The large mill off the highway is idle. Ironically, pineapple contributed to the demise of sugar here. Sugar is an intensely thirsty crop, and the sugar company was never able to get as much water as they needed, in sharp contrast to HC&S's water bounty in Central Maui. Their single best source of water dried up when their water supplier decided to start growing pineapple and cut them off from their source.

Farther north, Kapalua is an incredibly manicured oasis of green in this windswept part of the island. The gardening bill must be immense because no dead leaf goes unpunished. *Expensive* is the operative word at these resorts. Some of the beaches, such as Kapalua Bay, are

excellent. The wind tends to be strong here, and it's also more prone to drizzle than any other leeward resort area.

Where Lower Honoapiilani Road becomes Office Road, there's a little road turnout with a parking lot. Walk toward the shoreline and a long point of lava separates two large beaches. Called Makalua-puna Point, it's worth the 5-minute walk along the grassy edge of the golf course. The lava is different than most Hawaiian lavas. Light colored, dense and fine grained, bleached white in some areas, it flowed during the dying days of the West Maui volcano. Salt spray on the upwind side has etched the lava into thrusting shapes known as Dragon's Teeth. Other areas on the point have other types of lava objects embedded in them. In some places the ocean has eroded holes completely through the lava rocks. Walk over to the left (west) side and look at Oneloa Bay, often calm and protected on the nearest side.

The huge lawn in front of Dragon's Teeth has a tumultuous history. The Ritz-Carlton Hotel inland was *supposed* to be an oceanfront hotel. The lawn was to be its location. The only things standing in their way were approximately 2,000 ancient Hawaiians buried in the area. The developers began digging up the graves and, when the Hawaiian community learned of it, they began a series of emotional protests. Nearly 900 remains were dug up before common sense prevailed, and the hotel decided to relocate the buildings and reinter the bones in 1990. A state law was enacted after this to prevent such a thing from ever happening again.

PAST KAPALUA; OVER THE TOP

Like the highway past Hana along the bottom of Haleakala, the drive along the top of West Maui suffers from a long out-of-date reputation. Chances are you'll read that the road is not passable in a rental car or the ridiculous statement that you need 4WD. Free tourist brochures need to update their write-ups. Years ago the road was nearly impossible to drive. Poor pavement gave way to no pavement, and the narrow spots would make a stunt driver sweat. But today the road is much better. The real caveats are the two sections where it is one-lane. About 1½ miles of the highway are a *very* narrow paved one-lane road, and another 2½ miles a narrow*ish* one lane. There are some turnouts on these stretches, and timid drivers may want to evaluate if this is for them. (If two cars meet where there's no turnout, etiquette dictates that the *uphill* driver needs to back up.) Just drive the one-lane portions very slowly.

For what it's worth, we think this is one of the least appreciated drives on

The Green Flash

Ever heard of the green flash? No, it's not a superhero. We'd heard of the green flash for years before we moved to Hawai'i. We assumed that it was an urban myth, or perhaps something seen through the bottom of a beer bottle. But now we know it to be a real phenomenon, complete with a scientific explanation. You may hear other ways to experience the green flash—but this is the only true way.

On days when the horizon is crisp and clear with no clouds in the way of the sun as it sets, you stand a reasonable chance of seeing it. Avoid looking directly at the sun until the very last part of the disk is about to slip below the horizon. Looking at it beforehand will burn a greenish image onto your retina, creating a "fool's flash" (and possibly wrecking your eyes). The instant before the last part of the sun's disk disappears, a vivid flash of green is often seen. This is because the sun's rays are passing through the thickest part of the atmosphere, and the light is bent and split into its different components the way it is in a rainbow. The light that is bent the most is the green and blue light, but the blue is less vivid and is overwhelmed by the flash of green, which lingers for the briefest of moments as the very last of the sun sets.

For a variety of reasons, including our latitude, Hawai'i is one of the best places in the world to observe the green flash. But if you aren't successful in seeing the real green flash, try the beer bottle method—at least it's better than nothing.

Like a jet engine firing into the sky,
Nakalele Blowhole rocks when the ocean rolls.

the island. It's like the Hana Highway without the traffic. Though nowhere *near* as lush as the Hana drive (nor as long), the windswept charm of this almost forgotten piece of Maui makes it worth the drive—if you can stand the curviness and the narrow sections. Along the way are some unforgettable sights, including one we discovered that amazed us with its perfection.

Our description assumes you will be driving this section from west to east, in a clockwise direction. We strongly suggest you do it this way for several reasons: The sights are better from that direction. Also, drivers rarely discover the road from the Wailuku side, so most traffic, sparse when compared to Hana traffic, will be flowing *with* you. Blind corners seem more blind when driving from Wailuku. Lastly, when on a narrow road, it's more comforting to be on the *inside* lane. Passengers can get uncomfortable when you're on the outside lane as you would if you came from Wailuku.

There are still some popular attractions past Kapalua. There's the *lovely sounding* Slaughterhouse Beach, after the 32 mile marker, with its concrete steps down to the shoreline and, before the 33 mile marker, Honolua Bay with its outrageous snorkeling in the summer and monstrous waves in the winter. Both are worth stopping for if your destination is the water. Both are described further under BEACHES. A dirt road along the sea cliffs after you've climbed above Honolua Bay past the 33 mile mark offers a tremendous view of Honolua. Try to ignore the voluminous black plastic embedded in the ground there. It's one of the less glamorous legacies of growing pineapple. It's used to reduce the amount of water and pesticides needed. Pretty ironic, isn't it? That plas-

tic litter is all over the place *to protect the environment*. (Gee, thanks guys.)

At times you'll see a yellow/orange stripe in the lava cut by the road or erosion. These are deposits of ash from the island's youth. At that time huge volcanic explosions covered much of the mountain in ash that was then covered with lava flows. Though quiet now, West Maui was very violent in its younger days.

Still one last beach remains along this stretch, though you'd have a hard time finding many visitors or even locals who know about it. Called Punalau Beach, the access is 7/10 mile past the 34 mile marker. It's always uncrowded during the week. Past here you won't find any sand beaches until you reach the other side of West Maui Mountain at Wailuku.

The road begins its sinuous 25-mile trek to central Maui from here. Dynamite coastal views are common. Now, 25 miles might not *seem* very far, but you're likely to drive slow and stop often, so don't assume you'll be there in an hour. There are countless places to pull over and gawk at the untamed shoreline—sometimes from cliffs above, sometimes from along the shore.

Past the 36 mile marker is the village of Honokohau. There's a road that leads to the back of the valley, but expect plenty of stink eye if you try to go. They don't seem too neighborly there.

Exactly ½ mile past the 38 mile marker is a wide turnout backed by rounded boulders. About 1,200 feet from the road (and 205 feet below you) is one of the more spectacular sights in West Maui. Called the Nakalele Blowhole, the **A REAL GEM** ocean here has undercut the shoreline, pounding underneath the lava shelf, where it spits through a man-sized hole in the lava. The blowhole varies *tremendously* with the tide and size of the surf. We were here once when the blowhole wasn't blowing a thing. Zero water was issuing from the hole. Four hours later we returned and found the blowhole shooting 70 feet into the air every few seconds with such vicious, explosive force it made the ground tremble, and we were convinced the earth was going to split beneath our feet. It was like a jet engine rocketing seawater into the air with amazing fury. High tide is your best bet, and high surf adds to the fury. The local newspaper has tide information on page 2.

Remember, this is wilderness. There's no guard-rail to stop you from shrinking the gene pool should you use bad judgment and fall into the hole. If the blowhole is pumping (which is quite common in the winter), get as close as common sense dictates. It's hard to predict which waves will make it scream. Huge waves sometimes produce nothing, while wimpy-looking waves sometimes surprise you. The area to the left (west) of the blowhole is some of the most amazing-looking landscape you'll ever see. It looks like an alien war zone where combatants fought with acid. Over countless eons, billions of tons of sea spray have shot through the blowhole and been blown on the wind. The spray attacks the fracturous rocks on contact, literally eating the land, and the results are never to be forgotten. Rock hounds will enjoy seeing how the elements have tortured the rocks into various bizarre and jagged formations.

If the blowhole isn't overly angry while you're there, you'll notice a whole community of life living off this phenomenon. Crabs tempt the ocean by lining the steamy hole during pauses, eating algae growing on the sides, in constant danger of being swept away from a wave. Primitive-looking blennies (also called rockskippers since they can leap from pool to pool) live their whole lives in the 3 inches of water that remain from the splashes that shoot out of the hole. There's a natural lava viewing ledge above the blowhole, but you are still in the potential wet zone there.

The trail starts at the turnout mentioned above and goes down toward the ocean slightly to the left. (It's not the more obvious-looking road cut slightly to the right; see map.) While on the trail, take note of the huge amount of olivine encrusted in much of the lava rock. We've found dime-sized specimens of this semiprecious gem in the area. If you're interested in a longer, more beautiful hike to the blowhole, see page 190.

This is probably a good time to warn you of the mindless cows that often wander onto the road. Cows aren't known for their smarts, but they seem especially clueless along this route, so be on the lookout for them. We've also seen a couple of donkeys on the road—and they're very friendly—so watch for them.

Nakalele Blowhole

2 pools
Light Beacon
Parking Lot
38
Trail
Several dirt roads are along here
30
Blowhole
21°01.621
156°35.314
Rounded Boulders
Trail
N
W — E
S
0   1/4 Mi.
39

© 2008 Wizard Publications, Inc.

When you reach the mushroom rock, you've reached a spectacular place to watch the ocean's fury.

Almost ½ mile past the 40 mile marker is a small turnout on the ocean side. It presents a truly kickin' view along the coast. If the blowhole is pumping, you'll see the results from here. The ocean is directly beneath you, and you don't need to go more than 10 feet from your car. Another ²/₁₀ mile along the highway is an even better lookout about 100 feet from the larger pullout. (You'll also see a trailhead for a strikingly *dull* state path called the Ohai Trail.) The coastline unravels beneath you. Look for the blowhole back the way you came. It's below and slightly to the left of a light beacon near the point. Of course, no surf means no blow. Many of the boulders in the area have been undercut by wind and salt and seem precariously balanced.

Almost ²/₁₀ mile past the 41 mile marker the road opens up around a corner exposing the majestic 636-foot high Kahakuloa Head off in the distance. More on that later. At that corner there's a 5-minute trail that leads to a point with a commanding view. (There's a cattle fence near the end of the trail that most people just climb over since it's not private land, it belongs to the state.) The real oddity on this point is the crumbling remains of an old Pontiac Grand Prix. Its presence seems inconceivable here. There's no way it could have been driven or rolled out onto the point. Let us know if you figure out how it got here.

If you notice a strange feeling in your lungs about now, there's a technical reason for it. It's called *perfectly clean air*. The air here has drifted over the landless Pacific for many weeks. Skies are often crystal clear along this part of the island. So when you're at a sea cliff, suck in a deep breath; this is as clean as air can get.

More than ½ mile past the 42 mile marker, you'll find a turnout and trails leading toward the shoreline. One leads to a mushroom-shaped rock. From there, you'll find one of the best places in West Maui from which to observe the beautiful ferocity of the ocean during high seas. The unchecked pounding violence has tortured and scarred the helpless lava into a fantastic array of grotesque and wonderful shapes and textures. It's mesmerizing from this secluded spot to watch the creation and destruction happening at the shoreline. Be careful on the trail down; it's slippery when wet. The ocean is 175 feet below you. 4WDs can go much of the way.

This area has some very nice hiking, though less structured and often trail-less. Just stop at any particularly inviting piece of shoreline and dig in. One very nice hike from here is described under HIKING on page 192.

After the 42 mile marker the road changes from state to county, and the mile markers will start at 16. At ¾ mile after the 42 mile marker, and before the 16 mile marker, on the mauka side of the road, is the Bellstone. This large, round boulder *can* make a mildly metallic clank if you hit it at the right spot on the mountain side. Odds are, however, you'll simply look like some fool mindlessly whacking on a rock.

Right after the Bellstone is a dirt road on the ocean side. (It's almost kitty-corner to a dirt road on the mauka side with a gate leading inland—see map.) If you walk the short distance toward the ocean (veering to the right at the second intersection), you'll come to some nicely placed rock platforms 150 feet above the shoreline. (See map on page 62.) People occasionally go there and then turn around because some maps erroneously label the area as containing the Nakalele Blowhole. Until we revealed this site, however, few, if any, realized what they were missing below.

When you write guidebooks for a living and actually *do* and experience the things you write about, you get used to discovering exciting new things. But we were unprepared for the grand perfection of this totally unexpected oasis, which had never appeared in print. Judging by its pristine appearance when we found it, we'd say that not more than a handful of people on the island even knew about it even though it's on public land.

We called it the Olivine Pools because of its gem-like quality, the color of the area and the ample amounts of a semi-precious gem called olivine encrusted in the surrounding lava and sandstone.

A REAL GEM

They are numerous natural lava swimming pools ensconced in an ancient lava shelf, offering an outrageous and often very safe place to swim with the restless ocean pounding at you on three sides. It's reminiscent of the Queen's Bath on Kaua'i but far more grand and with more pools. The setting is as idyllic as any we can imagine. One of the pools is extremely deep and cool with a natural step to enter and exit. From this pool, your vantage point to the ocean cauldron beyond makes you feel snug and smug. Another pool is just deep enough to sit in, which makes it shallow enough for the afternoon sun to occasionally heat it to about 90 degrees in the summer. Another pool has only one way in and out. Reef shoes are fine, but we've walked

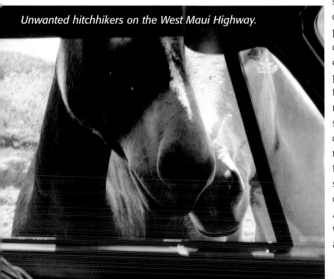

Unwanted hitchhikers on the West Maui Highway.

Some deep, some shallow, the Olivine Pools can be a calm playground in a restless sea.

around barefoot and not had a problem since the lava is pretty smooth, and there are no nasty sea urchins to kill your feet. It can be slippery, however. Perched above the pools is an amazingly flat platform, a perfect place to stretch out your towel to sun yourself. Natural lava steps lead to the pools themselves.

As the tide rises, splashes from the ocean may trickle into some of the pools and flow from one to another, sometimes forming small waterfalls. As far as we've observed, only high surf at high tide or prolonged heavy rain seems to ruin the area. (Big waves could make it—and any part of the shoreline—dangerous.) Big rains *occasionally* cause the pools to form one large silty pond that you'd never recognize from our above description. When spoiled like this, nature usually cleans it up within a week. *Rarely*, long periods of south winds and low surf may cause it to get a bit stagnant. Observe for yourself to see if conditions are good. Very high surf, above 12 feet, could spoil it during *all* tides. And don't get too close to the unpredictable ocean, which could always send a large wave to

pick you off. People standing at the water's edge instead of in the pools can *and have* been killed by large waves. And we've even heard of people getting scraped up *in the pools* when large waves came crashing ashore. In fact, after one such incident the state erected some dire-sounding warning signs to dissuade people from going.

There's a small blowhole off to the side that rarely does much, and next to it is the hole where most of the water drains to return to the ocean. (Be careful around the hole; falling into it would be a *big* problem!) This area tends to be windy, though it's partially blocked by some lava. Sometimes, especially during the summer, it can get so windy that you'll want to blow off this attraction (so to speak).

Since we revealed the Olivine Pools in our first edition, we no longer find it empty all the time like we used to. *Great!* You can't imagine how good it makes us feel to share this discovery with people. It seems tailor-made for recreation if the ocean's cooperating and, until now, it was unused.

Olivine Pools & Kahakuloa

Mushroom-shaped Rock

30 End State Hwy. 30

Olivine Pools
21°00.580
156°33.381

Walk to Overlook

Kahakuloa Head (636')

Bellstone (Big Boulder)
21°00.475
156°33.479

Kahekili's Leap

Narrow one-lane mountain road section

340

N
W E
S

0   1/2 Mi.   Kahakuloa Village

From the pools, take a look at the unusually intriguing lava formations around you. Some look like lava chessmen sentries. Above the pool is one formation that looks like a lava admiral's chair facing the ocean.

To get to the Olivine Pools from the rock platform overlook, look down the cliff and to your left for a lava bench below you. You should see a heart-shaped pool on the lava bench. There is faint trail leading down to the bench. Footing can be awkward and a bit slippery. Please be certain to bring everything out that you bring in. Also, it's easy to sunburn in the placid pools, but we're worried that too much suntan lotion may harm the pools. Try to refrain if you can while in the water. Though it's tempting to bring back rock souvenirs, you should know that Hawaiians strongly believe that any rocks that leave the islands bring bad luck due to a curse from the volcano goddess Pele. True or not, we can tell you that we personally receive numerous rocks from readers that are mailed to us when they experience a string of bad luck after returning. So it's up to you, but we advise you to leave everything where you find it.

Soon the highway gets narrow—*very* narrow—as it descends along the side of the mountain. Skittish passengers may *hate* this 1½ mile part. (We've seen some who had expressions as if they had just unexpectedly bungee-jumped into hell.) Soon their nightmare is over as they descend into Kahakuloa Village.

Kahakuloa is a tight-knit community isolated from the rest of the island, though some here commute to work out in the "real world." In the village on the left side is Panini Pua Kea Fruit Stand. They have an unusual handmade coconut candy that's pretty addictive. As you are leaving Kahakuloa and the road is just beginning to ascend, Julia's is a stand on the left next to a wet-looking taro patch that makes the best banana bread on the planet. Makes my mouth hurt just writing about it. (Hmm, raising the bar pretty high, aren't we?) When they're closed, Panini Pua Kea (above) often becomes their outlet.

As you're leaving Kahakuloa town, you ascend the valley walls on the narrow road. At the top of the road is a turnout, if your nerves are shot and you want a nice view of the village and bay. After this the road widens and you'll see a fence and gate with a path through a cattlestop leading down between the 636-foot high Kahakuloa Head (which means *the tall lord)* and a 547-foot high hill to the right called Pu'u Kahuli-'anapa. The short trail between the hills offers some good views of the back side of Kahakuloa Head towering above you.

If you're feeling adventurous, from near the cattlestop you could make your way to the top of the hill to the right. It's fairly steep and you won't pick up the cattle trails until toward the top. We've hiked to the top and the views are second to...well, one, actually. You see, the much steeper Kahakuloa Head to your left has a summit that can only be reached by a death-defying, 'okole-squeezing, nail-biting scaling of the crumbly rock wall. Thanks, but no thanks. But while exploring this area from the air in an ultralight I discovered something quite impressive. At the peak of the mountain were *two folding lawn chairs*. Someone apparently loved nothing better than to climb this beast in order to relax at the top while enjoying the views. Whoever you are, *bruddah*, you've earned it!

Part of Kahakuloa Head used to be called Kahekili's Leap. Why? Because the 18th-century Maui King Kahekili used to sometimes reside up here, according to legend. At a place part of the way down (but over 200 feet above the ocean) he would regularly dive into the water, then climb back up the cliff face for his breakfast.

After Kahakuloa Head you'll pass Kaukini Gallery. They have a nice selection of Maui-made jewelry, art and furniture (plus a restroom). Prices are expensive. (This is the place to buy that $14,000 koa wood rocking chair you've been looking for.)

Just after the 11 mile marker is the sharpest hairpin turn we've ever seen. Look as you're approaching it, and you'll see that the upper road is almost literally on top of the lower road. (We've tried photographing it but can't get a good vantage point.)

Just after the 10 mile marker is the Bruce Turnbull Studio and Sculpture Garden, an apt description. Their hours are squirrelly, and it's common to find them closed, but, if open, the area is replete with wood and bronze sculptures, and it's worth a stop.

Past the 8 mile marker is something you probably haven't seen on this side of the island—*a waterfall*. Lower Makamaka'ole Falls is visible from several turnouts; keep an eye out for it. It is a multi-tiered falls and is refreshing after all the dryness you've seen. Its name means *without friends*. (How sad.)

One last thing. For some odd reason, as you're pulling into Wailuku after the long drive, the last ¹⁄₁₀ mile of this road is one way—the *wrong* way—at the Vineyard intersection, and you're given no warning. We've seen some terribly close calls here as tired drivers plunge into oncoming traffic.

WEST MAUI SHOPPING

West Maui, or more specifically Lahaina, has the most extensive shopping on the island. The prime areas are along Front Street and at Lahaina Cannery Mall, but other intriguing options exist on side streets or down small alleys, so don't be afraid to explore.

At Lahaina Cannery Mall some notable stores are Footprints Maui for a large selection of sandals at less staggering prices than seen elsewhere on the island. One of our favorite stores there is Banana Wind. They have fine products made from natural materials like bamboo, sea grass, beach glass, etc. for your home. Maui WaterWear is a great place to pick up a new swim suit. Maui Toy Works will wow kids at every age. Hats Galore has hats...uh, galore. There's a Longs Drug here, too.

For shopping on Front Street in downtown Lahaina, park at one end (see map) and enjoy lunch at the other end and start back again. On some weekends there are locally-made products for sale under the Banyan Tree. The Visitors' Center and the Museum Store in the Old Courthouse Building have a good selection of Maui souvenirs.

There are way too many shops along or just off Front Street to list here but some stand-outs include Dan's Green House on Lahainaluna Road at Wainee Street. They'll ship (or you can carry back) plants that are grown on lava rock. (The birds they sell there are pretty entertaining, too.) Check out the Old Lahaina Book Emporium for a nice selection of Hawaiiana and used books. Glass Mango has outstanding glass jewelry. Lahaina Body & Bath carries locally-made soaps and lotions. Honolulu Cookie Company has yummy shortbread cookies in flavors like lilikoi, mango and Kona coffee.

For clothing try T-shirt Factory, Moonbow Tropics, Honolua Surf Co., Aunty Panty's Lingerie, J.J. Whitebird Resortwear, Hilo Hatties and Volcom.

There are tons of galleries on or near Front Street and some of the best (though hardly the least expensive) shopping can be found there. We suggest you leave plenty of time to peruse them.

In Ka'anapali, there is Whalers Village, a beachside shopping mall. Some stores worth a look are Martin & McArthur for koa wood items, Lids where you can get a custom-designed souvenir baseball cap. Endangered Species has lots of animal-themed items for little kids (and big ones, too), Totally Hawaiian has mostly (not "totally") Hawaiian-made products for your home and Lahaina Printsellers has antique maps.

WEST MAUI BEST BETS

Best Hike—Blowhole thru Acid Warzone

Best Hidden Gem—Olivine Pools

Best Sunset Stroll With Your Shoes On—Ka'anapali Beachside Path

Best Sunset Stroll With Your Shoes Off—Ka'anapali Beach

Best Breakfast for Cheap Cheap—Honolua Store

Best Beach to Start Your Day—Kahekili Beach Park

Best Place to Watch a Guy Jump Off a Rock—Black Rock from Sheraton at Sunset

Best Place to See the Ocean Explode—Nakalele Blowhole

Best Banana Bread (on the Planet)—Last Stand in Kahakuloa

Best Place to Find Golf Balls While Snorkeling—Oneloa Beach

Best Place to Kiss Off Snorkeling—14 Mile Marker

Best Place to Waste Your Money—Lahaina Ka'anapali Railroad

Best Beach to Frolic—Napili Bay

Best Protected Beach—Kapalua

Best Place to See Just How Narrow a Road Can Be—Hwy 340 Segment Going Toward Kahakuloa

Best Snorkeling—Right Side of Honolua Bay When Calm, or Black Rock from Sheraton Side

Best Parking Job—Abandoned Grand Prix on Cliff mentioned on page 59

Best Way to Recapture Mainland Road Rage—Trying to Park in Lahaina

Best Place to Sandblast Your Da Kines—D.T. Fleming Beach in Wind

Best Swimming Pool—Hyatt

Best Place to Lose Your Voice—Yelling at the Person Next to You at the Waterfall Grotto Bar at the Hyatt

Best Tree—Banyan Tree Park

Best Evening Show—Warren & Annabelle's

Ho'okipa Lookout is a great place to sit and watch big surf come crashing in.

Central Maui is your introduction to the island. You'll land here. You'll shop here. You'll also come through here when you head to Hana, up to the top of Haleakala or after circling West Maui. But with all that exposure, few people come to Central Maui just to see Central Maui. It's like the *Denver Airport* of Maui. Everyone passes through, yet few look around. But don't blow it off completely. Central Maui does have some reasons to stop and stay a while.

Since there's no logical way to organize this area, we're going to describe it in a scattershot manner.

WAILUKU

The county seat, center of power and, most important, home to a few good restaurant bargains. (How's *that* for a reason to come here?)

Think of it as a once-grand hub of island activity that's now in the shadow of Kahului, often forgotten and showing its age. There is a certain charm to Wailuku, but not enough to lure many visitors. Too bad. In its day, Wailuku was quite a place: where sugar barons wined and dined, island leaders made important proclamations, and people came from all over to be entertained. One part of town is known as **Happy Valley**, even to this day. The origin is uncertain, but the age-old rumor says it's related to the fact that the area was known for its collection of bordellos. (Hard to imagine in sleepy little Wailuku.)

Most people simply drive through Wailuku on their way to **'Iao Valley** and the **'Iao Needle**. This was a sacred burying place for chiefs and the location of Maui's last giant battle for supremacy.

Central Maui / Wailuku & Kahului

66

Hana map on page 90

Haleakala Hwy

Hana Hwy

Pa'ia 4 miles

Haleakala & Upcountry map on page 115

Kitesurfing prohibited

Spreckelsville Beach

Beginner Windsurfing

Kanaha Beach

Ka'a Point

Kitesurfing

Amala

Kanaha Pond

Tower

Kalo

Heliport

Terminal

Kahului Airport

Rental Car Return

Overflow Parking

Aalele

Keolani

Hana Hwy

Haleakala Hwy

Haleakala Hwy

Pulehu

Hansen Rd (short cut)

Sugar Mill

Costco & Kmart

Maui Marketplace

Wal-Mart

Home Depot

333 Dairy

Alamaha

Wakea

Huklike

Puunene Ave

Dairy Rd

Mokulele Hwy

To Kihei

Kihei map on page 129

Kuihelani Hwy

To Lahaina

Lono

Kamehameha

Dunes At Maui Lani Golf Course

Kahului Harbor

Kahului Beach Rd (Hotels along here)

Maui Mall

Kahului Mall

Kane

Wakea

Kaahumanu Center

Kahului

Wahinepio

Maui Arts & Cultural Center

Skateboard Park

Kanaloa

War Memorial

Papa

Mahalani

Maui Memorial Hospital

West Maui map on page 45

Waiehu Beach Rd

Waiehu Beach Park

Lower Waiehu

Kuhio

Hea

Haleki'i & Pihana Heiaus

Lower Main

Lower Main

Mill

Tao Stream

Banana Bungalow

Happy Valley

Central

Main

Church

Koahu

Wailuku

Maui Lani

Wai'ale Rd

Old Wailuku Inn

High

Kehalani Pkwy / Honoapi'ilani Hwy

Waihe'e Ridge & Valley Trails map on page 195

Waiehu Stream

Market St.

State Building (Camping Permits)

Bailey House Museum

To 'Iao Valley & 'Iao Needle

Vineyard

Kaahumanu

© 2008 Wizard Publications, Inc.

1 MILE

N W E S

37

3

0

36

2

1

1

350

32

350

311

380

2

2

380

2

1

2

32

1

1

1

30

320

340

2

330

2

3400

99

99

The king of the Big Island was Kamehameha the Great. In 1790 he decided that the time was right to invade Maui (again). After he had personally killed the leading chief of Maui, his forces swept into Kahului and Wailuku. The two sides were fairly equal except for one thing: the cannon Kamehameha had nabbed from the seized sloop belonging to Metcalf's son. (See page 16.) With this cannon, which the natives affectionately nicknamed Lopaka (Robert), and some captured (though now happily compliant) westerners as advisers, Kamehameha was able to utterly annihilate the Maui forces.

They steadily rolled Lopaka along the rocky trails into 'Iao Valley, backing the troops into a corner, and proceeded to murder almost everyone. Many of the women and children had been moved higher up the cliffs and saw their loved ones die as Robert, loaded with shells and sometimes rocks, blasted away. The carnage was so great that the bodies clogged up the stream. Even by Hawaiian standards of the time, the killing was appalling. The natives called the battle Ka'uwa'u-pali (clawed off the cliff) and Kapaniwai (damming of the waters).

Today 'Iao is a peaceful, beautiful valley. It seems impossible to imagine the death that once permeated the area. The valley stream is lovely, and there are short trails looping around the bottom. The 'Iao Needle is a prominent point sticking up from the valley. It's actually the end of a long, winding knife-edge ridge. (If you saw it from the side, you'd probably call it the 'Iao Plate.) This valley is what remains of the central caldera (crater) of the West Maui volcano. See map at left.

NOT TO BE MISSED!

The 'Iao Needle and stream make a splendid diversion in Central Maui.

Also nearby, if you have kids, they may like the Hawai'i Nature Center on your left on Hwy 320. See page 36 for more.

For the cerebral-oriented, the Bailey House Museum (244–3326) is the former mid-19th century home of missionary Edward Bailey. His home, now a museum, is a good place to check out artifacts from the past—such as a century-old surfboard, Hawaiian stone tools, spinning wheel, Hawaiian Bible, quilts, dresses almost two centuries old and even more surprising items, such as an opium scale and pipe. Bailey was also a painter, and his renditions of Maui in the 1800s are interesting. Entry fee is $5, $1 for kids. On Main Street on your way to 'Iao Valley. Closed Sunday.

Also in Wailuku are the remains of the Haleki'i and Pihana heiaus. These were former luakini temples (places of human sacrifice). The view from this strategic hill is impressive. You can see all of Wailuku and Kahului. As you gaze from the top of the heiau, your views of the mountains are mixed with views of the surrounding houses, creeping close to the heiau. Instead of houses, what would the ancient priests have seen when they looked out from here? Houses…and taro. This area was called Na Wai Eha, or Four Waters, and was one of the largest taro-growing areas in the state. The streams around here provided abundant water, so it would have looked similar to rice fields but with broad-leafed taro instead of rice. Thousands of Hawaiians lived here. Instead of shingles, they had thatch. Instead of a two-car garage, they had a two-canoe shed. But this area has always had lots of people.

The heiau park is not well maintained by the state, which is surprising, given how few ancient relics there are on Maui. (Well, except for the county council.)

To get there, take Waiehu Beach Road to Kuhio to Hea. (See map on page 66.)

KAHULUI

People who live here find themselves coming to Kahului all the time. What do they come for? Malls, movies, restaurants and—most important on an island where things cost a lot—*Costco*.

Kahului is where people come to take care of business. The biggest mall, Ka'ahumanu Center on Hwy 32, is a big draw. And Maui Marketplace on Dairy Road is where you'll find Borders Books and the island's biggest sporting goods store.

Finding someplace in Kahului is easy if you know one thing: Midas Mufflers is on Wakea and Hukilike. Why in the heck are we telling you this? Because every small town has a place like this. The *thing* that everything is relative to. Call up a business in Kahului and ask where they are, and, if it's not on a main street, invariably the response will be, *"You know where Midas is? Well, you take a left…"* We don't know why; it's just the way it is.

Kahului is nearly always windy. And on those few occasions that it's not windy—it's *real breezy.* If you rent a large vehicle, like a minivan, it'll often feel like someone's outside rocking your car.

THE VALLEY OF SUGAR

This is the reason Maui is called the Valley Isle—the large flatland separating East and West Maui. This area is dominated by only one thing—*sugar*. A single company—HC&S—is growing all that sugar you see—all 37,000 acres of it. Before people came to these islands, a thin, dryland forest existed here. The Hawaiians quickly cut down the trees when they discovered the island and the area became a barren desert, after which the Hawaiians had little to do with it. When western man arrived, he saw an opportunity to grow sugar in this unused region and began building ditches to bring water to this thirsty land. Today, the broad valley between the two great volcanoes is an ever-waving field of green trisected by the three highways.

At one time, all of the islands surrounding Maui formed a single large island. Then the ocean rose and the land sank to isolate each of the volcanoes into different islands. The valley separating East and West Maui is the last land bridge remaining, and its days are numbered, too. Given the present sinking rate, East and West Maui will be separate islands in about 15,000 years when this landbridge disappears. (Gives the realtors something to worry about, huh?)

On Honoapiʻilani Hwy (30) heading toward the west side, you'll find **Maui Tropical Plantation** (244–7643) between the 2 and 3 mile markers—60 acres of assorted tropical fruits and plants. It's a classic tourist trap, and it'll cost you $11 to ride the tram to see the gardens. (No walkers.) The place seems more geared to tour buses. The tour can be marginally interesting, but it's definitely *not* a must-see. They have a restaurant and a luʻau. The Molokaʻi coffee company that owns it plans to grow coffee on the slopes above the plantation.

If you drive along Hwy 311 on your way toward South Maui, you'll pass Maui's ugliest sight (except for the line at the rental car counter when you're late for your flight home). A sugar mill looking like it belongs more in the 19th century (which is when it was built) belches steam and sometimes black smoke into the air. The smoke is from the burning of bagasse, the fiber remaining after sugar has been removed from sugarcane. They produce all of their electricity that way and sell the excess to the local electric company. At the corner of Hwy 311 and Hansen Road you'll find the **Sugar Museum**

Sugar, sugar everywhere. This tall grass requires one ton of water to make one pound of sugar.

(871–8058). It has everything you ever wanted to know about sugar harvesting and refining, but were afraid to ask. It's $7 for admission, and they have lots of relics and artifacts. You'll feel hot and stuffy just *looking* at the outfits that field workers used to wear in the hot sun.

Along 311, the Maui Raceway Park between the 4 and 5 mile markers is often a happening place on weekends. (Ignore any errant HC&S NO TRESPASSING signs. They date back to when the *friendly* sugar company leased this government land. Today it's county land, and you *are* allowed access.) The Navy built the landing strip during WWII to land some of their carrier planes. Lots of the bunkers they dug into the ground still dot the area. Later the area was used by the sugar company for their crop dusters. Today, even smaller planes (the remote control kind) are flown out there. Sometimes they'll let you fly them through the use of a buddy box (so they can take over before you crash it). They also have drag races on weekends, go-cart races, motocross races on the dirt portion and other recreational activities. The county has lots of competing plans for this area, in addition to their new armory, so its use may change over time. You may find little going on there during the week—hard to say.

PA'IA

If you're heading in the direction of Hana, the last town you'll visit is Pa'ia. This town has accomplished something few Hawai'i towns can claim: It has become an attraction without any attractions other than itself. No great views, no waterfalls, no scenery, no big institutions like an aquarium. Pa'ia's sights lie in its character—and characters. The odd and bizarre add color to Pa'ia like no other Maui town. An example—one morning

we saw the following: a guy with a feather stuck in the top of his head (not his hat), a 90-year-old couple on a Harley (she was driving), a woman whose entire body was covered with tattoos, one gentleman with more dirt in his dreadlocks than a medium-sized canefield, a guy having a serious argument with himself (and losing), and a man in a hard hat carrying a full-sized cross. (Unfortunately, we *just missed* the naked woman painted green doing her Christmas shopping at the various shops.) Welcome to Pa'ia, where it's *still* the Age of Aquarius, and shoes are always optional in the streets. It's not a quiet town (even the name means *noisy* in Hawaiian), but it's unique.

Residents along these windward towns are so used to the frequent short passing showers that they don't even seem to notice when it starts to rain. They often just go about doing exactly what they were doing, oblivious to the falling drops.

In addition to people-watching, Pa'ia is probably second only to Lahaina for shopping. Though not as large, the selection is varied. Stores like Alice in Hulaland and Hemp House are situated near surf shops and the town's best-stocked liquor store. Every shop has its own flavor. Even men, who normally don't like shopping, may like wandering Pa'ia. And the town has some surprisingly good restaurants.

Up Baldwin Avenue Holy Rosary Church, across from Pa'ia School, is a beautiful birch and glass building. They also have a nice memorial to Father Damien of Moloka'i, the priest who worked at the leprosy settlement described on page 144.

While in Pa'ia, wave bye-bye to that last stoplight. If you're heading toward Hana, you won't see another light until you've almost completely circumnavigated Haleakala to Kula, 100 miles around.

Leaving Paʻia, the Hoʻokipa Lookout just before the 9 mile marker is a perfect place to watch the surf. When it's pounding, there's no better place to be than along this shoreline. Breakers can pound with such ferocity in the winter that it makes the ground tremble. Much of the year, expert windsurfers (see page 230) ride the waves after 11 a.m., often streaking faster than the wind, and it's quite a sight to see. Wind is so predictable here—and it runs almost parallel to the shore—that it's considered the single best beach in the United States to windsurf.

CENTRAL MAUI SHOPPING

Kahului is where residents do much of their shopping. The largest mall here is Queen Kaʻahumanu Mall on Hwy 32. You'll find department stores, such as Macy's and Sears, well-known chain stores and local businesses that offer island-made gifts and clothing.

Also on Hwy 32, Maui Mall has a couple of reasons to stop—a sherbet-type treat called Guri Guri at Tasaka's and kids will have a great time painting their own pottery souvenir at Kids & Company. There is also a Longs Drug here.

If you enjoy big outdoor swap meets, Maui's biggest is on Saturdays from 7 a.m. to noon. Park off Kamehameha and Puunene streets. The entrance is on Puunene next to the post office. They have lots of fresh fruits, baked goods and flowers, as well as coffees, T-shirts and other locally made items. 50¢ admission charge.

Costco and Kmart are at the corner of Hwys 380 and Dairy Road (see map.) You'll want to stop here to stock up on food if you're here for a few days or more. Kmart sells inexpensive film, sunblock, T-shirts and reef shoes. Wal-Mart is kind of hidden behind Maui Marketplace. You'll see it to the left of Home Depot off Dairy Road.

The town of Paʻia is one of the most eclectic places to shop on the island. There are many small boutiques offering amazing variety. If you can not find parking on the street, there is a parking lot on the mauka side as you enter town. Not all of Paʻia's business owners are early risers, so you may find some shops that don't open until 10 or 11 a.m.

Some clothing shops to look for are Mandala Ethnic Arts, Tamara Katz, Jaggers, Moonbow Tropics, Maui Girl & Co., Hemp House and Biasa Rose Boutique. For your keiki be sure and stop in at Tropikidz, which also has toys. For surf gear try Simmer Surf or Surfboard Maui.

The Wine Corner has an outstanding selection of beers (and wine, of course). Indigo is a great place to check out home accessories, as is Sand & Sea. If you like antiques, stop by the Paʻia Trading Co. Don't miss the outstanding jewelry from Israel at Dafna's. Maui Hands is found at several locations around the island, but this one is by far the best for its diverse selection of local artist works for sale. Stop in at Birken & Bailey's Boutique where Birken (or Bailey, for that matter) can help you sniff out just the right souvenir for your pet back home.

CENTRAL MAUI BEST BETS

Best Restaurant View—Mama's Fish House

Best Place to Watch Windsurfers Race the Wind—Hoʻokipa Beach Park

Best Place to Find Weird People Doing Odd Things in a Strange Way—Paʻia

Best Place to Watch Remote Control Planes Fly—Maui Raceway Park

If heaven had a highway…

The road to Hana is without question the most famous and desired drive in all Hawai'i, the crown jewel of driving. It's been compared to driving through the garden of Eden: a slow, winding road through a lush paradise that you always knew existed—somewhere.

If you're in a hurry to get to Hana, you're missing the point. Unless you're staying the night in Hana, you probably won't spend much time there. You're heading somewhere else. (Those who spend the night in Hana will have more time to sample its delights.) At the risk of sounding like a Chinese fortune cookie, fulfillment lies in the journey, not the destination. The whole reason to drive along this route is to see the Hawai'i of your dreams, the tropical fantasy that becomes reality along the way. This is a drive through wonderland, and the only thing at the end—is the end of your discovery. As you drive, don't feel the need to hurry up to get "there," because you may find that there is no there there.

If you're going to be staying in Hana for a couple of days (which we *highly* recommend), then you'll have a chance to see and do much of what the following two chapters present. But if you'll be seeing this part of the island on a one-day tour (as most do), then you won't have a chance to experience even a third of the things we've discovered on the road around Haleakala. If you're a one-dayer, we suggest you read through the following two chapters before you leave so you can prioritize the things that interest you most. For instance, if you're looking for a once-in-a-lifetime photo op of you at the top of a water-fall, check out the Infinity Pool on page 107. Maybe you want to do some body-surfing at the best beach on the island for it. Then Hamoa Beach on page 96 is what you want. If you want to see a drop dead gorgeous view of the coast, make sure you take Nahiku Road on page 88. If you want to dig your toes in a genuine volcanic black sand beach, then Wai'anapanapa on page 90 is a must-see. Maybe you'd like to swim in a freshwater cave. Page 91 is where you'll find it. Want to see crazy fools make daring leaps into the water? Gotta check out page 84. Want to take a pow-ered hang gliding flight along the coast? You need to see Armin on page 185. This is just a small portion of what's available. The point is, you can't do it all, so decide which adventure is most important to you.

The road to Hana is two lanes with lots of one-lane bridges. Tourist literature says there are 600 turns, though I don't know exactly how they classify a turn since the road is never straight. (Your steering wheel *certainly* changes direc-tion more than that.) Whether you find the Hana Highway wild or tame depends on your experience. We've noticed that people who have lived most of their lives in flat areas—where a straight line *really is* the closest distance between two points and you can always see what's a mile in front of you—find the constant winding road and blind turns unnerving. Those of us who grew up with crooked roads find it a joy. We once met some visitors from the midwest who were high-ly adventurous. They skydived, flew ultra-lights and thought nothing about jumping off the 60-foot bridge over 'Ohe'o Gulch into the water. But they refused to drive the Hana Highway again because it

"made them nervous." Ironically, they were traveling with timid couch potatoes who grew up in Northern California and loved the "relaxing feel" of the highway. So I guess it depends on what you're used to.

CAN A RENTAL CAR GO ALL THE WAY?

There are many myths associated with the Hana Highway. Let's dispense with the biggest and most entrenched.

Myth—You can't drive a regular car all the way around Haleakala; you need a 4WD vehicle and high clearance past Hana, and even if you could, it would vio-late your rental car agreement.

Fact—The road past Hana is nearly always perfectly driveable and *may* not violate your rental car agreement. You *don't* need high clearance or 4WD. Years ago, the road to Hana was a tortu-ous drive. The sadistic pavement was full of potholes and ill-conceived pothole fills beating up you and your car along the way. But today, the road to Hana is smooth, though a winding and narrow two lanes much of the way. *Yeah, but what about the part past Hana?* Well, 14 miles past Hana, after the 38 mile marker (the number sequence is altered at Hana), the road goes from pavement to gravel that is graded regularly. After less than 5 miles of sometimes bumpy gravel (its bumpiness depends on when you catch it during the maintenance cycle) it becomes blacktop again, textured rough from countless poor patch jobs. After a few miles of bumpy blacktop the smooth highway returns. *Very* rarely, extremely heavy rains (or an earthquake—see page 108) may close the road at one point where a normally dry stream crosses the road, but it is usually reopened as soon as they can get a crew out there.

Most rental car contracts we've seen restrict you from using the car on "unpaved" or sometimes "unimproved" roads and don't mention the road to Hana specifically. In the past that language certainly covered the latter part of the road. But now those terms don't sound as if they apply. After all, the paved portion would seem to be legitimate, and the gravel portion is certainly "improved" constantly. Besides, if it's so bad, how come large tour buses are able to drive all the way around? The fact is, the second half of the road has a very out-of-date reputation, and all the free magazines and maps that tell you otherwise need to have their people drive it for themselves. Even if you are violating your rental car agreement, what does that mean? According to the rental car companies we contacted, it means the extra insurance you took out *may* not cover you there (and you may not want to pay for that anyway because your own personal car insurance may cover you), and it means they won't come get you if you get into trouble.

Driving all the way to Hana and then turning around (which the vast majority of visitors do) means missing the windswept back of Haleakala in the late afternoon. The way the light casts deep shadows in the water-scoured gulches, the incredibly expansive views of the coastline, the impossibly blue sky against the brown and red upper slopes of the volcano, the angry, wind-ravaged seas, and the utter lack of civilized development—these are the things that make a drive along the bottom part of the island worthwhile. It won't look like the Hana drive; you just *saw* that. But it will pass from Eden-like lushness to the land of sun and wind. It's hard to believe that the backside is part of the same mountain.

DRIVING THE ROAD

You *definitely* want to drive in a clockwise direction so you can take advantage of the sun. The Hana side is sunny in the morning, shady in the afternoon, and its waterfalls are best before 11 a.m.

It's best to start the road to Hana *early,* so you'll have time to see and experience as much as possible. Unfortunately, we're not the only ones who give this advice, so everyone else seems to be leaving early, too. On average, between 1,500 and 2,000 cars per day drive the road to Hana. Most leave Kahului between 8:30 a.m. and 10 a.m. I know, I know. You're supposed to be here on vacation, and we *really* hate to suggest something as regimented as a timetable, but let us make one recommendation. If you're not going to be staying in Hana overnight, we strongly suggest you leave early enough to be passing Kahului by 8 a.m. This lets you avoid the crowds and see the sights in good light and allows you to take your time. If you're staying in Hana, leave after 10:30 a.m. when the road's more empty.

Both of these scenarios allow you to avoid being in a procession of cars. This can take away *much* for the driver. *We can't emphasize this enough.* Whether they realize it or not, drivers focus almost constantly on the car ahead. You can't help it; it's instinctive. But when no one's ahead of you, your eyes tend to sweep and record the road ahead and then fall onto the delicious scenery. That's why we're more than happy to pull over repeatedly to allow cars to get far enough ahead so that we can drive to Hana and enjoy ourselves. We've done informal surveys and found that people who drove behind another car didn't think the drive was *nearly* as nice as those who drove it with no one in front of them. And if you notice a long line behind you, pull over to allow the faster ones to get by. There's virtually no place for them to pass on this highway.

WATERFALLS

Everybody loves **waterfalls**. They seem to universally affect people with a peaceful, soothing feeling. On this drive, waterfalls near the road are easy to find. This part of Maui was tailor-made for waterfall production because it has the two necessary ingredients—constant elevation changes and lots of rain up the mountain. But many of the lovelier ones are off the road, often accessible from trails. We have identified many with this symbol.

We tried to photograph most of the waterfalls flowing about halfway between abnormally pumping and abnormally light. The only exceptions are Hanawi (we just *had* to show you what it looks like when it's really going) and Lower Puohokamoa. The others are fairly typical middle-of-the-road. Sometimes higher (usually winter), sometimes lower (usually summer).

One thing you need to understand is the extremely variable nature of waterfalls. At different times, the same falls can be an unimpressive trickle, a world-class waterfall in a lovely setting, or a brown, swollen mass of water and mud after a heavy rain. We have found most of these falls in all three states at different times. During some wet winter months, you may find more waterfalls than we mention. Sometimes, during dry months, some of our favorites may shrivel to a pathetic dribble, but you'll never see fewer than six falls between Kahului and Hana *if* you know when and where to look.

A FEW BASICS

East Maui Irrigation Company (EMI) has ditches that run most of the way to Hana. At times, they will turn off various falls as they divert the water to feed the thirsty cane fields in Central Maui and for some residential use. Be aware that some of these falls may be on land

Though many of the waterfalls flow year round, some, like Wailua Iki, flow only in the winter.

Serious jungle action, brah.

marked with NO TRESPASSING signs, usually EMI's. While crossing land gates here, remember that most of it is actually a *state-owned* forest reserve, not private. EMI merely leases the water rights. Their lease is supposed to be on a revocable year-to-year permit, but at press time it was only month-to-month, so perhaps they will have the authority to prevent public access, perhaps not. (In other words, who's to know if, by the time you read this, they have a lease on the land or not?) Hunters have used the land on weekends for years. Here and under HIKING we describe several awesome hikes in this area. You may want to contact EMI in advance to get permission to hike to some of the falls. You won't be able to get permission while at the falls themselves because you'll rarely find any EMI personnel around at the falls to ask. Remember, this is a watershed. So don't do anything in the streams you wouldn't do to your *own* water supply.

Car break-ins can occur at scenic spots such as waterfalls. Though not exactly common along the Hana road, all it takes is one or two scumbags smashing windows to create a problem. So avoid leaving valuables in the car, especially visible on the seat.

Many of the businesses along this road are closed on Sundays.

Start the trip with a full tank of gas.

The car of choice for the Hana Highway is the convertible. There are many times that you'll see striking greenery above you that others will miss.

The **weather** on the Hana Highway is notoriously difficult to predict. Parts of it get a *lot* of rain; that's why it's so beautiful and the waterfalls so plentiful. You can call 877–5111 for a weather update. One thing that Hana road veterans know is that as you start the drive, if you observe bad weather, it usually (but not always) gets better past Nahiku, so don't turn around assuming it will be raining the whole drive. More times than we can count, we've hit heavy rain much of the way only to have it disappear just before the Hana Airport.

This stretch of road, more than any other in the state, suffers from the lemming effect. (Lemmings are rodents known for going over cliffs *en masse* because the ones in front of them are doing it.) The drive is so special that everyone's afraid of missing something, so when you pull over, you'll likely see others pulling up behind you to see what they might be missing. We are well aware that many of the sights that we've discovered—some of them never mentioned anywhere else—will soon start attracting others who pull in behind our readers. But at least *you* know what to look for, and *they* are the lemmings. And just because you see others on the side of the road, don't think they know something you don't. Odds are, they don't.

PA'IA TO HIGHWAY 360

The first part of the drive starts on Hwy 36 after you've passed Pa'ia. (That town is described in CENTRAL MAUI SIGHTS.) The map on page 115 covers this first part. As you pass the 10 mile marker, you'll cross **Maliko Gulch**. An older bridge and train trestle were erected ½ mile up mauka (toward the mountain) in 1913. The sugar company that built it had lots of trouble getting workers to work on the foundations. It required swinging into the 300-foot gulch on ropes, and nervous workers kept refusing to go. Finally the boss/owner of the sugar company grabbed the rope and swung into the ravine. None of the other workers ever refused again. You see, the boss, Henry Baldwin, did it while recovering from a recent accident—where he had *lost an arm.* Baldwin had swung into the gulch armed with only...well, you know. After that, no worker had the nerve to refuse to do something with two arms that the boss man had done with one. The bridge was eventually torn down to prevent indestructible teenagers from repeating the feat.

While still on Hwy 36, you'll come upon the **Maui Grown Market** past the 14 mile marker with their sign saying, "Last Stop Before Hana." Don't you believe it! There's a better place 20 miles ahead.

ON HIGHWAY 360

Soon the highway changes its name to 360 (now it's a county road), and the mile markers start at 0. The map on the next page starts here. You should reset your odometer so you'll always have a general idea where you are, but bear in mind that the mile markers aren't always placed a mile apart as they should be. We refer to their *actual* location, not where they're *supposed* to be. So if we say something is ³/₁₀ past the 8 mile marker, check again at the 8 mile marker to see what the odometer reads.

The first half of the drive is more tightly enclosed by vegetation, so you won't get too many expansive views. There *may* be a fruit stand and lots of people just past the 2 mile marker. A series of roads and trails leads to **Twin Falls**, actually six or seven waterfalls, none very spectacular compared to what's ahead. People tend to spend too much time here because it's the first available falls and then rush by better opportunities. You should avoid them for the nicer, less-mobbed waterfalls later. But the fruit stand itself, when it's there, is pretty good with lots of fresh fruits and excellent banana bread.

Little more than a half mile past the 3 mile marker is a road which leads to **Kaulanapueo Church**. Built in 1853, it's still in use and is an excellent example of 19th-century churches, though it will probably be locked when you visit.

Hana Highway

Waipi'o Bay

Hoalua Bay

Huelo

Tunnel

Central Maui map on page 115

2

3

4
Missing

5

Twin Falls

Hana Highway

Diversion Ditch & Tunnels

36

16

360

1

Ditch Road

Diversion

Ditch

© 2008 Wizard Publications, Inc.

Waiokilo Falls

Ke'anae
Ching's Pond

Spring

Nua'ailua Bay

17

18

Honomanu Bay

Ke'anae Arboretum
Missing

Halfway to Hana Stand

Wailua

13

15

16

Benches

360

14

Wailua Valley State Wayside

19

Lower Waikani Falls

Honomanu Valley

Upper Waikani Falls

20

21

Wailua Iki Falls

Map continued on page 90

© 2008 Wizard Publications, Inc.

At 1⁹⁄₁₀ mile past the 5 mile marker (#6 is missing) is a dirt turnout. A trail leads to *four waterfalls*. Many of the waterfall trails along the highway are in this section. But this one's an exception and is in ADVENTURES on page 236.

Between the 9 and 10 mile markers on the Hana Highway is the **Waikamoi Nature Trail**. Two nature loops—one about 10 minutes, the other about 30—make a pleasant place to stretch your legs a bit, but it's not a hugely compelling hike. It's good for families and you gain, at most, 200 feet. See HIKING on page 200 for more. No restrooms here.

Waikamoi Stream near the 10 mile marker is usually dry, but after a heavy rain it can be a giant caldron with a large waterfall up the mountain and a slippery trail to a smaller one. You'll know whether to bother by the amount of water flowing under the bridge.

Soon you come to the **Garden of Eden** (572–9899). Pretty tough name to live up to; it's an arboretum and botanical garden. The $10 per person entrance fee

Kamehameha Fights to the Death

Just before Holokai Road between the 15 & 16 mile markers (on Hwy 36) there is a hill visible a mile up mauka. This hill became famous during the time of Kamehameha, the first king to conquer all the islands. While he was here battling for Maui in the late 1700s, the Maui king's top warrior was sent with troops to repel Kamehameha. One night Kamehameha camped at that hill and paraded his war god Ku around the camp to see how the feathers on the head of the god would look. They believed that the more erect the top feathers bristled, the better the battle would go. The feathers cooperated. The next day a fierce battle was fought beyond the hill at a place called Kokomo. Though most battles were fought by lower ranking soldiers, here Kamehameha himself fought in a battle to the death with Maui's top warrior. Kamehameha had practiced making war since he was a child, even going so far as to have some of his top men surprise him from time to time by throwing spears at him when he wasn't looking, just to keep him sharp. (He prided himself on being able to dodge or catch as many as five thrown at once.) The battle was begun as most Hawaiian battles were—both leaders on opposite sides of the battlefield hurled insults at each other to stir up the other. When the Maui warrior landed a particularly cruel blow (accusing Kamehameha of having no royal blood, but rather descending from slaves—yes, the Hawaiians did keep slaves), Kamehameha roared. Both leaders shot sling stones at each other. Then they charged each other with spears. Hand to hand, Kamehameha landed a vicious blow with his leiomanu, a club studded with shark's teeth, opening the Maui warrior's chest. The Maui warrior stabbed Kamehameha with a wooden dagger, but Hawai'i's future king finished off his opponent with his club. Maui's top warrior was slaughtered on the field of battle in front of the Maui troops. Those troops were so demoralized that the taking of Maui became inevitable.

seems a little high at first, but you soon realize that this is a meticulously maintained and very beautiful garden. Everything is scrupulously labeled. You can either drive it or walk a separate path. They have a picnic area with good views down the coast if you're looking for a place to eat that sandwich you brought with you, and there's a restroom.

At ⁸/₁₀ mile past the 10 mile marker on the ocean side of the road is a turnout with a telephone pole. There's a well-worn path. Take it for a couple of minutes, and you'll be treated to a view of a particularly large waterfall that the vast majority of drivers miss. Plunging about 200 feet, **Lower Puohokamoa Falls** drops into a large pool as drivers, blissfully unaware of its existence below, rush along on their way to Hana. The trail continues and gets steeper as it meanders into the valley, but that latter part is treacherous.

Just past the 11 mile marker is a path to **Upper Puohokamoa Falls**. The landowner (Garden of Eden) has

WATERFALL ALERT!

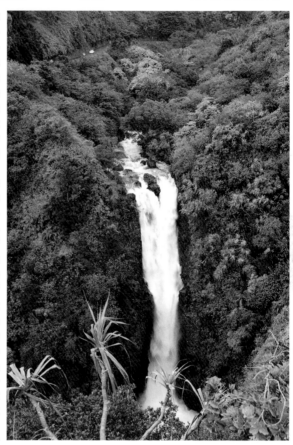

Most drivers (top) have no idea that they are passing Lower Puohokamoa Falls. A short trail takes you to this vantage point.

erected a wall and won't allow people to access it from the near side. Perhaps they simply want you to visit their garden and view the falls from their property instead. Fortunately, they don't own the land on the far side and from there you'll find a trail to the falls.

A half mile past the 11 mile marker there's a small turnout on the far side of the bridge and a trail that leads 30 seconds or so to a pool and small waterfall called **Haipua'ena Falls**. It's worth a

stop. There's another, larger falls just upstream, but the trail to the second falls, even on a dry day, has a short stretch where it's easy to fall. (An ugly fall at that.) Not worth it; stay at the first waterfall.

WATERFALL ALERT!

Past the 12 mile marker you come across the **Kaumahina State Wayside** with its restrooms. The **restrooms** at Ke'anae 5 miles ahead are usually less crowded even though there are fewer of

The raw, younger Ke'anae coastline is a beautiful place to imagine Maui in its younger years.

them. The wayside also has a series of short nature loops heading uphill from the ocean overlook.

There's a spot a half mile past the 12 mile marker where the road opens up, exposing the very scenic **Ke'anae Peninsula**, but there's no place to pull over. In another ¼ mile there's a place where you can quasi-pull over to have a peek. What a view!

As you cruise along, consider that cars couldn't make it to Hana from central Maui until an unpaved road was cut in 1926. Before that, Hana was isolated and quiet. Even with the new road, driving was only for the brave and the well insured. It remained unpaved until 1962. The paving job was awful, and the paved Hana Highway deteriorated until it was almost worse than the old unpaved road it replaced. The state finally did it right in the early 1980s, creating the smooth (though still narrow) ride you enjoy today.

If you've been itching for your very own private waterfall, you *may* be in luck. One quarter mile past the 13 mile marker there's a tiny turnout on the far side of the white 1911 bridge and another one farther along the road. Even when it looks dry, there *may* (or may not) be more water flowing unseen under the rocks near the highway, so it's hard to gauge the flow here. About 800 or so feet upstream is a pretty and lacy unnamed falls on the Punalau stream. (We'll call it **Punalau Falls**.)

WATERFALL ALERT! This is one of the few falls along the way that you can visit and have a reasonable chance of having it to yourself for three reasons: You can't see it from the road, it's never been written about as far as we know, and you'll have to walk on the (usually) dry stream boulders nearly the whole way. (When the boulders are wet, they're pretty slippery.) It'll take between 10 and 25 minutes to get there (depending on your rock-hopping aptitude). A pair of walking sticks is invaluable for stream walking; you'll go from being a two-legged animal to a four-legged one.

On the highway just past Punalau Falls there's a dirt road that leads to **Honomanu Bay**, though it takes you to the wrong side of the bay. (You would have to walk across the presumably low stream.) Another road just past the 14 mile marker takes you to the right (usable) side of the bay, though part of it may need 4WD clearance. The beach here is gravelly and the swimming poor, but in the early morning or late afternoon, the sun creates a magnificent golden green on the gouged-out valley walls, reminding you why you came to Hawai'i.

The present government road to Hana is by no means the first. Back in the 1500s a king named **Kihapi'ilani** decided that trips around the island were too perilous. Many of the gulches you have passed along the way were well known places for robberies, since the thieves could easily get away. So the king had trails cut and paved with smooth stream stones all around Haleakala—quite a feat at the time. It took years (though probably less time than the current county government seems to take these days when they repave it). It was said that the king didn't want to be forgotten when he died. His public works project succeeded, because five centuries later he is still remembered fondly, and another public works project, Pi'ilani Highway, bears his name and the name of a 17th-century governor. His 500-year-old stone road was still visible in places until the jungle consumed the last of it in the early 1900s.

At ⁴⁄₁₀ mile past the 14 mile marker is a large turnout offering exceptional views of the valley and highway ribbon draped across the mountain. Vegetation sometimes blocks it. The turnout another ²⁄₁₀ mile ahead is better. Actually, ¹⁄₁₀

mile past that are some old wooden benches buried in the overgrown ferns. There's a skinny semi-pullout in front of them, but a real pullout just ahead. If you walk to the dilapidated benches (be careful walking on the road), you'll find an amazingly tranquil view of Honomanu Bay and of the zig-zagging Hana Highway working its way up the cliffs. Take your time here and savor the smashing scene. The upper part of the valley you're looking at is full of burial sites. The old Hawaiians refused to walk there at night, believing that the spirits of chiefs buried there roamed the valley.

Off the highway just before the road into Ke'anae Peninsula is the **Ke'anae Arboretum**. Neglected for years, the state seems to have rediscovered this garden. Now plants and trees are well-marked and the formerly weed-infested taro field is making a comeback. The paved and unpaved path is a 25–30 minute stroll. It's not as nice as the Garden of Eden mentioned earlier, but it's free. Past the main path, a narrower, marginally interesting trail goes through a wilder, darker, more jungly terrain to a couple of very small waterfalls. Bring mosquito repellent unless you're a practiced bloodletter.

KE'ANAE TO NAHIKU

Next comes the road into **Ke'anae Peninsula** and village. (The YMCA camp you just passed has cabins for rent, see page 177.) The road hugs the coastline for a time, and at one place there's an excellent photo op with the ocean tearing through some jagged lava boulders. Very striking, especially at high tide. The impossibly blue water against the rich lushness of the Hana coast is a feast for the eyes. Farther ahead are some rest-

DIVERSION ALERT!

rooms near the ballpark. (Before the ballpark, a stand on the right sells **banana bread** that's even better than the stuff described below at Halfway to Hana.) The coastline across from the restrooms is a good place to watch the waves beat up the shoreline. The land here is younger than the rest of the island, and it shows.

There's an extraordinary legend about the origin of the taro fields at Ke'anae that can't be confirmed but ties in nicely with what we know about the geology of the land. The legend states that in ancient times there was a chief who was constantly at war with the neighboring village of Wailua. At that time Ke'anae was mostly a barren lava field. The chief decided that he needed more taro-growing land and more people living in the area. So he decreed that every man, woman and child would go to the upper valley, gather soil in baskets and fill the peninsula with enough soil to grow taro. In time, the peninsula became a prime taro-growing area. True story? Who knows? It's a legend. But what a task it would have been. Imagine hiking miles up the valley, hauling a basket of heavy dirt back, dumping it on the lava rock and heading back uphill. The definition of a thankless Dilbert-like job!

Ke'anae was nearly wiped out by the tsunami (tidal wave) of 1946. Nearly every building was destroyed, leaving only the immovable stone church.

Back on the highway, just before the 17 mile marker, is a bridge and pullout. The path about 75 feet to the left leads down to a marvelous pool, known locally as **Ching's Pond**. The swimming is particularly good, and most drivers never even see this pond. Above the narrow stream portion (just before it opens up to the pool) there's a concrete platform on the right side. We've seen daring young locals *diving* out and away from the cliff into the tiny part they claim is deep enough so you don't hit rocks. We're talking about a 25 foot or so drop with *zero* margin for error. *That's* what we call an 'okole squeezer. (We'll let you guess what an 'okole is.) Obviously you shouldn't do this unless you name us as beneficiaries on your life insurance.

WATERFALL ALERT!

A cliff diver at Ching's Pond lands in the only space deep enough.

About ⅓ mile past the 17 mile marker is a stand generally known as **Halfway to Hana**. (Actually, you're ⅔ of the way from Kahului.) They have justifiably famous banana bread (moist, sweet and tasty) that we like to review every time we travel the road. (Just to be thorough, you understand. We do it for you, only for you.) They also have fruits, beverages, some sandwiches and so-so burgers, and other snacks. If you're hungry, consider stocking up here for snacks. Hana has relatively few food options. By the way, take a peek at the house behind the stand to see if they still have all those pigs' heads hanging on the wall.

About ⅔ mile past the 17 mile mark, pull over and walk to the white concrete bridge. Look down on the ocean side of the bridge, and you see water gushing out of the mountain, surrounded by flowers and some huge elephant ears (called 'ape) in a garden setting tailor-made for a postcard (though they sometimes let the flowers overgrow). This is a **spring-fed gusher**, originating here. Any pipes you see under the flowers are tapping the water, not feeding it. When they keep it well tended, it's a lovely sight.

The tiny settlement of **Wailua** is off the road not long past the 18 mile marker. This quaint community is mostly built around taro growing. (Taro is the plant Hawaiians use to make poi, the purple, less-than-tasty paste you may try—once— at lu'aus.) That road is dead-on straight. (Bowlers may get sweaty palms imagining the possibilities. It's strange to be driving on straight pavement again; your hands are searching for something to do.) Keep an eye on your right for a glimpse of the enormous, multi-tiered **Waikani Falls**, which drop 1,000 feet in several stages just under the highway. (You can't see the large lower falls from the highway.) The only other thing of interest in Wailua is a small, pretty church.

Just before the 19 mile marker, most people blow by without even noticing the **Wailua Valley State Wayside** on the mauka (mountain) side. Take the stairs to the right to the top, and on the ocean side you'll see the quaint village of Wailua with its fields of taro beneath you. Turn around and look up mauka. You'll see (clouds permitting) the Ko'olau Gap at the top of the mountain. Notice how steep the valley walls are, yet the floor is so broad and flat? This valley used to be thousands of feet deep, cutting into the very core of the volcano. It was filled in at the same time as the Kaupo Gap on the other side of the volcano. (See page 111 for the full story.) The relatively new lands of Wailua and the Ke'anae Peninsula were formed by the same flows that filled the gaps.

Many of the one-lane bridges along here are close to 100 years old. The county wants to replace them, but there's a hitch. In order to get federal (meaning your) dollars, the bridges usually need to be two-lane. (The feds don't like paying for one-lane bridges.) The problem is that Hana residents don't *want* two-lane bridges. Since the county is perpetually short of funds, it's a safe bet that some two-lane bridges are on their way. In fact, in Kaupo on the bottom of the island before the 28 mile marker you'll notice two new expensive concrete two-lane bridges—connecting two halves of a one-lane road. We Maui residents thank you for your support.

Between the 19 and 20 mile markers there's a very popular waterfall to photograph called **Upper Waikani Falls**, sometimes called **Three Bears Falls** (the upper cousin to the huge falls partially visible from Wailua village).

WATERFALL ALERT!

These falls vary dramatically, depending on flow. In case you're wondering, yes, you *can* get to the falls themselves. At the far side of the bridge (on the mauka side) is a fairly easy short path—it's just the first step that's ugly. Standing near the falls, you'll realize that they're a lot bigger than you thought.

Remember, the secret to shooting waterfalls is a long exposure. If your camera has adjustable shutter speeds, the longer the exposure (say around ¹⁄₁₀ second), the better the shot looks—if you can hold the camera still enough. If you flunked out of surgeon school because your hands shake, use a tripod or prop the camera on a rock. Also, see page 33 for precautions on swimming in streams. This is probably a good time to tell you that, while swimming in natural pools, use

your hands as much as possible to avoid kicking unseen rocks. (Voice of experience with the stubbed toes to prove it.)

The stream just before the 21 mile marker is sometimes almost dry. That's because most of the water is diverted less than a ½ mile upstream. But ²⁄₁₀ mile past the 21 mile marker is a hunters' road called **Wailua Iki**. A 10-minute walk from there (at the top of the dirt road turn right) leads to a very nice waterfall and pool, as well as a *gorgeous* valley. (See page 75 for hiking in this EMI area.) There are two more falls farther up the stream, but they're harder to reach. By the way, *if* there's water flowing at the highway, the real view is from about 250 feet up the highway (there's a one-car turnout just up the hill), where the water

WATERFALL ALERT!

Most people seem to think that the heavier the water flow, the prettier the waterfall. These two shots of Waikani Falls (AKA the 3 Bears) are an example of how sometimes less is more.

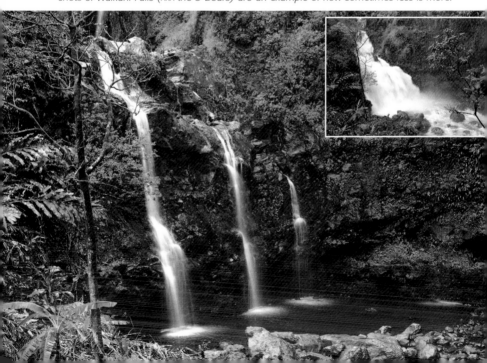

that flows under the highway plunges off the cliff in a very dramatic fashion.

At ⁹⁄₁₀ mile past the 21 mile marker is one of the heavier-flowing falls along the coast. (It's heavy because there's no ditch upstream robbing its water.) Unfortunately, it's just barely out of sight (except maybe the top as you're driving up) 500 feet inland. This whole area is part of the Ko'olau Forest Reserve, but EMI, which has the water rights, has infrastructure there that dissuades you from visiting the falls. Assuming they give you their blessing to hike to it, you'll find a trail on the right side of the stream leading most of the way to the falls. You'll have to find a way to scramble up the rock wall in front of you to get to it.

Between the 22 and 23 mile markers is **Pua'a Ka'a State Park**. (*That's* a hard one to say.) Two easily visited small waterfalls make good photo ops, and there are **restrooms**. The falls are often fairly light, but it's not for lack of water. If you're adventurous, we have a surprise for you. There's an awkward trail on the right side of the upper falls. It first leads to a short path to the top of the falls, but if you go past it for 5–10 squishy minutes (it's usually muddy), there's a much heavier untapped falls and pool just above the diversion ditch that's taking much of the lower falls' water. When the trail gets to the elevated waterway (viaduct), you have to walk along it (which those afraid of heights will *hate*), then across. Only 100 more feet upstream is your prize. The falls make an ideal photo op—you know, the *me under a waterfall* shot, if the flow's not too heavy—and it's a pretty dependable waterfall, even during the driest times. The

trail goes around a hill and narrows as it goes down to the pool.

By the way, there are boreholes in the Pua'a Ka'a highway bridge to answer that question that's troubled you all your life—how thick are these bridges anyway?

After the 23 mile mark you pass a couple caves, a bridge, then a bigger cave covered with large white roots. You can follow one of these to the back of the cave and exit the cave into the jungle next to a stream. These are **lava tubes**, created when lava from volcanic vents forms a river that crusts over on top. These tubes can transport the lava for over 20 miles, losing a mere 20°F along the way. Lava tubes tend to collapse over time, so young islands, like the Big Island, are loaded with them, whereas older islands, like Kaua'i, have relatively few.

After the 24 mile marker, yet another pretty waterfall called **Hanawi Falls** awaits. It's particularly attractive. If you take a photo from the bridge, be careful. The guard-rail is shorter than it looks. There have been people who have sat on the rail for a photo, only to careen backward onto the rocks. When the flow is heavy, this becomes one of the nicest waterfalls on the whole coast. It splits around the rocks, and the portion on the left adds to the portion on the right, making it a dream.

OK, OK. I know you've probably seen a number of nice waterfalls by now. Been there, done that. But *when it's flowing,* this next one is different. Pull over on the far side of the bridge shortly past the 25 mile marker. If you walk out to the bridge (there's no walkway for you), from the middle of the ocean side, look straight down. (Be *really* careful not to topple over.) You'll see something you don't normally get to see. You are *directly* above

Hanawi Falls, when it's really pumping like it is here, is glorious even when you don't get out of your car. At other times, only the right side flows.

the spot where **Makapipi Falls** plunges unfettered into a large pool. Excellent vantage point as you follow the stream with your eyes as it burrows through the vegetation on its way to the ocean. Makapipi is more seasonal than most falls and is dry about half the time.

WATERFALL ALERT!

NAHIKU

Next to the falls, **Nahiku Road** leads 2½ miles down through the luxuriant community of Nahiku. If you think the road to Hana looked lush and beautiful, wait till you see Nahiku. When plants go to heaven, Nahiku must be their destination. Everything green seems so happy and healthy, you can almost hear them giggling. Life bursts from every corner at the bottom half of the road. Nahiku was formed in 1905 as a rubber tree plantation, but the effort went flat a decade later.

DIVERSION ALERT!

Drive slowly; children play in the streets. Several honor-system fruit stands are usually present. Once at the bottom of Nahiku Road, you're in for a treat—a jaw-dropping view of the shoreline all the way back to Ke'anae. There's a little path on the left that leads to a variable but charming little artesian waterfall and pool, right next to the ocean. What a spot! As you stand there in your own private paradise, you can't help but wonder if there's a more beautiful place in the world. Perhaps you can't see forever, but you can see all the way to paradise. This is one of our favorite spots to sit and gaze along the Hana coast. Miles of coastline are revealed as the sounds of the surf and the small falls make everything just perfect. A grassy area near the ocean makes a good place to have lunch.

As you depart and the road leaves the shoreline, you may think that Nahiku has delivered everything it can. But during rainy times there's one surprise left. Pull the car over about 150 feet uphill from the shoreline guard-rail. The stream to your left forms a big pool with a small waterfall. (It can dry up in the summertime.) The whole setting is ensconced in an area packed with more shades of green than you ever knew existed. There was even a rope swing there when last we checked, where local children sometimes play. The scene is as wholesome and idyllic as any you may encounter. It's a flawlessly sculpted natural setting. Only the mosquitoes remind you that it's still the real world. There's a short path down to the pool.

NAHIKU TO HANA

Back on the highway, you'll notice that the terrain is changing. It's less eroded because the land is relatively new here. You'll soon come to some food stands called the **Nahiku Marketplace**. They have fresh fruit, candy, other food and overpriced art. The taco stand with a smoker is the best reason to stop here. For $6 their kalua pork tacos will ease your hunger. (Good smoked fish, too.) Even if you don't stop, at least slow down. Parking is tight and cars pulling out might not see you.

Near the 31 mile marker is 'Ula'ino Road, Drive a couple miles down 'Ula'ino and you come to **Kahanu Garden** (248–8912), part of the National Tropical Botanical Garden. They have self-guided tours (which take around 30 minutes) between 10 a.m. and 2 p.m. for $10, Mon–Fri. The garden is set among spacious grounds, and the emphasis is on native and Polynesian-introduced plants, not ornamental flowers. The love and care is evident. They take good care of this place, and the plants are well labeled.

A REAL GEM The most extraordinary feature is not a plant at all, but rather the **Pi'ilanihale Heiau** (shown on page 14). This massive temple, the largest in the state, was largely forgotten and buried under vegetation until the garden restored it in the late '90s. The first time we saw it, we were unprepared for its immensity. When you first spot it, it looks enormous. But after you get close and go around a corner, you realize how utterly colossal it really is. It covers almost *three acres* and it took an estimated 128,000 man-days to build, starting in the late 1200s A.D. The second phase was completed around

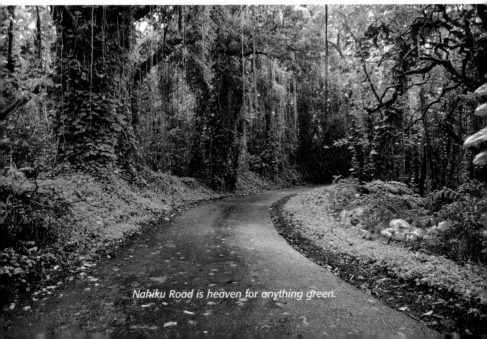

Nahiku Road is heaven for anything green.

1570. You won't be allowed to walk on it, and your vantage point isn't as good as our aerial photo, but you'll get a feel for its sheer size.

There are some nice coastal views from parts of the garden, as well as some Hawaiian stone implements and tools. Begin your walk at exhibit #4.

Near Kahanu Garden is **Maui Cave Adventures** (248–7308). See page 242 for more on that.

Past here the road eventually becomes private, ending at a stream crossing. You may read about a lovely waterfall past the crossing called **Blue Pool**. It's a fantastic site with a tall, delicious waterfall on one side of the pool and the ocean on the other. Unfortunately, access has become a tangled mess. It's on one large single parcel with dozens of owners. Some of the owners of this single parcel are inviting you onto their land, evidenced by their signs near the end of the road saying you can park for $2. At least one of their fellow owners apparently *doesn't* want you

there, evidenced by a purportedly grumpy greeting at the end of the road and sometimes even threats, according to numerous e-mails we've gotten from readers. We're very concerned about someone getting hurt and can't recommend going to Blue Pool any longer.

Back on the highway, you'll pass the tiny **Hana Airport**. If you want a thrilling adventure, consider a **powered hang glider flight** in a seated ultralight along the Hana coast. The views along the coast are unreal. See page 185 for more.

WAI'ANAPANAPA BLACK SAND BEACH

Just past the 32 mile marker is the road to **Wai'anapanapa Park**. (Gee, that really rolls off the tongue, huh? Blew a gasket in the old spellchecker on *that* one. It sounds like WHY-A-NAH-PAH NAH-PAH.) The park is clean and well maintained. They even have cabins for rent. Other facilities include restrooms, showers, picnic tables and camping. It's got

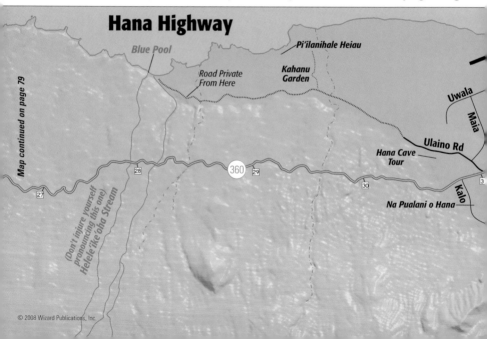

Hana Highway

Blue Pool

Pi'ilanihale Heiau

Road Private From Here

Kahanu Garden

Uwala

Map continued on page 79

Maia

Ulaino Rd

Hana Cave Tour

360   29

28

27

Kalo

(Don't injure yourself pronouncing this one) Helele'ike'oha Stream

30

Na Pualani o Hana

© 2008 Wizard Publications, Inc.

An idyllic Nahiku pond that looks so perfect it can't possibly be real.

two other things going for it. One, there is a freshwater cave that makes a great place for a dip. Two, it has a volcanic black sand beach.

First, the **spring-fed freshwater caves**: these are probably the remnants of lava tubes. There are two, though only one is suitable for swimming. The water level rises and falls each day with the tide, which the fresh water floats on. A little sea water mixes with the fresh water, meaning the water is slightly brackish but crystal clear. The temperature is very cool, though not painfully so. There are two small chambers that snake their way back a bit. A short loop trail drops three

Hana Airport

Powered Hang Glider Flights

Trail

Wai'anapanapa **Black** Sand Beach

Sea Arch

Freshwater Caves

Cabins

Trail

Footing rougher from here

Alalele

360 32

Hana Highway

Heavenly Hana Inn

Trail ends, becomes undefined shoreline hike

Hana Maui Vacation Rental 33

Waikoloa

0   1 MILE

Uakea Rd

34

Hana

Hana Bay

Keanini
Keawa

Uakea

Hauoli

Ka'uiki Head

Red Sand (Kaihalulu) Beach

N
W   E
S

⌒\ Indicates Foot Trails
⊡ Roadside mile markers
⋅⋅⋅ Unpaved Roads

Map continued on page 97

Wai'anapanapa State Park has the only volcanic black sand beach (created from a lava flow) on Maui. Good facilities, freshwater caves; the only thing difficult about this park is pronouncing it.

stories and circles the two caves. There's a Hawaiian legend posted on a sign near the loop trail. Occasionally, prolonged dry spells combined with low tide translates to little water in the cave.

If you've heard of a **volcanic black sand beach**, you may have thought they were all on the Big Island. *Au contraire.* Pa'iloa Beach here at Wai- **A REAL GEM** 'anapanapa Park is 100 or so feet wide and attests to the newness of the land here. The beach was formed when lava flowed and fountained into the sea near here, shattering on contact with the ocean. Fragments smashed against each other and formed the sand you see. (Don't believe books that tell you that the beach was formed by cliff erosion.) Maybe Rome wasn't built in a day, but this beach may have been, because these type of beaches are often formed in days or weeks. We've watched black sand beach-

es being created on the Big Island, and it's an awesome sight. They usually have a short life span since the source of the sand stops as soon as the lava stops flowing. Usually within a few hundred to a thousand years they vanish as the ocean gradually sweeps the precious sand away. (White sand beaches have organic sources, like coral and shells, which are renewed.) Occasionally the sand is deposited in a perfectly shaped bay, like this one, which allows it to stay a little longer. Some lava flows nearby are 500 years old, according to a dated sample taken a mile south of here. There's a pretty coastal hike that leads to the source of all this sand. It's described under HIKING on page 199.

Older islands like Kaua'i and O'ahu have no volcanic black sand beaches. (They can sometimes have the other type of black sand beaches, like the one at Hana Bay, caused when water chips flecks of lava from stream beds and piles it up onshore.) Since the sand supply here is finite, please try to refrain from taking samples back home with you, except the stowaways lodged in your bathing suit. Don't swim during high surf as currents can form in the bay.

HANA

Hana doesn't hit you, it seeps into you. Living on Maui, we had driven through Hana many times and thought we knew it well. But it wasn't until the first time we spent a week in Hana that we truly connected with it. The peace that Hana exudes can only penetrate when you're here at leisure, not on a mission. Today, Hana is one of our favorite places to go to get away from the hellacious rigors of guidebook writing. (You have no idea how hard it was to write that last sentence with a straight face.) If you're on Maui for a week or more, we strongly suggest you consider spending the last couple of days in Hana.

Hana has a reputation of being a rainy place. In fact, they get just over 80 inches a year at the Hana Airport, though it varies quite a bit. That may sound like a lot (actually it *is* a lot), but hidden in that number are two things you need to know. First, it's *way* less rain than what they get farther up the mountain (which is what feeds the waterfalls), and it's less than what they get to the northwest, around Nahiku. This is because Hana is relatively flat and the orographic rain engine that waters most of Hawai'i misses Hana more than most people think. (The photo on the cover is typical. Notice how Hana itself is sunny, with the clouds starting farther uphill?) Second, the great majority of the rain falls at night and early mornings due to the same effect. During the day, heavy five-minute showers also contribute to those rain numbers. Don't

get us wrong. You can still come for a week and have it rain every day. They occasionally get monstrous rains, especially in the winter. It can happen anywhere in Hawai'i. But it's much less likely in Hana than you may guess by simply looking at raw numbers.

Things move slowly in Hana, and if you try to rush, you'll only end up frustrated. Businesses may close for any reason. The only bank is open 1½ hours a day. (How's *that* for bankers' hours?)

Here are some of the things you'll want to check out near Hana.

HANA BAY

Hana Bay has a large, black sand beach. The sand source is lava eroded from a nearby stream. This is usually the safest place to swim along the coast. You can grab something to eat here (see Tutu's, page 98) and eat it at the shore.

On the north (left) side of the bay you may spot an area where the waves come in and seem to die at a certain place. Called **Ke'anini**, Hawaiian legend says there was once a visiting Tahitian chief who wanted to go surfing there. He asked the gods to give him waves, and this they did. As he was surfing, two beautiful local girls saw the handsome chief from shore and fell in love with him. Competing with each other for his attention, they both removed their pa'us—skirts—the only things they wore. The chief saw them and was so startled by the sight that he stopped right there in the water, and the wave went no farther. That is why the waves always stop at that surf site today.

On the right side of the bay is the **Hana Pier**. Nearby, there is a trail that leads 200 or so yards along **Ka'uiki Hill**. There's a plaque at the end of the trail marking the spot near a cave where Ka'ahumanu (King Kamehameha the

Little gems, like this tiny red sand pocket beach near Hana Bay (not the larger, more famous Red Sand Beach), are here to be discovered for those not in a hurry to get to the "Seven Sacred Pools."

Great's "favorite" wife) was born. The real reasons to take the trail are to visit a small but unknown **red sand pocket beach** that varies seasonally (not *the* Red Sand Beach mentioned later) and to get up close and personal with the geology of this part of the island a little farther along. This hill was formed in geologically recent times when a volcanic vent sprayed lava high into the air. The hill came into being as airborne gas-frothed lava was caught by the trade winds and piled up here. Near the plaque area you see places where globs of lava plopped and piled up. The deep burgundy color (especially at the small beach) is from iron in the lava. It's literally rusting before your eyes. There's an isthmus connecting the end of the trail to a small islet that houses a light beacon. During real calm seas you can cross it. One caveat: The beginning part of the trail near the pier was faint to non-existent at press time thanks to a small landslide, so

be careful there. The cove below the end of the trail is an excellent snorkel spot, and it's common to see kayakers there.

If you ever decide that you need to make a stand somewhere, this hill is the place to do it. For generations invaders from the Big Island would capture this hill and were nearly impossible to dislodge due to the hill's easy defense. From up top they could harass area residents and plan general mischief.

RED SAND BEACH

Though we usually describe all beaches in the BEACHES chapter, Hana is so far that you'd never come here simply for a day at the beach. So we're deviating from our usual format and describing Hana's beaches here. The other side of Ka'uiki Hill hides one the area's more exotic looking beaches, **Red Sand Beach** (Hawaiian name is **Kaihalulu**). There's a photo on page 169. It's made from the same crumbling red and black cinders that make up the hill. The swimming is often poor except during calm seas. There's a strip of jagged lava that forms a semi-pool at the head of the beach, but it sometimes has the perverse effect during high seas and high tide of making the water more chaotic and disorienting, like swimming in a washing machine. The snorkeling opportunities are usually marginal. To make matters worse, the trail is on the side of the hill, with loose cinders making the footing awkward in several spots. (And you wouldn't want to slip and fall down the side of the hill—regular shoes are preferred over beach shoes). Lastly, there may be a sign from Hana Ranch telling you not to trespass.

This must be the most violated sign in all east Maui, because everyone, young and old alike, tourists and locals walk to this beach, and we've never heard of anyone being denied entry. So we often have marginal swimming much of the time, marginal snorkeling, an awkward, poten- tially injurious five-minute walk, and a NO TRESPASSING sign. Is it worth going to? To us, it sure is! This is a striking beach, at least worth a look. The rainbow of colors in the lava cinders along the way, the electric blue waters outside the cove, the menacing-looking lava rock inside the bay, the ironwood trees, the layered cinder walls and the untouched beauty make this a memorable place to visit. It's popular and sometimes used by nudists, though nudity is particularly resented by the Hana community and locals sometimes make their displeasure known in a big way, so you might want to take your bare *da kines* elsewhere.

To get there, park on Uakea near Hauoli. (See map on page 97.) Even though it's a dead-end street, make sure you park facing the correct direction. Furiously *under*worked Hana cops will give tickets for this heinous crime. Just before the Sea Ranch Cottages there's a large lawn area owned by the county. Look past the second lamp post on

Gobs of life, gobs of color. The Hana Highway rarely disappoints.

the right for a path leading downhill. Continue straight down, taking a left just near the shore. It's easier to navigate than it sounds. Don't hike if the trail is muddy, and be careful on the slippery cinders. All told, it's about a 5-minute walk.

KOKI BEACH

This beach is a mixture of red and black sand (from the nearby crumbling hill) along with white sand from pulverized coral. It's a good place to sit and observe the ocean under the nearby trees with a dramatic view of the red hill behind you, a sea arch off to the left and the coconut tree-topped 'Alau Island off to the right. Swimming is unprotected and can be hazardous, except when calm. Boogie boarding can be good here. The shape and direction the beach faces makes it a good place for beach-combing. Fishing nets, Japanese net glass floats and other flotsam often wash ashore. Unfortunately, litter seems to be more common here than other beaches.

The large hill next to the beach is called **Ka Iwi o Pele**, said to contain the bones of the volcano goddess Pele, left behind after she had a battle with her sister. The hill and adjacent land is currently owned by Oprah Winfrey.

HAMOA BEACH

A great beach! Tons and tons of fine salt and pepper sand, some shade, showers, clear water and the best **bodysurfing** on the island make this one of the island's primo beaches. The thickness of the sand toward the middle is so great that you don't have to worry as much about stubbing your toe on rocks as at most north- or east-facing Hawai'i beaches. (Though it's always possible.) Toward the center of the beach the sand drops abruptly a little ways offshore, meaning

A REAL GEM

Hamoa Beach, in the early morning, is where you'll find the best bodysurfing on the island.

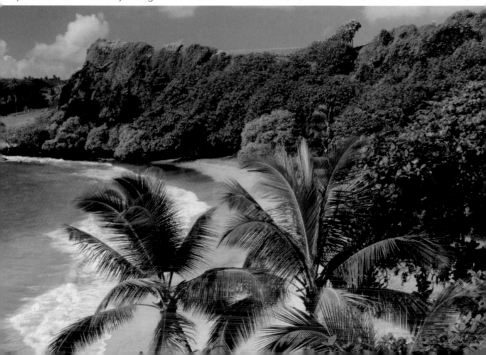

that the waves tend to break at the same spot each time—exactly what you want for bodysurfing. If you've never done this before, be real careful and only do it on small waves. The ocean is unprotected here—no reef to break things up—so the waves have more power here and can drill you into the sand if you're not cautious.

To bodysurf, you simply stand in place, wait for a wave to break right about where you are, and jump forward with your arms extended, turning yourself into a surfboard. I use a mask and snorkel while doing it to keep the salt out of my eyes since I wear contacts. (The mask sometimes gets torn off, so to keep from losing it, I bite down harder on the snorkel when I feel the wave coming.) Many an hour we've spent bodysurfing this beach. Don't try it during high surf; it's too dangerous. Snorkeling is marginal, and there are currents at the two ends of the beach; best to stay in the middle. Located at the south end of Haneo'o Road, there's a paved path leading down. Make sure you park facing the right way. There are other facilities that are for guests of Hotel Hana Maui, but the showers and restrooms are used by all.

Around the rocks to the right (south) is another beach, which is usually deserted. Best to swim to it as the rock scrambling may be difficult.

DINING IN HANA

We normally put dining reviews in the DINING chapter, but we're putting them here for the same reason we put beaches here. Hana is so far out, *nobody* drives there just for the food.

Hana Ranch House (248–8255)

This used to arguably be the worst restaurant on Maui and our criticism, however harsh, was understated (in our opinion) but became notorious on Maui. (OK,

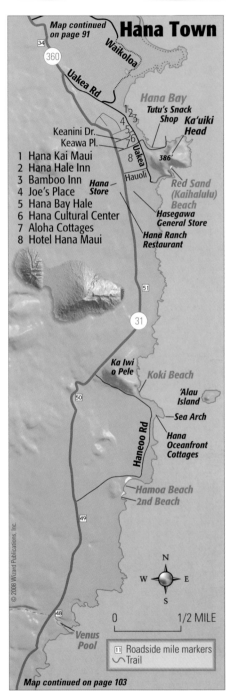

Map continued on page 91

Hana Town

Waikoloa

34
360
Uakea Rd

Hana Bay
Tutu's Snack
Shop   Ka'uiki
Head

Keanini Dr.
Keawa Pl.

1 Hana Kai Maui
2 Hana Hale Inn
3 Bamboo Inn   Hana
4 Joe's Place   Store
5 Hana Bay Hale
6 Hana Cultural Center
7 Aloha Cottages
8 Hotel Hana Maui

Uakea
Hauoli
386'

Red Sand
(Kaihalulu)
Beach

Hasegawa
General Store

Hana Ranch
Restaurant

51

31

Ka Iwi
o Pele   Koki Beach

'Alau
Island

Sea Arch

Hana
Oceanfront
Cottages

Haneoo Rd

50

49

Hamoa Beach
2nd Beach

© 2008 Wizard Publications, Inc.

N
W   E
S

0   1/2 MILE

48

Venus
Pool

11 Roadside mile markers
Trail

Map continued on page 103

Hana's offshore 'Alau Island.

perhaps we were a bit over the top when we begged *don't eat lunch here, don't eat lunch here, don't eat lunch here* at the beginning of the review.) Anyway there are only three places to eat lunch in Hana and this place had the luxury to be as bad as they wanted and still get away with it. We're pleased to report, however, that they have improved *a lot* since then. The menu is mostly ½-pound burgers, some sandwiches and salads inside; add some local-style items and shave a few bucks at the outside window. The burgers aren't great, but hey…they're just burgers. And their salads are downright decent and usually fresh-tasting. Overall, Hana lunch dining is still a three-horse town, but at least now this horse isn't lame. Dinner is only served Wednesdays and Fridays. The setting at the restaurant outdoor tables is quite nice. $7–$11 for breakfast, $13–$18 for lunch, $10–$20 for dinner. No tank tops or bathing suits.

Tutu's Snack Shop (248-8224)

Located at the beach at Hana Bay, this is the best place to go for lunch in Hana. Though essentially a burger shack, it's right on Hana Bay. Open 8:30–4, they have burgers, very good fries (when they don't overcook them), hot dogs, chili, plate lunches, sometimes teriyaki chicken, etc. In the morning they have surprisingly good breakfast sandwiches. Take the food to the little tables next to the water if it's a nice day. The service can be achingly slow, and the place is pretty disheveled. If they were anywhere else, we'd be more critical, but your options are limited in Hana. $4–$8. By the way, the dark cliff just before Tutu's at the base of the hill was used as a bake-oven to cook the warriors taken captive here during a battle for the hill in 1782. No, they weren't eaten, and let's not hear any cracks about what the special of the day at Tutu's is, huh?

Hotel Hana Maui (248-8211)

This is Hana's version of fine dining, and it's open for breakfast, lunch and dinner. The food has really improved and is quite excellent, though pricey. Breakfast and lunch have small menus, and they're around $15. Dinner selections are limited (but tasty), and it'll run you about $35–$50. Is it overpriced? Yeah...so? *Whaddayagonnado?* It's Hana and this may be your only choice for dinner. Dress code is enforced. Collared shirts and slacks or nice shorts for men and a similar caliber of clothing for women. Otherwise, you'll have to eat at the adjacent bar. Reservations are *required* (even when things are slow).

As an alternative, if you're staying in Hana, you can always pick up something cookable at Hasegawa's Store and fix it back at your hotel/condo/house.

ALSO IN HANA

The **Hana Cultural Center** (248–8622) is a tiny museum on Ke'anini Street with a small display of Hawaiian stone tools, quilts, shells, Chinese and Japanese bottles as well as re-creations of thatched huts and a canoe shed. (Dugout canoes required serious labor, and the ancients always built a garage for them.) The museum is somewhat interesting but expendable if your time is precious.

Hina Malailena's Hana Village Marketplace is a series of market stalls built years ago but never occupied. There are rumblings that, after more than a decade of the bureaucratic two-step, it'll finally be opening, but that rumbling has been going on for a long time.

Hana-Maui Sea Sports (248–7711) has short, fun kayak/snorkel trips at Hana Bay. For $120 you take a 2-hour tour of Hana Bay and/or some nearby areas. Some areas have nice snorkeling, and owner Kevin is a good guide.

Hasegawa General Store (248–8231) has the most widely diverse assortment of...stuff we've ever seen. That's the only word that describes it. Stuff. Where would you find men's dress socks?

Next to the shower curtain rings, of course. And the aloha shirts? To the right of the epoxy. How about fishing spears? Across from the movie rentals. Really need some muffler tape? Turn right when you see the red cabbage; it's between the dried cuttlefish and the lawn mowers. By the way, they also have tabis, great for walking on wet rocks. (They're next to the galvanized pipe.) Some items are a decent deal. Milk was actually cheaper here than at the confiscatory Safeway in Kahului. Other items can be breathtakingly expensive. (I remember going in for a few items once. When I checked out, the total came to $68. I was convinced that the total must represent the last few customers... *it didn't*.)

Incidentally, if your radio has faded and you miss music, stations from the Big Island are your only choices here. And if you need to use your cell phone, depending on your carrier, it might work in most of Hana or you may need to stop at the school on the left side of the highway in Hana, stand on your right foot, raise your left arm, stick out your tongue, and you *might* get a signal.

HANA HIGHWAY BEST BETS

Best View of Coastline—End Nahiku Rd.
Best Bodysurfing—Hamoa Beach
Best Breakfast Experience—Eating Tutu's Breakfast Sandwich at the Cement Tables at Hana Bay
Best Exotic Beach—Red Sand Beach
Best Place for a Cool Dip—Cave #1 at Wai'anapanapa
Best Place to see Every Shade of Green—Nahiku
Best Place to See a Cliff Diver— Ching's Pond
Best Attraction to Skip—Twin Falls
Best Breakfast on the Way—Charleys, or Anthony's in Pa'ia

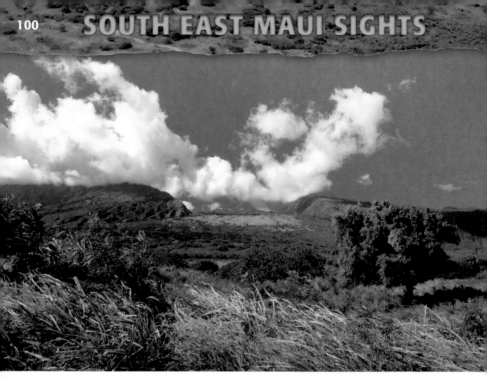

What a difference from the wet, windward side. The dry mountaintop above Kaupo is 9,000 feet high.

After the inspiring drive to Hana, what else can there be? *Plenty!* Past Hana the road goes through beautiful Kipahulu, past the 'Ohe'o Gulch (formerly called the Seven Sacred Pools) and along the bottom of the island, where jungly forest is replaced with wide open expansiveness. The road to the pools is good. Past that you have a decision to make. To go around the bottom...or not to go? The answer is on page 73.

KIPAHULU

If you've driven the entire Hana Highway today, it's easy to fall into a sort of beauty fatigue by now. In fact, it wasn't until we stayed in Hana the first time and drove this part of the road in the morning that we realized how utterly gorgeous it was. Only when we were fresh and had

allowed Hana to melt our bones did Kipahulu seep in. The mountains are so stunning, the waterfalls unspoiled, it's hard to believe that the highway can still deliver after all these miles. Those making the all-day drive are now getting tired. It's after noon and they are looking for the payoff at 'Ohe'o Gulch, AKA Seven Sacred Pools. But if you're lucky enough to be in Kipahulu in the morning, when the light is best, you have the highway pretty much to yourself, and any waterfalls you find are yours and yours alone.

The mile markers have changed and are now counting down. (Until 15, then they jump back to 20 and start going down again—*go figga.*) Leaving Hana, there is a surprise waiting for you if you have time to venture to it. It's one of the largest and nicest freshwater pools on the island. Called **Waioka** by the Hawaiians, its physical appearance has spawned a new age name that seems to have stuck—**Venus Pool**. It looks like a painting that you would normally dismiss as being too contrived, too per- **A REAL GEM** fect, yet here it is. It's located next to the ocean with a hala tree-capped ball of lava symmetrically dividing the sea view. There you'll find numerous places that people jump from, deep water in several spots, the pounding ocean just on the other side of the gravel and some perfect areas on the mountain side from which to sit and cogitate. The aura is unforgettable. If you go in the morning or late afternoon, you'll sometimes have it to yourself. The water is slightly brackish (salty) from the ocean but usually very clean since it is partially spring-fed and not dependent on the seasonal

stream it resides in. During whale season we've seen the leviathans breaching close to shore. All told, it's a fifteen-minute hike from your car. If you're looking for a unique place to swim or ponder, this will definitely ring your WOW meter.

To get there, park on the side of the highway just past the 48 mile marker. Near the Hana side of the bridge is a trail toward the ocean near a sign erected by Hana Ranch saying that VENUS POOL IS CLOSED. With all due respect, we checked, and they don't own the land where Venus Pool is, they own the *trailhead*. We appreciate their concern about liability, but if you look to the right and go down into the gulch you're on *state* land, so Hana Ranch has nothing to fear. Stay on the left side of the gulch the whole way, and although it'll be awkward and potentially hazardous in spots, resist

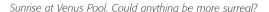

Sunrise at Venus Pool. Could anything be more surreal?

the urge to use Hana Ranch's much easier path which is at the edge of their property. Venus Pool is the large pool at the bottom of the gulch next to the ocean. Be careful of slippery rocks, and don't jump unless you've checked out what's below. (Look around to find the best place to get in and out of the water.) Avoid if the flow is too heavy from the stream. Occasionally, very long dry spells make the water a bit stagnant.

Weather permitting, look for the Big Island peeking above the clouds. Its mas-sive mountains, over 13,000 feet tall, are impressive to see.

Back on the highway, there may be a small waterfall at the 46 mile mark-er. Then, before the 45 mile marker, you'll notice a **cross** erected in memory of Helio Koaeloa, one of the earliest Hawaiian Catholic priests. The trail lead-ing to the bottom is treacherous and not worth the bother. There's sometimes a pretty little waterfall near the sign called **Paihi Falls**.

After you cross the Wailua Stream, yet another *(sigh)* sweet waterfall called

© 2008 Wizard Publications, Inc.

Wailua Falls on the next stream awaits. (Why isn't Wailua Falls on the nearby Wailua Stream?) Wailua is best in the morning when the sun shines on it. The flow varies *a lot*. (There's a photo of it on page 28.) Its water pattern can be exceptionally idyllic—even for Maui—or a light, pathetic trickle. Later in the day vendors sometimes congregate there, selling handmade souvenirs.

Are we at the Seven Sacred Pools yet? No, sorry. You'll have to endure

yet another falls called **Pua'a-lu'u Falls** just past here. We apologize for the inconvenience. The falls are to the left of the bridge and also fall under it. Driving past these falls, look for a **Blessed Mother Shrine** in a remnant from an old lava tube. It's lovingly maintained by a retired woman in the area. A priest chose this location because Pua'a-lu'u Falls always flows, so there's always water available nearby for blessings and for cleaning the statue.

Map continued on page 97

Hana

Haneoo

Hamoa Beach

Waiho'i Valley

Kipahulu Gap

Venus Pool

Wailua Stream

Honolewa Stream

Pipiwai Stream

Paihi Falls

Falls

Wailua Falls

Waimoku Falls

Pua'a-lu'u Falls

31

47

46

45

44

43

Pipiwai Trail

Falls

'Ohe'o Gulch (AKA 7 Sacred Pools)

Infinity Pool/ Makahiku Falls

42

Visitor Center

Kipahulu

41

Lindbergh's Grave

Popoiwi Heiau

Alelele Falls

39

40

36

37

38

Kukui'ula Falls

Narrow section of road.

Mokulau

Less than 5 miles of regularly graded gravel road.

N
W   E
S

⌒ Indicates Foot Trails
11 Roadside mile markers
⸱⸱⸱ Unpaved Roads

Southeast Maui/Kipahulu & Kaupo

Those Seven Sacred Pools are just ahead before the 42 mile marker.

'OHE'O GULCH– AKA SEVEN SACRED POOLS

OK, enough of these serene waterfalls; now it's *playtime*. This series of waterfalls and pools at the shoreline is the most popular attraction in all of east Maui. Why? Because the old name, Seven Sacred Pools, sounds so appealing you just gotta check 'em out. Also **A REAL GEM** because the swimming is usually so good and the setting so beautiful. What's not to love? Back when nobody had ever heard of Hana, the owner of the Hotel Hana Maui wanted desperately to attract people here. He had a choice: Tell people they could visit the fabulous *'Ohe'o Gulch* or the wondrous *Seven Sacred Pools* (which he made up). Which do *you* think looked better on a brochure? (For the record, there are not seven of them, and they never were sacred.)

When a retired airline executive from the mainland named Sam Pryor planned to build a house right near the pools back in 1960, articles began to appear in local papers warning that access to the pools would become a thing of the past. Pryor realized that the pools were so beloved by residents that he contacted the people who sold him the land and insisted that they trade it for land elsewhere, saying the pools should belong to everyone. He later contacted his old friend Laurance Rockefeller and convinced him to buy 52 acres around the pools and eventually donate it to Haleakala National Park. So today, the pools are forever protected.

The pools near the highway are incredibly user-friendly. Falls, pool, falls, pool, falls, pool. It's an ideal playground. The bridge over the first pool is a popular place where daring young dudes (why is it usually us males who do this?) jump off the bridge into the pool around 60 or so feet below. Then they jump the waterfall, then the next. It makes for good entertainment. Other, shorter places to jump are also present. By the way, need a new watch? There are rock platforms of various heights where people jump into the water, and the pools beneath them are good places to look for watches, new (loose) wedding rings and other jewelry torn from jumpers during their plunge. (If you see a silver watch with my initials on it, can you send it to me?) Whether you want to jump, swim, hike or just watch, this natural playground is a great place to polish off a day. People *staying* in Hana have it best, because they can get here before the crowds do. When we took the photo on the facing page, we got there at 10 a.m. and had to wait an hour before *anyone* showed up to photograph. In the afternoon, expect *a lot* of people to join you in the fun.

Park at the lot past the 42 mile marker. The lot sometimes fills up around peak time (2 p.m.). The loop trail from the lot to the pools and back is just over ½ mile.

Part of Haleakala National Park, it's $10 per car for entrance here, sometimes on a quasi-honor system. This fee also gets you into the park at Haleakala's summit and vice versa, so save your receipt.

We explain leptospirosis on page 33, which can be found in any of nature's freshwater streams or pools. The rangers told us there has never been a confirmed case here due to their control efforts.

Camping is available; see page 177. There are restrooms at the park *but no water*.

Playtime!

The Infinity Pool rests at the top of a 200-foot waterfall. Just make sure you stay at the right end.

The huge valley above the pools, stretching all the way up the mountain to Haleakala Crater, is a wondrous area. Called **Kipahulu Gap**, it has resisted the introduction of most foreign plants brought by man, making it one of the more pristine forests in the state. Endemic birds and plants, found nowhere else in the world, thrive in the waterlogged rain forest above you. It has been designated a biological reserve, and entry past the end of the Pipiwai Trail is closed. Park officials are in a never-ending battle with pigs in this valley. Despite their best efforts, pigs abound here and can wreak havoc with endemic plants.

PIPIWAI TRAIL

Above the pools lies one of the best hikes on the island. You certainly won't have it to yourself, but you get more wowie views and settings per mile on this trail than almost any other. All told, it's almost 2 miles each way and you gain 650 feet (not 800, as the park brochure says) from the highway, though the grade is fairly gentle. (The first part is the steep-est, and it's not that steep.) Called the **Pipiwai Trail**, it's smashing and takes anywhere from 2½–5 hours, depending on how much of a hurry you're in.

Trails are usually described in HIKING, but we deviate here to make things simpler because there's no chance you woke up, decided you wanted a good hike and drove way over to these-here parts to do it. The trailhead is down the highway toward the 'Ohe'o Bridge near the 42 mile marker. (See map on page 103.)

The trail basically follows the stream. You'll want mosquito repellent in places if you deviate from the main path. Early into the hike you see a concrete derrick with a pulley on top. Another is on the far side of the bridge. Back when sugar was king, they were used to haul sugar cane across the gorge on its way to the mill down the road. Around ⅔ mile into the hike you come to the **Makahiku Falls** overlook. This massive falls drops 200 feet.

Shortly past this you have an opportunity to deviate onto a side path to the right of the main trail. The park doesn't seem to be actively encouraging people to take this side trail much anymore because of liability concerns after an accident awhile back. If you take it anyway and if conditions are right, it makes for the kind of photo that you can put on your desk and be assured that people walking by will stop and exclaim, *My God, where is that?!* If you've ever seen an infinity pool at a resort—the kind that have no lip to give the impression while inside that it goes on forever—imagine that very same pool at the top of a 200-foot waterfall! This **Infinity Pool** has a row of thick rocks to the right that keeps you from going over during normal flows. To the left is where water cascades over during normal flows (so don't go there!). Needless to say, you need to evaluate the setting for yourself. Too much water flow would be ugly, and you always need to be aware in any stream of the potential for flash floods. While in the pool, all you see is the ocean beyond as you hear the water cascading beneath you. We've seen airplanes dip below the field of view—flying below us—and white-tailed tropic birds soar in the valley beyond the falls. What a scene!

DIVERSION ALERT!

Sometimes the flow grinds to a trickle, making it less dramatic. Behind the pool is a surreal, plant-draped bend in the stream. If you're feeling adventurous, you can scramble over the rockface on the right side, swim across a pool, then scramble over another rockface, and you'll find a large, pretty waterfall that flows even when the Infinity Pool doesn't. (Much of its water percolates under the rocks and gurgles out at the base of the falls below the Infinity Pool.)

Back on the trail, you'll go through a gate, and in a few minutes there's a confusing intersection. Confusing coming back, not going up, so remember it.

Check out the wise-looking banyan tree with its aerial roots along the way. Without a doubt, banyans are the most ancient-looking trees you'll ever see.

After the banyan you can take a side trail to one of the louder waterfalls you'll find. It free falls and smacks onto rocks, then runs into a particularly emerald green pool that has undercut the mountain, forming a cave. You can see more of the falls by following the rock steps to the right.

More diversions await, including a pool at least a football field long. Then a pair of bridges soon enable you to cross the magnificent stream you've been following. (And yes, foolhardy buggas jump off the first one here, too.) The vantage point from the bridge is tongue-wagging.

What next? Why, a thick, vigorous bamboo forest, of course. (Bamboo, which is a grass, makes an excellent walking stick.) After the boardwalk—constructed to keep you out of the perpetually muddy areas—you eventually come to the end of the line. (Well, you still have to go back, of course.) Slicing 400 feet down the back of a three-way sheer wall of lava, **Waimoku Falls** marks the instantaneous beginning of this canyon. What a way to end a trail! You could walk under the falls, but remember that any debris falling from above will feel like getting hit by a meteorite. Did you bring your hard hat? Best to view it from a little distance. During abnormally dry times in the summer the water flow can diminish somewhat, but it's mostly spring-fed, so its flow is not as rain-dependent.

PAST THE PARK

Back on the highway, about $\frac{1}{10}$ mile past the 41 mile marker is an easy-to-miss road that leads to **Palapala Ho'omau Church** where the world's greatest aviator, **Charles Lindbergh**, is buried. See box on the page 109.

DIVERSION ALERT!

Towering Waimoku Falls dwarfs a lowly hiker.

Lindbergh's grave is through the cement post openings, and straight past the older graves on the corner. Just past the grave is a tiny park. Walk to the far end for a scrumptious view of the jagged coastline, or munch on a snack at the shaded picnic tables.

At ³/₁₀ mile past the 41 mile marker you'll see the Laulima Fruit Stand. For two decades (supposedly) they've used a bicycle to power their blender. That's kind of misleading because *you* have to do the peddling. Makes you wonder where they hide the team of cyclists that must be necessary to power their refrigerator and coffee machine. The smoothies aren't that great, even after you work up a sweat to grind them up.

Back in 2006 an earthquake caused the closure of the road shortly past the park. Even after all this time, the road was still closed at press time with alternating predictions from state officials about when it would reopen. Assuming they *git 'er done* by the time you read this, here's what you'll encounter.

At ⁶/₁₀ mile past the 40 mile marker there's a small one-car pullout. If you walk across the street, there's an utterly glorious view of the Kipahulu coastline. The road's about to get narrower for a few miles with many blind turns, so be alert for oncoming cars.

At the bottom of this first valley, pull over past the second set of guard-rails into the short gravel driveway to the ocean. Looking back the way you came, you'll *usually* see Kukui'ula Falls plunging into the ocean. (You can't reach the falls by land, and we have the scars to prove it.) It only occasionally runs dry.

OK, here's your last chance to frolic at a waterfall, and it's a sweet one. About ⅓ mile past the 39 mile marker is a white bridge with the word ALELELE on it. There are several trails, all leading

Where Legends Come to Die

Kipahulu will be forever distinguished as the final resting place of aviation great Charles Lindbergh. Most of those from our generation know very little about Lindbergh, and that's a shame. In 1927 the world held its collective breath as this 25-year-old air mail carrier fought weather and fatigue-induced hallucinations for 33^1/$_2$ hours to become the first man to cross the Atlantic in an airplane. One of the greatest feats of his time, he did it solo, and it was celebrated as much in its day as the moonshot was years later. Lindbergh hadn't been able to sleep the night before his flight left New York, so when he landed in Paris, he had been awake for nearly 60 hours. Some 150,000 screaming well-wishers met his plane when it landed in France. (More than 4 million later turned out for him when he returned to New York.) He had no idea when he landed in Paris that he had the world in the palm of his hand. All he wanted was to take a nap.

After the flight, Charles Lindbergh became the century's first media superstar. His life was followed with more interest than any man alive at the time. He represented the very heart and soul of aviation and was a worldwide hero. When his baby was kidnapped a few years later, the ransom demands went on for 2^1/$_2$ months, and the baby was eventually found dead just a few miles from his house. (The infant never even made it out of the house alive; he died when the kidnapper's ladder broke on the way out the window.) The Lindbergh baby kidnapping trial was called the trial of the century (before anybody had ever heard of O.J.).

In later life, when Lindbergh's old friend Sam Pryor told him, "I have found heaven on earth, and it is at Kipahulu, Maui," Lindbergh visited his friend and was immediately smitten with this part of Maui. He built a home here and spent the last six years of his life in East Maui.

In 1972 Lindbergh was diagnosed with lymphosarcoma. Over time he tried various treatments in New York, but the cancer eventually spread to his lungs. His doctors told him his time was very short. He phoned his physician in Hawai'i and told him, "I have 8 to 10 days to live, and I want to come back home to die. I would rather spend two days alive on Maui than two months alive here in New York." Against his New York doctors' wishes, he was flown on a stretcher in a commercial 747 (the other passengers had no idea who was behind the curtain in first class) back to his beloved Maui. He spent the next week meticulously planning all facets of his funeral, even designing his coffin and picking the lining. Lindbergh wanted the wild plum tree next to his grave removed, but his grave digger convinced him to let it live there with him. Just over a week later, on August 26, 1974, he died. As the small funeral procession passed the tourists visiting the "Seven Sacred Pools," none had any idea who it was for. Fewer than 15 people were invited to attend, and Lindbergh had asked that his pallbearers wear their work clothes. A Hawaiian hymn was sung as the casket was lowered into the ground, and one of his sons said the hymn "just soared out and away with the wind and the crashing of the waves below us."

A short distance from Lindbergh are the graves of Sam Pryor (the friend who lured Lindbergh to Maui) and his wife. Between Pryor's and Lindbergh's graves you'll find six small graves. These were Sam's "children," including Keiki, George, Lani, and his favorite, Kippy. None have last names because his "children" (as he always referred to them) were actually Asian gibbons. Sam took these apes with him wherever he went. Townsfolk rarely saw him without one of his children.

The inscription on Lindbergh's grave, from the 139th Psalm, reads, "If I take the wings of the morning, and dwell in the uttermost parts of the sea." The rest of that passage, not on the stone, is, "Even there would Thy hand lead me. And Thy right hand would hold me."

In remote and sparsely populated Kaupo, St. Joseph's Church, built in 1862, only holds services if there's a 5th Sunday in a month.

5–10 minutes inland. It's fairly easy (though you'll have to cross the stream at one point, usually keeping your feet dry). **Alelele Falls** is around 40–50 feet high and has the cleanest, clearest and coldest water you'll find. We believe that it's partially spring fed, which accounts for its clarity. The lower pool is lined with lots of pebbles, making entry easy on your feet. The pool's about 6 feet deep. Bring your camera; you'll really like this one. It occasionally slows to a trickle, but not often.

WATERFALL ALERT!

Past the grassy road around the corner, look up the hill in front of you, and you'll see what looks like a rock wall near the top. That's the **Popoiwi Heiau**, a religious structure. What's unusual about it is that it wasn't made by the Hawaiians. It was made by the people who were here *before* them. You see, when the first people arrived here from the Marquesas Islands around 300 A.D., they lived untouched for about 700 years. Then another group came, this time from Tahiti. They killed and subdued the first inhabitants, driving them ever farther northwest. (The first inhabitants were called Menehune by the second arrivals, a derogatory term denoting small in class and stature. The legend was later distorted by westerners who didn't understand, and Menehunes became the Hawaiian equivalent of elves.) The last remnants the Menehunes left behind are some decidedly un-Hawaiian carvings on tiny islands northwest of the main Hawaiian Islands.

Before the 35 mile marker there's a road on your left that angles back toward the ocean and leads to a church and cemetery. It's a dirt road, but 2WD vehicles are usually OK unless it's been raining. Drive to the end and you'll see why it's called **Mokulau**, or "many islets." Dozens of lava outcroppings in the water defying the relentless waves make a dramatic photo op as the water pounds and twists to get past them. Keep an eye out for Hawaiian monk seals that sometimes beach themselves here. The church at Mokulau has restrooms.

DIVERSION ALERT!

Kaupo Store past the 35 mile marker is your last chance to pick up snacks. Mostly sodas, chips, ice cream and candy mixed with an interesting collection of antique cameras, clocks and assorted knickknacks. There's also a restroom out back. Check the dates on any food here as freshness this far out can be hard to maintain.

We were once at the Kaupo Store when a visitor noted to the woman behind the counter how much Kaupo had *grown* in the 30 years since her last visit. "How has it grown?" asked the woman behind the counter. Lots of new buildings, the visitor replied. The counter woman and I exchanged confused glances, and then she patiently explained to the visitor that the only thing that had changed in Kaupo in the last 30 years was that so-and-so had added a new room to his house and Auntie Jane opened a lunch wagon (which is now gone). That's it! The moral of the story: *Nothing* ever changes in Kaupo.

Looking around in this part of the island, it's easy to think that nothing important ever happened along here. Actually, this area was subject to a vicious invasion in 1775 by the king of the Big Island. He occupied the area and treated his captives so badly, they called it the war of Kalaehohoa (meaning, roughly, *the war where they beat our brains out with clubs*). When Maui's king responded, he routed the Big Island king along the shoreline below the 33 mile marker. One of his Big Island lieutenants in this defeat was Kamehameha, who would later become king of all the islands. Kamehameha barely escaped with his life.

Just over ⁴⁄₁₀ mile past the 32 mile marker is one of our favorite spots to pull over and enjoy the views of Haleakala and the broad expanse of shoreline in the late afternoon. The deep gorges, formed by sporadic but intense rain, show up well in the afternoon. Look to the top of the mountain and you'll see the **Kaupo Gap**, the large, wide opening at the top of the mountain. At one time the gap, caused by erosion, was at least 5,000 feet deep, perhaps deeper, and cut into the very core of

Even in the harsh waters off Kaupo, a net fisherman has to eat. This one was knocked down several times before he successfully caught his dinner.

the mountain. (There's a similar gap on the other side of the mountain, meaning the volcano was essentially cut into two halves.) Later, lava again poured from the summit, filling the great Kaupo canyon to the shallow level you see now. If you look at the left side of the gap, it's not hard to imagine how the lava dammed up against the side of the older mountain and flooded the canyon and the plains below.

Wind is almost always present along here as the trade winds pile up along the flank of the great mountain. We once saw three helicopters struggling to land on a barren, grassy field next to the road. We soon learned that a wedding coordinator had convinced a group of Germans that this would be an ideal place for a wedding reception, so they chartered the expensive helicopters to fly everyone in. We can still picture them standing there, with the wind blowing champagne all over their shirts, as they looked around asking each other, "Whose *stupid* idea was this?"

Just before the 31 mile marker there's a gate. This leads to Nu'u Bay, the only decent ocean swimming area along this entire stretch of coastline. You can open the gate and proceed, but you'll either need 4WD for the ²/₁₀ mile road or you'll have to walk it. The road terminates at an old cement landing. The snorkeling is fairly good to the left (away from the shore), but don't venture beyond the protected point where the water is rougher and there's a current. The only thing marring the plentiful coral scenery is an unusually large number of fishing nets. Local fishermen thoughtlessly abandon them when they become entangled on coral heads, which creates a permanent hazard for sea life. We once found a dead reef shark (a normally docile animal) entangled on the bottom here. That's not a sight we'd like to see again.

If the surf is up, the short dirt road just before the 30 mile marker leads to a great place to listen to the surf. Huakini Bay is lined with small- and medium-sized rounded stones. When large waves rake at the shoreline, these stones make a deep rumbling sound that you won't soon forget. The bigger the waves, the better. Just don't get too close to the water. The cliffs behind the bay are said to contain ancient Hawaiian petroglyphs, according to a 19th-century archeological report we read, but we must confess we haven't been able to find them. Let us know if you're more successful. Be careful of the wicked kiawe (mesquite) thorns.

DIVERSION ALERT!

Modern man is not the first to traverse the island along this route. The ancient Hawaiians built a highway centuries ago, paved with lava stones and wide enough

Dry and desolate. Nothing in common with Hana, on the other side of the mountain, except the beauty.

for two. This was how they went from east to west. Keep an eye out on the right side for remnants of it.

At ⅔ mile past the 30 mile marker, a dirt road angles back to the shoreline. This is it—the *last* beach on the island. It's a small, **unnamed black sand beach** about 60 feet wide. Its sand source is a nearby intermittent stream patiently dismantling its lava streambed. Cloudy water, but the sand has an exotic look. Sometimes storms remove the sand for months at a time.

Past the 29 mile marker you'll spot the **Pokowai Sea Arch**, but don't pull over until the road descends to the shoreline. From there you can get out and get a closer look at the arch and shoreline. Though the ocean is almost always whipped and frothed here, we've seen throw-net fishermen braving the water for their catch.

After the 28 mile marker you'll find a brand new two-lane bridge on this one-lane road. (As with Hana Highway bridges, federal dollars will only pay for two-lane bridges, even if they are on one-lane roads.) The gulch that the bridge spans is beautiful, showing the layers of the different lava flows.

As the road leaves the sea on its way up to the 3,000-foot level, you may wonder what you are missing with all that land and shoreline below. The answer is *nothing!* The land below the highway past here is the most wretched you'll find on Maui. Harsh and unforgiving lava fields, sparse and scrubby brown grass—there is nothing visually pleasing about this area other than some marginally interesting lava rock ruins. (Even paradise has to have an ugly side—this is it.) The shoreline, though rich in fish, is lashed by heavy seas, making it hazardous. Many maps show a trail that goes from South Maui all the way to where the highway started leaving the

shoreline. Yeah, the trail's there, but it's sporadic, miserable and ugly and passes almost nothing of interest.

Surprisingly, this area used to be heavily populated by Hawaiians. Thousands took advantage of the fishing area and the good sweet potato growing conditions in some pockets where there was soil. There was even a forest in those days, before cattle were introduced. Hawaiian ruins are scattered about the rocky fields. Today, native Hawaiians are in the process of trying to repopulate the area. Over 100 families are working as a group to rebuild this part of Maui, called **Kahikinui**. It won't be easy. Life was always difficult in this land of little rain and ever-present winds. Easier life elsewhere lured their grandfathers for a reason and they abandoned the land. Even today the homesteaders live with no power or running water and only time will tell if they are successful.

Past the 15 mile marker (the 18–15 markers are only visible to traffic coming the other way) you see the **Tedeschi Winery**. They have a nice wine-tasting room and gift shop (albeit with fairly unremarkable wine, some made from pineapple), and it's worth a stop. The grounds are pretty and serene. Across the street is the **Ranch Store**, a deli/grill if you're hungry.

SOUTHEAST MAUI BEST BETS

Best Surreal Sunrise—Venus Pool
Best Place to Watch Someone Make a Giant Leap for Mankind—'Ohe'o Bridge
Best Hike—Pipiwai Trail
Best 'Okole Squeezing View—Infinity Pool
Best Place to Play—Pools at 'Ohe'o (Seven Sacred Pools)
Best Place to Lose a New Wedding Ring—Jumping in the Water at 'Ohe'o
Best Place to Hear the Ocean—Huakini Bay if the Surf's Up

Sunrise from Haleakala Crater can be a surreal, ethereal experience.

People come to Maui for the ocean, palm trees and balmy weather. So why on earth would you want to use up one of your precious vacation days in the center of the island where you won't find *any* of that? Simple. This part of the island has green, rolling hills, switchback roads, cool mountain air and a *lump-in-your-throat* crater. It may not be typical Hawai'i, but it's definitely worth visiting.

UPCOUNTRY

Upcountry refers to the cluster of towns located 2,000–4,000 feet up the slope of Haleakala. They aren't pointing directly into the trade winds, so rain is less frequent. Drought happens on occasion, sparking water rationing. Since tempera-tures fall almost 3° with every thousand feet, it's cooler up here than at the shore. It's popular with people who want to work or play in the tropics but don't want to *live* there.

Don't tell people who live upcountry this, but in ancient times, Kula residents were considered dim-witted and dense and were the butt of jokes throughout the islands. It stems from the fact that they lived so far from the water that they possessed little sea knowledge, and were thought of as stupid and backward. Sort of the ancient equivalent of *how many Kulans does it take to pound poi? Five! One to hold the pounder and four to raise the bowl over and over. Ha, ha, ha...*

Haleakala & Upcountry

Ho'okipa Beach Park

Jaws

Pa'uwela

Inn at Mama's Fish House

Ku'au

M.A. Baldwin Park

Nalu Kai Lodge

Ha'iku

Breckelsville Beach

Pa'ia

Holomua

Maliko Gulch

Ha'iku Rd

Ha'iku

Kauhikoa

West Kuiaha

East Kuiaha

Ulumalu

Holokai

Kokomo

Hana Hwy

36

360

Hana Hwy

Hana Hwy

390

Baldwin Ave

4th Marine Division Memorial Park

365

Kaupakalua

Map continued on page 78

37

Haleakala Hwy

Hali'imaile

Makawao

Makawao

Olinda Rd

Pi'iholo Rd

Old Haleakala Hwy

Pukalani

Golf Course

2,000'

Hanamu

Haleakala Hwy (Upper Hwy)

Pulehu Rd

(Slow—Not a shortcut)

377

37

Kula Hwy (Lower Hwy)

Omaopio Rd

Lower Kula Rd

Surfing Goat Dairy

Enchanted Floral Garden

Kimo

Kula Lodge

Skyline Eco-Adventures & Haleakala ATV

Entrance to Haleakala National Park

Pulehu Rd

3,000'

Pulehuiki

4,000'

Crater Road/Haleakala Hwy

378

6,000'

8,000'

L. Kula Rd

Kula

377

Kula Botanical Garden

Waipoli Rd

Haleakala Crater

3,000'

Ali'i Kula Lavender Garden

Gate (which you can drive through)

10,023' Gate

Haleakala Crater Map on page 120

Polipoli State Park

Gate

Skyline Road (closed 4WD Road)

Gate

2,000'

37

31

Tedeschi Winery

© 2008 Wizard Publications, Inc.

N **W** **E** **S**

0   2 MILES

∿ Indicates Foot Trails
11 Roadside mile markers
⋯ Unpaved Roads

To get upcountry, most people head up the Haleakala Highway on 37. (The term *Haleakala Highway* and the signs are misleading because it is actually composed of segments from *three different highways,* 37 to 377 to 378.) If it's clear, between the 4 and 5 mile markers you get a perspective of just how *big* this mountain really is. It's over 10,000 feet high, and from here you can tell by the width that this single mountain hides a monstrous amount of rock.

Why are the Days 24 Hours Long? Thank Maui.

The Hawaiians believed that in ancient times there was a demigod named Maui. (A demigod is the offspring of a god and a mortal.) Maui noticed that his mother used to complain that the days were too short for her to dry her tapa cloth. So young Maui set his mind to lasso the sun as it streaked across the sky. He went to Hana to watch the sun rise, then tried to catch it at Haleakala but failed. Later, near Kahului, Maui cut down all the coconuts he could find and made a long fiber rope. He climbed Haleakala and hid at a place across the crater called Hanakauhi. When the sun streaked by, he lassoed many of the sun's rays, weakening it. Maui told the sun, "Now I will kill you for hurrying so fast." The sun answered, "Let me live, and I promise that from now on I'll walk instead of run across the sky." Maui agreed and the sun kept his promise. Today the days are 24 hours long as a result of this agreement. (Weekends were apparently exempt from the deal because they seem much shorter.)

There are areas mentioned in this chapter that you won't pass by coming up Hwy 37, the most notable being Ha'iku and Makawao.

HA'IKU

Ha'iku is just below the area normally considered upcountry and is probably the least discovered town in Maui. The population is around 10,000, consisting of a mix of old-time locals, hippie-turned-farmers, wealthy mainlanders, Maui business owners and computer commuters. Green, wet and quiet is what they come for, and they're not disappointed. Their higher-elevation neighbors sometimes look longingly at Ha'iku's abundance of water. The roads here tend to be narrow. Twenty feet was considered wide enough in the horse and buggy days, and parts of some roads have maintained that width. There's usually very little traffic on Ha'iku roads during the week. Look at the map on the previous page if you're interested in driving (for no particular reason) some of these pretty roads like Ha'iku or Ulumalu roads. The town is worth visiting if you're in a wandering mood or want a treat from the Ha'iku Marketplace.

MAKAWAO

Makawao is a major upcountry hub. It's supposed to be the island's cowboy town. Most visitor information conveys the impression that you'll see old cowpokes riding horses through town. Not likely. If you see anybody on a horse, it'll probably be a teenage girl wearing a sports bra and pastel pants picking up some brie for her mom's get-together. And try to get a good burger in this "cowboy" town,

The mystic forest along the upper part of Waipoli Road.

and you'll likely be offered a tofu burger. (Stopwatch has the best *real* burgers.) But it's an interesting place to wander and shop, with some unusual finds. For instance, the Rodeo General Store sells "island coconut-flavored gourmet kosher Maui-grown coffee." (You know, it's kind of hard to picture a grizzled old Hawaiian cowboy saying, *Hey, Kimo, pass the gourmet kosher coffee, will ya?)* Around town you'll also find Hot Island Glass which blows their own glass art works, Supernatural with their vast selection of crystals and lots of treats. The absolute best is **Komoda Bakery** on Baldwin Avenue. Unimpressive on the outside, but unreal baked goods at reasonable prices. You can purchase $3.50 sandwiches at **Kitada's** at the edge of town on Baldwin Avenue. Makawao is where people with dreadlocks, backpacks and bare feet share the streets with the well-groomed, iPhone-toting business crowd.

Galleries are also common here, though they seem to take themselves pretty seriously. Like the one that claims to be for "peace and the enrichment of humankind with their visions" and they "accept the aloneness in the creative process and celebrate the aloha with their togetherness." Well, damn, that's really good to know. But hey, do you folks sell that velvet painting of the dogs playing poker?

Be aware that mornings can be a zoo in Makawao since the downhill bicycle tours race through town. Also, if you're trying to park and find all those two-hour stalls filled, look across from Ai Street off Makawao Avenue for a free lot.

By the way, no self-respecting Hawaiian cowboy (called paniolo) would ever be caught dead saying, *Get along, little dogie.* Here he would say, *hele makai* (go to the ocean). Other local cowboy terminology are:

Hemo kapuka—open the gate
Pipi—cattle
Lio—horse
Oni—let's move out
Kau ka lio—mount your horses
Waha!—yeehaa!

KULA

Think of Kula as everything past **Pukalani** (which itself offers little other than golfing). Kula has some downright tasty views of the central valley as well as restaurants and flower farms. Overall, it's not huge on the visitor hit parade, but you may want to consider some of these attractions:

Kula Lodge (878–1535) is the most renowned landmark up here. In addition to its accommodations it has a beautiful (though pricey) restaurant with great views, a pretty garden terrace and a confiscatory gift shop.

Though there are numerous flower farm and gardens, not all are worth stopping for. The best is probably the **Kula Botanical Garden** (878–1715) on Hwy 377 between the 8 and 9 mile markers. It's well maintained, well marked and there's a nice assortment of tropical plants scattered over 6 acres. Well worth the $7.50 if you're into gardens. Another garden, **Enchanting Floral Gardens** (878–2531), has a setting that isn't as pretty as Kula Botanical. It, too, is $7.50 and is just past the 10 mile marker on Hwy 37. **Sunrise Market and Protea Farm** (876–0200) just up Hwy 378 is a small but well-tended collection of proteas, gift shop and snack bar.

Polipoli State Park is at the end of that *other* winding road (Waipoli Road) working its way up Haleakala. It's the road few people ever take. (See map.) At the end is an unexpected redwood forest in the middle of this tropical island. The trails are described under HIKING on page 197. It's cool and misty and would seem to belong more to Northern California than the center of Maui.

Also on Waipoli Road just before a gate and cattle guard is the **Ali'i Kula Lavender** (878–8090). You never knew you could do so much with lavender until you come here. They sell lavender chocolates, sherbet (yummy), scones (also yummy), coffee, lotions, lemonade (not so good), candles, face pillows and more. The staff is exceptionally nice and they are generous with samples, so it's hard not to buy something at their gift shop. They have pricey guided tours at 10 a.m. and 2 p.m. each day (arrange in advance) for $25 (it's an extra $25 if you want to be fed, which is hard to justify) and takes just under an hour. Overall, they do a good job.

Past main Kula on your way toward the bottom of the island, the **Sun Yat-sen Park** is not far from the 18 mile marker on Hwy 37. History buffs will remember that Sun lived in Hawai'i, attended school here where he learned about democracy, and went back to China to overthrow its last emperor in 1912. If you drive down the road next to the park, you'll (literally) find yourself on EASY STREET.

Past the park the last thing between you and the vast lands of Kaupo is the **Tedeschi Winery**, described on page 113.

HALEAKALA NATIONAL PARK

From Hwy 37 you took 377 then 378, right? (See map on page 115.) You now

begin the endless switchbacks necessary to scale the steep slopes of Haleakala. A donut

A REAL GEM ring of clouds often forms part of the way up, fooling people into thinking the summit's socked in. Most of the time the clouds clear before the summit. Watch for mindless, wayward cows on this stretch. It's an open ranch, and the witless bovines often wander onto the road. They're occasionally turned into hamburger prematurely by cars traveling too fast in the fog. You will be afforded many outstanding views of West Maui and the

Sunrise From Haleakala—Is it *Really* That Good?

Sunrises from atop Haleakala have taken on legendary status. They are said to be comparable to a religious experience, that they will heal your soul, rejuvenate your spirit and perhaps even fix that ingrown toenail you've had lately. In short, they are said to be the best in the world. As a result, sunrises from up here are considered must-dos.

The first time we came to watch the sunrise up here, we thought it was the most overrated, overhyped event we'd seen. Pleasant, yes, but hardly worth the effort. Those around us seemed to agree. Also, the first time we were so wretchedly cold that we couldn't have appreciated winning the lottery, much less seeing a sunrise. The second time we did it, however, we were blown away by its majesty. Wouldn't have missed it for the world. What's the difference between pleasant and wow? Multiple trips have cemented a theory. It's simple—clouds. A sea of clouds below you with the sun rising from beneath makes a glorious canvas for the sun to paint. It's like nothing you've seen, and when it's good, it's as good as a sunrise can get. Other times, when it's too clear, it's simply…nice…and cold. And for nice it's hard to justify the hardship. Fortunately, clouds below you are fairly common.

To get the time of sunrise and a weather forecast, call 877–5111. You'll want to get there at least half an hour before sunrise. However, if you don't arrive about an hour before, you run the real risk of not getting a parking spot at the actual summit. You'll have to park at the upper visitor center instead, where all the bike riders stop. If you try to park in the dirt, you may get a monstrous ticket. If you park at the visitor center, consider walking the short distance to the Sliding Sands trailhead. (See map on the next page.) It's less crowded, and you may find the wind partially blocked by White Hill next to you. Allow just under two hours from Kihei, a bit over two hours from Ka'anapali. If you don't allow enough time, you'll be one of the poor saps who woke up at 3 a.m. and still missed the good stuff. Bring a small flashlight if possible; it's easy to fall down in the dark and numbing cold. If you get here while it's still inky dark, you'll probably see more stars than you've ever seen in your life. No matter how warmly you think you need to dress, dress warmer. Bring every piece of clothing you brought from the mainland, if necessary. If you rented an open-air JEEP, here's where you pay the piper. You'll freeze your nuggies off. (In fact, look on the side of the road and you'll see mounds of nuggies frozen off from past visitors.) If the wind's blowing at that high altitude (which it often is), it'll make a penguin scream. We bring our ski clothes, gloves and a wool cap and even still, we sometimes get cold. The temperature rises quickly when the sun does, but few visitors are properly prepared for the morning cold, even in summer. At the summit there's an enclosed viewing area, but it's usually crowded and noisy in there, and the views are more restricted. If properly prepared, consider toughing it outside.

valley between the mountains. (Unless you're heading here for the sunrise; then you'll have to see many of the sights mentioned here on your way down.)

If you ever want to *see* what **turbulence** looks like, take a look at the cloud formations as you drive up and down Haleakala. As a pilot, this is the only place I know of on the island where I can come to and *see* turbulence (as opposed to feeling it) close up as the clouds roil and boil in all directions. While coming down, around the 8 mile marker is often a good place to see it.

After the 10 mile marker you'll pay your $10 per car entrance fee and enter the park. Try to smile at the poor slob at the entrance gate freezing his/her 'okole off in the booth. For years admittance

was often free because (only the government could come up with this kind of logic) they "didn't have the budget for someone to collect money all the time." Can you imagine Disneyland making that policy? Now they've installed an honor system pay box when personnel are absent. Anyway, the visitor center and campground are the first things you pass. The visitor center has restrooms and the only phone available. This is where you make camping arrangements.

Camping is allowed at several places in the park, including the coveted cabins at the bottom of the crater. See CAMPING on page 177 for more. The campsite at **Hosmer Grove** as you entered the park has a 25-minute **nature loop**, though it seems more neglected than the rest of the

Haleakala Crater

The crater area is hard to visualize, so it's shown here on an angle. Think of it as a casting of the crater sitting on a table top. The smaller map is how it looks from the other side.

Pohaku Palaha
Kipahulu Gap
Hanakauhi (8,907')
Dinosaur Spine
Paliku Cabin
Ko'olau Gap
Halemau'u
Kaupo Trail (To the coast)
Hosmer Grove Campgrounds
Halemau'u Trailhead
6,600'
Kawilinau (Bottomless Pit)
Sliding Sands
Kaupo Gap
Leleiwi Overlook
Silversword Loop
8,000'
378
Holua Cabin
Halemau'u
Ka Moa o Pele
Kapalaoa Cabin
Pu'u o Maui
Spur Trail
Kalahaku Overlook
Park Headquarters/ Visitor Center 7,000'
Ka-lu'u-o-ka-'o'o
Pu'u o Pele
7,500'
8,000'
Upper Visitor Center
9,000'
Sliding Sands Trail
From the other side..
Summit (Red Hill) 10,023'
To Skyline Road (closed 4WD Road)
Science City

© 2008 Wizard Publications, Inc.

park. Consider it dispensable. This campsite is a good place to see **moonbows**, when the full moon's rising in the east and it's raining toward the west.

As you've ascended the mountain, note how much the vegetation has changed. You're not in Hawai'i anymore; you're in Alaska. Cold, windy and arid conditions favor plants with needles and very small leaves. One plant that looks like a whisk broom has powder-filled spore casings. Ancient Hawaiians used to come up here and gather the powder to rub into their *da kines* to prevent chafing on long walks.

The visitor center at 7,000 feet has an average high temperature of 59° and low of 41° in February. In August it averages a high of just 66° and a low of 47°. It's about 10° colder at the summit, and every few years they even get a light dusting of snow or ice. Most of the rain at the summit falls in the winter months, but it's still not nearly as rainy as the lower elevations can be with 54 inches at the 7,000 foot level and much drier at the summit. (If you have computer access, our Web site, wizardpub.com, has a link to current weather readings on Haleakala, including temperature and wind speed.)

HALEAKALA SUMMIT

After the 17 mile mark you'll see a parking lot for the **Leleiwi Lookout**. Most people blow right by in their frenzy to get to the summit, assuming

DIVERSION ALERT!

Walking down Sliding Sands Trail will transport you to another world.

Leleiwi merely gives them another nice view down the mountain to the coast. Too bad, because Leleiwi is nothing of the sort. Walk five minutes to the end and the crater itself suddenly explodes into view. What a startling sight! It looks very different than the more traditional view at the top and is well worth the diversion. A small shelter protects you from any wind that may be present.

As you near the summit, keep an eye out for **silverswords** ('ahinahina). You'll know them when you see them. This plant, unique to Hawai'i, first arrived as a California tarweed seed in the feathers of a wayward bird a million years ago and evolved into this striking round silver wonder. They developed their dense covering of silver hairs to live in this difficult environment. It allows them to retain water and ward off the intense sun at this altitude. If you see one blooming with a large stalk of flowers, pay your respects. Silverswords may live up to 50 years, but, like salmon, they only reproduce once then die. At one time silverswords were endangered when thoughtless people plucked them out of the ground for all sorts of ornamental purposes. Today they are protected and their numbers have rebounded. Be careful walking around them, however, as the fine for damaging them is more than the cost of your whole vacation. For the ancient Hawaiians, there was nothing silver in their universe until they met this plant. Their name for it, 'ahinahina, literally means *gray gray*. That's as close as they could get.

Though perfectly adapted to live their life above the clouds, the endemic nene is one of the world's most accomplished beggars. Try to resist their charm.

There are several trails that are supposed to highlight silverswords, like the one at the **Kalahaku Overlook** up ahead. But you're more likely to see them from the side of the road nearer the summit. While at Kalahaku, take the time to enjoy the view of the crater, which already looks a bit different than at Leleiwi.

There aren't many types of birds that can live up here. Flying in thin 30 mph winds, which is common, is not a very efficient means of transportation. So they walk most of the time. The three most successful are the native **nene** and the imported **chukar** and **ring-necked pheasant**. A nene is what results when you take wayward geese from Canada and stick them on an island for a few million years. They've left the water and adapted to high, arid lands, losing much of the webbing on their feet in the process. They were almost extinct at the beginning of this century. Today they are protected, but are often accidentally killed because of their laid-back attitude toward cars. They just don't seem impressed with an auto's size, like frogs at night looking into your headlights as they're squashed. People often accidentally back over them. As a result, it's more important than usual not to feed them, or they'll get even cozier with cars. They'll likely come up and beg if they see you, and they're hard to resist, but try. They're often visible at the **Halemau'u Trailhead** between the 14 and 15 mile markers.

Most visitor information refers to **Haleakala Crater** as the *largest extinct volcanic crater in the world*. Cool! Too bad none of that statement is true. It's not the largest, it's not extinct, and the crater is not volcanic in origin. (In fact, the park now prefers to call this a *basin, valley* or *wilderness area*, but we refer it as a *crater* because people will look at you funny if you mention *Haleakala Valley.)*

After Haleakala built itself up, it went to sleep for several hundred thousand years as most Hawaiian volcanoes do. During its snooze, two great valleys formed on either side due to erosion. These valleys cut at least 5,000 feet deep, into the very core of the volcano. They worked their way up the mountain until they met at the summit, back to back. Now the mountain was essentially cracked down the middle, separating the east and west sides, with only a thin ridge between the two great canyons. Then Haleakala awoke for one last series of eruptions before it falls forever silent and eventually sinks under its weight back into the sea. That's what will happen to all of the Hawaiian Islands. (This last series of eruptions is in its final phase, having last erupted around 1790.)

When it awoke, it did so from the summit, filling the enormous canyons with lava and raising the summit floor you see before you. So, you see, Haleakala Crater is an *erosion* crater that was partially filled with lava and gravel from the crumbling sides, not a volcanic crater like those on the Big Island. When you drive around the bottom of the island, you'll be able to see, from around the 32 mile marker, where and how the lava flowed through the Kaupo Gap and flooded the plains below in an ever-widening flow of molten rock hitting the sea between the 30 and 35 mile markers.

As you approach the top of the mountain, you may find yourself a bit breathless. You've gone from sea level to almost 2 miles high with no time to acclimate. Take it easy and drink plenty of water. You dehydrate very quickly without noticing at this altitude. If you've been SCUBA diving in the last 24

hours and your blood feels a bit carbonated up here, remember—as far as your body's concerned, you may as well be flying. *You got da bends, brah; go back down.*

The upper visitor center after the 20 mile marker has kickin' views, a place to park and restrooms. (Though the latter are inadequate for the number of bikers and tour buses that come up here. Expect lines. There's also a restroom at Kalahaku Overlook and at the Halemau'u Trailhead.) Early morning bike rides commence from up here. They travel 38 miles, downhill virtually the whole way, and end up in Makawao or at the sea. See BIKING on page 173 for more.

The way the clouds race by, clawing at some of the nearby peaks, you could be looking at Mt. Everest instead of a Hawaiian peak across the crater. The beauty **A REAL GEM** is hard to describe, but it's unlike any other place we've seen. Adjectives that describe it include desolate, wondrous, arid, majestic, colorful, harsh, peaceful, vast, spiritual, exciting, scary, ancient...all of these and more can be applied to Haleakala Crater. If you were smart enough to dress warmly and can concentrate on things other than the temperature, you'll come up with your own adjectives.

If you're here in late afternoon to see the **sunset** (which can be fantastic and not nearly as crowded as a sunrise), you may be treated to something available in only a few places in the world. It happens as you're standing at the crater's edge, and there's cloud below and in front of you while the sun is low and directly behind you. (Leleiwi Lookout is a good place to see it since it's close to the Ko'olau Gap's clouds.) Called **Spectre of the Brocken** or **akaku anuenue** in

Sharp contrasts, impossibly blue skies and a myriad of colors; your eyes will be dining on a feast.

Hawaiian, it's when you see your own shadow on the clouds with a rainbow surrounding your shadow. It's an *incredible* sight. The Hawaiians felt blessed to experience it because they believed that what they were seeing was their actual soul, and the rainbow was a promise from heaven that their souls would be taken care of. If you're lucky, maybe you'll be blessed, too.

The ancient Hawaiians never lived up here, but they did visit for religious purposes and to hunt birds. Many artifacts have been found in the crater. The Hawaiian historian Kamakau says that commoners used to come up here to toss the remains of their loved ones into a pit at the bottom they called Ka'a'awa, now called **Bottomless Pit** or **Kawilinau.** (Hawaiians were always fearful that others would desecrate the bones of their ancestors, so this bottomless pit was a perfect place to assure that their remains wouldn't be tampered with.) People who lived at the bottom of the mountain in Kaupo believed that their water came from Haleakala Crater, and

they used to bitterly complain that the reason their water tasted so insipid was because of this practice. (Hmm, sort of makes you want *bottled* water while driving through Kaupo.)

Hawaiians also came for the rock. Most lava rock is relatively soft. There are several deposits of harder stone that the Hawaiians used to make adzes (a stone ax) for shaping other tools.

Lastly, Hawaiians came to Haleakala to hide the umbilical cords of their newborns. Hawaiians strongly felt that if rats, notorious thieves, were to steal their baby's umbilical cords, the child would grow up to be a thief. So they hiked to some of the smaller volcanic pits in Haleakala to keep the cords from rats (which aren't native—the Hawaiians brought the Polynesian rat with them from the South Pacific).

At one time imported goats were a huge problem in the crater, eating everything in sight and tearing up the ground with their hooves. You may read that the park has completely eradicated them, though that's not entirely correct. They purposely left a few sterilized males marked with radio transmitters to roam the wilderness. Referred to affectionately as *Judas Goats,* the theory is that lonely males are *far* more effective (and motivated) at locating any unaccounted-for female goats than park personnel could ever hope to be.

Past the upper visitor center parking lot, the road leads to the actual summit itself at 10,023 feet. Winds can be strong up here and can cause windburn if you're exposed to them for an extended period. If it's not windy, as is often the case later in the morning and afternoon, it's tempting to shed your warm clothes. You should know that sunburn happens very quickly up here since the light filters through a thinner atmosphere. (OK, OK, no more nagging.) The peak directly southeast of the summit is called **Magnetic Peak**. Can't find southeast? That's because the iron in Magnetic Peak is messing with your compass.

At the 21 mile marker, if you avoid the turnoff up to the summit and instead stay to your left, you're heading to **Science City**. The Air Force and the University of Hawai'i have astronomical observatories up here, but they're not open to the public. The Air Force uses their 12-foot diameter scope to optically sweep space, tracking space junk that could collide with existing satellites. The optics alone for this cost $40 million, and it can spot items the size of golf balls in space. (The space shuttle has reportedly lost very few golf balls, but the Air Force *is* tracking a wayward glove.) Astronomers also bounce laser beams off retro-reflectors left on the moon by the Apollo astronauts in the '70s. By timing the reflection, they can measure the speed of continental drift. Maui's Pacific plate moves northwest at the same rate that your fingernails grow. (Apparently, their procurement office moves at about the same speed. It wasn't until this millennium that they finally replaced their '70s-era 4mhz computers with newer ones that were only five years out of date. Now *that's* progress!)

We came up here once in the middle of the night to watch a meteor shower, but the shower was mostly a bust. After dozing for a few minutes in the car, we awoke and thought we were hallucinating. *How can this be?* It looked like thousands of shooting stars in line with each other, like a special effect from a *Star Wars* movie. It took a minute to realize it was a pulsating laser shooting all the way to the horizon from one of the university's many science experiments.

On this road to Science City, at the next intersection, the FAA has a sign say-ing that trespassers will be tortured and maimed, or something to that effect. It's apparently incorrect, unauthorized and contradicted by the fact that the state has established a *public access* to Skyline Road (mentioned below). Few people have been to this part of the summit in the past because of the sign. Too bad. We did a little digging and found that the FAA erected the sign to prevent *tour buses* from using the narrow washboard road for (c'mon, everybody, you know the words to this song) *liability reasons.* The FAA doesn't have a problem with smaller vehicles using the road since it's necessary to access **Skyline Road**, a fantastic and lightly used dirt road that meanders down the spine of Haleakala, ending at Polipoli Park. (See BIKING in ADVENTURES or HIKING in ACTIVITIES.)

If you take the federal road (the sign may vanish since the state's considering taking over the road), you'll come to a dirt road on your left. That's Skyline, and if you walk on it around the corner for a few minutes, you're treated to a magnificent view of most of Kahoʻolawe. Though you're almost 10,000 feet up, the ocean is only 6 miles away. What a sweeping vista! The Big Island—at 4,000 square miles it's almost as big as Connecticut— lives up to its name. It looks positively *huge* from up here.

After all these beautiful sights, it's (literally) all downhill from here. Remember to use a lower gear driving back down; the slope will burn your brakes.

INSIDE THE CRATER

On the other side of the hill next to the upper visitor center is **Sliding Sands Trail**. If you're only going to do one hike at Haleakala, this is the one. The trail descends 2,400 feet fairly evenly over a span of almost 4 miles to the crater floor, but you don't need to go that far to see some of the gorgeous views from your slow but constant descent. Just go as far as you want, and you'll see how much larger and grander the crater looks from inside. At times it looks big enough to hold another island. The colors inside are amazing. Everything from green, yellow, red, brown, grey and blue are represented. If you don't want to hike it, there's a company that takes people down on horseback, all the way to the bottom. It's an *outstanding* ride, showcasing the crater at its best, and is the coolest horseback ride we've done in Hawaiʻi. See HORSEBACK RIDING on page 202. The trail leading into the crater is far less windy than up above. The weather **A REAL GEM** is usually sunny, especially in the morning. Clouds will push up from the Koʻolau and Kipahulu gaps as the day progresses. From inside you'll often see the clouds roiling at the head of the Kipahulu Gap at the far end, like a white waterfall, but passing no farther. Quiet prevails inside the crater, and the ever-eroding walls provide endless gravel. In fact, it's been necessary to dig up the horse hitch at the bottom of the crater several times. Erosion from the sides of the crater keeps raising the basin floor, creating the illusion that the hitch is sinking.

Inside are numerous hiking trails described under HIKING. Though Haleakala's most recent eruption in 1790 was at the coast, the crater is far from dead. Lava flowed in the crater 900 years ago while Hawaiians occupied the island, and perhaps even more recently. And it probably will erupt again.

There are cabins in the crater for the lucky lottery winners. If you get one, enjoy that complimentary firewood. It'll make the most expensive stove fire you've ever had because the park service gets it there by helicopter. Other maintenance is done by rangers on horse and mule.

HALEAKALA & UPCOUNTRY BEST BETS

Best Tour—Horseback Ride Down Sliding Sands into the Crater

Best Hike—Sliding Sands as Far as Your Heart Takes You

Best Coup—Getting a Cabin in the Crater

Best Decadent Treat—Komoda's Bakery in Makawao

Best Sign to Ignore—FAA Sign to Skyline

Best Place to See Someone Shoot at Klingons—From Science City at Night

Best Way to Freeze Your Da Kines Off— Wear Shorts to Watch the Sunrise

Best Place to Get a Glimpse of Your Soul—Leleiwi Overlook

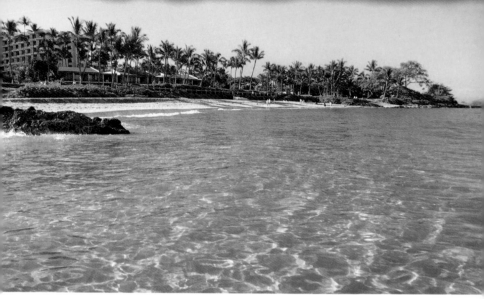

Crystal clear water, luscious beaches like Mokapu and swanky resorts are why people love South Maui.

Ahh, South Maui. Land of sun and beaches and visions of offshore islands.

Until the mid-1900s, there were few people living in South Maui. Lack of water made it difficult to grow things, and, after all, what else was land good for? Today we know it's good for growing Hawai'i's most important cash crop—*visitors!* South Maui gets so little rain (many years it may only rain three or four times), and its beaches are so extraordinary that it's a mecca for anyone looking for a dreamy, dependable tropical vacation.

If you look at the graphic above, the first thing you notice is that the term *South Maui* is not very geographically correct. *South Central Maui* seems more accurate. But South Maui is what the region has been historically called, so who are we to quibble?

We're going to describe it from Ma'alaea at the top of Hwy 31 heading south as far as you can go.

MA'ALAEA

At the intersection of Hwys 30 and 31, Ma'alaea was feared and despised by early airborne visitors. Because it was here, where the Kealia Pond now exists, that clueless aviation officials chose to place Maui's first airport in 1929. (It looked geographically convenient on a map to early planners.) It didn't last long because this is the windiest spot in Hawai'i. The scouring wind ensured that the inbound flight experience would be as terrifying as possible. (So if you think your landing at Kahului was bumpy—*brah, dat's nothing!*)

Ma'alaea is still a transportation hub, only now it's for boats. If you take a snorkel or whale watching trip, odds are very good you'll leave from here.

Maui Ocean Center (270–7000) is the other big attraction here and is definitely worth a stop. Opened in 1998, this is a relatively small (compared to some mainland aquariums) but extremely well-done aquarium. The living reef exhibit has a fantastic collection of fish found around the Hawaiian islands, and the sealife seems remarkably well cared for. Turtle Lagoon has lots of turtles roaming around that you can view from above or from a glass wall below the surface. Elsewhere there is a glass tunnel that passes right through a large tank, complete with sharks. Stop in the tunnel's center, and the sharks pass right beneath the glass floor. The gift shop has a surprisingly fine and vast assortment of gift items, many locally made. It's one of the more impressive gift shops we've seen on the island. The aquarium is more crowded when the weather is bad. The $24 entrance fee may seem excessive due to the small size, but the quality shines. (Kids are $17.)

Ma'alaea's greatest natural asset is its 3-mile long Ma'alaea Beach, stretching all the way to north Kihei. If you're looking for a great walking or jogging beach, this is the one. Early mornings and early evenings are best, as winds punish the area during the day. You won't have it to yourself, but you will have an amazingly peaceful stroll.

While *you* may have come to Maui for the beaches, *birds* visit us for Kealia Pond. This important wetland is home to several species of native birds. There's a turnout and boardwalk trail *(if* it's open—*long* story) between the 1 and 2 mile markers on Hwy 31. (Also labeled as Hwy 310 as some signs are marked.) This is a good place to bird watch. During the summer the ponds dry up.

In past years around the area of Hwy 31/310 clouds of mindless midges (a tiny, irritating, imported bug that often flies up your nose) would sometimes

Though it may dry up in the summer, the existence of Kealia Pond, a wetland in perennially dry South Maui, is a surprise to everyone except the birds.

swarm the area and sound like rain as they pepper your car. They've made great efforts to minimize them lately by utilizing hormones in the Kealia Ponds, and it's made a difference.

Even still, we believe staying in Ma'alaea is not advised. Though conveniently located, the wind, intermittent smoke and dust from sugar operations, a nearby power plant and a landfill upwind—none of which are probably in the brochures you've seen—make Ma'alaea a pretty dicey proposition. They better offer you an outrageous deal; otherwise, consider the offerings farther south.

Until they installed that picket fence lining the shoreline, hawksbill turtles would occasionally cross the road here in late spring/early summer to lay eggs in the Kealia Pond. Today they lay their eggs on the beach. But that's the only time you're likely to see them. They live and feed in deeper waters, far from shore. The turtles you see while snorkeling are usually green sea turtles, which rarely nest here, preferring French Frigate Shoals, 700 miles away. (Like restless teenagers, sea creatures rarely want to hang around the place they were born.)

As you're entering Kihei, you have a choice of either taking South Kihei Road

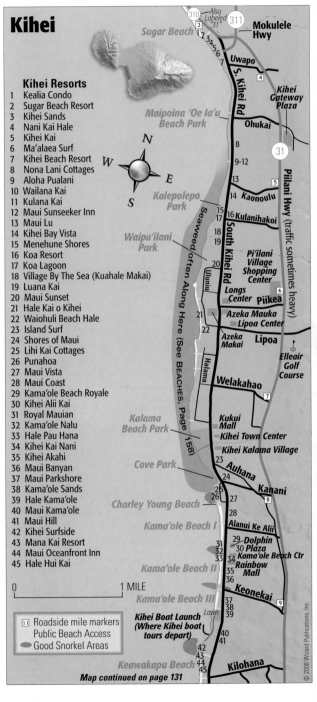

Kihei

Kihei Resorts
1 Kealia Condo
2 Sugar Beach Resort
3 Kihei Sands
4 Nani Kai Hale
5 Kihei Kai
6 Ma'alaea Surf
7 Kihei Beach Resort
8 Nona Lani Cottages
9 Aloha Pualani
10 Wailana Kai
11 Kulana Kai
12 Maui Sunseeker Inn
13 Maui Lu
14 Kihei Bay Vista
15 Menehune Shores
16 Koa Resort
17 Koa Lagoon
18 Village By The Sea (Kuahale Makai)
19 Luana Kai
20 Maui Sunset
21 Hale Kai o Kihei
22 Waiohuli Beach Hale
23 Island Surf
24 Shores of Maui
25 Lihi Kai Cottages
26 Punahoa
27 Maui Vista
28 Maui Coast
29 Kama'ole Beach Royale
30 Kihei Alii Kai
31 Royal Mauian
32 Kama'ole Nalu
33 Hale Pau Hana
34 Kihei Kai Nani
35 Kihei Akahi
36 Maui Banyan
37 Maui Parkshore
38 Kama'ole Sands
39 Hale Kama'ole
40 Maui Kama'ole
41 Maui Hill
42 Kihei Surfside
43 Mana Kai Resort
44 Maui Oceanfront Inn
45 Hale Hui Kai

0 ——————— 1 MILE

11 Roadside mile markers
Public Beach Access
Good Snorkel Areas

Map continued on page 131

© 2008 Wizard Publications, Inc.

along the shore or staying on the highway. The latter you'll use when you're simply interested in getting farther south. Though you won't take it every time, we'll describe South Kihei Road from here because that's where all the goodies are. The maps show all the connecting roads.

KIHEI

Kihei is the unplanned outcome of South Maui's explosion of popularity during the 1970s and '80s. It's a linear collection of condos and strip malls. While it certainly lacks the old world charm of Lahaina, Kihei doesn't try to be anything other than what it is—a beach town—where everything is water-related. As for downtown Kihei, there is no such animal. The closest you could come to defining the town center is the shopping center area near Lipoa and South Kihei Road. And that's a stretch.

Before it was developed, Kihei looked like what you see up the mountain: dry, scrubby and not overly attractive. Water was scarce. With no water to tap from this dry side of Haleakala, planners drilled wells over in water-rich West Maui and piped it in under the central plain. Most people who live here don't even know this and, when Upcountry experiences its occasional droughts, they look resentfully down the hill at the green of Kihei and Wailea and wonder where *they* seem to get all their water.

South Kihei Road is quite a sight for first-timers. It's so close to the ocean and beaches, you recognize immediately how important the sea is to this town.

When the Big Island's King Kamehameha invaded Maui for the last (and ultimately successful) time, he came ashore in Kihei at one point. The fighting was fierce with Maui warriors employing a novel weapon—*heated* sling-stones.

Kamehameha's forces were a bit intimidated by the hot rocks and contemplated retreating. So Kamehameha ordered all of their canoes destroyed. The message was simple—win or die. With newfound motivation his troops eventually won (with the help of some western cannons) and went on to conquer all the islands.

Since we've already made some residents mad with our Ma'alaea comments, we might as well go for broke. Though south Kihei and Wailea have some of the *best* beaches on the island, north Kihei has some of the *worst*. In short, don't swim in most of the water from just south of the intersection of South Kihei Road and Ohukai down to Cove Park, 3 miles south. We explain the gory details under BEACHES on page 158. Simply put, the water is yucky.

As you pass Cove Park, note the color of the water. Brownish, right? Less than 200 feet south the water will get clean and clear again, and the next beach, Kama'ole Beach I, offers fine swimming. From here on, it's nothing but great beach after great beach. All are described under BEACHES. Outstanding Keawakapu is the last beach you pass on South Kihei Road. Here the road veers away from the shoreline. You'll take a right on Wailea Alanui Road to continue your southward journey.

Breezes usually stiffen into winds in the afternoon in South Maui. (See WEATHER on page 26.) Most beach activities are best in the morning or late afternoon just before sunset.

If you're watching a sunset from South Maui and the sky is clear of clouds, take a look behind you as soon as the sun sets. If Haleakala's free of clouds, too, you'll see that the sun still shines there. It's so tall that the sun sets several minutes later on Haleakala, bathing it in sunlight when it has vanished from your eyes.

WAILEA

This is the premier resort area on the island (Kapalua's and Ka'anapali's claims notwithstanding). Expensive resorts line its heavenly beaches. Some, like the Fairrmont Kea Lani, are so posh and **A REAL GEM** exotic, you'll weep when you finally have to go back to the *real* world. While Kihei was an *every man for himself* development, the Wailea area had a single owner with a single vision: grand, green, groomed and golf. With splendid weather (cooler than Kihei and the afternoon winds aren't as strong), phenomenal beaches, clean water and kickin' views of Molokini and Kaho'olawe, Wailea is a grand success.

There are no mile markers here, and some places don't have signs. If you reset your odometer at the corner of Wailea Ike and Wailea Alanui, we've marked distances on the maps.

Many of the best beaches on the island are found right here. In addition to its beaches, Wailea has a glorious beachside path. Though not as long or as well known as Ka'anapali's path, it stretches between the Renaissance and Fairmont Kea Lani resorts (Mokapu and Polo Beaches) and is a perfect way for visitors at one Wailea resort to dine at another without messing with cars. It also makes a great place for a sunset stroll or a sunrise jogging path.

Wailea Alanui becomes Makena Alanui past the Fairmont Kea Lani. (That's the goofy-looking, though very luxurious, resort past the Four Seasons—someone was reading *Arabian Nights* when they designed *that* one.) Segments of the old Makena Road visit less known beaches, such as Palauea and Makena, as well as snorkeling and diving areas like Five Graves. Kayakers often launch at Makena Landing.

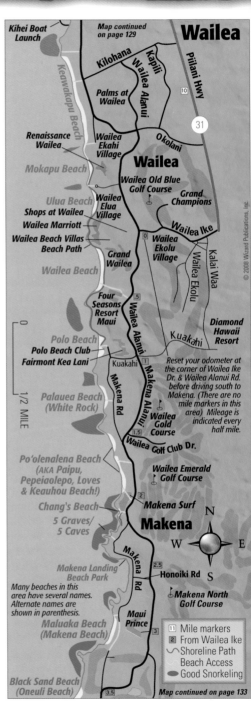

Map continued on page 129

Wailea

Kihei Boat Launch

Keawakapu Beach

Kilohana

Wailea Alanui

Kapili

Piilani Hwy

Palms at Wailea

10

31

Renaissance Wailea

Wailea Ekahi Village

Okolani

Wailea

Mokapu Beach

Wailea Old Blue Golf Course

Grand Champions

Ulua Beach

Wailea Elua Village

Shops at Wailea

Wailea Marriott

Wailea Beach Villas

Beach Path

Grand Wailea

Wailea Ike

Wailea Ekolu Village

Kalai Waa

Wailea Ekolu

Wailea Beach

Four Seasons Resort Maui

.5

Wailea Alanui

Kuakahi

Diamond Hawaii Resort

Polo Beach

Polo Beach Club

Fairmont Kea Lani

Kuakahi

1

Reset your odometer at the corner of Wailea Ike Dr. & Wailea Alanui Rd. before driving south to Makena. (There are no mile markers in this area) Mileage is indicated every half mile.

1/2 MILE

Makena Rd

Makena Alanui

Palauea Beach (White Rock)

Wailea Gold Course

1.5

Wailea Golf Club Dr.

Po'olenalena Beach (AKA Paipu, Pepeiaolepo, Loves & Keauhou Beach!)

Wailea Emerald Golf Course

Chang's Beach

2

Makena Surf

5 Graves/ 5 Caves

Makena

N

W   E

S

Makena Rd

2.5

Honoiki Rd

Makena Landing Beach Park

Makena North Golf Course

Many beaches in this area have several names. Alternate names are shown in parenthesis.

Maui Prince

3

Maluaka Beach (Makena Beach)

11 Mile markers

2 From Wailea Ike

Shoreline Path

Beach Access

Good Snorkeling

Black Sand Beach (Oneuli Beach)

3.5

Map continued on page 133

© 2008 Wizard Publications, Inc.

Who would expect an oasis of life in a young lava field, like this one at Cape Kina'u?

One sound that's common in South Maui is the call of the gray francolin. This bird starts every morning with a surprisingly vigorous call, which sounds something like a car alarm.

MAKENA

Leaving Wailea and passing the Maui Prince, as you round the corner you'll notice a large hill near the ocean. The drama that created that hill was probably witnessed by the ancient Hawaiians.

Haleakala is in its twilight years as an active volcano. Its time is almost up. The typical life cycle for a Hawaiian volcano is to grow slowly beneath the sea through sporadic eruptions. It then begins vigorous, near-constant growth, building an island. Later it falls asleep for 500,000 to 1 million years and then awakens for its last hurrah before dying and eventually sinking beneath the sea under its own weight. Oahu's Diamond Head is a product of its last gasp 300,000 years ago. Here, on Haleakala's southwestern flank, we see a volcano in its death throes. Its last eruption was around 1790 at the end

of the road ahead. It was a "typical" surface flow; lava squeezed from a vent and flowed downhill. The eruption that created the large hill toward the sea, called Pu'u Ola'i, or Earthquake Hill, was not.

Hawaiian legend states that before the 1790 eruption, this was the last place on the island to erupt. Imagine how it must have looked if there were villagers living here at the time. Lava began quietly pooling beneath the surface in what was supposed to be just another "typical" surface flow. But because it was so close to the shoreline, sea water seeped into the magma pool. This water immediately flashed into steam, building up the pressure in the lava pool. Earthquakes began rumbling as the earth struggled to contain the pressure. Villagers may have begun to notice small amounts of steam coming from the ground. As more lava and sea water combined, something had to give. Suddenly, the ground ripped open with a tremendous explosion as fountains of bright orange and red lava shot into the sky. It must have been spectacularly large, because the entire hill you see before you was created as the gas-frothed lava fell to earth and piled up to form the 360-foot Pu'u Ola'i, perhaps in as little as a week. (Looks taller, doesn't it?)

Hiking up Pu'u Ola'i is more difficult than it looks. The trail to the top marches through the cinders (called *tephra* by geologists, in case you just *had* to know) that make up this mass. So, as you take a step up, the tendency is to fall back a few inches, making the climb more tiring. But the view from the top is magnificent. You can see Big Beach below on one side and much of Wailea on the other. At press time the state had the trail closed for safety evaluation.

You may see signs in the area warning of deer crossing. These aren't a joke. Five axis deer from India were brought here in 1959. They were supposed to have a low reproductive potential. Apparently somebody missed the fine print in their warranty, because in the brief time they've been here, they've multiplied to around 10,000 and are considered a nuisance. Many of them live in this area and are occasionally whacked by passing cars. Golfers at Wailea's courses may find additional hazards on the greens as the deer come down from the mountains during times of drought upcountry and leave souvenirs on the greens. They're most plentiful on Pu'u Ola'i.

There might be a few food stands on the side of the road in Makena. The best is Makena Grill after Big Beach across from the lava rock wall at Secret Cove. Awesome fish tacos.

MOLOKINI

To residents and visitors in the know, the name Molokini conjures up images of crystal clear water and bright, vivid coral. If nature hadn't made this off-

A REAL GEM

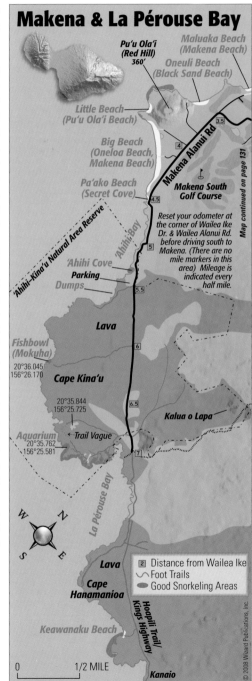

Makena & La Pérouse Bay

Pu'u Ola'i (Red Hill) 360'
Maluaka Beach (Makena Beach)
Oneuli Beach (Black Sand Beach)
Little Beach (Pu'u Ola'i Beach)
Big Beach (Oneloa Beach, Makena Beach)
Pa'ako Beach (Secret Cove)
Makena Alanui Rd
3.5
4
Makena South Golf Course
'Ahihi-Kina'u Natural Area Reserve
'Ahihi Bay
4.5
Map continued on page 131
Reset your odometer at the corner of Wailea Ike Dr. & Wailea Alanui Rd. before driving south to Makena. (There are no mile markers in this area) Mileage is indicated every half mile.
5
'Ahihi Cove
Parking
Dumps
5.5
Lava
6
Fishbowl (Mokuha)
20°36.045 156°26.170
Cape Kina'u
20°35.844 156°25.725
6.5
Kalua o Lapa
Aquarium
20°35.762 156°25.581
Trail Vague
7
La Pérouse Bay
Lava
Cape Hanamanioa
Hoopili Trail/ Kings Highway
Keawanaku Beach

2 Distance from Wailea Ike
Foot Trails
Good Snorkeling Areas

0   1/2 MILE
Kanaio

© 2008 Wizard Publications, Inc.

Perfect days end with a perfect sunset.

shore island, the Hawai'i Visitors Bureau would have. This aquatic wonder was created when an undersea vent, held under pressure by the ocean's weight, busted loose with lava and ash, building up what we call a tuff cone. The northern half has been eroded away by wave action, creating a semi-circular reef far enough offshore to be clear of runoff or sand. So underwater visibility is nearly always 100 feet, sometimes 180.

Visiting Molokini means taking a boat from either Ma'alaea (10 miles away) or Kihei Boat Ramp (6 miles). Though it seems close to Maui, don't try to take a kayak there. Currents and winds between Molokini and Maui are too strong for most kayakers.

The crater is a marine and bird sanctuary. You're not allowed to walk on the island. Once inside the crescent, you'll find the water inviting. See page 209 for more on snorkeling and diving Molokini. In the past, the crater used to be visited often by a lonely monk seal who was famous for swimming right up to divers. Boat captains nicknamed him Humpy because of his...*unusually* friendly gestures toward swimmers. The seal was apparently unaware of the law prohibiting human contact with monk seals. If any monk seals visit Molokini while you're there, just remember that *they* have to initiate any contact.

The horizontal notch on the back of the crater is caused by wave cuts. If you were to SCUBA dive down 250 feet, you'd find a similar wave cut, evidence that the ocean was *much* lower during a past ice age.

According to lore, the 19th-century King Kalakaua wagered Molokini in a hand of poker with a local rancher. When the king lost the hand, he reneged, proclaiming that he hadn't wagered Molokini, but rather *omole kini,* which is a bottle of gin.

LA PÉROUSE BAY

As you approach the end of the road, look on both sides of you. It appears to be a lumpy tilled field, just waiting to be planted. That's a field of a'a lava rock, and it looks just the way it did when it erupted two centuries ago. Turn your attention to the split lava mound uphill just before the road's end. This was where the last eruption took place on Maui. Local legend states that there was a family living there at the time. An old woman came one day and asked for a chicken to eat. The family refused, saying that they first had to sacrifice some to the volcano goddess, Pele.

The old woman raged, saying that *she* was Pele and how dare they refuse her. She sent lava flowing their way. The mother and daughter fled toward the mountain, but Pele seized the two and turned them into stone. The hill you see, split in two, is made up of the mother and daughter, forever separated by a vengeful Pele.

La Pérouse Bay is as far as you can go by car in South Maui. It's renowned for two things: dolphins and wind. Dolphins are relatively common early in the morn-

When was the Last Eruption of Haleakala? 1790... Or is it 1490?

Ask most people on Maui when was the last time there was an eruption here, and you'll be told 1790. It's said so often it's considered an unchallenged fact. The truth is, we don't know when it happened. The 1790 date is based on the fact that when George Vancouver visited here in 1794, he drew a map showing the lava flow at Cape Kina'u (at the end of the road in South Maui). But when the French explorer La Pérouse visited in 1786, his map didn't show the cape. This, coupled with the fact that the flow looks very young, allowed people to divided the time and conclude that the eruption occurred "around 1790."

The problem is this: As a mapmaker, La Pérouse was terrible. He didn't get anything right. And his map of the shoreline was so crude and inaccurate, you can't use it to determine anything—other than the fact that La Pérouse probably flunked out of cartography school. You'd never recognize these islands from his map. Recent carbon-14 dating puts the eruption closer to 500 years ago, give or take a century. And by analyzing crystals in the lava, they can check the direction of the earth's ever-changing magnetic field. The crystals don't match the flows that we know happened on the Big Island in 1801.

What about historical accounts? There were people living here and, after all, two centuries isn't that long. Didn't they witness it? Sure, they did, but nobody wrote it down. The Hawaiians didn't have a written language until western man invented one in the 1800s. The only known historical accounts come from two sources. One was an American missionary who came to Maui in 1841. He said the native Hawaiians had told him their "grandparents witnessed it." Hmm, pretty slim. The only other account was from a Hawaiian cowboy named Charlie Ako. In 1906 he told a reporter that his father-in-law told him that his grandfather had seen the flow when he was "old enough to carry two coconuts from the sea to the upper road," which was 4–5 miles. The reporter plugged in the various ages and dates, assuming 33 years per generation, and came up with around 1750.

So we have map readers saying 1790, historical accounts saying 1750, and some scientific tests saying around 1490. Since we had to use some date, we mention the 1790 date in this book. But now you know the full story.

So now if someone tells you that the last eruption took place in 1790, you can look them directly in the eye and tell them with smug certainty...maybe.

ing. A pod patrols the area, and we often see them here around 7 a.m. and at Big Beach by around 10 a.m. But we often go months without seeing them at all. (Maybe dolphins take vacations, too.) Scientists think that, while resting, dolphins are able to turn off much of their brain (including the part that runs their echolocation abilities). They do a sort of snooze-and-cruise at La Pérouse in the early hours, counting on the fact that the shallow water and a light bottom will alert them to predators in the absence of their sonars. This means that, in the morning, dolphins are *literally* operating on half a brain. (Come to think of it, so am I before my coffee.)

It is illegal to chase or harass dolphins or do anything that disrupts their natural behavior. It may be hard to imagine slow, clumsy swimmers harassing sleek, fast dolphins, like a lowly crop duster harassing an F-16 fighter. If you're swimming near them, dolphins can distance themselves from you almost instantly and with very little effort. But when they're resting, they're not in a very fast mood. They don't *want* to work to distance themselves. So if you swim in the same water near them, don't shoot like a shotgun in their direction. You can slowly meander toward their general vicinity, but you shouldn't try to box them in or head them off at the pass. They may initiate the contact, if they are interested. Many times we've been in the water and had dolphins come over to check us out. Most of the time, however, they keep themselves at a cautious distance. If they don't stay away, you can only interpret their actions as curiosity. In short, don't harass or chase them or try to grab them if they come close. If people continually bug them, they'll simply stop coming to La Pérouse and we'll all lose.

Wind is also a La Pérouse trademark. If you look at the front cover map, you can see that wind coming from the northeast (our usual trade direction) will build up along the bottom of Haleakala and get ejected where the flank ends here at La Pérouse Bay, shooting out toward Kaho'olawe island. (You can actually *see* the windline in that photo.) The wind-caused chop on the water will usually start at the south end of the bay and work its way north throughout the day. The dividing line between choppy and calm water is often sharp, often around 100 feet wide.

La Pérouse Bay was well known in ancient times as a place where night marchers could be found. Called Huaka'i po, it refers to spirits who are still trapped on earth and generally cause mischief at night. To this day, there are places Hawaiians avoid at night because of night marchers. On Kaua'i there was a night marcher area that had an unusual string of bad car wrecks, which many believed were due to these spirits. (Police, however, blamed the wrecks on the other type of spirits—the kind in a bottle.)

Past La Pérouse there is a hike to a usually deserted black, white and green sand beach called Keawanaku. The snorkeling is great there, but the hiking trail has some obnoxious footing. See HIKING on page 201.

Looking at the map you'll see the upper highway less than 3 miles uphill from Wailea. Access to Haleakala, Upcountry and the Hana Highway is so near and yet so far. There's a very handy dirt road connecting the upper highway to Wailea, but the company that owns it won't let anyone use it. (They blame that old demon—liability.) The county is *discussing* the *concept* of *planning* to *talk* about *considering* a bypass, but in the meantime, it's a 30-mile detour through Kahului to get up the hill.

SOUTH MAUI SHOPPING

The Ma'alaea Harbor Village is near the Maui Ocean Center. A good stop after your boat trip from the harbor. Just make sure you tie down your kids, or you'll watch them careen off the island from the wind here. Moonbow Tropics has a good selection of island-style clothing. Island Soap & Candleworks is just what the name implies.

If you're short of time and have a long list of souvenirs to purchase, try the Kihei Kalama Village across from Kalama Park. There's parking in the back. This covered arcade has lots of small stall-type shops that carry a wide variety of Hawaiian-style items from art glass to coconut carvings.

If your shopping time is a little more leisurely, try Kihei Gateway Plaza off Piilani Highway behind the Tesoro Gas Station. You'll find Maui Golf for club rentals. Maui Clothing Co. is a huge store with items for the whole family.

Up Piikea Avenue is Piilani Village Shopping Center, featuring Hilo Hatties, which is a great place for aloha wear. They also have tons of souvenir gifts. There's also a Borders Express for a nice selection of Hawaiiana books.

Back on South Kihei Road you'll find Longs Drug Kihei Center that has Longs Drug, a good stop for souvenirs, mac nut candies and coffee and they're open until midnight. They also have reef shoes and tabis. Next door in Azeka Mauka, Who Cut The Cheese (besides having a daring name) has a gourmet selection of cheese and wines. Shoe lovers will feel right at home at Paradise Sandal Co. Across the street in Azeka Makai, White Pebbles has a blinding selection of beads—finished strings or loose—and for the quilter, check out Maui Quilt Shop. Farther south, Kama'ole Beach Center has Honolua Surf Co., a good place for excellent surf wear. Their long-sleeved T-shirts are wonderful to don after snorkeling or diving. Hawaiian Moons has health foods and snacks.

South Maui's upscale shopping venue is The Shops at Wailea at Wailea Iki and Wailea Alanui. Here you can find Gucci, Tiffany, Fendi, etc., not to mention a hot pink, feather boa and rhinestone-trimmed Princess phone for $450. For the rest of us, there is a great selection of sunglasses at Shades of Hawai'i. Martin & MacArthur has well-crafted koa items. Consider Blue Ginger for adorable cotton kids' clothes (and moms', too) and Sand People has nice items with a beach theme for the home. If you've run short of cash after your shopping spree, consider picking up a salad, drink and a bag of chips at Whaler's General Store. Take it to the beach in the new swim suit you just bought at Maui WaterWear.

SOUTH MAUI BEST BETS

Best Place for a Stroll—Shoreline Path From Mokapu Beach to Polo Beach

Best Snorkeling—Between Po'olenalena and Palauea or North End of La Pérouse

Best Cold Treat—Homemade Ice Cream Sandwich at Hula Cookies

Best Place to Toast Your Da Kines— Little Beach

Best Place to Chew Up Your Hiking Boots—Kalua o Lapa Lava Vent Hike

Best Sunday Brunch—Maui Prince

Best Example of What Should Be a Misplaced Decimal Point...But Isn't— $250 to Use a Cabana Chair *For One Day* at the Grand Wailea

Best Long Beach Stroll—Ma'alaea Bay

Best Boogie Boarding—Kama'ole III

Best Place to See Richie Valens Roll in His Grave—Hearing *La Bamba* at Kahale

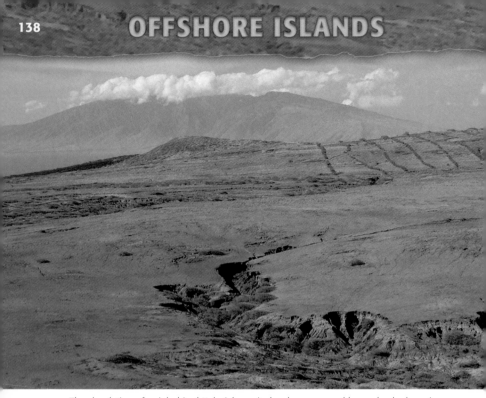

The desolation of uninhabited Kahoʻolawe, its hardpan exposed by unchecked erosion, is a vivid reminder of what both indigenous and modern man can do to the land. West Maui is in the background.

One of things that adds to the exotic nature of Maui is the abundance of offshore islands. Somehow, seeing multiple islands across the water adds mystery to the scene. Islands are never more intriguing than when they are tantalizingly out of reach. Because of the way they are sprinkled about, no other Hawaiian island has such great views of offshore islands. For instance, when you awaken for your first day at Kaʻanapali, you are confronted by islands dominating your view. Is that Kahoʻolawe? No wait...that's the other part of Maui; the land bridge is below the horizon. Is that Lanaʻi? No, Molokaʻi is where Lanaʻi should be. Take a look at the fold-out back cover map and the graphic above to orient yourself. Molokaʻi dominates the view from Kapalua, Lanaʻi is offshore of Lahaina, and Kahoʻolawe is the closest to South Maui.

We haven't attempted to make this a complete guide to other nearby islands, but you may want to know a little about your neighbors. Some can even be visited by boat trips listed on page 208 or by helicopter trips listed on page 189. Since Maui is the gateway to the resorts of Lanaʻi, we're including some information on them here.

KAHOʻOLAWE

If you're staying in Kihei, Kahoʻolawe is the impressive island offshore behind the tiny crescent islet of Molokini. Though it looks enticing from afar, Kahoʻolawe is an ecological mess.

History revisionists (most of whom have almost certainly never visited Kahoʻolawe) attribute Kahoʻolawe's ecological woes to either the military or Western man in general. The truth can be a little more embarrassing. When the ancient Hawaiians discovered these islands, they found on Kahoʻolawe a fragile dryland forest. It was a marginal environment to live in due to its location in the rain shadow of Maui. Dry, thin soil populated by hearty but water-starved trees and shrubs marked the island. In the course of their settlement, the Hawaiians cut down most of the trees on the island to make canoes, for firewood and for other purposes. Without roots to hold the soil together, erosion became the thief that stole the essence of Kahoʻolawe.

In fact, by the time Captain Cook first encountered the islands in the 1770s, Kahoʻolawe was no longer inhabited and was instead used only as a campsite for visiting fishermen. When the king of the Big Island invaded Maui in the 1780s, he made a separate trip over to Kahoʻolawe and was furious when he discovered there was nothing to steal or plunder there and only a few fishermen to terrorize. When Maui children of that era asked their parents why nobody lived on the island across the waters, they were told it was because the island was sacred. Perhaps, but it was also used up.

In the mid-1800s the Hawaiian government used Kahoʻolawe and Lanaʻi as penal colonies. Crimes that got you banished to Kahoʻolawe included rebellion, theft, divorce, breaking marriage vows and murder. Starvation was rampant there, and desperate escape attempts were common.

Later, western man introduced feral animals: goats, pigs and cattle. Their hooves and grazing quickly completed the ecological rampage.

During WWII the military took control of Kahoʻolawe and used it for target practice. It was later seized by direct presidential order for exclusive use by the military. But the damage from their target practice was minimal compared to what the island had already experienced and was mostly limited to a smaller area. (Hitting a stationary island of 44½ square miles is, after all, a pretty poor demonstration of marksmanship. Their goal was to hit a certain *part* of the island.) Often, the military would put an old jeep in an open area and fire at it. Residents of Kihei grew up to the booming sound coming from 7 miles across the water. After a half-century of live fire, President Bush (Sr.) signed an executive order in 1990 halting all target practice on the island. There are a number of unexploded small ordnance scattered about the entire island, enough to make it a dangerous place to wander around.

The result today is an island robbed of her topsoil in many places, leaving nothing but an unforgiving hardpan layer. The areas that still harbor plants feature mostly gray shrubs and grasses. There is no permanent source of water other than wells. But despite that, there is a stark beauty to the place. It looks nothing like the rest of Hawaiʻi. Cleanup of most of the unexploded ordnance has been completed, but don't count on booking your Kahoʻolawe vacation anytime soon. The island was transferred to native Hawaiian control in 1994. They are trying to replant the island with native plants and increase the amount of soil. It's a hot, tiring job, but it's hoped that future generations will find a Kahoʻolawe that is much like what the initial Hawaiians found. Going back in time is a rare event in this world, and islands don't often get a second chance. Maybe this time Kahoʻolawe will benefit from our hindsight and our diligence.

LANA'I

For most of the 20th century Lana'i was known as the pineapple island. Almost 98% of the island was owned by Dole Pineapple, and pineapple dominated this 140½-square-mile island. In the late '80s the owners (the island is now privately owned by a mainland family named Murdock) decided that owning a secluded Hawaiian island was more valuable than owning pineapple fields. So they got out of pineapple and began marketing Lana'i as the "private island," complete with two high-end resorts and excellent golfing.

The population is around 3,200 and most work for the landowner, often paying cheap, subsidized rent. More than once we've seen residents taking the ferry to Lahaina to pick up stacks of pizzas for delivery back to Lana'i City. (Lana'i is a tad out of Domino's delivery range.)

Lying in the rain shadow of West Maui, Lana'i is arid, receiving only 10–20 inches of rain annually in most locations, and it's certainly not the most attractive island you'll visit. Some of its beaches, however, are excellent (though occasional heavy storms from the south can muck up the water for as long as six months at a time). Taking the Expeditions Maui–Lana'i Ferry (661–3756) for $25 each way is the most popular way to get there. (Sit on the right/starboard side.) There are also flights into the airport.

Lana'i is an amazingly relaxing place to stay. The second day into our first visit, we were tempted to call the front desk and complain that someone had broken into our room and surgically removed our bones. You can actually *feel* motivation and ambition draining from your body. The downside to the relaxing nature is the lack of options available to you here. The island is dominated by a few players who have more control over you than you may realize. For instance, the company that

does most of the boat activities, Trilogy, also owns the island's Dollar Rent-a-Car (800–533–7808) and the only gas station, and you may find yourself wondering if they prefer that you take a profitable tour, rather than rent a car. Because renting a car can be difficult—there are less than 3 dozen vehicles to accommodate all 362 rooms. (Moloka'i has *10 times* that number of cars for a similar visitor count.) And rental car prices will shock you. In fact, *everything* is expensive on Lana'i. (You'll be forgiven if you start to wonder if Lana'i is the Hawaiian word for, "It costs *how* much?") It's easy to let expenses get away from you since nearly every place on the island lets you charge things to your room. (It's called check-out shock, and it can be fatal for those with weak hearts.)

Though resort personnel "aren't supposed to tell you this," there is another company renting JEEPs on the island with prices better than Dollar's. Adventure Lana'i Ecocentre (565–7373) also gives coolers, etc., with the JEEP, has fewer restrictions on where you can drive (*that's important*) and their mud tires are better than Dollar's. Sure, their JEEPs are a bit more banged up. But that's because they allow *you* to bang 'em. They also have ATV and bicycle rentals and tours.

If you rent a JEEP, use it! Although Lana'i's not the prettiest island, if you don't mind eating some dust and getting your hands dirty, it's a JEEP-lover's dream. Especially recommended is the 4WD Munro Trail that skirts the island's misty upper ridge. The views of Maui and Moloka'i are awesome up here, and the pine trees, ferns, wild turkeys and pheasant transport you to another world.

The main beach at the hotel is probably among the top 10 beaches in the state. Called Hulopo'e Beach, it has a huge sand deposit and good swimming coupled with unreal snorkeling on the left (southeast) end of the beach.

Venture along the rocky shoreline away from the beach, and you're treated to some very dramatic underwater scenery. Not because of the coral (which is sparse) or the fish (which are abundant) or visibility (often a bit cloudy), but because of the canyon-like lattice structure of the lava and dead coral. Chasms, holes, stacks and arches create a miniature Bryce Canyon with exciting possibilities. Avoid during moderate to high surf, however, or it may get *too* exciting due to surginess. Occasionally, large Kona storm runoff causes severe water cloudiness that can last for many months. You can easily walk to the beach from the ferry landing.

Staying on Lana'i

The island has only three places to stay, and two are Four Seasons Resorts. Manele Bay (800–321–4666), which is actually on harder-to-pronounce Hulopo'e Bay, has the more Hawaiian feel. At check-in your credit card is momentarily whisked away to be run through their spe-cial NASA-designed hydraulic credit card press, capable of pumping more money out of your credit card than you ever imagined. The resort is very pretty and tropical and the restaurants are good, though pricey. (There's a dress code at one of the two restaurants.) Rates are from $445–$7,000 per night.

The Lodge at Ko'ele (800–321–4666) is the most expensive lodge you ever saw and certainly the ritziest. Located 1,700 feet up in the misty, cool center of the island, the lodge is for those who want a formal, less Hawaiian experi-ence. (Some Hawai'i residents like it for this very reason. They consider it a get-away.) The place looks more like an English manor than a Hawaiian hotel. Tea time is from 3–5 p.m. We're partial to the blackcurrant tea with scones while sitting next to the fireplace reading Tennyson or Shelley. (OK, so we don't *really* read those dudes, but *dang,* the tea sure is good.) Food is the weak spot here. It's worth nowhere near the $45–$65 you'll spend in the formal

Renting a JEEP on Lana'i allows you to discover the mouth-watering views of Moloka'i and Maui during your drive down to the north coast.

dining room. Even the bar charges $6 for pineapple juice. Room rates are $345–$1,500.

At press time many Lana'i residents were of the opinion that the island's owner wanted to turn Lana'i into another Aspen, Colorado. Long-time shopkeepers (who rent from the island's owner) were closing, making way for newer shops that would cater to upscale visitors. Whatever Lana'i's fate, change is on its way. Already, land prices have ballooned. Simple plantation houses with tin roofs around Lana'i city are now selling for $400,000-plus, and old-time residents are either selling and moving out or scrambling to figure out how to buy one on salaries that can't meet the mortgages.

As an aside, you can always tell when the owner of the island is flying in on his private jet. Lawns around the island get mowed; trash is swept up.

Hotel Lana'i (800–795–7211) is a 10-room hotel that predates the large resorts. It's for the "budget traveler" to Lana'i. (If there is such an animal.) Rates are around $139 per night and up, 2-night minimum. Their Lana'i City Grille restaurant isn't much cheaper than the other resorts, but the food is good. Prices are $35–$50. Other Lana'i restaurants, such as Blue Ginger Café, are cheap but unremarkable.

Lana'i is the last place you would expect to get worldwide attention. But on New Year's Day 1994, the island became the most exclusive place on earth. The event? A wedding. The groom wanted privacy and could *definitely* afford it. Willie Nelson was hired to perform the night before. The groom rented every hotel room on the island and kept most empty. He also chartered every helicopter on nearby Maui and paid them to stay on the ground. Then he hired a private security force to patrol the island. No one was allowed on or off Lana'i. (A cameraman who was nabbed by the private security force was later awarded an out-of-court settlement by the groom when it was pointed out that he was in a *public* area.) After all the preparations the groom married his sweetheart on the 12th hole of the island's oceanside golf course. Only 130 people were allowed to attend the wedding of the richest man in the history of the world, Bill Gates. The man who could marry at (and probably buy) any place on the planet chose Lana'i to tie the knot. It cost him over $1 million. (Probably a mere rounding error in his checkbook.)

MOLOKA'I

Moloka'i is a long, skinny island of immense beauty and unimaginable sea cliffs. It's 260 square miles, though it was once much larger. The island owes its shape to the type of cataclysmic event that sometimes occurs with Hawaiian volcanoes. Much of the volcano from east Moloka'i broke off and fell into the sea hundreds of thousands of years ago, where *half-mile-sized* chunks of rock rolled to a stop 100 miles away. The landslide created awesome sea cliffs that are up to 3,000 feet high—the highest in the world—which are continually undercut by the ocean's waves. Think about the mind-boggling forces involved in that event. The entire Pacific rim was affected as tidal waves of skyscraper heights ravaged shorelines thousands of miles away. Moloka'i is not alone in experiencing these kind of apocalyptic events. The Big Island had a slide 120,000 years ago, and the resulting wave swept over Kaho'olawe and tossed chunks of coral up to the 1,000 foot elevation level on Lana'i. Kaho'olawe and probably Lana'i and Ni'ihau also experienced monster landslides.

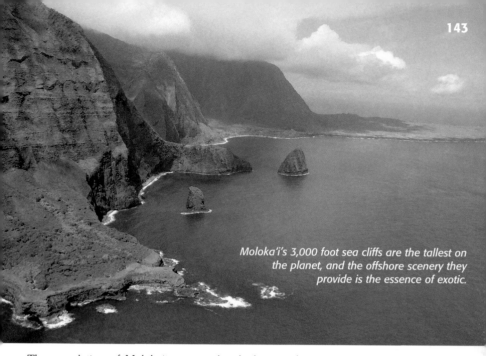

Moloka'i's 3,000 foot sea cliffs are the tallest on the planet, and the offshore scenery they provide is the essence of exotic.

The population of Moloka'i is around 7,500, and there is not a single traffic light on the whole island. Not all is rosy on Moloka'i, however. The island has a perpetually dismal economy. Most of the residents are on some kind of government assistance. Though the island's nickname is "the friendly island," you may find just the opposite. Though they are very friendly with each other (the only repetitive motion injury residents are likely to suffer is from drivers constantly waving at each other), many (though by no means all) tend to be pretty reserved with visitors. In fact, more stink eye greets visitors to this island than any other. (It's a favorite of many visitors due to its undeveloped nature, but many complain of feeling unwelcome.) NO TRESPASSING signs are conspicuously few. You either belong somewhere or you don't, and residents don't need signs to tell them that.

Local residents, many of whom are adamantly opposed to more visitors, had a nasty little war going on with the island's largest landowner, Moloka'i Ranch, which owns over *a third* of the island (mostly on the drier western half). When the ranch

built a pipeline to carry water to another part of the island, vandals destroyed it. While the ranch suffered tens of millions of dollars in losses from their operations, residents stopped them from doing any development. As a last ditch effort to save the the business, Moloka'i Ranch threw a Hail Mary. They proposed developing a 500-acre strip of land at La'au Point on the extreme southwestern tip. They agreed to use proceeds from the sale of luxury lots at the otherwise inaccessible land to rebuild the long-closed Sheraton resort and to set aside 50,000 acres (over ¾ of all their land holdings) for conservation. But residents wouldn't hear of it. Hand-made SAVE LA'AU signs went up all over the island and local activists influenced the land use commission to turn down Moloka'i Ranch's plans.

So in 2008 the company essentially quit the island. They closed their two remaining resorts, got rid of their cattle operations, shut down the gas station and movie complex in Maunaloa and closed off indefinitely access to their ⅓ of the island. The foreign owners say they will sit on the land until the business environment warms up on Moloka'i, but locals think they'll ultimately sell it.

Visiting Moloka'i

The two best ways to visit from Maui are either a boat/car trip, or fly over for the mule ride to Kalaupapa.

Maui Princess (667–6165) will take you over several days a week (call for the changing schedule) and give you a car for five hours of exploring; it's $212 for the first person, $85 for others. Kids are $43. They also have van tours, but you'll probably prefer your own car. Once on island, your biggest decision is which way to go. Either turn right (east) if the weather's good, or left if it's not. East wanders along the dry, southern part of the island. Private fishponds line almost the entire shoreline. With no one in front and no one in your rear-view mirror, Moloka'i feels like it's all yours. Once 20 miles out of Kaunakakai, the scenery turns dramatic (and the road narrows). The sweet payoff 30 miles from Kaunakakai is the end of the road, and the vista alone is almost worth the trip. Halawa Valley is isolated, quaint and strikingly beautiful. Backed by tall waterfalls, the descent into the valley is marvelous. Once inside, Moloka'i's "friendly" nickname becomes laughable. There's a good dirt road and path leading back to the falls, but makeshift signs tell you not to go. (Unless you pay someone for a guided tour, of course.) Just revel in the bayside scenery. It's as good as the waterfall anyway.

Toward the middle of the island, a 6-mile detour from the highway leads to Moloka'i's biggest must-see. The Kalaupapa Overlook. Moloka'i was notorious in the 1800s as the site of the state's leprosy settlement. Leprosy may have been brought back to Hawai'i by a chief who had visited abroad in 1840 or by Chinese laborers a bit later. Located on an isolated peninsula called Kalaupapa, stricken patients were banished there when their condition was discovered. They didn't come here to live with the disease; they came to die. It was a hideous and vile place in those days, com-

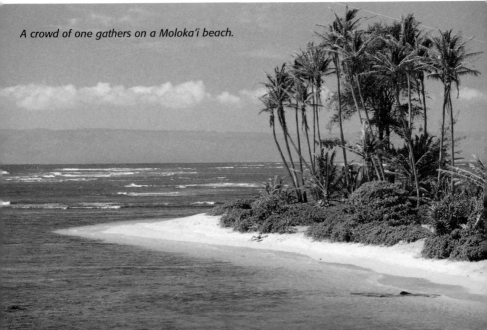

A crowd of one gathers on a Moloka'i beach.

pletely neglected by a government that only wanted to forget it existed. A 33-year-old priest from Belgium named Father Damien arrived in 1873 and tended to the unfortunates, living closely with them. Giving no thought to his own safety, he eventually contracted the disease and died there in 1889. The method of transmission was baffling to 19th-century doctors. They had no way of knowing that over 95% of the human population is naturally immune to the disease, which means that 19 out of 20 priests sent to Kalaupapa could never have contracted it. Damien was genetically unfortunate to be among the 5% who could.

Though his last 16 years of life were a selfless dedication to the most reviled and abused people among us, Damien was tormented on his deathbed with the fear that he was unworthy of heaven. According to today's Catholic Church, he had nothing to fear. The church is in the final process of making him a saint.

Though the disease has a cure now, there are still former leprosy patients living at Kalaupapa, which is now a national park. (Some Kalaupapa residents prefer the more modern term, Hansen's Disease; others prefer to leave it as *leprosy*. All hate the term *leper*.) Mule rides down into the area are the most popular activity on Moloka'i. (See ADVENTURES on page 241.) If you get a chance, rent the 1999 movie, *Moloka'i: The Story of Father Damien*.

From the unbelievably beautiful overlook, you realize why 19th-century Hawaiian officials chose this place. After the volcano collapsed and created the sea cliffs, the apparently cold magma chamber came back to life for one last creation. It erupted at the base of the cliff and created land that is adjacent to, but utterly apart from, the rest of the island. Only a manmade trail, gouged in the side of the cliffs, allows land access.

As you stand at the overlook, with the wind whistling through the trees, the ghosts of misery and pain that were banished there a century ago can seem all too real. It's ironic that a place once so despised is today a visitor attraction. Perhaps that's the only way to completely clear away the haze of despair that once filled the air.

Most of the workers at Kalaupapa live there, but there are a half dozen workers who hike in every day. *Big deal,* you say! Well, yeah, it is. The hike includes going down and then up a 1,700-foot-high mountain—*every day*. They say the biggest hazards are the mules on the trail that don't like to be passed and have a nasty habit of kicking them when they try. Now *that's* a commute!

The other attraction near the overlook is Ka-ule-o-Nanahoa or Phallic Rock. It's a 5-minute uphill walk. To the ancient Hawaiians, the 6-foot-tall stone in the shape of a gigantic...well, *you* know... represents fertility. It's really quite a remarkable...uh, formation. (It may have had some human help.) Even today, some Hawaiians believe that if you sit or sleep on it, it will make you conceive. Legend states that it's what remains of a husband who should have kept his eye on his work.

The west side of Moloka'i is drier and flatter. Vast beaches line much of the shoreline. You'll have the opportunity to create the only footprints in long stretches of sand though some of the west side beaches can get pretty windy. If you're returning your car from either the west or Kalaupapa, don't bother driving back to Kaunakakai to gas up. Save the 20 minutes and eat the extra few of bucks to have the rental car company gas up.

While in Kaunakakai, the best food is Moloka'i Pizza Café. The pizza is definitely as good as any you'd find on Maui. Very good sauce and fresh, light crust. They also have sandwiches and pasta.

BEACHES

Ideally shaped to provide calm swimming much of the time, Kapalua Beach is a West Maui winner.

Of all the Hawaiian islands, Maui probably has the most user-friendly beaches. Nearly all of the sand beaches on the island are concentrated in the more protected leeward areas of West and South Maui. If you were designing your own island, that's *exactly* where you'd put them, because the other side of the island is exposed to more surf and runoff. The few beaches in Hana are good, but the remaining windward beaches near Kahului won't ring your chimes.

Because of this topographic blessing, Maui is considered by many to be the *Ocean Island*. In fact, so much of the Maui experience is centered around beaches (to a greater degree than any of the other Hawaiian islands) that we've had to endure countless hours assessing the characteristics of each individual beach. Which ones worked best for snorkeling, boogie boarding, swimming or just plain frolicking? Sometimes this research was as simple as determining if a sunset mai tai worked better at one beach than another. (See, and you thought that writing guidebooks was all fun and games. There's a *serious* work ethic involved.)

Here, you can snorkel exceptional reefs, boogie board till you're raw, take a 3-mile beach walk, dig your fingers into genuine volcanic black sand, catch rays on a red sand beach, and sip a cocktail under a palm tree on a golden sand beach. Maui's beaches have earned their legendary status.

BEACH SAFETY

The biggest danger you will face at the beach is the **surf**. Though most beaches are on the calmer part of the island, that's a relative term. Most mainlanders are unprepared for the strength of Hawai'i's surf. We're out in the middle of the biggest ocean in the world, and the surf has lots of room to build up. We have our calm days when the water is like glass. We often have days where the surf is moderate, calling for respect and diligence on the part of the swimmer. And we have the high surf days, perfect for sitting on the beach, watching the experienced and the audacious tempt the ocean's patience. To get **current weather forecasts**, call 877–5111. For a **surf forecast**, call 877–3611 or see page 2 of the *Maui News*. Don't make the mistake of underestimating the ocean's power here. Hawai'i is the undisputed drowning capital of the United States, and we don't want you to join the statistics.

Other hazards include rip currents, which can form, cease and form again with no warning. Large "rogue waves" can come ashore with no warning. These usually occur when two or more waves fuse at sea, becoming a larger wave. Even calm seas are no guarantee of safety. Many people have been caught unaware by large waves during ostensibly "calm seas." We have swum and snorkeled the beaches described in this book on at least two occasions (usually more than two). But beaches change. The underwater topography changes throughout the year. Storms can take a very safe beach and rearrange the sand, turning it into a dangerous beach. Just because we describe a beach as being in a certain condition does not mean it will be in that same condition when you visit it.

Consequently, you should take the beach descriptions as a snapshot in calm times. If seas aren't calm, you probably shouldn't go in the water. If you observe a rip current, you probably shouldn't go in the water. If you aren't a comfortable swimmer, you should probably never go in the water, except at those beaches that have lifeguards. There is no way we can tell you that a certain beach will be swimmable on a certain day, and we claim no such prescience. For instance, a strong storm and accompanying swells one year swept lots of sand from South Maui beaches and mucked up the water so badly, it took months to recover making beachgoing a different experience. There is no substitution for your own observations and judgment.

A few standard safety tips: Never turn your back on the ocean. Never swim alone. Never swim in the mouth of a river. Never swim in murky water. Never swim when the seas are not calm. Don't walk too close to the shorebreak; a large wave can come and knock you over and pull you in. Observe ocean conditions carefully. Don't let small children play in the water unsupervised. Fins give you far more power and speed and are a good safety device in addition to being more fun. If you're comfortable in a mask and snorkel, they provide considerable peace of mind in addition to opening up the underwater world. Lastly, don't let Hawai'i's idyllic environment cloud your judgment. Recognize the ocean for what it is—a powerful force that needs to be respected.

This is a good time to repeat that reef shoes, a water-friendly shoe that goes under many brand names, make entering and exiting beaches that aren't 100% sandy *much* easier. Kmart in Kahului, Longs Drugs and lots of other stores sell them. Even if you *think* a beach has a completely sandy bottom, toes have well-known magnetic properties and will often attract that lone jagged rock, ruining an otherwise perfect beach day. While snorkeling, we like to use reef shoes and fins that fit over them. See SNORKELING on page 225 for more.

Theft can be a problem when visiting beaches. Visitors like to lock their cars at all beaches, but piles of glass on the ground usually dissuade island residents from doing that at secluded beaches. We usually remove anything we can't bear to have stolen and leave the car with the windows rolled up but unlocked. That way, we're less likely to get our windows broken by a curious thief. Regardless, don't leave anything of value in your car. (Well...maybe the seats can stay.) While in the water, we use a waterproof fanny pack (easy to find on the Internet) for our wallet, checkbook and keys, and leave everything else on the beach. Sometimes we only bring car keys and tie them to bathing suit drawstrings. We don't take a camera (except disposables) to the beach unless we are willing to stay there on the sand and baby-sit it. This way, when we swim, snorkel or just walk, we don't have to constantly watch our things.

Use sunblock early and often. Don't pay any attention to the claims from sunblock makers that their product is waterproof, rubproof, sandblast proof, powerwash proof, etc. Reapply it every couple of hours and after you get out of the ocean. The ocean water will hide sunburn symptoms until after you're toast. Then you can look forward to agony for the rest of your trip. (And yes, you *can* get burned while in the water; that's where most people here get cooked.) Of the sunblocks we've tried, Bullfrog and Neutrogena seem to work the best. Use *gel*-based (not lotion) products for better waterproof results.

Water quality around most of Maui can be amazingly clear. (Just look at the photo on pages 2–3.) The Pacific Ocean is kind enough to provide a roughly east-to-west current that constantly replaces our water with clean, clear, open ocean water. There are, however, several spots where geography and human action conspire to mess up the water, and we don't recommend swimming there. They are: north Kihei, off Lahaina (especially the north part of town), Kahana (sometimes), Kahului Harbor and around Pa'ia. Waters in these areas can be unpleasant, so avoid them.

Consider using one of those disposable underwater cameras. Even if you don't go in the water, they will withstand the elements. Their quality is better than most people think. Between the Kodak and the Fuji, we give a slight quality edge to the Fuji. The closeup dolphin shot in this book was taken with one.

Always remember that in Hawai'i, all beaches are public beaches. This means that you can park yourself on any stretch of sand you like. The trick, sometimes, is finding the legal public access and finding a parking spot. We'll try to point out a way to all of the island's beaches.

In general, surf is higher and stronger during the winter, calmer in the summer, but there are exceptions during all seasons. Compared to the rest of the island, South Maui waters *tend* to be calmer year round. When we mention that a beach has facilities, it usually includes restrooms, showers, picnic tables and drinking water.

Mornings are almost always best. Wind in South Maui and north of Lahaina in West Maui picks up in the late morning and early afternoon.

Beaches with lifeguards are D.T. Fleming and Hanaka'o'o in West Maui, the three Kama'oles in Kihei, and H.A. Baldwin, Ho'okipa and Kanaha near Kahului. Also Hana Bay in the summer.

Lastly, remember that just because *you* may be on vacation doesn't mean that residents are. Consequently, beaches are more crowded on weekends.

We're starting our BEACHES section at the upper left side of the island and working our way down the coast in a counter-clockwise direction.

WEST MAUI BEACHES

West Maui doesn't have *as many* good beaches or good snorkeling areas as South Maui, but the best ones here really shine.

❖ Punalau Beach

How appropriate that we start the beaches section with a beach that almost nobody's heard of. Also called **Keonehelele'i Beach** and sometimes Windmill Beach, it's ⅓ mile long and backed by abundant shade trees. During high surf (usually in the winter), large, well-formed waves break on a lava bench particularly close to shore, making it a perfect place to watch the surf. During calm seas, the beach is fronted by a bouldery tide-pool and clean water, making the snorkeling interesting, though shallow. Swimming and snorkeling are only advisable during very calm seas since unusually strong currents can form during higher seas. Access is from a 4WD dirt road ⁷⁄₁₀ mile past (east of) the 34 mile marker. You'll have to walk a few minutes down to the beach. During the week few visit this beach compared to other beaches in the area. Public access has historically been tolerated by the large private landowner.

❖ Honolua Bay

A REAL GEM

This is one of the more awkward areas to describe. That's because water conditions are more variable than most, and there's no sand beach here. It's a popular snorkeling and diving destination. At times Honolua has breathtaking underwater scenery—tons of fish, turtles and coral—and great visibility. (See photo on pages 2–3.) Other times, for a variety of reasons, you can't see diddly here. If there's been a lot of rain lately, a stream on the left (west) side of the bay will generally muck up the water. Snorkelers are usually steered to

OK, OK. So the name Slaughterhouse Beach doesn't exactly look good on a postcard. But the beach sure does.

the left side of the bay, but the right side has better coral and visibility, though it's deeper and used often by SCUBA divers.

Honolua Bay is a reserve, making fishing and spearing illegal, so fish counts *can* be high here. Water is colder due to freshwater springs percolating up from the ground. Unlike most island beaches, mornings aren't *necessarily* best here. Summer is better than winter. If you see lots of surfers out around the point to the right, it means snorkeling conditions aren't at their best.

Parking may be a problem here. You probably won't see the 32 mile marker on Hwy 30, but past it are the stairs down to Slaughterhouse Beach (described below). Then the road descends and at the bottom of the descent (½ mile past Slaughterhouse) are several small turnouts and a road on the ocean side. You can walk that road around a gate then go 4 minutes to the water. Enter the water at an old boat ramp. Water is always cloudy at the shoreline, but usually improves as you go farther out.

If those turnouts are full, you'll have to drive past them and park where you can.

Honolua is occasionally canvassed by car break-in maggots, so don't leave anything valuable in your car.

While at your car, you may wonder why so many cars seem to *honk* here. It's because a road sign around the corner tells drivers to do just that. Wouldn't you just *love* to live next to a road sign telling all passing drivers to honk?

❖ Slaughterhouse Beach

Ooh, doesn't *that* sound inviting? Hawaiian name **Mokule'ia Bay** (which itself is often misspelled as **Makuleia**), this beach gets its commonly used name from a long-gone slaughterhouse that used to be above the cliffs. This relatively small pocket beach has lots of sand in the summer,

which can almost disappear during winter surf. The snorkeling to the right *can* be good, but the beach is subject to water-clouding runoff from an intermittent stream to the left (southwest). There's some shade in the mornings, but none in the afternoon, and the beach is *partially* protected from afternoon winds. The morning views of Moloka'i are stunning; you won't see more detail from anywhere else on Maui. Located north of the 32 mile marker on Hwy 30; access to the beach, 100 feet below the road, is via a concrete stairway.

❖ D.T. Fleming Beach Park

Swimming is similar to Oneloa below: good during calm seas, but vulnerable to rip currents when the surf picks up. In fact, these two beaches used to be one, until the West Maui volcano, in its dying days, sent lava to the coast to form Makalua-puna Point, splitting the bay in two. D.T. Fleming is long and wide. There's lots of shade, courtesy of ironwood trees. Picnic tables, BBQs, lifeguards, showers and restrooms all make the beach very popular with locals who come to relax and talk story (shoot the breeze), so weekends can be very crowded. Park facilities aren't as well kept as other area parks. The right side gets occasional runoff, so the ocean isn't as clear as nearby Oneloa. Boogie boarding can be good. Afternoons can bring an irritating wind, so be sure to bring that old BBQ grill you've been meaning to have sandblasted. (Mornings are calmest.)

❖ Oneloa Beach

A REAL GEM

Not to be confused with the other beach of the same name in South Maui. Despite the huge number of resort dwellings behind this long, luxurious beach, it is surprisingly

Where is everybody? Certainly not at often-forgotten Oneloa in West Maui.

uncrowded most of the time. It's a deceptive beach. The public access deposits you on the eastern (right) third of the beach and you quickly conclude that this ¼-mile long, wide sandy beach has bad swimming and snorkeling because of a lava bench in the near-shore waters seemingly extending the whole length. Visitors often turn around and leave at this point. What they can't see is that the left third of the beach usually has a padded sandy bottom, making the swimming delightful when calm. (Occasionally, the winter surf can temporarily erase some of the sandy bottom.) The snorkeling around the left end can also be very good with lots of fish and some wild rock formations, but don't do it when the surf's up, or a washing machine effect will bounce you around. Plus a rip current forms. Take time to climb up the rocks on the left side to poke around the tide-pools and cove. Boogie boarding on the left side can be good for the intermediate *sponger* (local slang). This beach is sus-

ceptible to wind. (The GEM designation only applies when the wind and surf are low.) Early mornings are best. The extreme right side is somewhat protected from the wind, but, of course, the swimming and snorkeling aren't very good there. (But we do like hunting for lost golf balls there, from the nearby golf course. If you find a club, you know the guy was having an off day.) No shade or facilities except for a shower and *powerful* faucet and sometimes a hose near the parking lot. From the highway, take Office Road till it dead ends, turn left, then right on Ironwood Lane. If it's too windy for a day here, consider the more protected Napili Bay or perhaps Kapalua Beach.

❖ **Kapalua Beach**

A REAL GEM

Well known as one of the best swimming beaches on Maui, the bay is usually very protected, making timid swimmers happy. The water isn't necessarily the clearest, so snorkeling is not that hot, and the offshore waters can be rocky. You'll do well to bring your reef shoes so you can walk about in the water without fear of stubbing your toe. But Kapalua is a great place to wade into the ocean without worrying about getting beaten up by the surf most of the time, and the palm trees behind the beach are very picturesque (helping to disguise the surprisingly ugly ultra-expensive condos there). There are two access paths—one at the north end (which was closed at press time due to construction) and the other near the Sea House Restaurant at Napili Kai condos. The sign says NAPILI LANI and there's a yellow fire hydrant nearby. Drive down and look for a blue beach access sign.

❖ Napili Beach

An excellent beach that seems to generate more fun per square foot than any other beach in the area. It's very

A REAL GEM recessed into the shoreline, which blocks much of the afternoon wind along here. The sand is steep, so the waves slap the shoreline then recede quickly, creating an impressive undertow during high surf. The offshore waters are quite sandy. This combination creates the best beach on the island for an activity called Monastery Tag (named after a beach in California where we invented it one day after a SCUBA dive.) Now bear with me here, it's going to sound strange, but we've shown others how to do this and they *love* it. The three ingredients you need are a steep beach, unchecked (unprotected) waves and a padded, sandy bottom. Basically you lie in the water at the surf's edge and zip up and down the beach up to 40 feet each way on a thin

Grain for grain, Napili Bay seems to invite more fun than any other beach in the area.

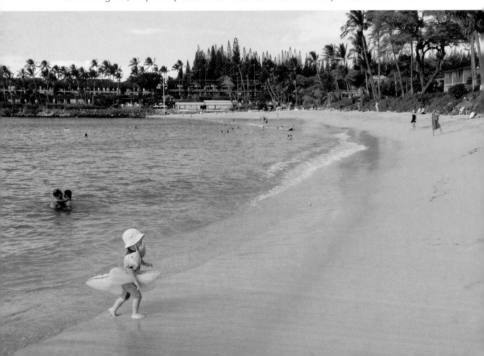

cushion of water, digging feet or hands into the sand to control your ascent and descent. Like a low-to-the-ground sports car, the sensation of speed is greater. Here, you're only inches above the sand and the trick is to go as far up the shore as possible without getting beached. To people on the beach it looks like you're scraping along the sand, but actually you're unscathed as you orient the shape of your body for maximum efficiency. As with all worthwhile and important endeavors, it takes years of practice and dedication. (You see, and you thought we spent all our time doing only *frivolous* stuff.) A mask and snorkel make it easier. On your back, front, head first or feet first, it's important to master them all. You really feel the power of the ocean this way. Best conditions are usually at the center/right portion of the beach.

The beach can get fairly crowded. Two accesses to the middle and south end are from Hui Drive (cutting through Napili Sunset) and Napili Place (limited parking and the public access sign is sometimes *conveniently* missing), both off Lower Honoapiilani Road. See map on page 53.

❖ Keonenui Beach

Usually a respectably wide white pocket of sand and fairly attractive. Sometimes natural sand migration strips away much of the beach, making it narrow. Slightly cloudy water, sandy bottom, steep shorebreak. On occasion, seaweed blooms create marginal water quality. Fronting the Kahana Sunset on Lower Honoapiilani Road. Only public access is from the north along the shoreline path.

❖ Ka'opala Beach

Nasty, uninviting piece of shoreline beach, that gets its water from a foul creek ½ mile south of here. (Current runs north.) How appropriate that Ka'opala translates to *trash*. We see uninformed visitors swimming here and can't help wonder if they bring something exotic back from the islands that they didn't count on. Occasionally, the creek runs dry, and the ocean cleans out a bit here.

❖ Kahana Beach

Not a bad beach, not a great one. In the past they've had problems with seaweed washing ashore here, but the seaweed blooms have been minimal lately.

❖ Pohaku Park

Pretty little park for picnics or sunsets, but the water is another must-miss. Yucky. Also called **S-Turns Park**. Located just north of the Noelani condos.

❖ Honokowai Beach Park

The swimming and snorkeling are poor, but it's a good place to come with your lunch (Honokowai Okazuya Deli is nearby) and eat to the sound of the surf. On the southern end of Lower Honoapiilani Road.

❖ Keka'a / North Beach / Airport Beach

This stretch of sand fronts what used to be the old Ka'anapali Airport and runs to Honokowai Beach Park. In general, it's a somewhat narrow sandy beach and the nearshore waters are rocky, so swimming is only marginal. Reef shoes will help protect your feet. The (preferred) southern section is accessible from Halawai Drive between the 25 and 26 mile markers. The northern stretch has an access next to the Embassy Vacation Resort. (See map on page 51.) A large timeshare project was being built behind the beach at press time. Snorkeling is fairly good at the southern section once you get 100 or so

The south end of Kahekili Beach Park has the sandiest bottom—and the dreamiest water.

feet offshore. The northern stretch of the beach gets small amounts of the seaweed that is so common (and heavier) farther north. That seaweed is the norm until you get to Napili Bay, which is clean.

❖ Kahekili Beach Park

A REAL GEM

A superb park, glorious beach and excellent facilities, including covered tables, a large parking area, restrooms, showers and lawn area. A windbreak running north of here *partially* protects you from afternoon winds. Kahekili is a popular place for SCUBA diving. Several companies do introductory shore dives here.

Conveniently, the best snorkeling is directly offshore of the pavilion, about 75 or so feet where a nice variety of coral and some fish await. Just plain ol' swimming offshore of the park facilities is not so good, suffering from hidden rocks at the water's edge that you can't see without polarized sunglasses. But if you walk down the concrete path south (left) toward Black Rock, you'll find that when the sidewalk ends, so do the hidden rocks in the water (for the most part), and from there all the way to the end of the beach

(¼ mile) is a sandy, frolicker's delight. (Winter surf sometimes temporarily erases some of the sand, exposing rocks not normally present.) A stream near Black Rock brings colder, fresh water onto the surface a few dozen feet from shore but doesn't affect things *near* the shore. There's a rumor that an airplane went into the water between the pavilion and Black Rock. (Ka'anapali Airport used to be to your right.) We've spent many hours looking for it and have been unsuccessful. Let us know if you find it. When surf's up, there's a current that runs from Black Rock along the shore heading north. Bigger surf can make the water cloudy and difficult to enter. If it's not calm and you choose to swim anyway, better to walk down and let the current aid you coming back to the pavilion.

Kahekili is a magnificent place for an early morning swim, or just bring your cup of coffee and set the day's tone here. Lana'i and Moloka'i are usually bathed in bright light, and the often-tranquil waters create an unusually serene atmosphere.

Access is off Hwy 30 between 25 & 26 mile markers. Take Kai Ala Drive. (Puukoli Street is across the street.)

❖ Black Rock

This is the large, black lava rock (called **Pu'u Keka'a**) that separates the two halves of Ka'anapali Beach. (It's also where Hawaiian spirits went to meet their ancestors. See page 50 for more.) The snorkeling around the rock is legendary and mostly lives up to the hype. Lots of fish and a decent amount of coral. Start from the Sheraton side and work your way around the rock; it's mostly a wall of coral-encrusted lava. The part nearest the beach is the *least* interesting. Only one area around the corner has a lava shelf. Be careful there of surges. Watch for turtles that come to the area as customers of cleaner wrasse fish stations. When returning back to the Sheraton side, if you notice a current around the corner, swim away from the rock along the beach about 75 feet. The current should end, and you can swim back to the beach. (That current is from the weak longshore current that bumps up against Black Rock and slithers around it.)

❖ Ka'anapali Beach

This beach has a dozen different, often conflicting names. Pick a handful of free magazines around the island and each may have a different name. Some names were apparently invented out of the blue. Technically, Ka'anapali Beach is everything from Keka'a (North Beach) to Hanake'o'o (Canoe) Beach, but we'll bow to the more common usage and designate it as the sandy beach from Black Rock south to Canoe Beach, including a section known as **Dig Me Beach**. (See map on page 51.) Ka'anapali is one of the finest beaches you'll find on Maui. This portion fronts most of the Ka'anapali resorts and Whalers Village. There's a **concrete path** running the entire length of Ka'anapali Beach, from the Sheraton to the Hyatt. It's a *great* place to be at sunset. This beach turns into a kickin', hoppin', happenin' place as all eyes are cast toward the sunset. Dinner cruises ply the waters, beachside restaurants hum, and couples walk the glorious beachside path holding hands and waiting to greet the night. It's busy but not offensively loud. If you're staying in West Maui, you should

It might not be a hidden, untrampled beach, but Ka'anapali never disappoints.

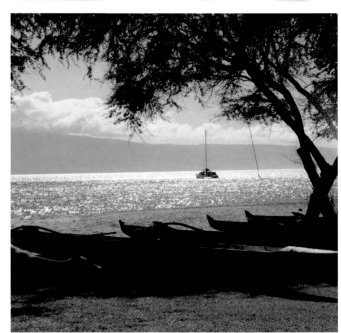

Hanaka'o'o/Canoe Beach is the resting place for many of the island's competition canoes.

surf's up, waves break on the somewhat steep beach with greater force and swimming is not advised.

The north end of the beach is the best, from Ka'anapali Ali'i Resort to Black Rock. It's a lovely plain of sand and clean water. The southern end in front of the Hyatt and Marriott has a foot-gouging reef near shore and sometimes seaweed in the water.

❖ Hanaka'o'o / Canoe Beach

A major hub of West Maui activity, you have your choice of jet skiing, boogie boarding, body surfing, watching canoe races and...oh, yeah, swimming. Snorkeling is poor due to bad visibility. There are covered picnic tables and facilities, and the beach is popular with locals, especially on weekends. Access is from the parking lot between the 23 and 24 mile marker. Wander north from the lot.

❖ Wahikuli Wayside Park

South of Ka'anapali, this long sliver of shoreline is wedged between the highway and the sea. Often nearly empty during the week, there are restrooms and showers, but the restrooms can be pretty scary. (County parks are notorious for their bad restroom maintenance.) The northern end is best, but fairly yucky water and little sand make it a forgettable beach park unless you're just looking for a place to eat your picnic lunch. Between Lahaina and Ka'anapali. Wahi-

strongly consider spending one evening doing a stroll along this path, then dining at one of the restaurants along here. There are five free parking lots along the beach. Since the north end of the beach is best, check for vacancies from north to south. The last one, at the Hyatt, usually has empty spots and, since we often see employees parking there (which they're not *supposed* to do), I'm sure they won't mind if you take one of *their* regular spots. You can also park at the Whalers Village Shopping Center. Any shop will validate if you spend around $20 (which is *easy* to do).

The waters at Ka'anapali are great when calm. Snorkeling at Black Rock on the north end is good. The middle offers a nice sandy bottom and good **bodysurfing** when the waves are right. When kuli means *noisy place,* an appropriate name given how close the beach is to the highway.

❖ Lahaina

Lahaina is good for a lot of things, but beach-going ain't one of 'em. The waters off this busy town are usually murky and not suitable for swimming. **Pu'unoa Beach** at the north end is also known as **Baby Beach**, but you probably won't want to spend time there. **Kamehameha Iki Park** (formerly Armory Park) near 505 Front St. is also a place where you could slip into the water, but why would you want to? West Maui has better beaches elsewhere.

Just south of Lahaina town near the 18 mile marker is **Launiupoko Park**, a popular place for beginner surf lessons, though water quality makes it unsuitable for snorkeling. Nearshore waters slope gently, so even small waves last a while. Picnic tables and BBQs make it a good place to bring cookables.

❖ 14 Mile Marker

Many dive shops and free magazines steer snorkelers to a spot on Hwy 30 called Mile 14 (referring to the mile marker). To put it bluntly, the snorkeling there usually bites. In fact, we wonder if they have even snorkeled there in the last 10 years, because its reputation is based on something that doesn't exist anymore: Namely, clear water and live coral. Visibility *may* be 20 feet *on a great day*; it's 5 feet on more days than we'd care to admit. And though there is coral, more than 90% of it is dead, perhaps choked to death by runoff from a now-defunct sugar company.

From the highway, it *looks* like it will be wonderful. Driving along, you see lots of reef and contrast, giving the *illusion* of good snorkeling, but it's usually cloudy. It varies with the tides and seasons and is sometimes better, but odds are you're likely to be disappointed. However, if you're absolutely terrified of the ocean, this site has two things going for it: It's usually calm and protected and it's often shallow enough to stand up. You will see some fish up close, but *compared to other island snorkel sites*, it's only suitable for the ultra timid. (The state's shark warning signs here also ruin the moment.) The best snorkeling is 200 yards out to sea *west* of the 14 mile marker; snorkel boats take paying passengers here to a place called **Coral Gardens**. But it's too far away from shore, and the visibility, though improved, can still be topped elsewhere.

❖ Ukumehame & Papalaua Parks

These are stretches of beach lining Hwy 30 between the 11 and 13 mile markers. Access is easy: Just drive up, open your door and fall out. The only good snorkeling is where the road leaves the shoreline, ascending toward the tunnel heading southeast. The reef and visibility improve markedly. But you'll have to swim from the last stretch of sand at Papalaua, and that can be tiring. Best just to enjoy the beach for what it is—a good place to pull over and revel in the view.

❖ Scenic Lookout

Though not a beach, the snorkeling below the scenic lookout between the 8 and 9 mile markers 2 miles southwest of Ma'alaea on Hwy 30 is fantastic. Extraordinary fish counts often bless the area. The problem is getting in and out. The trail from the railings is the easy part. At the bottom, entry and especially exit from the water are difficult. Do so only when calm, wear reef shoes into the water, and pick your spot carefully. While exiting, remember the difficult-exit rule: Work with the ocean and let it do the work for you. You can use a surge to bring you up onto a rock if you do it right. While in the water, snorkeling to the right is best. Be careful of surginess. Divers will find deeper waters fairly quickly.

SOUTH MAUI BEACHES

When it comes to good beaches, South Maui has an embarrassment of riches. This is where the tropical beach dream comes true. Perfect stretches of thickly padded sand normally kissed by gentle surf, clear water and palm trees create an instantly pleasing atmosphere. The surf is usually flat in the winter and very small in the summer. The only downside to South Maui beaches is afternoon wind. Shielded by Haleakala during the morning, winds tend to start slithering around the mountain at north Kihei in the late morning and work their way south throughout the afternoon. At the other end, La Pérouse Bay is where the morning wind starts and works its way northward as the day progresses. This means that *morning* almost always offers the best conditions, both for swimming and snorkeling. The last area to get windy and choppy is usually around Wailea, and that's also where the best beaches are, so we're in luck.

❖ Ma'alaea Bay

If you're looking for a long beach stroll, have we got a beach for you. Stretching all the way from Ma'alaea Harbor 3 miles down to north Kihei, this beach is a walker's delight. The waters off the Ma'alaea end aren't the friendliest, and winds in the early afternoon can be irritating, but morning and sunset strolls are great here. As you near Kihei, a portion of the beach is known as **Sugar Beach**. Here you

can sometimes rent windsurfing boards and other beach paraphernalia.

❖ Maipoina 'Oe Ia'u Beach Park to Kalama Beach & Cove Park

One of the dirty little secrets (literally) about Kihei is that you can't—or at least in our opinion often wouldn't *want* to—swim along the coastline anywhere from the northern part of Kihei town to Cove Park. We've shown it on the map as a SEAWEED area. We've caught *a lot* of flack from politicians, the media and local bigwigs for printing this, but none of them have disputed it. We've learned that much of the criticism we've received from locals about *Maui Revealed* is really misdirected fury at this disclosure. People in power here simply don't want us to tell you about it. But here's the skinny, anyway. The water in much of that area is nasty. This problem has been going on for over 30 years, and anyone who tells you it's a thing of the past should be looked at skeptically since they probably have an agenda. A discharge ditch running through the center of Kalama Park sometimes drains nasty water into the area. Slow but ever-present northward currents take the nutrient-rich water north until it dissipates. Algae flourishes in this water, making the ocean here a bit smelly, murky, full of seaweed and generally unpleasant. (From Kama'ole I all the way south, the water is *completely* unaffected.) Even when the ditch is dry, nutrients may be seeping into the ground and out to sea, and the alien seaweed in the area flourishes. We hate to tell you this, especially if you're renting a wonderful-sounding beachfront place in this area, but it's something you need to know. There are times when the water clears up, such as when storms flush the area or light winds affect the currents. But don't count on it. Avoid Cove Park, Kalama Beach and everything up to and including Kalepolepo Park (and *sometimes* Maipoina 'Oe Ia'u Beach Park). Some of the beaches, such as the one in front of Koa Lagoon, have the dead seaweed scraped off each day. Others don't. Surfing lessons are common at Cove Park, but we don't recommend the water there except in the winter. Cove Park is not quite as bad in the morning since the ocean current has cleaned the water that has been driven south by afternoon winds, and winter's lighter winds also keep Cove Park a bit cleaner. (Surfers use the whole area, but hard-core surfers will surf in *anything*.)

❖ Kama'ole Beach

A REAL GEM

Kama'ole Beach is broken into three parts, cleverly named Kama'ole Beach I, II and III. **Kama'ole I** is the biggest and best of the three—a long and pretty stretch of fine sand with good swimming much of the time, restrooms, showers and a lifeguard. Access is a snap, and your car is very close to the water. Across the street is a convenience store, in case you get hungry or thirsty, and there's a lawn area at the south end of the park. You'll find very good snorkeling around the rocks bracketing each end, especially the north (right) end. (That end is also called **Charley Young Beach**.) **Kama'ole II** is also a good beach, though not quite as long or as nice as Kama'ole I. Here, too, good snorkeling exists around the rocky points defining the beach. Of the three Kama'oles, **Kama'ole III** is the most popular with locals. There is a small spot here where waves focus, even during calm seas, which makes the boogie boarding as reliable as you're gonna get in South Maui. There's some decent snorkeling at the north end near the rocks, but beware of a particularly bad surge there if the sea's not calm. There is a *huge* lawn at the south end of Kama'ole III, which makes a great place to fly a kite or toss a Frisbee or football, and there's a limited playground for the keiki. Unfortunately, Kama'ole III is also the messiest of the three due to its usage, and the sand beach

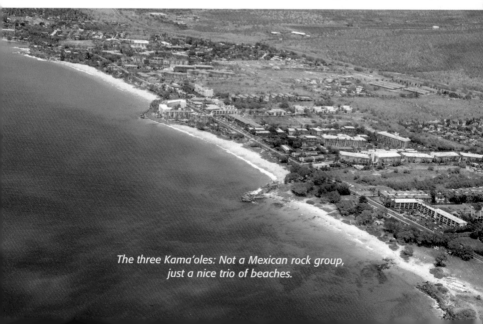

The three Kama'oles: Not a Mexican rock group, just a nice trio of beaches.

area is relatively small. All three Kama-ʻoles are easily identified from South Kihei Road between Alanui Ke Alii and Keonekai roads. All have showers and restrooms. On S. Kihei Road. See map on page 129.

❖ Keawakapu Beach

A REAL GEM

One of the most criminally underrated beaches in South Maui. Very long with gobs of fine sand on and offshore. The only resorts on the beach are at the north end. The rest is lined with *very* expensive houses (some selling for over $10 million!). The area in front of the main public access has a huge, well-padded sandy bottom, perfect for frolicking with minimal fear of stubbing your toe on a rock. (You've never *really* cursed until you've cursed a beach rock that has attacked your foot.) If you walk to the south (left), the beach widens and you'll find another large sandy bottom area. This part of the beach is amazingly underused. Farther south is the third Keawakapu entrance. (The first two have parking lots at the intersection of South Kihei Road and Kilohana and near the Mana Kai Resort.) Few people other than locals even know about this third entrance (which has a shower) at the unnoticed end of South Kihei Road, and the water offshore is very well sanded. (This is probably a good time to tell you that sunglasses that are *polarized* are amazing at detecting dark rocks on the sandy bottom.) Mornings are best; afternoons can be windy. One caveat about Keawakapu: Some plants on the backshore attract bees, which usually aren't a problem, but it's sometimes possible to step on an errant bee blown onto the sandy shoreline, especially in the windy afternoon. At the south end of S. Kihei Road. See maps on pages 129 and 131.

❖ Mokapu & Ulua Beach

These two beaches are usually spoken of in the same sentence since they share the same parking lot just south of the old Renaissance Hotel. When you take the short path down, the beach on your left is Ulua, on the right is Mokapu. The sand at Ulua doesn't extend as far offshore as most of the other beaches in the area. We prefer Mokapu; it's more picturesque, used a bit less and has slightly clearer water. Ulua is a popular dive spot. Though a tad overdived, it's nice with a lot of coral, albeit crowded, and the visibility is often poor. Night dives have pretty easy access—a big plus. The 51 parking stalls fill up *early* since most slots are snagged by dive companies that take students here for introductory SCUBA lessons. Access to Mokapu isn't dependent on the parking lot, however. You can park at the southern Keawakapu lot and stroll around the corner along the beach to the left to get to Mokapu. You're at Mokapu when you see a hotel and wooden walkway inland.

❖ Wailea Beach

A REAL GEM

An outstanding beach! Over ⅓ mile long, this classic crescent of sand has been ranked by several beach rankings (yes, there *are* people who do that) as the best beach in America. Terrific clear water, fine-grained sand, picturesque setting, calm waters most of the time, excellent swimming; Wailea should be on your short list of beaches to visit while here. The biggest problem at Wailea is parking. The resort has provided a parking lot, accessed just past the Grand Wailea, but it may fill up if you don't get there early. (However, the Wailea parking lot usually fills up *after* the Ulua/Mokapu Beach parking lot.) Showers and restrooms are provided. As with

*Sigh! Lovely Wailea, just another kickin'
South Maui beach.*

all South Maui beaches, morning is better than afternoon, though Wailea won't get windy as early as beaches farther north. Snorkeling can be decent at each end when calm. Boogie boarding can be very good for novices at the far south (left) side when there's a little surf. (But remember, small surf is often a South Maui hallmark, so boogie boarding is not always possible.) Waves at Wailea are short, close to shore and easy to catch without fins. Just stand there and jump with them. Stay just far enough away from the rocks at the end of the beach to avoid them. The tiny cove just past the rocks at the south end has a rocky bottom. Good for sunbathing, but not for swimming.

❖ **Polo Beach**

Easy access and more parking than other Wailea beaches, Polo has restrooms, a shower, picnic tables and BBQ grills on the lawn above the beach. The beach isn't as deep as some other Wailea beaches and there are a few more hidden rocks in the sand, but it's a fine beach nonetheless, and the water is usually clear. Parking is ample and rarely fills up. There are beach chairs lining the beach, though they're *presumably*

for guests of the Fairmont Kea Lani, which backs the beach. Located two miles from the Wailea Ike intersection; see map on page 131.

❖ **Palauea Beach**

A REAL GEM

Used primarily by local residents who take the short path through the trees to this lesser-known beach, it's not usually crowded during the week. Also called **White Rock**, the snorkeling around the rocky point on the left is *very* good. It's also good on the right side, though the water isn't as clear as the left side. The gently sloping shoreline is loaded with sand in the middle and provides excellent swimming much of the time. The bay is recessed, so it doesn't get as windy in the afternoon as other beaches. No facilities, but the easy access and quality of the beach make it a winner. Off Makena Road; see map on page 131.

❖ **Po'olenalena Beach**

A REAL GEM

Probably the least known and certainly least used large beach in the Wailua/ Makena area. It's also known locally as Paipu Beach, Pepeiaolepo

Beach, Love Beach, Keauhou Beach and sometimes Makena Surf Beach. *(How can something so little known have so many names?)* Nearly ½ mile long, there have been times when we've found other Wailea beaches crowded and found this beach nearly empty during the week. (Weekends are busy here, as all beaches can be.) The water offshore is mostly a broad, flat, gentle, sandy bottom with only occasional outcroppings of rock. The beach is gently sloping, making the water especially good for swimming during the normally calm seas. When there's a little surf, the left (south) side can offer good boogie boarding. The beach is interrupted toward the right (north) side by lava. Scramble over the lava rocks or take a shoreline trail, and you may have the northern third of the beach to yourself.

The beach is bracketed by lava points on each side, and the snorkeling around them is exceptional and little used compared to other snorkel sites. Tons of fish and a very healthy coral community, especially as you venture away from shore along the points, make it a worthy snorkel destination. Usually *lots* of **turtles** at the left and right sides and even the occasional lobster. (By the way, lobsters are sometimes known locally as *bugs*. When you hear someone say, *Hey, brah, we go catch bugs,* it means he's going lobster diving.) The right end of the beach is rarely snorkeled and is one of our favorite snorkel sites on the island. So let's see… We have great swimming, great snorkeling, easy access, good boogie boarding when there's surf and a general lack of crowds. *What's not to love?* The two accesses are on either side of our "imaginary" 2 mile marker on the map on page 131. The second one is a bit farther south at the Makena Surf and, though limited to nine stalls, is often unused. It's better since it has showers nearby. Go through the unlocked gate

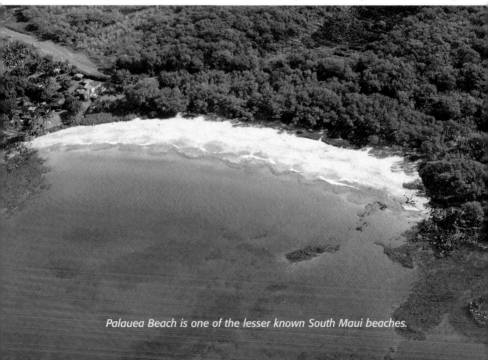

Palauea Beach is one of the lesser known South Maui beaches.

and along the walkway. If they're full, use the first access.

One quick nag: The coral and fish in this area haven't been exposed to lots of people. The coral isn't trampled and broken, and the fish haven't been fed much. Please don't start the tradition. Fish feeding completely messes up the balance, leaving only a few aggressive species while driving away the meeker fish. And while snorkeling, be *real* careful not to bump into the coral with your fins, and don't stand on it or grab it. This will keep the reef here pristine and beautiful. (OK, end of nag.)

Just south of Po'olenalena is a public access (with only six parking stalls) that leads to **Chang's Beach**. Cut off from Po'olenalena, it's a wonderful little cove with fantastic snorkeling offshore and a sandy beach to lie on. When there's some surf, the boogie boarding here can be awesome.

❖ 5 Graves / 5 Caves

A good SCUBA site and fairly good snorkeling. Turtles are common, and there are several caves. Once in the water, divers should head straight out, slightly to the right and look for the caves along the wall. Entry is from a small, semi-protected rocky cove off Makena Road. See map on page 131. You'll walk by a small graveyard (with *seven* graves that we counted, and probably more in the faint lava rock outlines). Sometimes referred to as 5 Caves, sometimes 5 Graves, but neither seems to be accurate. On Makena Road; see map on page 131. If you're lucky on a SCUBA dive, you'll find the elusive bubble cave near the shoreline. The air pocket inside is sealed and the ocean's surge constantly changes the pressure, causing your ears to continuously flux and a cloud of pressure-induced haze to form and dissolve instantly with every surge. *Real* cool.

❖ Makena Landing Beach Park

A marginal place for snorkeling, but it's usually calm with easy entry making it a popular place to launch kayaks and do intro or night SCUBA dives. The visibility is best on the north side, which also has good coral.

❖ Maluaka Beach / Makena

A REAL GEM

You'll be forgiven if you get confused as to where Makena Beach is. So is everyone else. Ask a local for directions, and you could end up in one of *four* places. Oneloa Beach, also called Big Beach, is often called Makena Beach or sometimes Big Makena Beach. (It's also called Makena State Park.) Makena Bay, just north of here, which also contains Makena Landing, is sometimes called Makena Beach. Sometimes Po'olenalena Beach is called Makena Surf Beach. And lastly this beach is sometimes called Makena Beach. It's usually called Maluaka Beach, as the signs often say. Hey, don't blame us, we're just the messengers. For clarification *(ha!)* we'll call this beach Maluaka Beach.

Fronting the Maui Prince Hotel, this wide, pretty beach slopes gently, providing good swimming during calm seas, especially toward the center of the beach where a thick padding of sand awaits. During calm seas keiki (kids) splash about with abandon. There is shade at the south (left) end, as well as restrooms, showers and picnic tables. Parking is past the Maui Prince Hotel, where Makena Road backtracks, 3⁶⁄₁₀ miles south of the Wailea Alanui/Wailea Ike intersection. (See map on page 131.) If the lot's full, try using Makena Road just south of Honoiki. There's a drop-off area right at the sand, then you can park your car about 100 yards from the drop-off area, near the

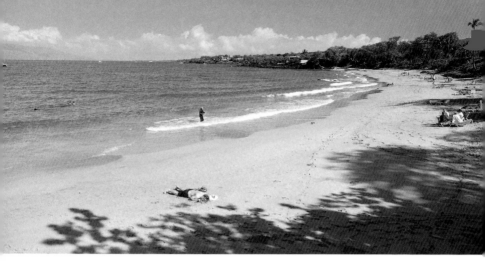

Why aren't you wet yet? Maluaka Beach in front of the Maui Prince has shade, good swimming and great snorkeling.

Keawala'i Church. Don't walk through the church cemetery.

The snorkeling off to the left (south) is very good with good coral and fish, and usually *lots* of turtles. In fact, this area is one of the famed *turtle towns* that some snorkel boats take people to. Off to the right also offers good snorkeling.

❖ Oneuli Beach / Black Sand Beach

A REAL GEM Less known than other beaches in the area since it's not well marked and can't be seen from the road. Those who do know about it usually call it simply *Black Sand Beach.* It's on the north (right) side of that large hill in Makena called Pu'u Ola'i, and you access it from the short, bumpy, but usually passable dirt road shown on the map on page 133. (Keep an eye out for deer on this road.) Once at the salt and pepper beach it's easy to see how it formed. Pu'u Ola'i is essentially a large mound of lava cinders created from an enormous lava fountain. Wave action has bitten into the cinder cone, causing the loose black cinders to fall into the ocean where they are ground into black sand. Over the years shells have been pulverized into sand and coral has been...well, *processed* by parrotfish, adding salt to the pepper.

The water at Black Sand Beach is usually calm, but the sand gives way to a lava shelf at the water's edge, making the swimming marginal. However, the snorkeling can be great, and turtles are very common on the left side near the hill. Visibility is usually cloudy near the shore, so head out and to the left for lots of coral, turtles and fish. If it's calm, you can snorkel all the way around Pu'u Ola'i, and it gets even better. Beware of any currents by occasionally stopping to see if you are drifting. Kayakers sometimes visit the beach, but it's rarely crowded.

❖ Big Beach / Oneloa / Makena

A REAL GEM Big Beach is what many people think of when they think of a Hawaiian beach. It is considered by many to be *the* beach on Maui. (Not to be confused with another beach in West Maui also called **Oneloa Beach**.) Almost ⅔ mile long and over 100 feet wide, this beautiful crescent of golden sand is a dream for swimmers, snorkelers, frolickers and sometimes boogie boarders. When seas are calm, the water is very inviting. You won't find it empty; it's one of the more popular beaches. But you *will* find it enchanting.

During the '60s hippies from the mainland came to Maui looking to get back to nature, and they found their nirvana at what was then an isolated beach. Unable to remember its Hawaiian name, Oneloa (meaning *long sands*), they referred to it as simply Big Beach, a name that has stuck. (They also called it **Makena Beach**, which is incorrect. Makena Beach is farther north, but that name, too, has stuck.) After several years of hippie occupation, disease outbreaks from a lack of hygiene, lack of proper waste disposal and contaminated water supplies, along with rampant drug use, authorities raided and evicted the illegal "campers" in 1972. Today Big Beach is a state park. Porta-potties and picnic tables are available.

The large hill on the north (right) end of the beach is called Pu'u Ola'i, or Earthquake Hill. It was the site of the huge eruption described on page 132.

From the right side of the beach, you can take a short trail to a promontory. (Walk up a little, then turn left rather than continuing up the steeper gravel portion.) On the lava promontory, 20 feet above the water, there are several short trails leading shoreward that end at nice places to watch the sunset. The views of Big Beach from up here are delicious. On the other side of the promontory is a smaller beach. Let's see. The big beach is known as Big Beach, so what do you think the hippies called the little beach? Hmm, that's a toughie. How about **Little Beach**? (Darned clever, they were.) This ideal pocket of sand tucked away in a nook of Pu'u Ola'i offers great swimming, snorkeling, boogie boarding and bodysurfing. As it's not visible from the road, it is often used by nudists, which, by the way, is illegal in Hawai'i. (We tell you this so that if nudity bothers you, you may want to pass

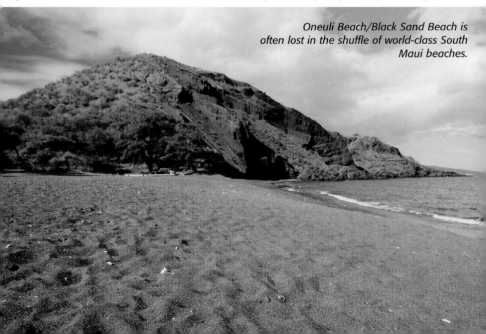

Oneuli Beach/Black Sand Beach is often lost in the shuffle of world-class South Maui beaches.

on Little Beach. Hmm. I wonder if there's another reason they call it Little Beach…) Another thing you need to know is that Little Beach is occasionally (but not too often) occupied by squatters in makeshift tents, creating an unfriendly atmosphere. Aside from these caveats, you may want to take a peek at Little Beach from the trail on the promontory overlooking the sand to see if it's right for you that day. If it is, head on down and stake a claim to some sand. Weekends at Little Beach can be packed. The ocean has a sandy shoreline bottom, excellent for swimming, and the snorkeling around the points at both ends of the beach is good during calm seas. If you swim to Little Beach from Big Beach, the current can make swimming back annoying. Consider walking back if it's a problem that day.

There are two parking lots for Big Beach that you'll see from the road. Actually, if you're not going to Little Beach, consider driving past the second one and park on the road at the south (left) end of the beach where there's shade on the beach and less crowds.

You have several **food options** via road stands nearby. Your best bet is Makena Grill, closer to Secret Cove (below), or the plate lunch stands. Avoid Jawz Tacos.

❖ Pa'ako Beach / Secret Cove

A REAL GEM   This beach is *literally* a hole in the wall, or at least access to it is. That impressive rock wall you see just past (south of) Big Beach hides some impressive beachfront homes. But across from telephone pole #E2–3 (the first pole you encounter past Big Beach, in case someone steals the marking) is an opening in the wall, a legal public access. Walk through and you find a beautiful little pocket of sand. This is a popular place to get married, and for good reason. In the morning the views of Kaho'olawe and Molokini from this pocket are outstanding, and the little beach simply looks charming. Since it's small, it doesn't take much to fill it up; mornings are best. Off to the left, in front of a beach house, is a smaller pocket of sand. The beach doesn't really have a name other than Secret

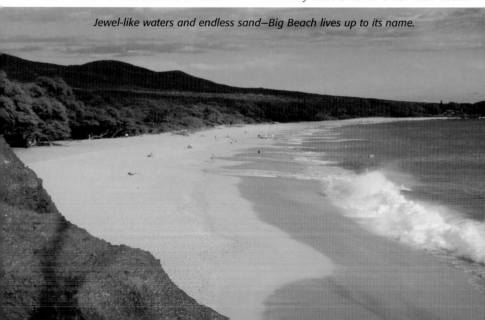

Jewel-like waters and endless sand—Big Beach lives up to its name.

Imagine getting married in this spot.
Secret Cove is in the hearts and photo albums
of couples all across America.

Cove. But the point on your right is called Paʻako, so we'll call it that.

❖ 'Ahihi Cove

Located just inside the ʻAhihi–Kinaʻu Natural Area Reserve (where it's illegal to capture or spear fish), the fish life here can be excellent, though visibility tends to be cloudy. No sand beach, but the cove is usually protected from wind and surf and access and water entry are easier than at Fishbowl below. Dumps (below) offers better snorkeling for those who are experienced. South of Wailea; see map on page 133.

❖ Dumps

Yeah, I went snorkeling on Maui at a place called Dumps. Makes you want to brag to all your buddies back home, huh? Well, the state actually *wants* you to snorkel here. They're hoping it'll keep you from snorkeling at nearby Fishbowl which has tons of political baggage associated with it. Located just past impossible-to-miss ʻAhihi Cove, Dumps (named after a now-vanished rubbish dump) has pretty mature coral and bigger but fewer fish than fishbowl. Visibility usually isn't great.

The winds can blow you out to sea and the surge can get rough near the shore. Though you'll see lots of life, we suggest this spot to intermediate snorkelers and even then only on light wind and surf days. After your 5-minute walk to the shore (and the only spit of sand near the center of the cove), kick out past the exposed rock, 25 yards out, and go right. The best area is near the low black cliffs.

❖ Fishbowl / Mokuha / Kanahena

First, it's not really much of a beach. Just a sprinkling of sand is all you'll find. But the snorkeling here is excellent. (You probably already figured that out from the name.) This tiny cove out on Cape Kinaʻu offers protected, clear water and lots of fish (though not much coral; the land here is very young). If you venture outside the cove, stay to the right where it's at least partially protected. Outside to the left exposes you to much of the ocean's tumult. Solo kayakers might arrive here in the late morning. By this time the wind may start blowing since you're right on the edge of the La Pérouse wind machine. We strongly recommend you come nice and early to possibly have it all to yourself and see it at its best. Access is not easy. It requires a 20–35-minute trek (each way) along a mile-long lava trail. It's a good trail but fades from the obvious in one or two spots, then quickly resumes. Some may find the footing tiring. (Wear *shoes*, not flip-flops, gloves if you fall down and bring water.) Part of the lava is encrusted with a green semiprecious gem called olivine, which sparkles in the sunlight. No shade at the cove. The trailhead at the road is not visually obvious from your car, but it's there. The trail starts 7/10 mile past 'Ahihi Cove, 45 feet *before* (north of) telephone pole #18 (which is the second to last pole on the ocean side before they change to the other side of the road). Sorry, there's no clearer way to explain it. See map on page 133 for some guidance. The trailhead is about 1/2 mile past the parking lot for Dumps, and you'll have to park there and walk the road to the trailhead since there's no parking on the side of the road. Don't try to hike across the lava field from Dumps. This is a protected reserve, not a park, so please make sure you don't leave anything behind and stay on the trail.

❖ La Pérouse Bay

In South Maui, this is as far as you can go by car. There's no sand beach here except for some small pockets at the south end of the bay, but the fish life is rich. La Pérouse Bay is a great example of incomplete information. We won't even guess how many times we've been there and seen visitors carrying their snorkel bag to the shore, only to come out several minutes later dejected, saying they couldn't see anything. All they were told, either in the snorkel shop or from one of the free magazines, is that there is good snorkeling "at La Pérouse Bay." But the visitors saw diddly. That's because the visibility there at the end of

the road is *terrible*. The private estate, situated on the bay to the right, is where visibility is the worst. But if you go *past* their little cove, staying along the shoreline on the right, each successive cove gets clearer (though never crystal clear), and the fish life gets better and better. About four coves down, the fish life is some of the best you'll find *anywhere on the island*. The variety is incomparable. (See the great hike/snorkel trip listed on page 233 for more.) The farther out you go, the better the fish life, but the water can get rougher as you go farther, too.

Go *early* in the morning. During normal trade winds, the bay fills in with wind and chop as the morning progresses, and by afternoon it can be cranking. 8 a.m. is better than 9 a.m. To get there, drive to the end of Makena Alanui Road, just past the La Pérouse monument where the road becomes rocky. Enter just to the left of where the fence posts go into the water. There's a nice lava shelf that works well for entry if the surf's not high. Keep an eye out for pin cushion-like sea urchins. (Or enter from the beach area to the right, though the water is not nice there.) Be cautious of surf and surges along the shoreline past the private cove. Many of the coves past there are protected, but the water outside of them is not.

The area past the end of the road is a popular fishing spot for locals, and more than once we've seen them try to talk visitors out of swimming at La Pérouse. (Assuming we were visitors, we've had fishermen try to convince us that dolphins were *leaping out of the water*...just down the road at 'Ahihi Cove.)

Past the end of the regular road, hikers can proceed to a number of small coves that you can claim for the morning.

La Pérouse is a common place to see dolphins in the early morning. A large pod seems to cruise this area, heading northward as the morning progresses. We often see them here around 7 a.m., then at Big Beach around 10 a.m. Turtles are also relatively common, though more so just north in 'Ahihi Cove. Remember that this area is a natural area reserve, meaning that it's protected and cherished. Although the government has allowed a private estate and an old *rubbish dump* to exist here, the state has written us to ask us to remind you to be respectful and to keep the area as pristine as you find it.

❖ Keawanaku

Any local reading this will say, *where?* That's because this beach really has no name and has been virtually unknown until now. It's past the end of the road in South Maui. You need to hike to it. See ACTIVITIES on page 201 for more. At times the ocean reclaims the sand here.

THE BOTTOM OF MAUI

Past Keawanaku the shoreline is rocky and windy, and the seas are usually harsh. Other than one inaccessible pocket at the base of a cliff and a tiny seasonal sand patch, you could explore the entire 30 miles of shoreline (which we've done), and you won't find *one* sand beach until you get to Hana. The only area frequently accessed (mostly by locals) is **Nu'u Bay**, described on page 112 and the unnamed black sand patch between the 29 and 30 mile markers.

HANA BEACHES

Hana has only a few beaches. *Ahh,* but what beaches! A red sand beach, a black sand beach and the best body surfing beach on the island. Since there's no way you'd ever drive all the way to Hana just for a day at the beach, we've deviat-

Hana doesn't have many beaches, but the few it does have, like Red Sand Beach, are exceptional. The shoreline trail on the left is a little tricky.

ed from our usual format and listed them under Hana Highway Sights.

THE NORTH SHORE OF HALEAKALA–FROM HANA TO CENTRAL MAUI

Hana is on the eastern tip of the island, and once you're west of Hana, the shoreline turns rocky. There are a few bays that you can visit (listed in the driving tours), but they don't have sand and are exposed to the higher surf normally present all along this windward coast. Not until the towns of Pa'ia and Kahului will you find beaches, and they are *not* in the same league as South and West Maui's beaches.

❖ Ho'okipa Beach Park

This is the only beach on this coast that visitors will probably be interested in. Near the 9 mile marker on Hwy 36, it's upcurrent of most of the runoff that plagues other area beaches. It's widely recognized as perhaps the best place in the world to windsurf, and boarders from everywhere make their pilgrimage to this spot. If you're not an expert, don't try. If the ocean doesn't get you, the surprisingly snobbish windsurfers will. (Novices use Kanaha Beach.) But this is a *great* place to watch the hordes of windsurfers as well as the pounding surf that often racks the shore. (Windsurfing is not allowed until 11 a.m.) It's uncommon *not* to have wind here. Car break-ins are a problem, so don't leave any valuables in your car.

❖ H.A. Baldwin Park

At the 6 mile marker on Hwy 36, it has a huge lawn, a long crescent of sand, good body surfing (though it's easy to get pounded into the sand here), lifeguard, full facilities, pavilion and nice views of West Maui. The downside is cloudy water from nearby runoff and very crowded conditions on the weekend. During the week it's good for a beach stroll, though

you *may* find this one of the smellier beaches due to the seaweed thriving from the runoff. Farther east, **Lower Pa'ia** is simply a disgusting beach access $2/10$ mile west of the 7 mile marker. 'Nuff said.

❖ Spreckelsville Beach

A mixed bag. On the plus side, it's a long, attractive beach with unusually firm sand, deserted most of the time during the week with nice views of the north coast. Several areas have a bench of lithified sand (sandstone) near the water's edge that provides some protection for keiki (kids) and nervous swimmers after you check for safety. On the negative side, current and wind are pretty dependable companions all day long, the water is cloudy, and (this is the clincher) jets departing the island fly over part of the beach, which can rattle your jaw. The best part of the beach (farthest from the airport) is at the 5 mile marker on Hwy 36. Take Nonohe to Kealakai. The other part, off the unmarked road between the 4 and 5 mile marker, is more avoidable.

❖ Kanaha Beach

This is where most visitors do their **windsurfing** and **kitesurfing** lessons. (See page 231 for more on these.) As a beach destination it won't twirl your tassels, but it's perfect for these wind-related activities. In front of Kahului Airport off Amala Street. See map on page 66.

❖ Waiehu Beach

This beach and nearby **Waihe'e Beach** are the last beaches on the windward side. Kind of anti-climactic to end it this way after so many great beaches, but these beaches are mostly used by shoreline fishermen and local residents and don't offer much for visitors. The water's a bit murky, the shoreline rocky, and currents can be a problem.

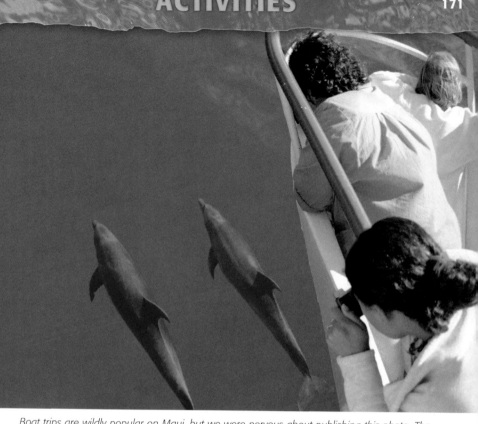

Boat trips are wildly popular on Maui, but we were nervous about publishing this photo. The water is so clean, clear and calm, it makes the photo look like it was retouched. We promise, we don't use tricky photographic filters or computers. This is really how it looks on a good morning.

Pick your fantasy; name your dream. If you had to pick the one thing that keeps people coming back to Maui year after year, this would probably be it. Just about everything you dream of doing in the tropics is available here. This is where it all comes true. But where should you go, and whom should you go with?

Most sources of visitor information, free and not free, tend to steer visitors to the same group of large activity providers, such as boat tours and helicopter companies. Some of these are good companies, but we've found some to be large, arrogant visitor-processing machines that seem to take their status for granted. We've spent countless hours *anonymously* reviewing smaller companies in addition to the larger ones to give you options you won't find elsewhere.

Be *skeptical* when looking at advertisements from different companies. Everyone claims to be the "best." Everyone is "world famous." Everyone claims to have been "voted number one." You could drown in their sea of hype.

Activity providers in Hawai'i are also notorious for using computers to put leaping whales on their ocean tour brochures or showing kayakers paddling up to waterfalls where it's not possible. Or how about the tour company that advertises that with their jungle tour they'll show you "hidden waterfalls" in Hana? Wow, sounds intriguing. Too bad the "hidden waterfall" photo on their brochure is actually the artificial falls in front of the Grand Wailea Hotel in South Maui. There are shameless attempts to capture your business, and you need to be vigilant in picking who you go with.

The activity industry on Maui is *massive*. Be suspicious of recommendations from activity desks and activity booths that often only "recommend" companies that give them the biggest commissions. (Those commissions are *30–50%* of the total cost of the activity.) Some are contractually bound to certain companies. Even many hotel concierges work this way. Our reviews reflect our personal observations, opinions and experiences. We actually see and *do* this stuff (always anonymously), and this section reflects what we saw. We don't get any money for steering you in a certain direction, a claim that very few can make. While it's true you can *sometimes* get good deals booking though activity companies (or get good deals if you trade some of your precious Maui time for a timeshare presentation), we *strongly* suggest you decide which company you want to go with *before* you see them, and don't let them steer you elsewhere. Also, some companies will give you a discount if you book directly, cutting out the activity brokers.

July, August and Christmas are busy times on Maui, and it may be difficult getting what you want on short notice. If you have your heart set on a particular activity, consider reserving it from the mainland (by phone or Internet; the latter often has discounts), just to make sure there's room for you. For all local phone numbers, the area code is 808.

These are those four-wheeled things that look like Tonka Toys on steroids with knobby tires. They are often used by ranchers these days to chase cows. And they're quite a bit of fun to ride. Two companies provide two very different trips.

Haleakala ATV Tours (661–0288) is 2½ miles up Hwy 378 in Kula. They are the best *run* of the two. Guides are friendly and professional, and they are very gentle and patient with nervous riders. Their trip is an out-and-back (on the same route), culminating in a peek at a native rain forest high on the slopes. They won't take more than 10 in a group, and they go *real* slow. Early rides usually offer better weather. 3½-hour trip with lunch is $145, 2-hour trip is $105.

Kahoma Ranch ATV (667–1978), is an entirely different experience, both good and bad. On the good side, the scenery is better. You climb 1,700 feet in 30 minutes along a dusty road. (If you're looking for a Maui souvenir, you'll end up with several pounds of Maui dirt embedded in every part of your body.) There are reservoirs, views of Moloka'i and Lana'i and the awesome Kahoma Valley. (It's to the left of the giant *L* above Lahaina.) The ATVs are large, 2-seater side-by-side models which drive more like a car. The down side is the way they're run. Guides are quiet and not overly personable. Their idea of feeding you is water and pineapple. Groups can get large and unwieldy. (Ask to be in a smaller group, if possible.)

Their 2½-hour tour (2 hours is what we got) is $129 per per person if you're a couple. Singles pay $199.

You *will* get dirty on both of these tours, so dress accordingly with closed-toe shoes and long pants. You'll go faster with Kahoma on their wider, smoother roads. We liked their terrain better and their halfway point makes for a good break. Haleakala ATV is a slower technical ride on a rough trail through a monotonous area. And if you're prone to hay fever, remember these are cattle ranches, which are essentially grass farms with living, edible lawn mowers.

The biking scene on Maui is certainly more varied than on the other Hawaiian islands. In addition to simply peddling around the neighborhood, there's the famous Haleakala downhill ride and the less-famous Skyline downhill mountain bike ride.

From Haleakala

This is probably the one you've heard about since more than 70,000 people per year do this, and you need to know how dramatically it has changed since what are affectionately known as "the old days." Back then you started near the summit of 10,000-foot-high Haleakala and cruised downhill virtually the whole way all the way to the ocean. If you opted for the sunrise tours, you'd get to see sunrise from the mountain the Hawaiians called *house of the sun*, which can be glorious. (Unless you don't dress warmly enough.)

Well, in 2007 the park service banned the tours from within the park

The view of clouds, ocean and Central Maui below are tempting, but don't take your eyes off the road.

boundaries, citing safety concerns. Today, the biking companies are forced to start their tour from the 6,500-foot level. You'll still see the sunrise if you opt to, but afterward you'll drive down a third of the mountain's elevation and start your tour lower. Most of the companies were not as up front as we'd like about the tours as they are currently done.

Most people are picked up at their hotels or condos between 2 a.m. and 3 a.m. A quiet or surly stupor fills the van during the 2-hour or so drive up the mountain, as thoughts such as "Whose stupid idea was this?" or, "There better not be any darned sing-alongs on the van" dominate the morning.

Once at the top, most people soon learn that they are seriously underdressed. Temperatures from the low 30s to the upper 40s coupled with 30 mph winds can turn the rarefied air to a symphony of groans and brrrs. See page 119 for more on the sunrise and how to prepare for it. When you get cold, you can sit in the van and drink coffee to keep warm.

There are three large companies that do this tour. The big guys are: **Mountain Riders** (242–9739), **Maui Downhill** (871–2155) and **Maui Mountain Cruisers** (871–6014). They take 13 people per trip, with a guide in front setting the pace and a van (called a sag wagon) pulling up the rear. Anyone who gets uncomfortable can climb in the van at any time. All three companies use comparable bikes whose wide seats are appreciated if you haven't been on a bike in a while. It's about $155 for the sunrise trip, cheaper if you want to sleep in a few hours later. **Cruiser Phil** (893–2332) is smaller and a bit more personalized. At press time, only Mountain Riders and Maui Mountain Cruisers took customers all the way

to sea level. The others end it upcountry, making this activity a mere shadow of what it used to be.

A Word of Warning: Because so many people do this, it's tempting to think that the danger must be minimal. It's not. According to the local paper, at least one serious accident *per week* occurs during these downhill rides. From road rash to broken bones to deaths, this activity has taken its toll on visitors. The first time we did it, we invited visiting relatives to go. Back then you went from the summit and we brought our 15-year-old niece. With only 2 miles left on the ride, a bee landed on her (not an uncommon occurrence) and, distracted, she failed to negotiate a turn and took a vicious tumble end-over-end right in front of us, landing on boulders 15 to 20 feet from the road. Even with a motorcycle helmet, she had head injuries (a deep gash all the way to the skull) and was hospitalized. It literally took over a year before her head injury symptoms abated.

Part of the problem is that riders in groups are strongly prodded to ride at least 20 mph, or the tour companies claim they'll be ticketed. And 20 mph (often faster) is pretty fast on some stretches, especially when you're still stiff from the cold and for many who haven't ridden a bike in several years. Though the age limit is 12 years old, we don't recommend it to anyone below 16. (Incidentally, those generous souls at Mountain Riders refused to refund her parents' money even though they spent much of the day at the hospital. Also, in case they're reading this, our niece is still waiting for your promised complimentary *I Survived the Haleakala Downhill Ride* T-shirt, which seemed particularly appropriate considering how it ended.)

A Few Thoughts: Mountain Riders tends to get there early, a plus if you want to leave right after sunrise since groups are spaced 10 minutes apart on a first-come basis, a minus if you want to sleep as late as possible. Late arrivals, such as Maui Downhill, may need to wait several hours after sunrise before beginning their descent or travel downhill by van a ways before starting. You won't see quite as many views on the way down as you might expect simply because you're concentrating on the road so much. A small flashlight can be handy at the nearly lightless pre-sunrise summit; many people hurt themselves stumbling around. Sunglasses are recommended on the ride because most helmets don't have eye protection. Contact lens wearers should bring drops. The colder you allow yourself to get before the ride, the stiffer you'll be during the ride. Lastly, if you're going to do the sunrise trip, do it early in your trip, when your body clock is still on mainland time.

An alternative to the massive downhill companies is to bike it on your own. Companies will take you to the edge of the park (at the 6,500-foot level) and let you ride down on your own, after perhaps first visiting the summit for a sunrise. The increased risk of not having a guide in front of you blocking tackle is balanced by the fact that you get to go *at your own pace*. Also, you can choose a different route if you want. For instance, **Haleakala Bike Company** (575–9575) is located in Ha'iku. So instead of stopping at the 2,000-foot level or taking uninteresting Baldwin Avenue at the end, you can take the more scenic Kokomo Road (first stop sign outside of Makawao) into Ha'iku with just a little uphill riding past Makawao. It's $69 for the drop-off at the park boundary; for $109 add a sunrise at the summit. A pretty decent outfit, and they have some of the better bikes on the summit complete with disk brakes and front suspension. Remember, if you have trouble with your bike, you won't have a van coming along to save your bacon.

Mountain Bike Haleakala's Spine

One of the most interesting bike rides in Hawai'i is down the lesser-known spiny side of Haleakala. See ADVENTURES on page 237 for more.

Renting a Bike

If you just want to rent a bike, in West Maui try **West Maui Cycles** (661–9005) and in South Maui call **South Maui Bicycles** (874–0068). It's around $50 for road bikes, $22–$40 for mountain bikes. Consider renting in advance.

BOAT TOURS

See OCEAN TOURS, page 207.

Boogie boarding (riders are derisively referred to as *spongers* by surfers) is where you ride a wave on what is essentially a sawed-off surfboard. It can be a real blast. You need short, stubby fins to catch bigger waves (which break in deeper water), but you can snare small waves by simply standing in shallow water and lurching forward as the wave is breaking. If you've never done it before, stay away from big waves; they can drill you. Smooth-bottom boards work best. If you're not going to boogie board with boogie fins (which some consider difficult to learn), then

Sponger shreddin' 'em. (Surfer lingo translation: Boogie boarder riding waves.)

you should boogie board with reef shoes or some other kind of water footwear. It allows you to scramble around in the water without fear of tearing your feet up on a rock or urchin. Shirts are very important, especially for men. (Women already have this problem covered.) Sand and the board itself can rub you so raw your *da kines* will glow in the dark.

In **South Maui**, if the surf is low (as is often the case), your best chance to catch waves is at Kama'ole Beach III. You also stand a good chance at the far south end of Wailea Beach. If there are moderate waves, Kama'ole III is probably too strong. Consider the middle of the beach at Kama'ole I, midway along Wailea Beach, Mokapu Beach, Keawakapu Beach (especially in the middle just south of the two-story house with the blue tile roof) and Big Beach. A great spot when the swells are right is at Chang's Beach next to Po'olenalena Beach. (See page 163.)

In **West Maui**, consider Hanake'o'o/ Canoe Beach, Ka'anapali Beach, left side of Oneloa Beach, and Slaughterhouse Beach in the summer. Some shoreline stretches south of Lahaina can be great. Just drive along and look for conditions.

Boards are easy to rent anywhere. It should cost about $5–$10 per day, $15–$20 per week.

CAMPING

Ah, camping in the tropics. The ultimate in low-cost housing. Although Maui isn't loaded with camping opportunities, there are several places worth noting.

Haleakala National Park has some of the best camping on the island. Drive-up campgrounds are at the seashore at Kipahulu (near the pools at 'Ohe'o, but there's no water) and at Hosmer Grove near the crater. Three-night maximum. *Inside* the crater, overnight tent camping at Holua and Paliku requires free permits. Apply in person at the park the day of your trip; no advance reservations. If they're booked up, tough toenails. Same 3-night max (2 nights at a site).

There are three *highly* coveted cabins inside Haleakala Crater, with free wood for the wood-burning stove, and *everybody* wants them. We know people who schedule a trip to Maui simply because they were able to get reservations at a cabin. The cabins hold up to 12, but it's only one party per cabin. The application process is complicated and involves a lottery. You may also have to entertain park officials with juggling or magic tricks and perhaps wash their cars. Call the number below to find out how to apply in writing at least two months in advance. You can call between 1 and 3 p.m. to check on cancellations if you're not too choosy about which cabin you end up with. Cabins cost $75 per night ($60 if you get a cancellation).

Haleakala National Park
Attention: Cabins
P.O. 369
Makawao, HI 96768
(808) 572–4400

State campgrounds are near Wai-'anapanapa Black Sand Beach and at Polipoli Park (high in the mountain). Call **State Parks** at (808) 984–8109 for permits. $5 per night per party. Five-night max. Wai'anapanapa has 12 cabins available for $45 (they're *real* basic), and there's one at Polipoli for $45.

There's only one **county campground** at Kanaha Beach Park (near Kahului Airport). Call 270–7389 for $3 per person permits. Restrooms, water and shower.

The **YMCA** in Ke'anae is one of the best deals on the island. For $17 per person you can share a cabin (tent camping is $35 *per family*). They also have 2 more modern ocean view cottages for $125 per night. BBQ grill available (bring food). Spring and summer are the busiest; book in advance by calling 248–8355.

Camp Olowalu (661–4303) on the way to Lahaina in Olowalu has tent camping for $10 per person per night. The grounds can feel crowded if just half of the 20 sites are taken. Basic amenities and cold water showers.

Camp stove gas can usually be found at **Airgas/Gaspro** (661–1480) in West Maui, **Sports Authority** (871–2558) in Kahului, and **Wal-Mart** (871–7820).

Deep sea fishing is synonymous with Hawai'i. Reeling in a massive marlin, tuna or tough-fighting ono is a dream of many fishermen. When there's a strike, the adrenaline level of everyone on board shoots through the roof. Most talked about are the marlin (very hard fighters known for multiple runs). These goliaths can tip the scales at over 1,000 pounds. Also in abundance are ono, also called wahoo (one of the fastest fish in the ocean and indescribably delicious), mahimahi (vigorous fighters—excellent on light tackle), ahi (delicious yellowfin tuna) and billfish.

Most big fish like to cruise through deeper waters than those found off the leeward side of Maui. (The Big Island is blessed with deep water right off the Kona shore.) The shallow water here that the whales love tends to be shunned by large pelagics. On Maui you'll have to take a 30–60 minute boat trip to areas where the undersea topography drops off steeply. But fear not. Once there, large game fish await.

Most boats troll nonstop since the lure darting out of the water simulates a panicky bait fish—the favored meal for large game fish. On some boats, each person is assigned a certain reel. Experienced anglers usually vie for the corner poles with the assumption that strikes coming from the sides are more likely to hit corners first.

You should know in advance that in Hawai'i, the fish belongs to the boat. What happens to the fish is entirely up to the captain, and he usually keeps it. You could catch a 1,000-pound marlin and be told that you can't have as much as a steak from it. If this bothers you, you're out of luck. If the ono or other small fish are striking a lot and there is a glut of them, you might be allowed to keep it—or half of it. You *may* be able to make arrangements in advance to the contrary.

Charters leave from Lahaina and Ma'alaea. Though there are 4-, 6- and 8-hour charters, many won't do 4 hours since half the time is eaten traveling to and from the fishing grounds. We recommend the 6-hour trips. Mornings offer best conditions. Prices are $150+ per person for a 4-hour shared charter. You can do a private 6-hour charter for $800–$1,000. 8-hour private charters go for $925–$1,200 or more for the big boats. Usually, the bigger the boat, the higher the price since nearly all are licensed to take only 6 passengers. Individual boat rates can change often depending on the season, fishing conditions and whims of the owners. Consequently, we'll forgo listing individual boat rates since this information is so perishable and instead list a few companies that we recommend. Call them directly to get current rates. If you have 4 or more people, make it a private charter so you can exercise more control.

If you're easy-queasy, take an anti-seasickness medication. There are people who never get sick regardless of conditions, and those who turn green just watching A Perfect Storm on DVD. Nothing can ruin an ocean outing quicker than being hunched over the stern feeding the fish. Scopolamine patches prescribed by doctors can have side effects, including (occasionally) blurred vision that can last a week. Dramamine II or Bonine taken the night before and the morning of a trip also seems to work well for many, though some drowsiness may occur. Ginger is a mild preventative. Try powdered ginger, ginger pills or even *real* ginger ale—can't hurt, right?

Tipping: 10–15% split between the captain and deck hand is customary if you are pleased with their performance. If the captain is a jerk and the deck hand throws up on you, you're not obligated to give 'em diddly.

Boats to consider in West Maui are **Absolute Sportfishing** (669–1449), **Aerial Sportfishing** (667–9089), **Finest Kind** (661–0338) and **Luckey Strike** (661–4606). The later takes more than a dozen anglers.

In Ma'alaea there's **Makoa Kai** (573–0383), **Piper Sportfishing** (242–8350), and **Rascal** (874–8633). The latter is a typical 6-pack. Their fighting chair looks more like an electric chair, but at least they let you keep most of the fish. Expensive at $250 per person or $950 for the boat for 6 hours. They'll also tag and release.

GOLFING

OK, OK, let's be honest. A place that's known as the *windsurfing* capital of the world surely can't have world-class golf, right? So you'd think. But the truth is the golfing on Maui can be outrageous. Granted, it's probably not *quite* as good as some on the Big Island or the Prince Course on Kaua'i, but some courses are pretty close and will blow away most of the courses you've ever played on the mainland. The trick here is to play *early*. Wind can be the instrument of your doom here, and the later you play, the greater the doom.

Overall, South Maui courses offer the best golf and are usually calm in the mornings with winds picking up around 11 a.m. or later. Sunshine is almost guaranteed. West Maui courses at Ka'anapali can offer similar weather with more wind. West Maui's Kapalua courses are *very* windy nearly *all* the time, but best in the morning. Passing showers are common.

At both South and West Maui courses, *greens break toward the ocean*, no matter what your eye tells you. They may even break uphill if it's toward the sea. Also, dress codes (collared shirts) are enforced more here. **Carts** are included and mandatory, unless otherwise noted.

SOUTH MAUI COURSES

If you only get a chance to golf once on Maui, we'd recommend South Maui. The exceptional morning weather, views of Kaho'olawe and Molokini, and three of the best courses on Maui make the

Course	Par	Yards	Rating	Fees
Dunes at Maui Lani	72	6,413	71.6	$125
Ka'anapali Royal (North)	71	6,700	71.8	$225
Ka'anapali Kai (South)	71	6,388	70.7	$185
Kahili	72	6,570	72.3	$125
Kapalua Bay	72	6,600	71.7	$215
Kapalua Plantation	73	7,263	75.2	$295
Makena Resort North	72	6,567	72.0	$200
Makena Resort South	72	6,630	70.7	$200
Pukalani Country Club	72	6,882	72.9	$78
Waiehu Municipal	72	6,330	70.1	$55
Wailea Golf Club Old Blue	72	6,797	72.2	$185
Wailea Golf Club Emerald	72	6,407	69.6	$225
Wailea Golf Club Gold	72	6,653	71.6	$225

Carts are included and mandatory at all courses except Waiehu.
Metal spikes aren't allowed in South Maui.
Yards and ratings are from the blue tees.

golfing incredible. If you're a great golfer, you'll prefer Makena South. If you're a decent golfer, you'll probably prefer Wailea's Gold or Emerald courses. We'll start at the extreme south and work our way up.

Makena Resort (879–3344)

One of the two Makena courses is among the best on the island, and both Makena courses are ego bruisers. The **South Course** is the most fun of the two. Slower greens than the north, and the hazards are more successfully implemented here. The close ocean proximity is delightful, and the views of Molokini and Kahoʻolawe are tasty. Few adjoining fairways. Hole 3 has a pretty scary view of eight bunkers guarding the green. A relatively short but potentially deadly par 4. Hole 7 is a wonderful 599-yard journey from the champ tees. After the drive, just shoot straight toward Molokini offshore and stop when you find a flag. Hole 13 has some magnetic water to shoot over. Most seem to underestimate it for some reason. Hole 15 is a dreamy 180 yards from the blues to the ocean. Club down for the steep downhill, but club up for the usual headwind. Hmm, maybe it's a wash. Regardless, it's a classic Hawaiian hole, guaranteed to elicit a contented sigh. Walk to the edge of the green for a beautiful view of the black sand beach. What a day it's been. Can it really almost be over?

The **North Course** is nice, but not as fun as the South, and the maintenance doesn't seem as good at the North Course. Really good golfers prefer the North, however, with its narrowness and adjoining fairways keeping it tight. But the rest of us mere mortals still like the South. Hole 6 is an odd split fairway. Stay on the left side during your drive to give you a better shot at the green, but not so far left you roll into the gorge. Be sure to look behind you at the view of Molokini. Some of the greens are as fast as pool tables, so be careful. The back nine is much nicer on this course. At 13 you have a

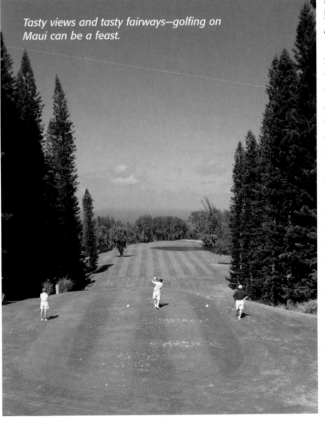

Tasty views and tasty fairways—golfing on Maui can be a feast.

splendid elevated vantage from the blues to the fairway below with scattered bunkers and a nice wide spot to shoot for. Number 14 is an incredible 611-yard romp downhill. Just blast away on your drive, and pat yourself on the back for your distance. 15 is pretty narrow and likely to bite you on the butt.

Both courses are excellent (though both could use better marked paths), but if you can only do one, do the South. No metal spikes.

Rates are $200 for the south course, $200 for north. $155 for south or north twilight. $130 for south or north for guests of Maui Prince. $70 kama'aina for south or north. Walkers are allowed on South after 3 p.m. Located just south of Maui Prince, see map on page 131.

Wailea Golf Club

Gold and Emerald (875–7450)
Old Blue (875–5155)

The Wailea courses are among the most beautifully maintained courses on the island, with fewer hazards and more forgiving play than the Makena courses (though they're still very challenging). The first two are Robert Trent Jones, Jr. layouts, whereas the older Blue Course is an Arthur Jack Snyder affair. All have GPS-equipped carts.

The most popular is the **Emerald Course.** It's wider than the Gold and starts things off nicely with a gently tapering 354-yard fairway march toward the ocean. Number 4 is another very picturesque hole. Kaho'olawe beckons from offshore. You may see other players on the 10th green, as it's shared with hole 17. Hole 15 is a tough 395 yard uphill par 4. Count yourself among the few who par this bugga. Too soon you come to the 18th. What a way to polish off a game! Smack toward the 360-foot

high Pu'u Ola'i. You're eventually rewarded with a half dozen bunkers surrounding the green. This course has been named the most "woman-friendly" in golf rankings in the past.

Wailea Gold also makes a good first impression as the fairway wanders down 400 yards with striking views of offshore islands. *Oh,* this is going to be a good day. There's only one small water body on the whole course, so live it up. Hole 7 is a long 567 yards with a nicely placed dogleg. Hole 8 is probably the most picturesque—a tough 188-yard par 3 lined up perfectly with offshore Molokini. This hole always reminds you that it's wonderful to be alive. Hole 9 has a pretty intimidating lava embankment in front of you, but it's not as far as it looks. Just give it your usual swing and don't try to kill the ball and you'll make it. It's the well-defended green that you should worry about. At #11 you might as well get your sand wedge ready. More sand around the par 3 green than many South Maui beaches. Both courses are off Wailea Golf Club Dr. See map page 131.

The **Old Blue Course**, set among luxury homes off Kaukahi, is (as the name implies) older and noticeably duller. When the course director feels the need to brag that the designer is still alive, you know it's not Maui's newest, hottest course. Don't get us wrong. If it were the only course on Maui, you'd tell everyone back home how great the golfing is here. But everything is relative, and compared to the Gold and Emerald courses, it's an also-ran. Individual holes don't stand out much, good or bad. They're all nice, but none great. Hole 4 at 562 yards offers a blind par 5, and the second shot may also be blind as well. At 14 slicers will need to drive carefully, lest you hit another driver on Wailea Alanui

Road. The Old Blue is easier on the ego and may lack pizazz, but it's still a fun, relaxing course.

Rates for the Gold and Emerald courses are $225 or $180 if you're staying at a Wailea resort. Old Blue course is $25 less for Wailea resort guests. No metal spikes. If you want **lessons**, Wailea has the best facilities and instructors in South Maui for $150 per hour.

WEST MAUI COURSES

West Maui offers nice courses in *extremely* windy Kapalua, or lesser courses in somewhat calmer Ka'anapali. We'll describe them from the farthest north heading south. At both Kapalua courses you can place food orders from your GPS cart and pick it up at the restaurants.

Kapalua (669–8044)

Wind, wind, wind. It's important to keep the ball low here, as 30–40 MPH winds *are common.* Kapalua courses are difficult and require concentration and strategy. At Kapalua, seriously consider keeping your scorecard in your pocket or bag because it's easy to lose it to the wind here. (Of course, if you're playing for a few bucks a hole and losing, here's your chance to get out of it.)

Kapalua Plantation Course has beautifully maintained fairways and greens. Of the two Kapalua courses, the wind seems strongest here. For what it's worth, it's been our observation that although some tough courses are still fun for higher handicap golfers, this one will eat them up and spit them out. Plantation is a serious course for serious golfers who seem to universally wear serious expressions. None of the dreamy glow of other courses; this is golfing to the death. Hole 3 is your first crack into the wind, and it's here where most learn the need to shoot those line drives. Pop it up, and it'll come right back at ya. At 4 your drive is uphill, into the wind and blind. Hey, nobody said this course would be easy. Hole 5 is 532 yards with a head/cross wind and a deep ravine to your right. At 6 they made wicked use of hills. Lose control near the green, and God knows where it will roll. Hole 8 requires a wonderful lob over a gorge onto the green littered with bunkers. One hazard not on the scorecard is the profusion of pineapple bugs that fly into your face while you are driving your cart. Don't open your mouth while cruising, or you'll see what I mean. Hole 10 is another blind, uphill, into-the-teeth-of-the-wind hole, with a cleverly located bunker near the green. Par 5 hole 15 has a healthy dogleg ending in a hungry dip well shy of the green. But if you pop it up too high coming out of the dip, no telling where the wind will take the ball. The course ends nicely with an endless 663-yard trek with the wind and elevation helping you. **Rates** are $295 *(hurt me!),* $200 for Kapalua guests, $150 for twilight. Past 31 mile marker on Hwy 30.

Kapalua Bay is closer to the ocean than the Plantation and the easier to play. There's not an overabundance of sand on this course. The fairways meander among several golf course communities. Hole 4 marches right toward the ocean, and glorious #5 actually shoots over the ocean. This 205-yard par 3 is one of our favorites on Maui. You have to hit over the strikingly blue ocean onto the green. Hole 9 shoots over a gentle hill toward the ocean—very picturesque. Note the unseen creek bisecting the fairway on hole 11. It's a ball-stopper. Hole 16 is most unusual. It's a 371-yard par 4 with a pond bisecting it and a creek running *down the center* of the fairway, right where you want to be. Add the wind and an undulating fairway, and you have a very interesting hole. On Kapalua Ave. **Rates** are $215, $175 for Kapalua guests, $130 for twilight.

Kapalua Golf Academy (669–6500) is armed with state-of-the-art teaching equipment. From private lessons to multi-day schools, this is the best place on Maui to earn your spikes.

Ka'anapali Golf Course (661–3691)

Golf in Ka'anapali goes back to the '60s, comparatively ancient by Hawai'i golf standards. And while the course is fun, it's overpriced for what you get, even for Maui. The course is flatter than the Kapalua courses and the greens certainly less pristine, but it's also a more relaxing play. Wind is far less of a factor (in the morning especially), and rain is uncommon. The Royal (North) Course is the most popular and difficult, with the Kai (South) Course having the reputation of being "woman-friendly." Cars and homes are always close by on the north. Ka'anapali's best asset is its location, so close and convenient to Ka'anapali resorts. Though not as nice as Kapalua, the diminished wind and rains are refreshing. Both courses have fewer hazards than Kapalua.

The **Royal Course** hole 5 is a pleasant 473 yards, with the second half straddling the beach (a large, but unlikely sand trap). Instead of Kapalua's ironwood and Cook Island pine trees, coconut trees are your floral companions here. (And they're a lot less intrusive, too.) Overall, the holes aren't as distinctive as other courses around the island. **Rates** are $225, it's $180 for Ka'anapali guests, $110 for twilight.

The **Kai Course** is certainly easier. The hardest thing is crossing Ka'anapali Parkway in your cart. Things start out

with a wide open 490-yard trot to the green. Greens are huge and only slightly undulating. Fewer people make more leisurely play, especially in the afternoon (though that may bring winds). The 4th green is right near the train trestle of the Lahaina Ka'anapali Railroad. The 8th fairway is one of the prettier ones on this course. It's 537 yards with short coconut trees most of the way. The South Course seems to receive a bit less maintenance than the north, but it's nice to have fewer houses and cars around. **Rates** are $185, $140 for Ka'anapali guests, $85 for twilight.

CENTRAL & UPCOUNTRY COURSES

There's one really good reason to consider golf outside the resort areas— *price!* No $200 greens fees here. Though the quality of the courses may be better elsewhere, if you can't stomach the price, consider some of these courses.

Dunes at Maui Lani (873–7911)

Maybe the most underrated course on the island. You get a lot of golfing for your $125. Granted, it's not close to the ocean and winds can be fierce here, but it's not as bad as at Kapalua. Opened in 1999, the course has a delightful layout and lots of character. The designer, Robin Nelson, made splendid use of the natural rolling terrain of this natural sand dune area. With a name like Dunes you shouldn't be surprised to find lots of sand, and you may end up wearing out your sand wedge. Well-placed, numerous and very deep bunkers, along with the wind, create a formidable challenge. Mornings are calmest.

This is an out-and-back design with the wind usually blowing to your left on the first 10 holes (except #6). Hole 4 has smashing views of the West Maui Mountains spiced with its steep, deep, vicious bunkers. Hole 6 is a nice 178-yard over-water par 3. The small but bottomless sand trap in front of the hole is unseen, and if you shoot too far, you may soar past the hill behind the green. At 10 you need to listen for the bell from the previous golfers telling you it's clear to shoot. It's a blind, downhill volley par 4, one of the best holes on the course. You end the game with a hideously difficult 558-yard par 5, probably into the wind as the angles have shifted a bit with a narrow strip of land between the lake and the bunkers. You par this one during afternoon winds, and you're my hero.

Rates are $125, $80 for twilight and $46 for kama'ainas. No metal spikes. On 380 1⁴⁄₁₀ miles south of Puunene Road.

Kahili (242–4653)

Located in Central Maui on the windy slope of the West Maui Mountains, the layout tends to avoid cross winds that could make life difficult here. Service is scant and there's no beverage cart, but the course is in nice shape and is not normally too crowded. There aren't any holes noteworthy enough to be considered signature holes, but yardages tend to be long and roughs fairly forgiving (most of the time). Views are dominated by distant Haleakala.

Rates are $125, $85 for twilight and $50 for kama'ainas. GPS carts included. On Hwy 330. See the right side of the West Maui map on page 45.

Waiehu Municipal (243–7400)

For a municipal course it's in pretty decent shape. The front 9 are at the ocean. Holes 5–8 are a delight as you hug the shoreline. The course was unmarked at press time, and visitors constantly ask, "Is this hole such and such?" The course is pretty light on hazards; bunkers are mainly around the greens, so the play is relatively easy and relaxing. In fact, the biggest hazard is its popularity. Weekends are a zoo, but weekdays aren't *too* bad, though certainly busier than resort courses. Winds are steadier here, not as gusty, and usually kick in around 11 a.m. The back nine was built several decades after the first and are up the mountain. Hole 13 is a beautiful elevated drive to the ocean with a dogleg right. Utterly spectacular. This is the only course on Maui where you can always walk; you don't have to use the $18 carts. (Pushcarts are $3.) **Rates** are $50 or $55 for weekends. Residents can play for half that, hence the popularity. North of Kahului on Hwy 340 1¼ miles north of Waiehu Beach Road. No credit cards.

Pukalani (572–1314)

You realize right off the bat how utterly straight this course is. The designers must have had an unusual fear of curves, but it's great for beginners. No fairway sand at all. Holes are mostly long but pretty straightforward. Even the greens read fairly true. None of this breaking-uphill-if-toward-the-ocean stuff, and most are pool-table flat. This is a great course to cut loose on. Accuracy and strategy aren't a big deal. Just hit the ball and have fun. Hole 3 is certainly the most interesting. Par 3 over a gulch onto the green. Don't like that option? Fine. Then hit to the *other* green below the hill. (It's nice to have choices.) If no one's behind you, play both and take the better score. (Did I say that?) Bring something warm as it gets chilly up here. **Rates** are $78; $63 for twilight, $39 for kama'ainas. At the end of Pukalani Street off Old Haleakala Highway in Pukalani. (See map on page 115.)

This section actually encompasses two activities. Powered hang gliding (you and your instructor sit in a seat in an ultralight aircraft using a specially designed hang glider wing pushed by a motor) and paragliding (similar to a parachute and is unpowered). I'm a little uncomfortable lumping them together because they are so radically different, but it seems more logical to organize it this way.

Powered Hang Gliding

First, I need to get something out of the way. Flying a powered hang glider (known as a trike) is different than any other type of aircraft. When I was growing up, I used to have a recurring dream that I could flap my arms and fly like a bird. My father flew little Cessnas, which, though fun, felt more to me like a car in the air than flying like a bird. I had forgotten my flying dreams until I reviewed a company on Kaua'i that gave lessons in this odd little craft called a trike. As soon as my instructor and I took off, I realized that a person *really could* fly like a bird. *This* was what the flying bug felt like! I was so smitten with the craft that I eventually hired the instructor on Kaua'i to teach me, and now I fly trikes myself. So although I have no personal interest in any company teaching trikes in Hawai'i, my perspective isn't as remote as it is for most activities. After all, it's not possible to

anonymously review some companies, like Hang Glide Maui, because I know the pilot. (We're both members of the small ultralight community.)

With that explanation, powered hang gliding is the activity I recommend, for several reasons. One, it's the safest of the two flying methods, *by far*. You have an engine, the craft is bigger and more stable, and it even has a powered parachute attached to the craft…just in case. (Even my dad's Cessna can't make that claim.) Trikes take off and land on regular runways (in this case at lovely Hana), and the ease and grace of the craft is glorious. (Rent the movie *Fly Away Home* if you want to see what they're like.) It's as close to flying like a bird as any form of flight I know. Trikes are what I have come to love so much and, in my opinion, are the safest form of ultralight flight available. (I'm not a daredevil and wouldn't fly them myself if I felt unsafe in them, though any time you're in the air you're potentially at risk, even on the airlines.) I grin like a fool every time I fly and have never reviewed an activity that generates more enthusiastic responses from other participants. It seems that whenever I see people coming off a trike (since I use the same airports that the trike companies do), passengers are frothing at the mouth with excitement, proclaiming that it's the best thing they've ever done on vacation.

The local company is **Hang Gliding Maui** (572–6557). Located out in lovely Hana, the pilot, Armin Engert, is certified as a Certified Flight Instructor and is well known and respected in the ultralight and hang gliding communities. I can't review him *anonymously*, but I can tell you that his skill as a pilot is something I aspire to. Armin has a camera mounted on the

Taking a lesson in a powered hang glider surrounded
by the waterfalls of Hana—what could be cooler?

wing to take a photo of you during your lesson for $30 or a DVD for $70—just in case no one back home believes you. There is a 240-pound weight limit. The cost of a half-hour, in-air lesson is $130. It's $220 for an hour. Reserve in advance. Expensive? Perhaps. But it's so unspeakably cool that the memories will stay with you for a lifetime.

Paragliding

Paragliding is, in my opinion, a much less safe method of flying. You are very susceptible to gusts of wind and to landing where you *don't* want to land. **Proflyght** (874–5433) jumps off Haleakala, hanging below what is essentially a gliding parachute. When we asked about passenger safety, we were told the *current* owner's safety record is perfect. That's fine, but as someone who flies various types of craft, I'll tell you that personally, I am too uncomfortable to fly with them. Not because of this particular company, but because of my skepticism regarding this type of flying as a whole. The chutes are prone to collapsing (unlike rigid or flex-wing flyers), and I know too many long time pilots who've only received injuries while flying this particular type of wing. If you choose to fly, it's $175 for a 15-minute 3,000-foot descent or $75 for a 1,000-foot descent. Have fun.

To see Maui from the sky is to explore areas you can't reach by land. Paradise in the tropics is a breathtaking experience from the air. There are rad-ically different reasons on each of the Hawaiian Islands to take a helicopter tour. We've never been shy in our strong advocacy for helicopter tours of Kaua'i and even the Big Island. Kaua'i, aside from being astoundingly beautiful, has three jaw-droppingly compelling reasons to take a helicopter tour: the Na Pali coast, Waimea Canyon and Wai'ale'ale Crater. The Big Island, too, has an aerial objective worth flying to: the active Kilauea volcano, which is awesome from the air. Maui has...some *very* pretty scenery. But is it worth the big bucks you'll have to shell out for a helicopter flight? It depends. As a pilot myself with hundreds of hours in the skies over Hawai'i, I can tell you that flying along the Hana coast and through the West Maui Mountains is fantastic, especially when it's been wet. It's incredible, but I don't get the same lump in my throat as when I fly over Kaua'i or the Big Island's Kilauea volcano. If a flight over Kaua'i doesn't move someone, then they can't be moved by anything. If a flight over the Big Island's volcano doesn't excite, then check your pulse. But a flight over Maui isn't like that. It's very nice, very pretty, but it's probably not an emotional event. It's simply cool. Maui has much to experience, but helicopters aren't as vital here as they are elsewhere.

Then there's the fact that helicopter flights are more expensive on Maui than the other islands. Even companies with outlets on the Big Island or Kaua'i charge more for air time on Maui. It might be because of the confiscatory commissions (up to 50%) paid to activity booths on Maui, and maybe it's also because that's what the market will bear here.

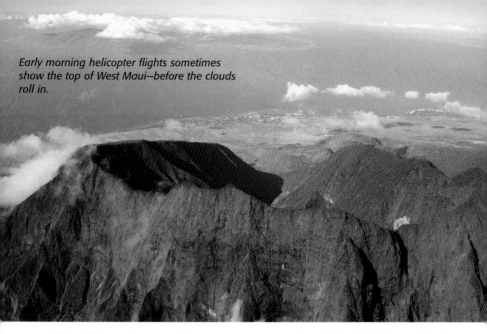

Early morning helicopter flights sometimes show the top of West Maui—before the clouds roll in.

The difference between Maui companies isn't as pronounced. They fly similar routes, charge similar prices, and mostly fly 6-passenger A-Stars. They have four main flights, listed with the best ones first.

#1 West Maui/Moloka'i Sea Cliffs

This is the best of the flights to take. After seeing West Maui and the beautiful and inaccessible Honokohau Falls, you fly across the channel and look at the stunning 3,000-foot sea cliffs of Moloka'i—an awesome sight, never to be forgotten. Then slip through the middle of Moloka'i, along the fringing reefs, then back to Maui. After going up Olowalu Valley, into the center of West Maui, you'll come out 'Iao Valley to end the hour-long flight for about $270.

#2 Circle Maui

You won't actually circle the island, and some companies see more of West Maui than others. For our Air Maui "complete island" flight, the West Maui portion only went into one valley before reversing back to the airport. The benefit over the Moloka'i flight is that you get to see East Maui, which, hopefully, includes a peek into Haleakala Crater (clouds permitting—they aren't allowed to fly *into* it but instead look over the rim) and the Hana coastline. An hour for about $270.

#3 West Maui

You'll see West Maui's 'Iao Valley, another valley with beautiful waterfalls called the Wall of Tears, and the pretty northeast coastline. It's 30 minutes of flight for $140 or more.

#4 East Maui

Similar to the circle island without West Maui. 45 minutes for about $200.

A Few Tips

These prices are list prices. Many companies will give some kind of discount if you ask them. Ask them about coupons, Internet discounts, or tell them you'll book through an activity booth if they don't discount it some. Sometimes they'll deeply discount if you book at the last minute, especially single passengers. In the late afternoon, call around and ask if they have room the next morning, and you may get a better rate.

If you decide to take a flight, consider doing it early in your trip. It'll help orient you to the island.

Morning is almost always best. Be done by 10:30 a.m. for best viewing conditions. Wind and clouds increase as the morning and afternoon progress, and conditions get bumpier.

For photos, use a fast film, such as ASA 400. Don't let the camera touch the vibrating window. Glare from the window can be a problem while filming. A circular polarizer can cut through almost all of it. Few point-and-shoot cameras will accommodate polarizers, but all SLR cameras will. Dark clothing also reduces glare.

Only two companies (see table) have a microphone so you can talk to the pilot. This is very nice because often you'll have a question about something you see. Others may say they don't have mikes for safety reasons, but that's laughable. For instance, one company has you hand notes to the pilot if you have questions. Which do *you* think is safer—the pilot *hearing* your questions, or *reading* your note while flying? Most probably don't have mikes for money reasons and because they don't want to be "annoyed" by your questions. One of the microphoned companies has a 4-passenger Hughes, which is a fun chopper to fly in.

For some reason, helicopter pilots are notoriously bad with their facts during narrations. Our Air Maui and Sunshine Helicopter flights had such bad "facts" that we bought the tapes of the flights to see how much conveyed was correct. The results were pretty poor, especially Air Maui's.

The state charges extra to park at the Kahului heliport, and the lot often fills up.

Don't wear earrings; they interfere with the headsets.

Here's the deal on seating: The best seats are up front—period. They may tell you otherwise in order to console you with your backseat position, but the front seat offers better visibility and allows the island to rush at you. But seating, especially up front, is dictated by weight, and lighter people usually go up front. Also, single riders often get placed up there since companies don't like to break up couples.

If you are sitting in the back, you want to be on the side where all the action is. On the West Maui/Moloka'i trip, the left seats are the best because of the route. On the Circle, East or West Maui trips, it depends on the direction they go. If they visit the south part of Haleakala and the crater first, then head up and then along the Hana coast, the left side is best. If they head straight for the Hana coastline, the right side is best. Talk to them on the phone and ask which route they're taking, then request a seat where the main

Company	Phone #	Tours	Aircraft Type	2-Way*
Air Maui	877-7005	1, 2 & 4	6-Pass. A-Star	No
Alexair Helicopters	877-4354	1, 2, 3 & 4	A-Star & Hughes	Yes
Blue Hawaiian	871-8844	1, 2, 3 & 4	A-Star & Eco-Star	Yes
MauiScape	877-7272	1, 2, & 4	A-Star	No
Pacific Wings	873-0877	Maui & Big Island	High Wing Plane	No
Paragon Air	244-3356	5 Island, Maui & Moloka'i	High Wing Plane	No
Sunshine	871-0722	1, 2, 3 & 4	A-Star & Eco-Star	No
Volcano Air Tours	877-5500	E. Maui, Big Island Kilauea	Low Wing Plane	No

Indicates whether craft contains a microphone for you to talk to the pilot

action will be on *your* side. They may not *guarantee* seats, but make sure they know that you'll consider them weasels if you don't get the seat you're looking for. Most of the time you'll be accommodated, even while they claim that "the computer assigns seats" or "the weather dictates our route." If they don't sound accommodating, go elsewhere.

Many companies now video the trip and will sell you the tape afterward. That's kind of cool, and you can hear your pilot on the tape, but the quality of these tapes won't match what you can buy from a pre-recorded tape, where sights were captured in their best light. It's your call as to which, if any, you want.

Most companies use 6-passenger A-Stars. **Blue Hawaiian** and **Sunshine** have some flights on their much-touted Eco-Star. It's larger inside and the windows are bigger, but it's 10% more than an already expensive standard flight, and is hard to justify unless you have extra cash burning a hole in your pocket.

AIRPLANE TOURS

Without as many narrow valleys as Kaua'i or the Big Island's Hamakua Coast, hovering isn't as important here, so airplane tours are a good alternative to more expensive helicopter flights.

Volcano Air Tours (877–5500) can leave from either Kahului or West Maui Airport and tours East Maui before heading to the Big Island to show you the active volcano. It's 2 hours in the air for $350–$400. (Depends on which airport you leave from, what time of day, what your hair style is, and if you can name all the state capitals.) The only ding is it's a low-wing 9-passenger aircraft, so the view is partially blocked, but the windows are very large and everyone gets a window seat.

Paragon Air (244–3356) does tours of Moloka'i and Maui. Their five-island tour covers Maui, Lana'i, Moloka'i and Kaho'olawe in a somewhat rushed 90 minutes for $305. Make sure you get their high-wing plane. (The "fifth" island is tiny Molokini.) They virtually never answer their phone, so you'll have to book online.

Pacific Wings (873–0877) does private charters and will go wherever you want to go, even interisland.

IMPORTANT NOTE

If this section seems shorter than you would expect, it's because we put *lots* of shorter hikes in the HANA HIGHWAY SIGHTS chapter and elsewhere. There are many 10–30 minute hikes sprinkled in those sections since we felt that you were more likely to hike them on a driving tour than head out there for that purpose alone. Also, one of the tastiest trails on the island, at 'Ohe'o Gulch (AKA **Seven Sacred Pools**) is under SOUTHEAST MAUI SIGHTS. See page 199 for more on HIKES DESCRIBED ELSEWHERE.

If you're going to do much stream hiking or wet rock hopping, pick up tabis (fuzzy mittens for your feet), which cling well. You'll find them at the various Longs Drugs or at Kmart in Kahului.

WEST MAUI HIKES
Acid War Zone to the Blowhole

There's a quicker way to reach the Nakalele Blowhole shown on page 56, but hiking to it along this route is definitely more fascinating. There is a small parking lot near the 38 mile marker past Kapalua near the northernmost point on the island on Hwy 30. You are allowed to hike on the old jeep road and past the light beacon that leads to the blowhole. This is not a long hike—at most 30 minutes each way without side trips—but the terrain is excellent.

See map on page 58. From the parking lot, make your way toward, then along, the sea cliffs. The trail is vague and spotty, but you shouldn't have trouble making your way as you first walk through a gulch toward your right before reaching the cliff. (Other paths are more inland but less interesting.) Keep going right. The cliffs are pockmarked with crags and caves, and the bouldery landscape around you is awesome. About 10–15 minutes into the walk, just before a light beacon, you'll notice some small pools below the cliffs. From down there you can see how big the sea arch you saw from the cliffs really is. Down at the pools there's decent swimming and a crack in the rock toward the sea that snorts air during high surf. The scenery is pretty down there, but access is tricky. You need to hop along boulders, then scale a questionable ladder with a questionable rope tied to a questionable rock. These pools might not be worth it. Infinitely better pools might be available at the Olivine Pools on page 60.

Back on the trail, you descend past the lighthouse and here the trail snags the uninformed. A small blowhole shooting from the notch of a lava shelf and wall fools most hikers. Probably 90% turn around here. But wait: This

ain't the blowhole! Continue along the shoreline and soon you come to an alien landscape. It looks like a war zone fought with acid. Billions of tons of sea spray, blown by the wind, has carved up the soft rock here. The land is literally being eaten in front of you. Take your time to examine some of the lava formations up close. This part of the island

Remember, there are lots of short hikes listed in HANA HIGHWAY SIGHTS, like this one at Pua'a Ka'a, and a longer, delightful hike listed under SOUTHEAST MAUI SIGHTS.

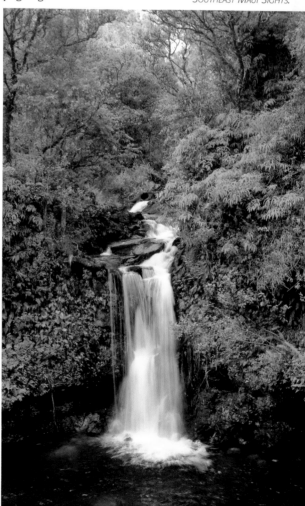

is like no other. The surroundings are so surreal that we're amazed no one has used this area in a movie yet.

About 20–30 minutes into the hike you come to the **Nakalele Blowhole**. There's a nice vantage point above and slightly upwind of the hole. (But you can still get wet when the ocean behind you occasionally explodes sea spray.) You can make your way around the lava to the bottom. Stay upwind to remain dry. See page 57 for more on the blowhole itself. Return the way you came.

Though not overly strenuous, this hike can be a windy affair, sometimes too windy. (Nakalele means *the leaning* because the wind is sometimes strong enough, especially during the summer, to lean into it.) If the wind is blowing you away and you still want to see the blowhole, see page 57 for a more direct (though less interesting) route. Wear good shoes; flip-flops are a bit too casual for this terrain.

Mushroom Rock Shore Hike

This is one of those *you're-on-your-own* hikes. Explore a wild, gorgeous shoreline, go as long as your desire takes you, then take the easy way back. The hiking is makeshift much of the way. Not much trail, just make your way, and be careful of the wind and crumbly soil and rock. It's not strenuous unless you want it to be. Like the blowhole hike, wind can sometimes be a problem here.

In West Maui 9/10 mile past the 41 mile marker on Hwy 30 there's a turnout on the ocean side. (See map on page 62.) From here, walk toward the ocean, then toward your left to a bluff overlooking the shoreline. The cliffs in front of you are striking, even for Maui. After overlooking a small islet, you'll see several discontiguous cow paths (and sometimes no paths) to your right. If you amble the right way, you'll quickly come to a cove with a shallow reef and a rusty old pole holder driven into the rock. The little

Though it looks too sculpted to be real, the upper tide-pool feeding the lower tide-pool creates a lovely setting for a cool, ocean dip.

rock sticking out is an enviable place to ponder the shoreline if you're not too afraid of heights. All is presided over by a mushroom-shaped rock to your right. By the way, the snorkeling on the downwind side of the reef below is exciting, but only when calm (which is not too often). Experts only. From here, either make your way back the way you came, or trudge up a gully-looking feature in the crumbly soil. Then make your way back to the shoreline to your right. Perhaps you'll stop at the mushroom-shaped rock before making your way around and then along the shoreline.

From here there's no real trail most of the time. You're exploring. Sometimes you're along the shore, sometimes you'll have to make your way inland around the large lava hills. The scenery is wild, raw, striking and, quite often, it's all yours. You can't really get lost since you're following the ocean, and the highway is not too far inland. You can spend from 30 minutes to several hours, depending on how far along the shore you want to go and how fast you go. But you won't soon forget this piece of shoreline. This is a delicious, secluded Maui ocean hike. The wind and spray have carved and chewed the landscape with unequaled artistry, and, with no crowds or trails, sometimes you feel like you're the only person in the world.

If you hike a mile along the shoreline (less as the crow flies), you'll come to the **Olivine Pools** described on page 60. Keep an eye out for yellow/orange stripes in the lava. These are deposits of ash from when the island was young and restless. Gigantic volcanic explosions caused the ash layers that were covered with later lava flows. Erosion now reveals what a violent volcano this was in its youth. Not far past here you'll have to ascend from the ocean and walk along the sea cliffs. Southeast of here there are areas where residents of Kahakuloa have dumped some of their garbage, the only mood spoiler. Continue as long as you want, then make your way inland to the highway and walk back to your car.

Two-Tiered Tide-Pools of Honolua

Most of the island is composed of a porous lava shoreline, making deep tide-pools a rarity. On page 60 we point out the Olivine Pools, which we discovered for our first edition. More recently, we found the heretofore unknown two-tiered tide-pools of Honolua.

The shoreline along these stretches looks somewhat artistic and exotic. It's made from a fine grain, light-colored rock and sandstone. At one area the ocean smashes against the shoreline, bathing an upper pool in a clean shower of seawater. As it fills, it overflows into the lower pool by way of a small but lovely waterfall, which is usually constant at high tide. This lower pool is attached to the ocean and the cycle is repeated. The results make a great place to take a dip and a wild, raw shoreline to explore.

These pools are best at high tide with the upper pool over 6 feet deep in places. This is not a good place to be when the ocean's raging. When 10-, 20- and even 30-foot waves tear up the shoreline, the pools would become a dangerous washing machine and you'd become a limp rag if you got near them. Use your good judgment when assessing the safety here. When smaller but still active surf prevails, it's fun to be in the lower pool as waves come charging into the cove next to (but separated by lava from) the lower pool. Wear reef shoes or, better yet, tabis so you can walk around the pools more easily. It's usually windy out here, but the lower pool is *partially* protected by some lava.

To get there, drive past Kapalua on Hwy 30, past the 34 mile marker and park at a turnout. Then walk back to the yellow gate you just passed. A publicly used road to the right parallels the private MAUI LAND AND PINEAPPLE road you see at the gate, but the first 100 yards of the publicly used road don't exist. You'll have to bushwhack that part to the right of the gate, or ask MLP if you can use their private road for a minute or so before ducking to the right to the publicly used road. You'll walk 550 yards toward the coast, through a gate and, just when the road veers left and starts to parallel the shoreline, look to the ocean. That large pool you see 100 yards away is your goal; make your way to it. Please don't pilfer any pineapples from nearby fields. MLP has been pretty cool about allowing access to areas under their domain, and we don't want to give them a reason to stop this practice.

The Waihe'e Valley hike crosses the stream on two swinging bridges.

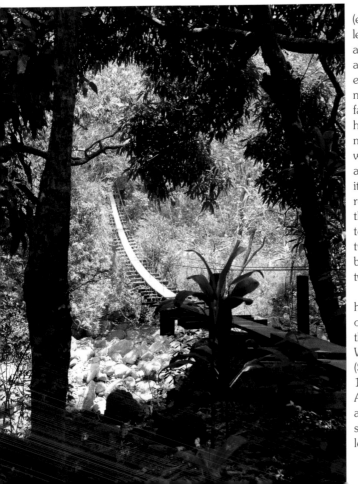

Waihe'e Valley Trail

This one's a 2-mile (each way) pretty valley hike that wanders along a dirt road, then a trail through forest, ending at a pleasing man-modified waterfall. It takes about 1½ hours each way. It's moderately strenuous with your only climbing at the beginning. Then it's fairly flat for the rest of the hike. Along the way you'll need to cross the stream twice on old swinging bridges, then cross twice without them.

To get there, you head north of Kahului on Hwy 340. Before the 5 mile marker is Waihe'e Valley Road. (See map on page 195.) Turn mauka. After ½ mile veer right at the Y and follow signs for Waihe'e Valley Plantation. At a

Waihe'e Ridge & Valley Trails

Next map on page 66

Makamaka'ole

Waihe'e Ridge Trail

Wailuku Ag land past here.

Swinging Bridges

Waihe'e Valley Trail

340

Waihe'e Valley Rd

'Ali'ele Falls

Abandoned Ditch

0   1/2 MILE

© 2008 Wizard Publications, Inc.

booth you'll be charged $6 per person to enter. The plantation land stops at the first bridge. Past that the land is owned by Wailuku Ag. and, though you'll be tempted to continue, a NO TRESPASSING sign is at the bridge. They used to grant access to *all* hikers, but after a dispute with the plantation they only extend their aloha to Maui Eco-Adventures tours. If you happened to go on their tours, this is what you can expect.

After your initial climbing (around 300 feet), the road levels and becomes prettier. This trail parallels two ditches built in the 1880s and 1905. Some of the tunnels bore through *blue rock,* a hard lava that required much more effort. Mostly Chinese immigrants worked on the ditches and tunnels, and they did it with dynamite, picks, compressed air and percussion drills. The various barricades along the way are there to prevent *vehicular* access, not hikers. Always stay on the main trail, not the sidetracks.

The trail soon becomes notched deep in the mountain, and the river's below you. Then you come to your first swinging bridge. (You may have to cross a small stream first if the water diverter is overflowing.) Use the guide wires, and walk with your knees bent to absorb your footfalls to minimize the swinging. If you're uncomfortable, the stream's probably dry here, and you can cross on its bed if you want. In a few minutes, the next bridge crosses the stream before it's diverted. A trail bypasses the bridge, but you'd have to boulder-hop.

Two more crossings (without bridges) require boulder-hopping a short distance. The beauty of the valley here is incredible. Mosquitoes are more numerous—did you bring your bug juice?

Just before the trail ends, an opening in the vegetation exposes the back of the valley with the gorgeous 2,000-foot **Mana-nole Falls** a mile away. (It looks farther.) An abandoned portion of the ditch leads you to the **'Ali'ele Falls**, modified as an abandoned diverter. (Also labeled as 'Ele'ele on some maps.) The roar of the falls can be delightfully loud. Local kids often come here on weekends or during the week in the summer. According to Hawaiian legend, you were supposed to throw a ti leaf in the water here. If it swirled around and around, you were permitted to jump. If it made a circle, then went under, then you shouldn't jump because a lizard god (called a mo'o) would seize and kill you.

Waihe'e Ridge Trail

A very pretty trail with smashing valley views and a vigorous forest to gawk at. You'll gain about 1,500 feet over the 2½ miles to the end (then return).

You'll want to do this hike early since clouds moving in later in the morning diminish the view. We like to be hiking this trail by 8 a.m. to maximize our weather chances.

From Kahului, get on Hwy 340 heading north. (See map on page 195.) At ⁹⁄₁₀ past the 6 mile marker is the road to Maluhia Boy Scout Camp. Another ⁹⁄₁₀ mile up that road is the trailhead.

The trail gets your heart pumping right away, as a cement road climbs 200 feet in short order, then the dirt path to the left ascends through a forest of guava, kukui, swamp mahogany and Cook Island pines. By ½ mile you've gained 400 feet. Shortly after, a switchback corner reveals a pretty gulch and a bench facing **Makamaka'ole Falls**. Ahead is a peak and the trail switchbacking up. Clouds often come up the gulch and down from the ridge, colliding right in front of you. (And sometimes *into* you.)

Soon you get your first incredible view of Waihe'e Valley. It's beautiful! Some paths through the grass afford closer looks. Look down and you may see the Waihe'e Valley Trail. Now the trail is along the ridge, and you're blessed with numerous commanding views (clouds permitting).

Several switchbacks and flat areas later, you'll eventually reach the end of the line—a hill called **Lani-lili** at 2,563 feet. If the clouds haven't moved in yet, the views are grand. If you've got your head in the clouds, enjoy the aural and visual silence.

Lahaina Pali

This is a trail that slips up over part of the West Maui Mountain, peaking at almost 1,600 feet. Along the way you get excellent elevated views. Unfortunately, this is a shuttle hike, with trailheads 6 miles apart (by car), a bit less by foot. Either hike to the top and return, or go one way if you've arranged transportation at the other end.

The biggest tip is to start from the Ma'alaea side in the morning. See map on page 45. You're already 200 feet up, and the sun will be at your back. The hike starts at the 5 mile marker on Hwy 30, heads toward the mountain to the left about 500 feet, then inland on a shaded trail. Enjoy the shade here because there won't be much more. As the trail gets progressively steeper, you'll start to get expansive views of Maui.

After climbing to the top, your vantage point changes as you descend to the other trailhead at Hwy 30's 11 mile marker. The ocean and offshore island views create an exotic landscape. Bring lots of water because you'll be exposed to the sun most of the time.

UPCOUNTRY & HALEAKALA HIKES
Haleakala Crater

There are 27 miles of trails inside Haleakala Crater, and the views from inside are incredible. The catch is that you need to descend 2,400 feet (and, of course, *ascend* on your return) down **Sliding Sands Trail** over a 3⁸⁄₁₀ mile span (each way) to get to the bottom. You can get to the bottom via **Hale-mau'u Trail** (which is only 1,400 feet down and 4 miles each way), but that trail, though beautiful, is more vulnerable to bad weather. If you want to hike many of the trails at the bottom, you'll need to camp inside. (See CAMPING.) Sliding Sands itself is incredibly scenic, even if you choose not to go all the way to the bottom. Consider just wandering down until just before you start to worry about the ascent. If you want a longer Haleakala hike, one of the best hikes on the island, see ADVENTURES on page 244.

At the far end of the crater is the **Kaupo Trail**, which descends all the way down the mountain. You'll only access it if you're camping. Though it's easy to look at a map and think that an all-downhill trail might be easy, don't be fooled. The footing in many places is slippery with soft dirt and loose rocks, and it can be steep. The constant downhill can put enormous strains on knees and other things you didn't think of—like your toenails. If your shoes don't fit right, you may find that the unrelenting tapping will cause you to lose them. (Trust me. Been there. Done that.)

Polipoli State Park

An example of the varied nature of the island, this is a hike through a redwood forest. Here? On Maui? Yup. Back in the 1920s and '30s the state and the Civilian Conservation Corps undertook a reforestation program in this area that had been destroyed by cattle. They planted redwood, sugi, cedar and many other types of trees (though these are not native to Hawai'i). The trees have since flourished.

Getting there is part of the fun—if you like narrow, winding roads. See map on page 115. From Kahului on Hwy 36, take 37 to the *second* 37/377 intersection (near the 14 mile marker on 37), and take 377 north for ⅓ mile or so then turn right on Waipoli Road. From here you'll have 6 miles of a winding paved road that offers smashing views of all of West Maui and the valley between the two great volcanoes. Believe the signs that tell you to watch for mindless cattle on the road. You'll even pass through an open gate with a cattle guard. After 6 miles (it'll seem longer), the road becomes unpaved. This last 4 miles is bumpy but *usually* driveable in regular cars despite the sign that says 4WD ONLY.

A forest of redwoods is the last thing you expect to find in the tropics, but Upcountry's Polipoli Park is one of Maui's surprises.

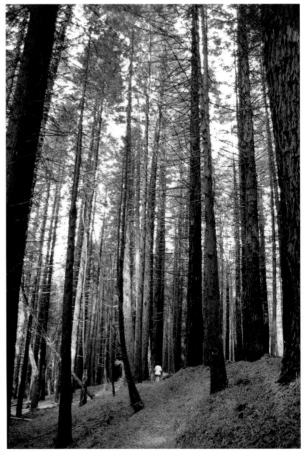

Once at the parking lot (you took the right fork near the end) you'll want to walk back up the road for 100 feet or so to the start of the **Redwood Trail**. After a couple of minutes you'll pass to the right of a cabin and begin your descent into forest. The area looks much more like Northern California than Hawai'i, and the coolness of the air at 6,000 feet is a refreshing change. The descent is fairly gentle and constant. Be aware of tree roots in the trail that may try to trip you. About 25 minutes into the hike you come to the large redwoods. Some of the redwood trees are around 100 feet tall and dead-on straight with trunks up to 6 feet in diameter. Pretty impressive growth in so short a time. When the Redwood Trail ends at 1⁷⁄₁₀ mile, either retrace your steps or take the **Plum Trail** and make it a 5-mile loop hike. (This is preferred.) A trail map to Polipoli is on page 238.

Assuming you make it a loop, the Plum Trail somewhat gently regains most of the 1,000 feet you lost on the Redwood Trail. When Plum Trail meets **Haleakala Ridge Trail**, take the left turn. (Plum is not well defined after it meets Haleakala, so don't follow it.) A ½ mile into Haleakala Ridge there's a sign saying, POLIPOLI PARK 1 MILE. Look for the short spur trail there, and then take the right fork. It leads to a smashing and very expansive view all the way down the mountain to the shoreline. Weather permitting, you'll see three of the Big Island's volcanoes—Mauna Kea (nearly 14,000 feet high), Kohala in front of it and Mauna Loa to the right. Up till now you probably haven't had any wind on this hike, protected by the ridge from the normal trade winds. But here on the ridge the wind can be howling. Back on the spur trail, the other fork leads to a cave.

Back on the Haleakala Ridge Trail, in another half mile is a confusing intersection. Take the left fork to go back to your car.

This trail is very nice when the weather is good, but dark when it gets really cloudy. Go early in the morning for the best conditions. It takes most people 3–4 hours to complete the loop, and it's moderately strenuous. Despite what you might hear, this trail is not open to mountain bikes.

Lava arches are common along the coast of the Wai'anapanapa hike.

HIKES DESCRIBED ELSEWHERE

Short and not-so-short trails are described in other parts of the book for several reasons, either because of their remoteness, adventurousness or shortness. They include **Punalau Falls** on page 82, the marvelous **Wailua Iki** on page 86 and **Upper Pua'a Ka'a Falls** on page 87, the **Red Sand Beach** on page 94, **Venus Pool** on page 101, the **Pipiwai Trail** with the waterfalls, including the **Infinity Pool** on page 106 and **Alelele Falls** on page 110. The ADVENTURES chapter starting on page 233 has the **La Pérouse Bay Lava/Snorkel/Hike**, the **Four Falls of Na'ili'ili-haele**, **Mountain Bike Haleakala's Spine** (which you can also hike), a **hike to the heart of an eruption**, a **hike in a lava tube**, and the **Haleakala Crater Grand Loop**. And West Maui has the **Olivine Pools** on page 60 and **'Iao Valley** on page 67. There's also the short trail around **Kealia Pond** on page 128.

OTHER EAST MAUI HIKES

In addition to the hikes mentioned above, there are a few other East Maui hikes worth noting.

Wai'anapanapa Coast Hike

One of the nicer coastal lava hikes you'll find. It displays the raw coastline, backed first by palm and hala trees, then showcases the most recent lava flow in the Hana area that created the black sand beach. Though there's no big climbing, the second portion of the trail is somewhat undulating, so you have lots of little climbs, and the latter footing is awkward. This hike can last anywhere from 30 minutes to 4 hours, depending on your thirst for scenery.

You start at Wai'anapanapa State Park near Hana (see page 90 for directions). Park to the right of the main beach, walk to the shoreline, and head right along the shore. Soon a low-hanging sea arch and a blowhole (that only blows during monster surf) indicate the kind of scenery you'll see. (Don't get too close to the tapered blowhole; it's a one-way trip down.)

About 10 minutes into the hike, at an area marked by some offshore rocks and a couple of arches, stop and listen for a hissing sound. The ocean's waves are undercutting the lava here in some places, and when the tide is right, waves will force air up through a tiny hole and you can actually hear and feel the ocean breathing. (Get too close, and you'll feel it spitting, too.)

The colors are very vivid as you walk along. The raw, black coastline smashed by white frothing water next to impossibly blue ocean all backed by lush, green palm trees makes a delicious meal for your camera. Soon you'll pass an enormous grove of hala trees, noted for their cage-like roots. Some locals cynically call them tourist pineapples, as their fruit does look similar. (Real pineapples grow on bushes, not trees.)

Angry seas can make this hike even more dramatic. The water is so clean and clear, and it's exhilarating to see large waves punish the shoreline here. At one point, the trail passes a natural split in the land. The lava bridge keeps you from falling in. A little farther the trail has a big step down; it's preferable to a vague trail going around.

In about 30 or so minutes you come to meager remains of a small heiau (temple). Nobody knows what it was used for. The trail gets vague for a minute, but should become clearer shortly after. Ahus (small piles of rock) help mark the trail. The footing has been pretty good up till now, but from here it becomes harsher and clumsier. Hiking shoes or boots can be helpful, as can a walking stick. You'll be walking on young (500-year-old) lava that created the black sand beach as lava shattered on contact with the sea and the new sand drifted into the bay.

Watch for columnar lava. These (usually) six-sided lava columns are at the shoreline in several places. They form when a lava pond cools, shrinks and cracks. The cracks work their way lower and lower as the rock cools, so the lava literally pulls itself apart. When you pass a community fishing shack (everyone pitches in to keep it up), it's 2 miles to Hana Bay. The prettiest part of the trail is behind you. Large red ants seem to be making a good living off the stark lava here. Keep walking until you're halfway to being tired, or you get to Hana Bay, whichever comes first, then turn around. It's about 7 miles (round trip) to Hana Bay, if you go that far. Make sure you bring water; lava fields make you thirsty.

Waikamoi Nature Trail

Between the 9 and 10 mile markers on the Hana Highway. Two nature loops, one about 10 minutes, the other about 30 minutes make a pleasant diversion on the Hana Highway drive if you need to stretch your legs a bit, but it's not worth driving out there just for this. This hike is good for families, and you gain, at most, 200 feet.

If you start from the left-most trail and work your way up the gradual incline, there are a few concrete benches scattered along the way. Sometimes there are nice views of the highway beneath you and the valley beyond. Patches of bamboo interrupt the hala, strawberry guava and huge, towering eucalyptus forest. At the intersection, either take a

right (back to your car for the 10 minute hike) or left for the longer one. The latter eventually leads to a picnic area with BBQ. The sign there says END OF TRAIL, though, in fact, the path continues. When it forks, take a left and walk a few minutes, and it leads down to a stream and dam. The view is nice there despite the lack of water flowing over the cliff.

Back at the picnic area, on your way down to your car on a 4WD road, if you veer to the left, it leads to a small reservoir. Otherwise, continue back to your car.

Wahinepe'e

This hike takes you up a hunters' road, through a bamboo forest and then links up with a road paralleling one of EMI's diversion ditches. During the first part you'll be climbing constantly, gaining about 250 feet. Note the density of the bamboo around you.

You start at the dirt road 2/10 mile past the 10 mile marker on Hwy 360 (Hana Hwy). Once at the top (about ¼ mile), take a left, and the road will pass 2 small waterfalls. The payoff for this hike isn't a single tongue-wagging view or falls, but rather a nice trek through a healthy forest of eucalyptus, koa and many other species, many draped with vines. About ½ mile into the ditch road, you come to an intersection. If you go right at this and every other intersection, it will bring you to the upper road. Straddling the upper road, the forest is even healthier and prettier up here at 1,200 feet. Take the road as long as your interest holds out, then retrace your steps by taking lefts at the intersections. Make mental notes where the intersections were; there are more than the map shows. We had a tough time mapping this area, even from the air. This hike is anywhere from 20 minutes to 6 hours, depending on how far you go. If you go all the way to the upper road, you gain 1,000 feet. It's a nice forest trek. As for access, this is a reserve, but EMI has the water rights. See page 75 for more on that.

SOUTH MAUI HIKES

Certainly not a hotbed of good hiking, but there are two that stand out. One is to the heart of on eruption in ADVENTURES. The other is below.

Keawanaku Beach

How about a hike along a lava trail that leads to a black and white sand beach that is usually deserted and was unnamed until this publication? From the end of the road in south Maui, where most cars park at La Pérouse Bay, a 4WD road (blocked by a gate but with a pedestrian pass-through) leads southeast for ⅔ mile, passing numerous small coves. When the road opens up to a relatively new lava flow (approximately 500 years old), you turn to the left, go through a wire fence, and the trail (now called the Hoapili Trail or

Some hikes require luscious treks through bamboo forests.

Kings Highway) shortcuts inland for a while, crossing Cape Hanamanioa. See map on page 135. This part of the 6-foot-wide trail was made in the early 1800s and was probably used to transport cattle across the harsh lava. As you walk this part of the trail, keep this in mind: The ancient Hawaiians crossed these types of trails *barefoot*. In fact, they often had to run through the sharp lava during battle, where there were no trails at all. But for the rest of us tenderfoots, we recommend hiking boots to protect the ankles. The footing on the Hoapili Trail is made of mostly fist-sized chunks of lava and is obnoxious.

An ancient phrase associated with this area is "the cloudless rain of Honuaula." Many a time we've hiked in this area and felt rain, though no cloud was even remotely nearby (due to the strong winds along the flank and the rain clouds up the mountain).

Just over a mile into the lava field trail you'll see lots of vegetation at the shoreline (700 feet away). A spur trail leading there starts at a small lava rock wall just to the right of the main trail. The main part of the spur trail leads to Keawanaku Beach. (Other vague trails leading off the spur trail are avoidable.) This area has several structures, including the remains of a Hawaiian heiau (religious site).

Normal trade winds build up along the southern flank of Haleakala and often howl along this part of the island. The beach itself is normally protected from these trade winds. We've hiked to this beach during unusually strong trade winds, when gusts exceeded 50 mph and the ocean was an ugly mess of whitecaps, only to find the bay at Keawanaku calm, windless and protected. (During less common Kona winds from the south, it would be a different story.) The snorkeling off to the left (east) of the bay is exceptional along the 10–20 foot lava wall, covered with coral and loaded with fish. The bay is usually (but not always) protected from much of the surf, and the water is beautiful and clear. The natural protective wall extends farther than it looks from the shore, bending around to the left and extending farther. The right side has several caves that you can explore if there's no surge or surf. (Surge would bounce you around in there.)

This beach is a jewel set amid the unforgiving lava, mostly black sand with white and a touch of green sand. (The latter comes from a semiprecious gem called olivine.) There are some beach boulders near the shoreline, but a generous repository of sand offshore *usually* keeps the shoreline relatively sandy, except after severe storms, which can temporarily move the sand offshore, usually during the summer. The area (and a nearby point) was called Keawanaku and some old-time Hawaiians used the name for the beach, but it is not listed in any of the old literature as having that name. (Perhaps because the flow is relatively recent and the beach so new, the Hawaiians never named it.) Nonetheless, we have deferred to the old-timers and called it Keawanaku Beach. (By the way, don't try camping here. At night the beach is *teeming* with cockroaches.)

Ten minutes farther along the Hoapili Trail is tiny Wawaloa Cove. Snorkeling there is not as good, and the currents are tricky. Just past Wawaloa are some excellent ruins, worth taking a look.

HORSEBACK RIDING

If you want to see the countryside but don't want to walk it yourself, you need your very own beast of burden. (I always loved that phrase.) Maui has lots of horseback rides, from forest to plains to lava fields to the inside of a crater. Some are awesome; some are a snore. Picking one depends on what you want to see.

Pony Express (667–2200) is our hands-down favorite. They go down Sliding Sands Trail to the bottom of Haleakala Crater. The views are unlike anything you've ever seen and positively drop-dead gorgeous. This is a *great* trip. They only take 8 people per day, so it's a good idea to book as far in advance as possible—3 weeks during busy times, 2 weeks during slow times. Call even earlier from the mainland to ensure your spot.

Since they want you near the summit of Haleakala at 9:30 a.m. (though they leave later), you might want to come up for the sunrise, then check out some of the short trails and overlooks before meeting them.

The ride is a single file, nose-to-tail affair, and you'll probably only trot a little coming up. But the way the unspeakably beautiful crater changes and unfolds effortlessly as you descend the trail will stay with you for a lifetime. Distances look huge as you descend the 3⁸⁄₁₀ miles to the floor 2,400 feet below. The air is usually crystal clear inside, almost like there's no air at all. Once at the bottom, you have lunch at a trail junction. Croissant sandwiches never tasted so delicious than when you've had them in the crater. There are some bees around, attracted to the horse droppings, but few people seemed to mind. On the way back up, you see the crater from the other direction. How is it that it can still enrapture someone after several hours?

The trail can be pretty dusty, and the sun is strong up here. Expect to pass envious hikers on the way back up. Wear a long-sleeved shirt, a jacket and a hat. Cheap gloves are also advisable since you can burn the back of your hands while holding the reins. Weather is usually good in the crater and winds far less than up above. Most of the rain here comes in the winter. There's no restroom at the bottom. At $182 for the 4-hour trip it may sound pricey, but the quality of the trip is unmatched. We've reviewed lots of horseback rides throughout the state, and we'd be hard-pressed to think of one we enjoyed more. They also have cheaper rides at their ranch, but the views can't compare.

Haleakala on Horseback (871–0990) has similar rides for similar prices, but we aren't as impressed with them.

Other Buckaroos

Mendes Ranch (871–5222) has a pretty nice ride on their beautiful ranch in West Maui. It's about 2 hours of riding followed by a BBQ lunch (for an extra

The first time we ever climbed 2,400 feet back up out of Haleakala Crater, we didn't even break a sweat. Of course, we had help.

$20) back at the stables. They ride up to a spectacular overlook of Waiheʻe Valley, then head to the ocean for more good views. It's a nose-to-tail ride (on sad and tired-looking horses) with only two *very* short runs allowed. (But hey, running is hard to come by on Maui rides.) Guides range from helpful and friendly to aloof. In all, a good trip for $115. Our only complaint is that they make outrageous and false claims to get you in, and it's really not necessary. For instance, their brochure says (and has for *years)* that you'll "gaze down into Eki Crater to view some of Maui's largest waterfalls." Well, *Eke* Crater is at 4,400 feet elevation, near the center of West Maui. Wow, what a view that would be! On the phone they say you'll ride up to 3,000 feet. Hmm, still pretty awesome. The guide says you'll make it to 2,000 feet. The reality? You go to *1,000* feet. C'mon, guys, just be accurate. The ride is good enough without the inflated claims. On Hwy 340 at 7 mile marker.

Makena Stables (879–0244) is in South Maui on the expansive Ulu-palakua Ranch. The small scale of this stable translates into very well cared for horses, good equipment and personal-ized attention. They seem proud and protective of their horses. The opposite of lush, this ride goes through kiawe (mesquite) groves and lava fields up to Kalua o Lapa Crater. Enjoy the nice views of Kahoʻolawe Island, La Pérouse Bay, ʻAhihi-Kinau and the lava flow from this intensely windy 500-foot ele-vation. Ride back down through shaded stretches of the King's Highway to the bay. The 2½-hour morning ride is $145; the sunset trip which goes a lit-tle longer is $170. Sincere, dedicated guides, but on our ride they were short on snacks and long on local politics. As

far as sunset rides go, this one has great views.

Lahaina Stables (667–2222) in West Maui is our least favorite due to the drab trailside scenery and destination. A thatched picnic hut beside a manmade reservoir provides the only shade you'll find on this ride, and views of the off-shore islands are their best asset. The guides do their best to make up for the unwelcoming trailside scenery. 2-hour morning ride for $110, $135 for the 2½-hour late morning ride gets you a modest deli lunch. The $120 sunset ride includes a snack. Higher maximum weight limit than many others.

Also in West Maui, **Ironwood Ranch** (669–4991) is a tidy stable and, al-though the greeter may be short on social graces, they are long on safety and use the info you give in a survey about your skills to match you up with one of their celebrity-named horses. The trail goes through some boring pineap-ple fields but is punctuated by ironwood groves and the Maile Pai Valley where you'll find ferns, dry creek beds and some nice rock outcroppings. You emerge from the valley onto the upper reaches of the plantation, providing grand views of offshore islands and the West Maui Mountains to your back. The contrasts are particularly nice at sunset. 1½-hour morning ride is $90; 2-hour morning or sunset rides are $120.

Upcountry there's **Piʻiholo Ranch** (357–5544) in Makawao. You drive up and away from the coastal plains into a cool eucalyptus forest, then arrive at their posh ranch center. Although this spread has a showy rodeo air, trail rides aren't second class status here. Their work shows in nicely laid trails and eager horses. On the trail, meander through forested valleys and wind-swept pasture lands. The climax of the ride (hold your hat) is the ascent to windy Pi'iholo Hill with 360-degree views. The elevation allows you to escape the extreme weather conditions that can accompany rides at lower and higher elevations, making it a particularly good choice for a midday ride. 2-hour morning and afternoon rides are $120. A 3½-hour picnic ride is $160.

Jet Skiing

Call them Jet Skis, Wave Runners (which are brand names) or personal watercraft—whatever your name for them, these motorcycles of the sea can be rented near Lahaina from **Pacific Jet Sports** (667–2066) from mid-May to mid-December. (They have to close during whale season.) Their attitude is kind of snotty, but you don't care much while you're riding. They use fairly powerful Yamahas and pretty much give you free rein in their circular course. That's good because it gives you more freedom…but it also leaves you free to hurt yourself. If you've never ridden before, these animals are a scream (literally for many riders).

Early morning is usually very smooth, late afternoon choppy. Late morning seems a good balance to give the water some texture. They offer ½ hour for $60, full hour $95. The half hour will tucker out most people, especially if you're like me and you drive it like it's stolen. Spend the extra few bucks for the goggles and experiment with different ways to hold your feet while you sit. Despite their brochure's claims, you're actually given little instruction, so be careful. Go fast enough during bumpy seas and turns will be like a controlled crash, so don't

turn too fast unless you know what you're doing. Extra riders are allowed for $15, but we recommend one person per craft. Doubling up seems to increase the risk of the passenger falling off, from what we observed. Some people seem to feel that these craft are hazardous to the ocean; others say modern jet skis are no different than regular boats. We honestly don't know which is the case; we're just saying what it's like to rent one. They meet off Canoe (Hanaka'o'o) Beach.

Kayaks are a fun way to see the coastline. None of Maui's rivers are fit for kayaking, but the shoreline offers lots to explore. The best areas are those that you can't reach by land without difficulty. One of the best trips is to the heretofore unnamed **Keawanaku Beach**, but it's a little tricky and is described in ADVENTURES on page 246.

Other areas to kayak are south of Olowalu in West Maui starting at Papalaua Wayside Park between the 11 and 12 mile markers. Paddle southeast along the pretty shoreline below the highway, staying close to land to keep winds from making your life more difficult. Most put in at the 14 mile marker, but it's much less interesting there.

If you can arrange it, in the afternoon it's nice to put in at Kihei and let the wind help you go down the coast, then come out at Makena Landing. Kihei winds tend to blow from north to south along the coast; West Maui winds tend to go from nothing to blowing offshore, which is more dangerous.

Also consider the coastline south of Big Beach at ʻAhihi Cove heading south. You can go around Cape Kinaʻu to Fishbowl, Aquarium and on into La Pérouse Bay, but be watchful of winds, especially in the afternoon.

Some companies put in at Makena Landing because it's so easy to launch. The kayaking from there is fairly good, though not great.

Winds will be your biggest factor. Don't let a breeze help you down a shoreline if you have to paddle back against it. Unless you've arranged for pickup, better to paddle in less breezy areas. The ocean can go from calm and light winds to wavy with strong winds over a span of about 100 feet. White-caps on the water are caused by wind, and it's easy to drift from a protected area to an exposed area. Stay alert.

Many of the big resorts rent kayaks by the hour for confiscatory amounts. At press time the state was in the middle of a permit crackdown, and many of the companies that rent kayaks had been driven out of business. We weren't able to find any reliable non-resort sources for renting kayaks in West Maui. In South Maui **South Pacific Kayaks** (875–4848) has singles for $40 and doubles for $60 at Makena Landing before noon. **Big Kahuna Adventures** (875–6395) in Kihei has singles for $40, doubles for $60.

For guided tours consider **Maui Eco Tours** (891–2223), **Maui Kayaks** (874–4000) and **South Pacific**.

In Hana, **Hana-Maui Sea Sports** (248–7711 or 264–9566) has short, kayak/snorkel trips at Hana Bay for $89.

KITEBOARDING
See WINDSURFING, page 231.

There are several companies that provide various types of land tours. Some are better than others. **Temptation Tours** (877–8888) does van tours of the Hana Coast for around $187. Though we recommend that you drive this yourself, if the winding road bothers you, this tour is better than not seeing the Hana Highway at all. Don't believe everything you hear, however. We've heard some *breathtakingly* bad information from them. We once had one of their drivers (not knowing who we were, of course) upon seeing a copy of this book tell us that "the authors of *Maui Revealed* have had their houses burned and their cars torched for revealing too many secret places on the island" and that the state of Hawaiʻi was "banning the book." Obviously, none of that's true, and we could only conclude that they simply make this stuff up as they go along.

Lahaina Kaʻanapali Railroad (661–0080) is listed as one of the "must-dos" in much of the free literature strewn about the island, but we can't help wonder if they've actually done it. Picture a slow-moving train that chugs through abandoned sugar cane fields, along a golf course and through a residential area. Dull, pointless and overpriced. Some kids may like it, but adults should blow their money elsewhere. In Lahaina. $22 for adults, $15 for kids.

Molokini is where you'll find the best water visibility in all Maui. Dive boats use the submerged corner and snorkel boats explore the inside.

Ocean Tours

This is probably the single biggest activity that people pay to do on Maui, and for good reason. The calm, clear waters make it a boater's heaven. Maui's boating conditions are superb due to the shape of its coastline, and it has close island neighbors to visit.

In some ways, this is one of the most difficult sections to write about. The section's length is a testament to your varied options. *So* many choices and fleeting characteristics make it dizzying. We may take a boat tour and rave about it, but the day after we go to press, the boating company may sell their 50-foot sailing yacht and begin taking passengers out on an inflatable raft from Wal-Mart. It's hard to keep up.

Most of the boats leave from Lahaina or Ma'alaea (close to Kihei). A few boats leave from the Kihei Boat Ramp and Ka'anapali Beach.

Boating trips can generally be broken down into four types:

Snorkel Trips
Pure Sailing Trips
Whale Watching *mid-Dec.–mid-May*
Dinner Cruises

Many of the snorkel trips *claim* they also whale watch, but that is mainly composed of making a beeline to their snorkeling spot and hoping to spot one of the buggers. That's like calling them fishing boats because they drag a lure behind them on their way to Molokini.

We need to clarify something up front. Taking a boat trip on Maui is like making a dessert with chocolate, ice cream and peanut butter. No matter how you combine the ingredients, you're gonna end up with something sweet and tasty. (See, *that's* what I get for writing while hungry.) The boater's ingredients are the boat, sun, water and fish. Unless the weather is horrible, even if you're boating with complete idiots, odds are you're still going to have a fun, relaxing time, because boating Maui's often-placid waters can't be beat. Since not all boating companies are created equal, our job is to steer you to the ones who seem to do the best job (and away from the idiots). We've anonymously ridden scads of boats off Maui, and the difference is striking. But remember as you read these critiques: Even bad boat trips are usually fun.

We've noticed that there seem to be two types of crews: Those composed of cocky guys and gals who spend all their time and energy showing their crewmates and you how impossibly cool they are. (The old *don't you wish you were as cool as me* syndrome.) Then there are crews who channel more of their effort to help ensure *you* have a good time. We obviously lean toward the latter.

SNORKEL TRIPS
Where They Go

Most boats go to two locations. Ma'alaea departures usually do their first stop at Molokini and the second at **Turtle Town**. *Where is Turtle Town?* you may ask. The answer seems to be, *Wherever they say it is.* Different companies take people to different "Turtle Towns," and it seems to be more of a marketing gimmick. (After all, doesn't the name *sound* intriguing?) For instance, a boat might call the area off Keawakapu "Turtle Town." Well, the snorkeling there is pretty boring, and you're not likely to see many turtles. Another "Turtle Town" (one of the better ones) is off the Maui Prince. One is near Ma'alaea. There are two near Po'olenalena, etc. Despite the picture the salemen paint of waters swarming with turtles, the odds are probably 50–50 that you'll actually see one. Don't go with the *expectation* that you'll swim with turtles. If you do, great. Otherwise, just enjoy the water,

Boat	Phone	Max. Passengers	Type of Boat	Departs	Wet Suits	Snorkel Stops	Rest Rooms	Food
Alii Nui	875-9259	36	60' Sailing Cat	Ma'alaea	Yes	1	Yes	BBC
America II	667-2133	24	40' Racing Yacht	Lahaina Sailing Trip				
Blue Water	879-7238	24	27' & 30' Raft-like	Kihei	No	1–4	No	De
Cinderella	244-0009	6	50' Sailing Sloop	Ma'alaea Sailing Trip				
Four Winds II	879-8188	130	55' Sailing Cat	Ma'alaea	Yes	1	Yes	BBC
Hawaiian Sail Canoe	280-9301	6	Sailing Canoe	Wailea	No	1	No	None
Kai Kanani II	879-7218	90	65' Sailing Cat	Maui Prince	No	2	Yes	De
Kapalua Kai	667-5980	49	53' Sailing Cat	Ka'anapali	Yes	1	Yes	De
Lahaina Princess	667-6165	149	65' Power Boat	Lahaina	No	2	Yes	BBC
Lani Kai	244-1979	70	53' Power Cat	Ma'alaea	Yes	2	Yes	De
Mahana Na'ia	871-8636	68	58' Sailing Cat	Ma'alaea	Yes	2	Yes	BBC
Ocean Riders	661-3586	18	28' Rigid Hull Raft	Lahaina	No	3	No	De
Pacific Whale	249-8811	Lots	Power Cats	Ma' & Lah	Some	2	Yes	BBC
Paragon	244-2087	38/24	47' Sailing Cat	Ma' & Lah	Yes	2	Yes	De
Pride of Maui	242-0955	140	65' Power Cat	Ma'alaea	Yes	2	Yes	BBC
Prince Kuhio	242-8777	149	92' Power Boat	Ma'alaea	Yes	2	Yes	De
Quicksilver	661-3333	105	55' Power Cat	Ma'alaea	Yes	2	Yes	BBC
Scotch Mist	661-0386	25	50' Sailing Sloop	Lahaina Sailing Trip				
Seafire	879-2201	22	25' Raft-like	Kihei	Yes	2	No	Barel
Trilogy I-VI	874-5649	Lots	Sailing Cats	Everywhere	No	2	Yes	Deli/BBC

coral and fish. Visibility will seem merely fair, but that's only because you probably just got spoiled for life at Molokini on the first stop. People who would have been *thrilled* with 80-foot visibility before, suddenly sniff indignantly because it's not 180 feet like Molokini on a good day. By the way, some are now using the name *Turtle Arches*, which sounds even better, doesn't it?

Molokini is 3 miles off Maui's coast and 10 miles from Ma'alaea Harbor. It's one of the most widely known snorkel and diving spots in Hawai'i. (See photo on page 207.) It's a sunken crater that is now a marine sanctuary. The floor is well coated with colorful coral. It's illegal to feed the fish here, though you'll quickly realize by their behavior that these little beggars *are* hand fed. (We've even seen boat personnel feeding them after telling passengers not to.) There's no need for you to do it; fish *assume* you will. The fish count inside isn't as great as other places on Maui, but it's still high, and with the incredibly clear visibility (usually 120–180 feet), it's a good place to snorkel. The bottom topography isn't overly interesting, just a gently sloping floor. We've repeatedly snorkeled the entire crater, and the best snorkeling is usually on the inside left (from the outside looking in—the side closest to Maui). Boats that park elsewhere usually tell you *they* park in the best spot, but they're wrong. (SCUBA diving is a different matter.) The inside right is second best, with the center the least interesting. (That's relative; the center still has lots of coral and fish.) Don't stay in one place; swim over near the shore for more coral, then to deeper water for more fish. During normal trade winds, the center/left (between the Prince Kuhio and Pacific Whale Foundation boats) is where winds may deposit any fine floating debris

and sometimes cloudy water, so it's best to avoid that part. It's *usually,* though not always, reasonably calm inside.

Molokini's biggest problem is its popularity. On a given day over 1,000 snorkelers may visit the crater—sometimes twice that many. Each boat moors in a certain spot, and you are asked to stay close to your boat. If you're in a less interesting part of the crater, you may need to swim through a sea of other snorkelers and violate the boat rules to get to a better part. But stay inside the crater and away from the far edges, especially the far right side (as you're looking inside) where the crater wall is submerged. Currents there can be bad.

Probably the best advice we can give about Molokini is to discard any preconceptions. So much has been written and said, so many exaggerated paintings exist, so many doctored photos, that people get a certain picture in their mind of what to expect. Best to go in with a blank slate, and you'll probably leave full of wonder.

If you take a boat from Lahaina, you usually stop at **Coral Gardens**. There's more than one, but one is offshore of the 14 mile marker. It offers lots of beautiful coral and decent, though not stellar, visibility. (But better visibility than shore-bound snorkelers will find.) Another Coral Gardens is below the Hwy 30 tunnel.

Lana'i is also a popular day destination. It can offer good snorkeling, but boats often go to a comparatively dull area called Shark Fin Cove, sometimes called Lighthouse Cove, instead of more exciting areas elsewhere. (This cove is a convenient place to park big boats.) Also, though the cause is debated, it's undeniable that the water quality around Lana'i has suffered in the past few years. We've seen heavy rainstorms muck up the water all around the island, and the effects can last well over six months. So, while Lana'i *can* be good, it's not guaranteed.

A Few Tips

Some companies, like Pacific Whale Foundation, can be real stingy with the food. After your first snorkel you're apt to be pretty hungry and may not be offered any food. Consider bringing your own stash of snacks with you. You may be able to sell them to other hungry customers at prices confiscatory enough to pay for your trip. *(I have a bid of $8 for a chocolate chip cookie. Do I hear $9?)*

Another consideration is warmth. Though the water temps range from 75° to 80°, you may want to consider renting a thin wetsuit from a dive shop to keep you snug. The second snorkel site tends to chill people, especially in the winter. (February has the coldest water.) Of course, boats that rent wetsuits tend to *under*-report the temperature about 5°–10° to convince you to rent.

Catamarans are twin-hulled and slice through the water much more cleanly than single-hull boats and, if wide enough, are more stable (less rocking) on the water.

If you're uncomfortable using the boat's snorkel gear (either for sanitary or fitting reasons), consider renting it elsewhere and bringing it along. Most boats have only one size mask. Also, when you defog your mask (using either dedicated goo or your own spit), rub it hard into the inside glass then rinse quickly.

If you want a towel, you'll probably have to bring your own.

Small, white tip reef sharks, which are essentially harmless, are sometimes seen at Molokini. *Don't worry* about them. Worry about getting sunburned.

Below deck is a bad place to be if you're worried about getting seasick.

Without a reference point, you're much more likely to let 'er rip down there. If you *tied one on* the night before, do yourself a favor and take Dramamine, Bonine or apply Scopolamine patches *before* you go. Ginger is also a very good preventative and treatment for seasickness.

People come off these trips *toasted,* especially in the summer. Make *sure* you slather on the sunscreen, or you'll be sorry for the rest of your trip.

Morning snorkel trips nearly always offer better snorkeling and calmer seas. The only upside for **afternoon snorkel trips** is price. The only time we recommend windier afternoon trips is when you only want to sail.

Allow enough time to find a **parking** spot. At Ma'alaea they can fill up if your boat isn't one of the first to leave, and you'll have to park at the aquarium, where some boats use buses to drive you back to the harbor. In Lahaina, the Mala Ramp can also tax parkers' patience. For Lahaina Harbor, consider the lot near Prison Street.

Don't take any inflatable raft trips out of Ma'alaea. Too much bumpy travel time across windy Ma'alaea Bay. Only go from the Kihei Boat Ramp and Lahaina. Inflatables from Lahaina to Lana'i are bumpy, too.

SNUBA (page 226) is often available. Inside Molokini Crater it's harder to justify the extra $45 or so as you really won't see much more than the snorkelers see a few feet above, but it's kind of fun. (Other locations make more sense for SNUBA.)

BEST SNORKEL BOATS OF THE BUNCH

Probably the best of the *big* boats is **Four Winds II** (879–8188). This is a 55-foot power catamaran that makes morning treks to Molokini. Though they take up to 130 people, the boat is nicely designed to accommodate many without feeling as crowded as some of the others. There's a good mix of sun and shade, and the upper deck perimeter bench seats allow you to spin around and face the water while resting on the railing—a nice touch. Their usual mooring spot at Molokini usually has clear water, though fish counts might be better elsewhere. Their food setup is also the best of the lot. All the BBQ burgers, chicken, hot dogs and veggie burgers you want are waiting for you when you get out of the water. Open bar (beer and wine only) longer than any of the others. One negative aspect—they don't go to a second site—can be a positive in that they spend more time at the crater, making it feel more leisurely. (Their second "turtle town stop" is where they stop just outside the harbor on the way back and point out turtles. In fairness, it *is* a good place to spot them—you just won't swim with them.) Our only real gripe is their unrelenting sales pitches throughout your voyage. All boat operators want to sell you T-shirts and DVDs, but these guys carry it to a level that starts to get annoying. All in all, however, Four Winds is a winner. Morning Molokini is $89, afternoon trip to Coral Gardens or occasionally Molokini is $42. SNUBA, Rx masks, underwater camera and wetsuits available for extra. Their hefty see-through seaboards are *very* nice for timid kids and adults. The "glass bottom" on the boat itself works well for kids, but adults might not be too impressed. Fresh-water hose shower on board, and there's a slide into the water.

Their other boat, **Maui Magic** is a very different product, and we're not as fond of it as we are the Four Winds II. The boat's older, less comfortable and feels more crowded. It's essentially a barge of cramped benches with almost no shade. Though they head down the interesting Kanaio Coast first, they stay so far from shore that you won't appreciate much detail. The boat doesn't handle swells well, either. Their second stop is at Molokini. $99. In short, stick with the Four Winds II.

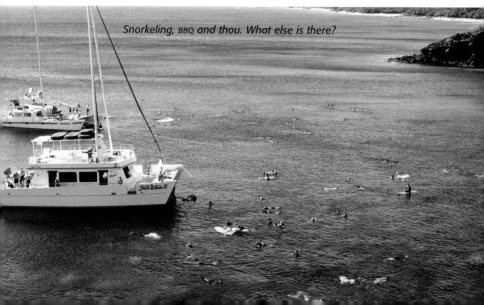

Snorkeling, BBQ and thou. What else is there?

The best big boat in *West* Maui is **Kapalua Kai** (667–5980). The crews are particularly laid back, and the boat's comfortable (though they don't have a shower). Try to snag one of the mats on the trampoline (an inside one), though you still may get wet at times. They have a deli lunch; cocktails and beer are included. They leave right from Ka'anapali Beach and go to either Honolua Bay or Olowalu for $97. They also have another boat, the **Shangrila**, though it's mainly used for private charters. It's *only* $1,000 *per hour*, so what the heck: Take it for the day.

The best of the medium-sized boats is **Paragon** (244–2087). They use 47-foot sailing catamarans and have good snorkel gear and crew. These guys *really* like sailing and are much quicker to raise and maintain their sails than most companies, often sailing both ways, not part of one way. (Their piddly 90 HP outboard is probably also a good reason to keep the sails up.) The boats hold 39, and there's shade for ⅓ of the passengers, plus what the sails provide. Riding the net (lying on the front trampolines) is a hoot on the way back. Soothing and dry if it's calm, thrilling and wet if seas are up. The outsides of the trampolines are the wettest. At Molokini they moor at a pretty good spot, and they let you roam the crater—no short leashes. The deli lunch isn't as satisfying as others' BBQ, and their ladder into the water is poor, but overall, this is a very good product. Since it's smaller, expect a slightly bumpier ride than Four Winds II. Wetsuits and Rx masks available for free. Ma'alaea to Molokini trips are $94, no second snorkel spot. For their Lana'i trip they snorkel outside Manele Bay, and then give you a picnic lunch to take ashore. $149 for the Lana'i trip, which only takes 24.

Four Winds II and Paragon don't snorkel at two spots. If that's a priority, **Pacific Whale Foundation (PWF)** (249–8811) has seven boats and a variety of tours. Started as a whale conservation eco-tour, PWF takes more people on the water than any other tour on Maui. If all their boats ran at full capacity, they could carry almost 1,000 people per day. Not bad for a nonprofit organization. We've noticed that the destination of each boat changes with the seasons. (Scheduling must be a nightmare for these people.) Call or visit their website for the most current matching of boats and tours.

Besides whale watching, PWF has snorkeling tours around the island. Their best selling excursion visits Molokini and "Turtle Arches" from Ma'alaea for $80. They also snorkel Lana'i from Lahaina for the same. A much longer 7-hour tour goes to both sites (weather permitting) for $95. On these trips you can expect to be on one of PWF's big double decker boats, the **Ocean Voyager**, **Ocean Odyssey** or **Ocean Quest**. These sister ships offer easy water entry, continental breakfast, BBQ lunch and beer, wine and mai tais for you and 129 of your closest friends. The **Ocean Spirit**, **Ocean Intrigue** and **Ocean Discovery**, all 65-foot power cats, are mainly whale watching boats that go snorkeling in the off season. They're scrawnier than their big boats and tend to rock more than most catamarans. Our last choice is the **Ocean Explorer**, whose real narrow design doesn't encourage walking around. Avoid it.

Their mooring spot at Molokini is not very good. Coral is sparser than at other spots, and the floating debris that sometimes accumulates in the center might be present.

Their food problem, alas, is still with them after all these years. Expect to get your hand slapped (figuratively) if you try to go back for seconds at lunch. They say it's "to make sure everyone gets something to eat," and that "there'll be seconds if there's anything left." Well, excuse us, but *bring more*, like nearly every other boat on Maui does. Because after that second snorkel, you're ready to tackle a shark, and getting *one* piece of chicken or *one* hot dog might not cut it. And at the end, just before the harbor, they'll hand you a cookie, rather than leave them out throughout the trip. Sheesh, guys, ease up on the food, will you?

Also, sometimes their eco-approach can get heavy-handed to the point of being silly. On a past trip to Lana'i a pod of dolphins cruised through a sea of snorkelers, went beyond a hundred yards, then came back to be with the swimmers again. Chance of a lifetime, right? But PWF yanked everyone out of the water! When we asked why, they piously responded, "We don't swim with dolphins; it's illegal." (Which is untrue. It *might* be illegal to jump in *after* you encounter them because it might alter their behavior, but it's perfectly legal and only common sense to *stay* in the water when the *dolphins* are clearly initiating the encounter.) We haven't seen any evidence that they've changed this policy.

Don't get us wrong. PWF does a good job for the most part. Their customers have fun, their bigger boats are inexpensively priced, they're *great* with kids, and their crew seem to be of a higher than normal caliber.

The longest running operator on the island is **Trilogy** (874–5649). We were very critical of them in the past, and they have systematically fixed nearly all of their flaws over the years. Their six big catamarans (all creatively named) leave from Lahaina, Ma'alaea, Ka'anapali and even Lana'i. They run with some of the friendliest crews we've encountered and offer services that no one else can. You can snorkel Molokini or cruise Ka'anapali, but their main attraction is an all-day trip to Lana'i. At $203, it's pricier than most, but worth it.

Once there, you have the option to go on a high speed rafting adventure to Shark's Fin Cove for an extra $45. (No snorkeling there.) It's much better than the free scenic ride into Lana'i City. Most of your time is spent relaxing and snorkeling at Hulopo'e Beach via a shuttle from the harbor. It's been reported that dolphins frequently mingle with guests here. The snorkeling isn't that great and the fact that they require you to wear a floatation device, even if you're a Navy Seal, doesn't help. This is the policy on all their tours and our only real gripe with them.

Before leaving Lana'i, you have a great BBQ lunch under their private pavilion. (The place is starting to look like Camp Trilogy.) Then they try to sail on the way home, depending on the winds. Usually they serve ice cream, but don't expect any drinks. None of their boats have a liquor license. Good if you're not interested; bad if you like a beer or mai tai as you cruise back to the harbor. They allow you to BYOB, but they don't call a lot of attention to that policy.

Trilogy is the sole company allowed to operate this kind of tour on Lana'i. Their service is top-notch and makes others look pedestrian. (You have to walk to the beach from the harbor if you go with anyone else.) Their other trips to Molokini and Ka'anapali are $118. They also do whale watching trips and provide SCUBA on some boats. Call for complicated rates.

Blue Water Rafting (879–7238) is a rigid-hull inflatable (a V-shaped hull surrounded by a rubber pontoon). They do

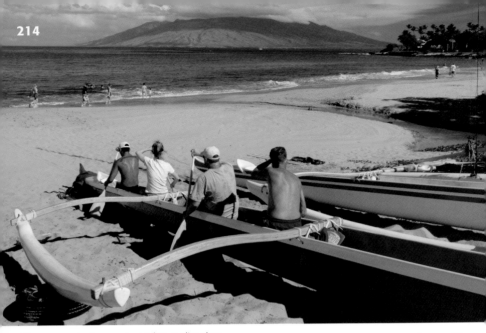

Newcomers to the sport need to realize that canoe paddling requires knowledge, experience, oh yeah, and a little water.

things different. From Kihei Boat Ramp you head down the coast, past La Pérouse Bay to a lava flow at Kanaio (which literally means *the bastard sandalwood tree*). After exploring the unusual lava formations, you head back, usually to La Pérouse Bay to a rather dull snorkeling area, then stop at another, better site for snorkeling and a deli lunch. The boat does a scorching 40 knots, and the ride is a blast (though less comfortable than a cushier boat and certainly wetter). Little shade. Consider a light, waterproof jacket for the morning trip out and wet riding later. $90 for 4 hours. They also have a 5½-hour trip for $115 that includes Molokini, but we recommend the shorter trip. Best seats are on the back, left side. Wind past La Pérouse can be fierce, hence their early start.

The **Kai Kanani II** (879–7218) is a beautiful new boat from the same manufacturer as the Shangrila. It's spacious but can get crowded when full. Rated to hold 90 passengers, even with just 60 it feels packed. Luckily the staff is helpful, the food is good and the open bar has beer, wine and mixed drinks. Their sleek boat takes much less time to get to Molokini than Ma'alaea boats and powers through big waves as if it were the calmest of days. Easy to recommend considering its launching point. It's also nice to pull into Molokini on one of the newest boats on island. $114 for Molokini and Turtle Town.

OTHER SNORKEL TRIPS FROM MA'ALAEA

Alii Nui (875–9259) is a 60-foot sailing catamaran. It's pretty pricey since you only go around the corner to "turtle town" (at Olowalu) for one snorkeling location for $109. A lousy deal, but at least they feed you fairly well.

Mahana Na'ia (871–8636) has an older 58-foot sailing cat. $85 for Molokini and "turtle town." Kind of crowded since it's one deck for up to 68 passengers.

Pride Charters (242–0955) uses a 50-foot, single-hull, rather spartan and uninspiring boat called **Leilani** and a 65-foot catamaran called **Pride of Maui**. The latter has a *very* crowded feel with 140 people packed on board: the quintessential cattle boat. Even with smaller crowds it feels like a lifeboat on the *Titanic*. Uncomfortable backless benches on top with no shade. On the plus side, they park in a good spot at Molokini. Their second spot, "Turtle Town," is at 5 Graves/5 Caves. They have a slide and SCUBA and SNUBA available, and a small number of wetsuit rentals for snorkeling. For their BBQ lunch they precook burgers, chicken, hot dogs and veggie burgers, wait till they're cold, then line you up and reheat them. Get in line early as it can take *forever*. Open bar after second stop. At $89, the trip is not a good deal.

Lani Kai through **Friendly Charters** (244–1979) has a 53-foot power cat with 69 people. Interior shade. $98 for Molokini and turtle town. You can do better.

Prince Kuhio (242–8777) is Maui's 92-foot, 149-passenger cattle boat. They do Molokini and Turtle Town (at the Maui Prince). Their mooring spot is one of the worst in the crater, right near the potentially junky area mentioned on page 209. Only positive is that the boat's real easy to get around on. $98.

Quicksilver (661–3333) is a 55-foot power cat that carries up to 105 people. It's crowded when full and the single stairway between decks is congested at almost all times. Most of the seats are in the shade. They have a good spot at Molokini but don't spend much time there. In the water their leash is so tight it's more like a choke chain. Don't even think about straying too far. And even though they advertise they go down to the Kanaio Coast to look for dolphins, we've only experienced them slowly cruising down the Makena Coast pointing out celebrity houses and making fun of other boat operators. Lastly their Turtle Town spot is too deep for snorkeling and had few turtles. In short, an easy trip to *not* recommend.

OTHER SNORKEL TRIPS FROM LAHAINA

Lahaina Princess (667–6165) is a 65-foot, single-hull boat that does morning trips to Molokini from Lahaina for $87. It's twice as far as a trip from Ma'alaea and their second stop is near Olowalu. Going to Molokini from Lahaina in this type of boat isn't a great way to go. Plus it really rocks when moored. Consider driving to Ma'alaea for your Molokini trips. Kids come for free.

Ocean Riders (661–3586) uses a 28-foot rigid hull inflatable to circumnavigate Lana'i for $135 (though they are oddly inconsistent on what they quote and charge for prices). These are rougher and wetter than more traditional craft, and shade is not too ample. But they snorkel three spots, and it's nice to see Lana'i's more interesting windward side. They even visit Lana'i's shipwrecks. Their most intriguing product is when they circumnavigate Moloka'i. Seeing the sea cliffs from the ocean is awesome. Unfortunately, they rarely do this because of winds. Even when calm, they seem reluctant to book the trip. Too bad. If you get lucky, you'll see quite a sight. Bring something to keep warm or dry.

OTHER SNORKEL TRIPS FROM KIHEI

If you just want to take a quick snorkel trip out to Molokini and don't want all the frills, **Maui Dive Shop** (879–3388) takes their 32-foot, single-hull boat from Kihei Boat Ramp to Molokini (only 4 miles) then "Turtle Town" for a 3-hour tour. (Just like Gilligan's Island.) Up to 24 people (which makes it *crowded*), continental breakfast and juices and sodas. No frills, but for $50 you ain't paying for frills. Snorkelers can accompany divers on their boat dive charter, but that costs $70 since you're taking up a diver's spot. By the way if you find yourself on their boat, the Kai Anela, it's had a more *intimate* relationship with Molokini than any other boat. Seems it sank there after an embarrassing incident and was later raised and is now used for tours.

Seafire (879-2201) is an unimpressive, raft-looking rigid-hull craft with minimal shade that goes to Molokini and Turtle Town for $55. Cheap, no frills, 3 hours, 2 stops. Only if price is paramount.

PURE SAILING TRIPS

You're not really heading anywhere and you aren't really interested in *doing* anything—you just want to sail. Most boats are sloops (single hull with little or no shade other than what the sail provides). If you're up front, sloops require you to move more often than the twin-hulled catamarans (cats). When it's too windy to go on a snorkel trip, it's probably great for sailing.

America II (667-2133) is the real deal—a genuine 12-meter racing yacht that participated in America's Cup. It's a fast, sleek sloop that takes 24 people (which is crowded). Price is cheap at $43 for 2-hour sails three times a day. Boat is usually full; reserve in advance. Snacks and drinks provided.

Scotch Mist (661-0386) is a 50-foot sailboat that accommodates 25 (which would be too crowded for comfort since it's not a wider catamaran), but they usually take about a dozen.

They'll go out with as few as 2 passengers, which makes for a relaxing time. Their 2-hour afternoon sail is just right to whet your nautical appetite. No shade except for the sail. Below deck is a bit dreary, but on top it's a nice, clean boat, and the experience is fun. Sodas and beer provided. Out of Lahaina; 3-hour afternoon or sunset sails are $40 and $50, 4-hour morning snorkel sail is $70.

Cinderella (244-0009) is a nice-looking sailing yacht. Comfortable in back, less so up front, it holds 6. Pricey at $250 per hour. Snorkeling available.

If want something a little different, **Hawaiian Sailing Canoe Adventures** (281-9301) takes up to 6 people on a genuine Hawaiian sailing canoe. It's not the fastest boat on the water, but it's a thrill to glide just above the surface on the boat's trampoline. Leave from Polo Beach and sail up and down the coast, snorkeling off the Grand Wailea. The captain has been sailing and racing since he was 16 and fills the trip with history and legends. It's very personal, relaxing and easy to recommend. $99 ($79 for kids). They go out at 8 a.m. and 10 a.m.

WHALE WATCHING

Is seasonal and described on page 229.

DINNER CRUISES

Are under NIGHTLIFE on page 287.

Parasailing is where you become a human kite, attached to a parachute and pulled by a boat via a long rope. It's a 7-10-minute ride though that includes reeling in and reeling out. It's been our experience that parasailing *looks* more fun and thrilling than it really is and doesn't seem worth the money. Think of it as a $65+ amusement ride. (People afraid of heights, however, will no doubt be properly terrified.) Off Lahaina, at least the view of town is grand. At press time, the companies all left from West Maui and only from mid-May to mid-December. (They have to close during whale season.) **West Maui Parasail** (661–4887) has 400- and 800-foot lines for $62 & $70. Tandom rides available. **UFO Parasailing** (661–7836) has a 7-minute 400-foot ride for $65 and a 10-minute 800-foot ride for $75. The latter gives no discounts for a second person.

One tip (*especially* for guys): Don't wear any slippery shorts, or you may cinch forward in your harness resulting in...the longest 7 minutes of your life.

OK, here's where Maui's often placid waters pays off. The diving here can be incredible. The usually calm morning waters off South and West Maui make boat rides short and sweet. In addition to its nearshore dives, Maui has two great offshore dives. West Maui has the awesome **Lana'i Cathedrals II** to journey to, and South Maui has the humbling **back wall of Molokini**.

We've noticed that, overall, the dive operations on Maui seem to be of a slightly higher caliber than the other islands, perhaps because there's so much competition. Prices can be lower, too. (It's good to see that *some* things are actually cheaper on Maui!) They're usually more professional here with less of the *dive shop attitude*. (You know the attitude—when you go into a shop, and the guy behind the counter never gets off his stool or takes off his sunglasses, doing everything he can to convey the impression: *I'm so cool—don't you wish you were just like me?*)

However, many of the dive companies have provocative brochures showing divers cavorting with all sorts of critters, including the holy grail of SCUBA encounters, the whale shark. We're not saying it doesn't happen, just don't *expect* it. People have been known to experience spontaneous human combustion, but we've never seen *that* happen either. We only know one friend who claims to have swum with a whale shark here. (And he lies a lot.)

So you'll know our perspective when we review companies, we should tell you what we do and don't like when we go on a dive. On a bad dive, the dive master takes the group on a nonstop excursion that keeps you kicking the whole time. No time to stop and explore the nooks and crannies. Good outfits will give you a briefing, tell you about some of the endemic species here, what to look for, and will point out various things on the dives, keeping it moving but not too fast. Bad outfits kick a lot. Good outfits explain the unique qualities of Hawai'i's environment. Bad dive masters may tell you what *they* saw (but you missed). Good companies work around your needs, wishes and desires. Bad companies keep everyone on a short leash. Good dive masters know their stuff and share it with you. Bad dive masters don't know squat but imply they know it all in order to impress you. As divers, we like companies that wander toward the boat for the latter part of the dive and allow you to go up when you are near the end of your tank, as opposed to everyone going up when the heaviest breather has burned up his/her bottle.

During times when we feel the diving conditions are bad (poor vis or big swells), we like to call around and ask about conditions. We appreciate the companies who admit it's bad, and we hold it against those who tell us how wonderful conditions are.

THE TOPS ON MAUI

The best companies we've found have been in South Maui. Regardless of the profession, it seems that the cream sooner or later rises to the top. So it is with the dive industry on Maui. Without question, the best dive outfits on the island are **Prodiver Maui** (875–4004) and **Mike Severns** (879–6596). **Prodiver** takes only 6 on their ample boat, so you never feel crowded. They have a good boat, good crew, good pace and a good attitude. They treat you well and handle the dives just right. The current owners have backed off a bit on snacks and beverages (feed me, feed me), but you can tell that the joy of diving hasn't left them. It's $129 per 2-tank, gear is $16. If they're full, **Mike Severns** is also a quality outfit top to bottom. Everyone gets a computer, good gear and plenty of snacks. Their knowledge is so accurate it borders on wisdom and their briefings are the most precise we've found. With perfectly led dives, a good 13-passenger boat (2 groups, which can get a bit cramped and clumsy) and the right attitude, this is a great company to go with. With so many years of experience, they are very adept at finding critters and showing them to you, and their knowledge is phenomenal. Since they know the sites so well, they key in on what to brief you on before the dives. Many companies do this, but nobody does it as

One of diving's Holy Grails—The elusive frogfish—straddles the forestays at the top of the sunken wreck, Carthaginian.

well. $139 for a 2-tank, $6 extra for gear. Book both in advance.

Ed Robinson (879–3584) is also a very well-run company and is a very acceptable alternative. Good ascent policy, good briefing, they go nice and slow during the dives, and their divemasters seem pretty knowledgeable if a bit cocky. But most do a good job and have a good attitude. They have two 12-passenger boats (groups of 6). As opposed to Mike Severns' bent toward education, these guys tend to stress the fun of diving more and lean toward finding rare stuff to round out your dive sightings résumé. They also do the best in the food department. Their boats, like most single-hull boats, rock a lot in heavy swells, but that's usually only relevant when they go to Lana'i. That Wednesday Lana'i trip from South Maui is, however, wonderful, though the trip is long. An easy company to recommend. It's $130 for 2-tank plus $20 for gear, but they usually won't do the Molokini back wall except on the $170 3-tank, which is a very good excursion. (They only want experienced divers on that 3-tank dive.)

Maui Dreams (874–5332) does good shore dives along South Maui. Their enthusiasm is evident and welcome. It's like you're diving with friends. They'll go out with only one person if

Sometimes swimming in a crowd isn't so bad.

necessary, even for a night dive. That's unusual for a dive company. (They could use a better briefing and maybe some food.) $59 for one tank, $89 for two, gear included.

Maui Dive Shop has several locations on the island, including the largest and best shop, which is in Kihei (879–3388) and another large shop in Lahaina (661–5388). Their shop personel can be snotty and short with customers, especially the Kihei location. Their rental gear is pretty good, though we've noticed that they adjust their regs real loose, and we've occasionally had problems with free-flow, even when the adjustment was backed off. Though you certainly won't find many steals, the Kihei shop is pretty complete.

As for diving, they do a pretty decent job, though it's a bit of a processing machine. Not bad, but not in the same league as the others mentioned above. They have boat, shore and night dives. They claim to be the only ones who will *guarantee* a Molokini back wall dive. Sure enough, we've seen them go when no one else would dare to go. Good or bad? You decide.

In **West Maui**, the best boat dive company is **Extended Horizons** (667–

Hawaiian Reefs—*Why is it That...?*

What is that crackling sound, like bacon frying, I always hear while snorkeling or diving?
For years this baffled people. In the early days of submarines, the sound interfered with sonar operations. Finally we know the answer. It's hidden snapping shrimp defining their territory. One variety is even responsible for all the dark cracks and channels you see in smooth lobe coral. A pair creates the channels, then "farms" algae inside.

Why are there so few shellfish in Hawai'i? It's too warm for some of the more familiar shellfish (which tend to be filter-feeders, and Hawaiian waters don't have as much stuff to filter). But Hawai'i has more shellfish than most people are aware of. They hide well under rocks and in sand. Also, people tend to collect shells (which is illegal), and that depletes the numbers.

Why do coral cuts take so long to heal? Coral contains a live animal. When you scrape coral, it leaves proteinaceous matter in your body, which takes much longer for your body to dispatch.

How did the early fish get here over the vast open ocean? Often in the form of larvae, which could travel in the ocean's current for long periods of time without the need to feed in the inhospitable open ocean.

What do turtles eat? Dolphins. (Just teasing.) They primarily eat plants growing on rocks, as well as jellyfish when they are lucky enough to encounter them. Unfortunately for turtles and lucky for us, jellyfish aren't numerous here.

Is it harmful when people play with an octopus? Yes, if the octopus gets harmed while trying to get it out of its hole. Best to leave them alone.

Why does the ocean rarely smell fishy here in Hawai'i? Two reasons. We have relatively small tide changes, so the ocean doesn't strand large amounts of smelly seaweed at low tide. Also, the water is fairly sterile compared to mainland water, which owes much of its smell to algae and seaweed that thrives in the bacteria-rich runoff from industrial sources.

Why is the water so clear here? Because relatively little junk is poured into our water compared to the mainland. Also, natural currents tend to flush the water with a continuous supply of fresh, clean ocean water.

Why do my ears hurt when I dive deep, and how are scuba divers able to get over it? Because the increasing weight of the ocean is pressing on your ears the farther down you go. Divers alleviate this by equalizing their ears. Sounds high tech, but that simply means holding your nose while trying to blow out of it. This forces air into the eustachian tubes, creating equal pressures with the outside ocean. (It doesn't work if your sinuses are clogged.) Anything with air between it gets compressed. So if you know someone who gets a headache whenever they go under water...well, they must be an airhead.

0611). It's not their services that shine. Light snacks for food, and their shorties are, frankly, insufficient for many people. And their sales pitch at the end of the dive, when they stop the boat, make speeches about how good the dive and crew were then start their tip jar ceremony while they strongly push the T-shirts and photo CDs is tacky and cheesy. What sets them apart is their lust to go to more than the standard dive sites. 12 divers max. They often go to Lana'i. $139 for 2-tank plus only $25 for gear. Shore dives are $89 for 1-tank.

Lahaina Divers (667–7496) is a big company, with fairly big boats that hold up to 24 people. If full, it's pretty crowded, but when there are fewer divers it's a good trip. They have a loose policy on keeping divers together underwater. Good unless you're a novice or want things pointed out. Friendly crews. We liked their Carthaginian (a sunken ship) sunset dive with the second tank at Mala Wharf where nightlife sometimes abounds. $109 for the shipwreck, $119 for their Lana'i trip. They also have the training to handle handicapped divers.

The best shore dive company in West Maui is **Pacific Dive** (667–5331). It's $59–$108, and they also do night and scooter dives.

WHERE TO DIVE

Though most boat captains will poll their customers asking where they want to go, they'll try to steer you to places they think are good that day. Three offshore places stand out as some of the best diving in Hawai'i.

One of the coolest is **Cathedrals II** off Lana'i. Most boats leave from Lahaina, but some, like Ed Robinson, do some trips from South Maui. Not only is the large lava room with several entrances here dramatic, but the sea life can be great. On a 2-tank dive here we saw, among other things, four reef sharks, two *huge* octopuses, a frogfish *(very cool)*, harlequin shrimp, ghost shrimp, pipefish, a titan scorpionfish, lots of black coral, slipper lobster and—oh, yes—*a pod of dolphins!* (This was one of the single greatest day dives we've ever done.) Obviously, Cathedrals won't always deliver dives like that, but it *can* be awesome. Not necessarily an advanced dive. You need to book this trip specifically. Boats leaving from Lahaina offer shorter treks. Dive lights are helpful. **Cathedrals I** is also great, but not as good as II.

Another standout location is the **back wall of Molokini**. This is *outside* the crater. It's not necessarily the fish life that makes this a good dive, though the fish are numerous. Rather, it's the dramatic way the wall plunges into the abyss. Its presence is never far from your mind. And as you round the corner from Molokini's shadow to the sunlight (penetrating to an incredible depth), it forms an awesome spectacle. Later, you may look down and see a black tip reef shark cruising the neighborhood 90 feet below you—and another one 90 feet above you. This is an easy dive to go deep, and most companies will screen to make sure you're up to the task. Since there's nothing much to stop you from going all the way, it's important that you be comfortable regulating your buoyancy. We don't want you setting any new depth records in your state of rapture of the deep. Bring a light for the shadow side.

The *inside* of Molokini isn't nearly as dramatic to dive as the outside, but it's easier. Either way, trips to Molokini are very short. It's only 7 miles from the Kihei Boat Ramp.

A newer dive site is the Carthaginian. Scuttled here in 2005, it rests in 95 feet of water. The boat was painted and rigged to resemble an old whaling boat and underwater the look makes the wreck appear older. The easily accessed inside is fairly wide-open and in time the fish count should increase.

Good Shore Dive Locations

From South Maui to West Maui, all are described in greater detail under BEACHES.

Black Sand Beach (Pu'u Ola'i) has good coral, turtle and fish life, but you'll have to swim along the hill's shoreline over 800 feet to get to the areas deep enough to justify SCUBA. Around the point, before Little Beach, there are some excellent caves. Ocean entry is over a lava shelf; try only during calm seas. Visibility is poor until you leave the shoreline area. Just follow the hill around as far as your will takes you. Dive boat captains call this site *Red Hill*.

Ulua is where intros usually take place in South Maui. There's lots of good reef, though visibility tends to be poor.

Makena Landing is usually calm with easy entry, making it a popular place for intro or night dives. The visibility is best on the north side which also has good coral.

5 Graves/5 Caves described on page 163 can be excellent.

Scenic Lookout described on page 157 can be exciting, though the gear-hauling and entry is a bit annoying.

Black Rock is fun, and there are dive companies at nearby resorts.

Kahekili Beach Park is a popular intro spot because of the easy entry. Kick straight out for best conditions.

Honolua Bay *can* be incredible. Though depths rarely exceed 40 feet, the right side of the bay has an extensive reef area and lots of fish. (The opening photo on pages 2–3 is Honolua Bay.) Eels are common. Head out 100–200 feet before dropping.

Mala Wharf is twisted pile of rubble from a badly constructed wharf that makes a great artificial reef. Night dives are best. At no deeper than 30 feet we've seen conger eels, octopi and even oval squid. From Mala Ramp, you can see the old broken wharf and how to get there.

IF YOU'VE NEVER DIVED BEFORE

Intro dives are how nearly all of us certified divers started. You'll get instruction, and a dive instructor will be nearby during the dive. Most do it as a shore dive. Though certified, we still do intros with companies to see how they do. Most intros take place at Ulua Beach in South Maui or Kahekili Beach in West Maui. If you have any asthma, heart disease, high blood pressure, ear problems or are on medication, call the dive company before you arrive. They may need a signoff from your doctor for some things.

Of the companies we've listed above, **Maui Dreams** (874–5332) in South Maui does the best job for intro dives, and they are very reasonably priced at $79 for a 1-tank, $99 for a 2-tank.

The two things that annoy us with companies doing intros are patronizing attitudes and the use of 63-cubic foot (or smaller) tanks. Most new divers suck a lot of air, and 80s, though heavier, are the way to go, not the smaller 63s. (Perhaps this is cynical, but maybe some use 63s so that they can get you in and out faster since your air won't last as long.)

OTHER DIVE COMPANIES

There are tons of them out there. We haven't been impressed with **Maui Dive**

Fishbowl makes for good, easy, protected snorkeling, if you don't mind the walk.

Shop's intros. There's absolutely nothing about **Boss Frog** that we like—pushy, rude and abrupt. **Makena Coast** is adequate. **Beach Activities** (662–8207) has painless shore dives at Black Rock for $69. **B&B SCUBA** (875–2861) has a pretty nice shop in Kihei. And their boat trip is…Did we mention that they have a pretty nice shop?

A FEW TIPS

Despite assurances that the gear has been checked out, if you rent gear to dive on your own, it's a good idea to hook the regulator to the tank before you drive away from the shop. Though we have our own gear, we often rent from shops and boats to evaluate the gear, and we've had problems with leaking regulators and tanks not filled completely with some shops. Anyone can have it happen once, but if it happens twice at a shop, we'll dump on them.

Dives, like snorkeling, are usually best in the morning. Afternoon winds can lower visibility and raise surf.

Some companies try to put you in 63-cubic foot tanks. If you don't want to be rushed, tell them you want 80s. Many will comply.

I'd like to pass on a tip that has helped my diving more than any other. I used to be a less-than-stellar breather, never the last one out. I tried skip breathing—holding your breath while not ascending, which, of course, you're _not_ supposed to do—but only got marginally better results at the cost of headaches caused by a buildup of CO_2. Then I learned the secret to make a tank last a long time. Breathe _continuously_, never stop, but do it slowly. A long, slow, deep inhalation followed immediately by a drawn out exhalation keeps CO_2 from building up and keeps your body from thinking it's low on air. (I use my tongue at the top of my mouth to spray the air out slowly.) You never feel deprived, and the tank lasts *oh, so long.* The only downside is less silence during your dive. Now, I'm almost always the last one out, and only the tables tell me when to come up, not my gauge. See your dive instructor. (That's the diving disclaimer equivalent of *see your doctor*.)

Here we go again, frothing at the mouth about the water. But give us the benefit of the doubt here. The truth is that snorkeling on Maui can be outrageous. Clean, clear water in many locations, calm surf much of the time, and gobs of fish and coral. The trick is knowing where to go. We've literally snorkeled miles and miles of coastline, from the top of West Maui to the bottom of South Maui, looking for good spots. If you look at our maps, the areas shaded in darker blue represent our best finds. In general, the best snorkeling is in South Maui, though the West does have a few gems.

We'll admit that we're snorkeling junkies and never tire of experiencing the water here. If you snorkel often, you can go right to our list below of recommended areas. But if you're completely or relatively inexperienced, you should read on.

For identifying ocean critters, the best books we've seen are *Shore Fishes of Hawai'i* by John Randall and *Hawaiian Reef Fish* by Casey Mahaney. They're

SNUBA is sort of like SCUBA-lite. Good for those nervous about taking the plunge. This is at Molokini.

what we use. You should see plenty of butterflyfish, wrasse, convict tang, achilles tang, parrotfish, angelfish, damselfish, Moorish idol, pufferfish, trumpetfish, moray eel, and humuhumunukunukuapu-a'a or Picasso triggerfish—a beautiful but very skittish fish. (It's as if they somehow *know* how good they look in aquariums.)

We know people who have a fear of putting on a mask and snorkel. Gives 'em the willies. For them, we recommend boogie boards with clear windows to observe the life below.

A FEW TIPS

- Feeding the fish is generally not recommended because it introduces unnatural behavior to the reef.
- Use *Sea Drops* or another brand of anti-fog goop. Spread it *thinly* on the inside of a dry mask, then do a quick rinse.
- Most damage to coral comes when people grab it or stand on it. If your mask starts to leak or you get water in your snorkel, be careful not to stand on the coral to clear them. Find a spot where you won't damage coral or drift into it. Fish and future snorkelers (not to mention the coral) will thank you.
- Don't use your arms much, or you will spook the fish. Just gentle fin motion. Any rapid motion can cause the little critters to scatter.
- Water temps range from 75° in February to 80° in September. The lower end may seem chilly; consider renting a short, thin wetsuit.
- We prefer using divers' fins (the kind that slip over reef shoes), so that we can walk easily into and out of the water without tearing up our feet. (If you wear socks or nylons under the shoes, it'll keep you from rubbing the tops of your toes raw.)

- If you have a mustache and have trouble with a leaking mask, try a little Vaseline. Don't get any on the glass—it can get *really* ugly.

THE BEST AREAS TO SNORKEL

See the writeups in BEACHES for info on each specific area. Some snorkeling sites have specifics you need to know.

South Maui Snorkeling

We recommend **Fishbowl** (see page 167 for directions), **Aquarium** and the excellent coves along the north side of **La Pérouse Bay** (see page 233). Don't bother with the part of La Pérouse nearest your car. The entire point separating **Po'olenalena Beach** from **Palauea Beach** is great, especially from the Po'olenalena side. Also, the south end of Po'olenalena is good. Between **Maluaka** and **Black Sand Beach** there's some good snorkeling. The point separating **Kama'ole I** and **II** is pretty decent. North of **Keawakapu** works pretty well as does south of **Wailea Beach**, though you'll have to go out farther there.

West Maui Snorkeling

The **scenic lookout** between the 8 and 9 mile marker is good if you can deal with the entry and exit. **Honolua Bay** offers excellent snorkeling about ⅔ of the time. **Black Rock** at Ka'anapali Beach can be superb. The south end of **Oneloa** in Kapalua is good much of the time. The 14 Mile Marker on Hwy 30 is ridiculously overrated, but the area below the cliffs southeast of the 11 mile marker is good if you can deal with the long swim.

ODDS & ENDS

Renting gear is easy. Maui is littered with rental places, and you won't have any trouble finding them. We probably lean toward **Maui Dive Shop's** many locations (879–3388). They also have wetsuits and divers' fins available for extra that will fit over your reef shoes. Most places charge about $2–$8 per day, $10–$25 per week for gear. Many shops have low prices in hopes of luring you in and then selling you other activities or timeshares. Also keep in mind that at some shops, the employee gets a commission for selling you more expensive gear. Get what *you* want, not what *they* want you to get. Make sure the mask fits without having to suck in too hard through your nose. Snorkels with drain valves and dry snorkels work better than ordinary tubes.

The most common way that visitors get bad **sunburns** is while snorkeling. You don't feel it coming because of the cool water. Do yourself a favor and consider wearing a T-shirt.

Don't judge a snorkeling site by the first 20 feet. Shorelines are often cloudy. You'll usually have to venture farther out for good quality.

It's a good idea to check on the **snorkeling conditions** the day before you plan to snorkel. Call 877–5111 for a weather forecast. For a surf forecast, call 877–3611 or check page 2 of the *Maui News* newspaper.

GUIDED SNORKEL TOURS

If you're intrigued but nervous about snorkeling, **Ann Fielding's Snorkel Maui** (572–8437) has a very patient and methodical lesson/tour. For $120 each (for two people). The price drops to $95 each for 3 or more. She'll spend several hours with you, getting you used to the gear and water, then lead you along a South Maui tour. Snacks included. Ann is a real-life marine biologist with great knowledge, so you'll learn much about our marine environment.

If you're a little hesitant about trying SCUBA, consider SNUBA. That's where you swim below a raft with tanks and a 20-foot hose, regulator in mouth and an instructor by your side. Anyone 8 and older can SNUBA. (You need to be age 12—or 10 through PADI—to SCUBA.) At press time we couldn't find anyone who was *reliably* doing SNUBA trips from the shore. But some of the boat trips listed under OCEAN TOURS have SNUBA available, usually for around $50. Specifically, read about **Four Winds II**, **Lani Kai**, **Prince Kuhio** and **Pride of Maui**. Groups of 4–6 per trip; expect about 30–40 minutes underwater.

If you're looking to be pampered, there are lots of spas on the island. Some are definitely better than others.

The grandest by far is appropriately named **Spa Grande** at Grand Wailea (875–1234, ext. 4949). It's the largest, most elaborately decorated, rich-feeling spa on the island. You name it, they've got it. They have a unique series of specialty baths that you partake before your treatment. Like most spas, you might feel a bit processed at the beginning, but once you start, they'll transform you from a raving lunatic to a smiling idiot. It's $30 extra if you're not staying at the hotel but includes parking and use of the gym.

The **Four Seasons** (874–8000), also in Wailea, is smaller but has a particular treatment called Mele Wailea, which is the closest you'll ever get to having your bones liquefied. They also have oceanside massages. The locker rooms are beautiful and are furnished with pretty much everything you'll need and then some. Outside guests have limited access to the fitness room.

In West Maui, the **Westin Maui's Heavenly Spa** (661–2525) rooms are dark, moody, quiet and relaxing. Services are are good. Non-Westin guests pay $15 extra for the fitness room.

Nearby **Spa Moana** (667–4725) at the Hyatt Ka'anapali has great massages, but the rooms are bright and unacceptably noisy. Hearing toilets flush, lawn mowers and screaming beachgoers sort of kills the moment.

submarine

You won't *Run Silent, Run Deep.* You won't hear the sound of sonar pinging away in the background. And it's rare that anyone shoots torpedoes at you. But if you want to see the undersea world and *refuse* to get wet, *dis is da buggah.* **Atlantis Submarine** (667–2224) uses a 48-passenger sub out of Lahaina that ambles about over a reef, which is, to be honest, a bit plainer than the type you'd choose to snorkel or SCUBA, but it's still cool. They also visit a sunken wreck called the Carthaginian. This is the opposite of an aquarium—this world belongs to the fish, and *you* are the oddity. This $85, 40-minute ride is a kick. Most kids like it if they are old enough to appreciate the sights. We took friends on this trip once, and a huge manta ray cruised by the window. Of course, their 2½-year-old son was *far* more impressed with the plastic fish card tied to the inside hull than the 14-foot ray just outside the window. But adults like it, and even certified divers like us get a kick out of it. Claustrophobics will probably be too busy staring through the windows to be nervous. Photographers will want to use fast (at least 400 speed) film and turn off the flash. Mornings are usually best. Wear a bright red shirt, and watch what happens to its color on the way down. Also, if you book the last trip of the day and it's whale season, you might get to spend extra time on the transport boat whale watching.

A cheaper substitute to a sub is the **Reefdancer** (667–2133). It's a semi-submersible—a boat with large windows below. After a 20-minute (each way) ride to the site, they glide over a shallow reef for 20 minutes as divers scavenge for critters to bring to the window. Kids under 8 will probably love it as will those too skittish to try snorkeling. It's also roomier than the sub. Only $33, and kids under 6 are free. The 1½ hour ride is too long; stick with the hour.

SURFING

Ho, da shreddin's da kine, brah. (Just trying to get you in the mood.) Surfing is synonymous with Hawai'i. And why not? Hawaiians invented da bugga. Lessons aren't as hard as you may think. They put you on a large, soft board the size of a garage door (well...almost), so it's fairly easy to master, at least at this level. Surf

A Punalau goofy foot grommet shreds one cherry bugga with Moloka'i behind 'im—dude.

is usually very small in South Maui, often too small even for beginners, and the wind that arrives late morning and in the afternoon complicates the learning process. Lahaina is a *much* better place to learn. Plus, the South Maui area where they teach—Cove Park because of its fairly reliable surf—has yucky water. (See page 158 for more on that.)

In Lahaina try **Goofy Foot Surf School** (244–9283). They're very good teachers and guarantee that you'll ride a wave or it's free. Two-hour lessons are $65 per person for groups of 5, $150 for a private lesson, $250 for a couple. By the way, a goofy footer is a person (in this case the owner) who surfs with his *right* foot forward instead of the usual left. Pretty goofy, huh? Also consider **Surf Dog Maui** (250–7873). Bigger groups; they, too, do a good job. We also liked **Girls Gone Surfing** (280–0103).

If you're in Kihei and don't want to drive to Lahaina, try **Big Kahuna** (875–6395). $60 for two hours.

If you're experienced, West Maui has easily accessible water, so you may want to simply drive along and look for the kind of waves that work best for you since it's very swell-direction dependent. Launiupoko State Park south of the 18 mile marker often has a good break, though it's kind of far out. The area south of the 19 mile marker can also be good.

Lahaina Harbor has a very dependable break, even in fairly low surf.

Honolua Bay is one of the best sites—if you know what you're doing.

One site that's received national attention in the last few years is **Jaws**. An unusual formation below the surface kicks in when the surf gets bigger than 15 feet (which happens about a dozen times a year in the winter). Then the waves become magnified and form a curved shape. They have been known to reach 70 feet here. Only a handful of experts can surf Jaws (using Jet Skis to tow them out and save their bacon when needed). Less than 15-foot surf means zippo is happening. (We're assuming you only want to *watch* at Jaws.) If the surf is pounding, the most direct route from Hwy 36 is Hahana Road (between the 13 and 14 mile markers). Go to the left on Hahana after the fork, and take the dirt road at the end of Hahana. It's along a gulch (there will be trees and such along your right). If it's real dry, a regular car *may* make it, but probably only 4WDs should try. If wet, consider one of the other roads among the pineapple fields. (See map on page 115.) It's private land, so ML&P may opt to close the road.

The best surf shops are in Kahului. They include **Second Wind** (877–7467) and **Hi-Tech** (877–2111). In Lahaina, try **Honolua Surf Co.** (661–8848) or their Kihei shop (874–0999).

By the way, a collection of surfboards is known in surfing lingo here as a *quiver*. A little kid surfer who doesn't have a job or car yet is called a *grommet*. Double *overhead* is when the waves are huge, double *overtoes* are when they're not. If someone says your girlfriend is *filthy*, it's a compliment. And a *landshark* is someone who says he surfs…but doesn't.

Lest you think of yourself as da best island surfer, consider this: Hawaiian legend states that Chief Kihapiilani once surfed a wave from Maui to Moloka'i. He was said to have been adorned with leis, and that no surf spray was found on the flowers. *(Hey, we don't make up the legends, we just report them.)*

Maui is the undisputed whale watching capital of Hawai'i. The shallow water between islands here is the whales' preferred birthing area. Few industries in Hawai'i bring as much shameless phony advertising as whale watching. Computers allow fake scenes with relative ease.

(For the record, we don't use computers to doctor our photos.) Some show whales leaping so close to boats you think they're going to get swamped. Just so you know, boats are forbidden by federal law from getting closer than 100 yards. The fine for violating a whale's personal space is obscene. Whales are allowed to initiate closer contact (and they're rarely fined), but in general, count on staying a football field away. That's OK, because these oversized buggas are so big that at that distance they're still incredibly impressive.

Though they're not the only whales here, **humpbacks** are the stars of whale watching. They work in Alaska during the summer, building up fat, then vacation here from December to March or April where the females bear their young and the males sing the blues. More than 1,000 whales come to the islands each year, and the mothers and calves stay close to shore. Only the males sing, and they all sing the same song, usually with their heads pointed down. No air bubbles come out while singing, and scientists aren't sure how they do it. Humpbacks don't eat while they're here and may lose 1/3 of their body weight during their stay in Hawai'i. (I doubt that very many *human* visitors can make that claim.)

There's no question that the whale watching varies from year to year. Some years the humpbacks are boisterous and raising hell, constantly breaching, blowing and generally having a good time. Other years they seem strangely subdued, as if hung over from their Alaska trip. What's really going on is that some years Maui's whales visit other Hawaiian islands. Perhaps whales, too, want to avoid getting into a rut.

See OCEAN TOURS on page 207 for a description of the different boats. The best whale watching company, not surprisingly, is **Pacific Whale Foundation** (249–8811). After all, this is their passion. It's $20–$32 for a 2-hour trip. Their knowledge is phenomenal, and the trips are fun. They even have hydrophones to listen to the beasts. Of their different crafts, the Ocean Spirit and Ocean Odyssey are their better boats. Avoid their Ocean Explorer. Narrow and tight.

Lots of other companies do whale watching trips. Most outings are 2 hours and they charge around $30. Bring binoculars if you have them.

From land, good places to spot whales are from the Scenic Lookout between the 8 and 9 mile markers or the light station at McGregor Point between the 7 and 8 mile markers, both on Hwy 30 past Ma'alaea. Whales are *much* easier to see when there are no whitecaps.

Windsurfing

Windsurfing is the result of taking a surfboard and attaching a sail to it. When properly instructed, you can zip along faster than the wind. It's a first-class adrenaline charge.

No matter where you go in the world, if you ask people where to find the best windsurfing on the planet, Maui is nearly always rated as the best. That's because of an accident of geography. Our amazingly consistent trade winds from the northeast are speeded up near Kahului by the venturi effect between the two mountains, so it's always windier there than the general trade speed. The shoreline orientation means the wind is usually along the shore to slightly onshore and parallel to the wave direction. Perfect!

By common agreement, no shortboard windsurfing (meaning everyone who's not a beginner) is allowed before 11 a.m. (Surfers get to use the waves up till then.) This is strictly enforced by local residents. Also, if you're interested in advanced lessons or simply renting your gear, local regs state that companies aren't allowed to deliver. You'll have to bring the gear yourself. (Beginners on longboards are exempt from the delivery rule and the 11 a.m. rule because winds after 11 are considered too difficult for learners.) Unless you're advanced, don't try to windsurf at Ho'okipa, the mecca of windsurf spots. Local users won't allow beginners at the sacred spot, and there is no shortage of young toughs there to enforce the ban on novices. Beginners, instead, will find Kanaha Beach near Kahului Airport the best place to learn.

A 2½ hour lesson is about $80 per person with 3 people per class. During that time you'll actually windsurf, though tacking and jibing (changing directions by heading into or away from the wind) may elude you. In general, it's a hard sport to master at the beginning, and you should expect to fall in the water 70 or so times during your lesson. So don't be discouraged if you're not streaking like the wind gods you see around the island. (Falling's not so bad; in fact, you'll probably get real good at it.) Shorter and slimmer people seem to learn board balance more quickly. During your lesson, don't be shy about asking your instructor to show you *exactly* what you're doing wrong.

The companies we've had good luck with are **HST** (871–5423) and **Action Sports** (283–7913). Also giving lessons is **Second Wind** (877–7467). All meet at Kanaha at 9 a.m., but you'll have to go to their nearby offices to pay. (No exchanging money at the beach.)

Maui Ocean Activities (875–1234) is in Wailea. Though conditions aren't

Hard-core windsurfers, you have arrived. You've reached the promised land at Ho'okipa.

as good as Kanaha, if the surf is high on north-facing shores (as happens often in the winter), you're probably better off there. They give lessons to up to 10 people every hour. For 1½ hours it's $69. Pick an early afternoon time.

Wear a T-shirt to keep the mandatory life jacket from rubbing you, and wear reef shoes while boarding. (Most provide.)

KITEBOARDING

Also called kitesurfing, it's a bit less known than windsurfing, so we're putting it here. Imagine a modified surfboard, shorter and boxier than a normal board, with fins at both ends and straps for your feet. Then let a special, controllable four-line kite drag you along. As in windsurfing, you don't have to go the direction the wind takes you—you have control. Despite what some instructors tell you when they want to sign you up, it's harder to get up on the board than windsurfing. But *oh,* what fun it is! More fun than windsurfing once you're comfortable on the board. One way you can prepare before you get here is to

buy a two-line kite and master it so that you can instinctively maneuver the kite. It's not that hard, but it helps if you can steer the kite without thinking.

Lessons are *expensive*. The best place to learn is either **Action Sports** (871–5857) or **Kiteboarding School of Maui** (873–0015), both in Kahului. Action Sports has a 3½-hour lesson for $210. This is a group lesson, but there's one instructor per student. KSM has a very comprehensive 4-hour lesson for $290 and a 7-hour lesson (over 2 days) for $490. We like the way KSM does their lessons early to minimize inadvertently staring at the sun as you operate your kite. Teaching methods differ. First you need to learn how to operate the kite (which is a hoot). Next comes body dragging. Though it sounds like something they do to you if your credit card is declined, it's actually when you let the kite drag you through the ocean while you manipulate it. Then comes the good part—*riding the board.*

Most companies claim you'll be riding the board after the first lesson, but don't be disappointed if that doesn't happen. It ain't easy, brah, and instructors privately concede that few are able to get on the board the first day.

If you want to *watch* kiteboarding, head over to Kanaha in Kahului. Kiteboarders use the west (left) end.

If you're already a kiteboarder, note that it's illegal to venture near the end of the runway at Kanaha in Kahului. See map on page 66.

Ever seen movies where military commandos don a harness, hook a pulley onto a steel cable and zip down into the action? This is similar—without the hostile fire at the end.

Skyline Eco-Adventures (878–8400) takes you down five different zipline cables, from super-short to super-long.

You'll hike for 5 minutes through a eucalyptus forest to the first cable, which is a fairly fun, if short, ride. Each cable gets a little better and more fun until the last one. That one is a grin and scream-inducing riot. It's 710 feet long over a gorge, and it's the coolest 18 seconds you can imagine. *Everyone* walks away from that one with a big ol' smile on their face.

The crew does a very good job; we just wish they didn't take 12 people at a shot, which causes fairly long waits between cables. It's $92. Non-zipping companions can hike along, but they'll have to pay $39. You need to be between 80 and 260 pounds, and if you're afraid of heights, you might want to think twice about this. On the road to Haleakala off Hwy 378. They book up *far* in advance, so call from the mainland.

Their other zipline tour is called **Skyline Eco-Adventures Ka'anapali** and has 8 lines with the longest one over 1,000 feet and you might reach speeds of 30 MPH. The environment is just the opposite of their Haleakala tour. Located on the Kahoma Ranch above Ka'anapali, there are sweeping views of West Maui, Moloka'i and Lana'i. Although the ziplines are high up on the mountain, it's dry and hot, so be sure to wear sunscreen. It's also one of the dustiest tours on island. They recommend not wearing white and hand out bandanas to wear like a bank robber. The guides are fun and help make the wait between zips a bit more interesting. One caveat is the price: it's $156 for this 4-hour tour which includes a meal, a free water bottle and all the dirt you can eat. Think of it as better than the $74 Haleakala tour, but not *that* much better.

Ziplining 700 feet over a gorge definitely qualifies as a yee-haw experience.

One of many coves hidden along the north shore of La Pérouse Bay.

Some of the activities described below are for the serious adventurer. They can be experiences of a lifetime. We are assuming that if you consider any of them that you are a person of sound judgment, capable of assessing risks. All adventures carry risks of one kind or another. Our descriptions below do not attempt to convey all risks associated with an activity. These *adventures* are not for everyone. Good preparation is essential. In the end, it comes down to your own good judgment. Also, please read our note on personal responsibility on page 42. It's particularly relevant to this chapter.

LA PÉROUSE BAY LAVA / SNORKEL / HIKE

La Pérouse is known around the island as the end of the road. This is as far south as you can go by car in South Maui. Some people also know that La Pérouse is where they stand a chance of seeing dolphins in the morning. But the one thing people *don't* know about La Pérouse is that the north end of the bay (located within a Natural Area Reserve) has some of the best hiking in South Maui, as well as some of the best snorkeling on Maui. (Granted South Maui is not renowned for its hiking. It's like being the best hockey player in all of Peru.) The snorkeling spots that most people use at La Pérouse are terrible. You need to know *where* to go.

The catch is that you have to hike to it, and the trail is on lava (which is sharp). The other catch is that if you want to make a loop hike out of it (not come back the same way), you'll have to make your way through about 400 yards of *very* vague trail. (You don't *have* to make it a loop.) And you need to stay on trail because the area's status as a Natural Area Reserve prohibits straying from the trail. But the exploration possibilities along this forgotten part of the coast are exciting.

La Pérouse Bay was formed when lava erupted from a vent just up the mountain around 1790, creating Cape Kina'u. All of the land around the cape is young. The shoreline here is starkly beautiful. The protected coves, the wind-blown bay, the views up the mountain, the lack of crowds, the odds of seeing dolphins dancing in the bay and the waters bursting with fish make this one of our favorite areas in South Maui.

See map on page 133. You start just before the end of Makena Alanui Road, 2/10 mile before the road's end. You'll see a turnout on the mauka (mountain) side and a trail on the ocean side where a barbed-wire fence ends. It passes through sand along a barbed wire fence at first, behind an enviously located private estate. This sand *used* to be the shoreline beach…before the 1790 lava flow cut it off and pushed the shoreline further out. The lava drooled down the mountain, ebbed up against the hill on the mauka side of the highway and flowed around it, creating the pointed shape of old land that you're now passing through. (The kiawe trees—mesquite—were brought in during the 1800s.) Once the sand ends, veer to the left and take the less worn trail along the shoreline for some truly *great* snorkeling and magnificent views.

The shoreline trail follows the coast out beyond the estate a short distance, becoming somewhat vague in spots. (But do try to stay on the trail.) The fish in the cove near the estate seem to love jumping out of the water; watch for them. You may see a few wasps in the area, but

we've never had any problem with them. Lest you be confused by the PRIVATE PROPERTY signs, the trail at the estate's cove is on public land; it's only toward the estate that the land is private. The next cove has somewhat cloudy water, but views from there are good. Look up the mountain and notice all those hills. Those are volcanic vents sprinkled up the hill that you probably never noticed from other perspectives. Each hill is from a separate eruption.

Staying along the shoreline, the next cove sometimes has some of the densest fish counts we've seen on Maui. You'll know you're at the right cove because there's a sign driven into the lava out on the left point of the bay aimed at kayakers. The sheer variety of fish here is dizzying and their numbers sometimes unrivaled. The quantity varies with the tides, seasons and how often some local residents come out to illegally fish in this reserve. But when conditions are right, we'd be hard pressed to think of another place in all Maui that's as fish-rich as this cove. One reason for the high fish count is that there isn't a tradition of fish-feeding here. So please, please don't start the precedent. Fish-feeding results in a few more aggressive species multiplying and driving out the meeker fish, dwindling the variety to a few audacious species. There's not much coral here—the land is too young. If you're coming out here early, as we recommend, wait to put on your sunscreen until after you've been in the water.

After this cove, more delightful coves present themselves, protected from the white, choppy water of La Pérouse Bay. A pair of inland ponds (cut off from the ocean) are lined with a white substance that looks like sand…but that ain't no sand. It's a phenomenon we call lava field quicksand, which doesn't occur too often, but we can tell you from experience that you don't want to go swimming in it. In fact, any inland pool that is completely cut off from the ocean is off-limits to swimming. (That's what the signs saying KEEP OUT OF THE PONDS are referring to.) They are fed from water seeping through the porous lava rock and are too fragile to accommodate recreational swimmers.

Farther along, past the golden pool, is another snorkel area open to the ocean. Here, too, you'll find a dazzling array of fish. Though not quite as dense as the last cove, the undulating underwater topography is even more beautiful than the first cove. The waters outside the cove and in the finger of water on the left side, are also loaded with fish, but currents there can be tricky. Best to stay in the cove on the right unless it's real calm.

The trail fades for a hundred feet or so past this cove. Regain it up the small lava hill just past the last small clear pool. The next cove is the largest yet. It's known as the Aquarium, and it doesn't disappoint. (Some people call this place Fishbowl and call Fishbowl Aquarium. Place names are often disputed on Maui.) It's a fairly large area to roam, and the cove and surrounding shoreline are usually protected from the wind by a lava embankment. Fish, eels and octopus are common here. Access is a little awkward since the trail doesn't quite go all the way to the shoreline. You'll have to scramble over a lava trail that isn't so obvious for a few dozen feet. Snorkel on the left side where the coral rubble is, and avoid the super shallow areas where there's coral. Once you've snorkeled, either turn around here, or, if you want to make a loop, you'll have to go in a direction parallel to the shoreline for 400 or so yards. The trail is super vague. It's tough terrain, and you'll probably take the occasion to curse us once or twice. Take your time and be careful on the sharp lava. See map on page 133 for orientation.

After your trek through lava hell, you'll come to two large ponds—one by the shoreline, the other inland. The ocean off the shoreline pond offers good snorkeling, but not as good as what you've seen so far. The trail back to your car is on the far side of the inland pond and will seem like a highway compared to the last 400 yards. The inland pond is golden-coated and surrounded by vegetation and a smattering of seabirds trolling for grubs in the gooey bottom. It's hard to believe that this oasis of life has erupted from the sterile lava over the span of a mere two centuries. Footprints near the shoreline can last for years, so don't venture beyond the surrounding rock.

Some Basics

Like everything at or near La Pérouse, the earlier you do this hike/snorkel, the better. We like to start hiking at 7:30 a.m. or 8 a.m. or do it in the late afternoon. That way we avoid the winds that kick up in the late morning and early afternoon, and we avoid the hot sun on this dark lava field. Early afternoons can be blustery, possibly even knocking you over on the rocks.

You'll also want to bring hiking shoes or boots; lava is murder on footwear. If you tend to be skittish while hiking, not as confident in your footing, some cheap garden gloves for grabbing the lava might come in handy. All told, you can spend anywhere from from 1 hour to 4 hours on this hike, depending on how long and often you snorkel, and if you make a loop of it. Though we usually use hiking sticks, we don't use them here as the lava tends to chew up the tips. And remember: This area is a cherished protected reserve, so please be sensitive and don't leave anything behind. Stay out of any inland ponds and stay on trails. And although you *are* allowed to walk this

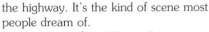

area, after a state site inspection found no damage being done to the area by visitors since mass kayak visits have been banned, some residents began lobbying to have the state make the lava trails even *more* vague to make things harder on you. Odd, we know, but true.

THE FOUR FALLS OF NA'ILI'ILI-HAELE

Quite a mouthful. But imagine *four* waterfalls, one right after another, in a beautiful setting, and all relatively near

This hiker (pictured at the bottom of the falls) reached the fourth, and best, falls at Na'ili'ili-haele. It's not too far, but it does include overcoming a hurdle. (Literally.)

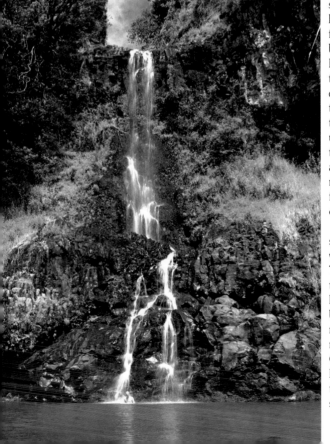

the highway. It's the kind of scene most people dream of.

First things first. The trail is on EMI land. (See page 75 for more on that.) Unlike most land EMI uses, they actually own this parcel. (Most of the rest is leased from the state.) Locals have simply been using the trail for years without a problem, but we'll leave it up to you to secure permission from them. The trailhead is 1⁶⁄₁₀ mile past the 5 mile marker (#6 is missing) on Hwy 360 across from some tall Cook Island pines. There's a dirt turnout on the right and a wire fence.

At first the trail can be slippery and awkward as it goes down through bamboo, across a ditch, through more bamboo, then directly to the stream. After you boulder-hop across—IMPORTANT!—follow the trail as it hugs the bank upstream to the left. Don't take one of the false trails heading up the hill. A downed tree fools you into thinking the trail doesn't hug the stream bank, but it opens up afterward. Go *through* the tree or around it. Soon after you might see an intermittent waterfall coming from a reservoir, but it's not one of the four falls.

Fairly soon an *apparent* spur trail leads to the first waterfall (which you'll hear). Take the spur, as the main trail will only peter out and lead you to impenetrable hau bush. The 15-foot falls are nice but a bit too small. (Oh, my, we're getting spoiled.) Cross the stream (boulder-hop again), and the trail continues on the other (east) side. Up through the bamboo (with a few awkward spots), and you'll soon come to waterfall #2. This is as far as many will go. Falls #2 has most of the ingredients people want. Very pretty with a nice swimming pool, rounded pebble shore with sun and shade. You may find yourself falling asleep to the sound of the water.

One of the things that separates a hike from an adventure is uncertainty of outcome. So it is here. On the left side of the falls, a trail leads up to...a dilemma. A fairly sheer 12-foot rock face is in your way. There are two more falls ahead. On our last visit there was a thick rope ladder (which we don't vouch for) to assist your climb, but it's not easy. And coming back down isn't much fun either. Most will probably settle for the first two falls. If you don't, here's what to expect.

It has probably taken you 30 minutes to get to falls #2. After overcoming the rockface, you'll soon come to a long pool. A trail on the right side through the wild ginger helps, but eventually you'll have to get in the water and swim 100 or so feet up the pool. (Have I lost you yet?) Then you'll scale a man-high waterfall (#3), walk around the bend, and claim your prize: a gorgeous waterfall, at least 35 feet high (maybe more) in a drop-dead gorgeous scene. It's official. You have now arrived at paradise.

Now, that's a lot to go through to get to a waterfall, even a beautiful one. Why do it? Because it's a lot to go through, and it rewards you with a beautiful waterfall. That's it. Nothing deeper than that. Just an adventure you never would have had back home.

In case you're wondering, *yes,* there are more waterfalls past #4. And *no,* you'll never see them. It would be crazy to scale falls #4. Don't even think about it.

Reef shoes or tabis are a big help for the last part of the journey. If you want to take a photo of falls #4, either get a waterproof bag, waterproof camera, or hold your camera high while swimming the length of the natural pool. (Hard to do.) Also, if you don't want to start the hike at the gate mentioned previously, you can start at the pullout 1³⁄₁₀ mile after the 5 mile marker and follow the stream. But this is much more difficult, and the first part of that trail is harder to follow.

MOUNTAIN BIKE HALEAKALA'S SPINE

OK, so everyone's heard of the Haleakala Downhill bike ride mentioned on page 173. But few are aware of this—there's a road called Skyline that meanders down the *other* side of the volcano, and it makes an incredible downhill *mountain bike* ride. After Skyline's downhill trek you have 2 miles of relatively flat dirt road, then almost 6 miles of paved downhill *yee-haw* riding. Best of all, there are no commercial operators clogging the roads. (Some might tell you you're not allowed to mountain bike it, but the truth is *they're* not allowed to do it *commercially.*)

Here's the deal. To do this you'll probably need two cars—one to leave at the end of Waipoli Road, the other to take you and your bikes to the summit of Haleakala. You'll probably find that renting a cheap-o car for a day is about the same price as renting a mountain bike (which is kind of odd when you think about it). Leave the car and a bike rack (which you get when you rent the mountain bikes) at Waipoli and Hwy 377 (the upper highway—see map on page 115), then head to the summit (not the upper visitor center).

Once at the top, ride your bikes down the short road, hang a right (the 21 mile marker is there), and at the next intersection stay to the left to get to Skyline Road. (If the nasty government sign bothers you, see page 125 for an explanation.) Skyline is just over a mile downhill from the summit.

Watch for the Mamane Trailhead at almost 5½ miles into Skyline; it's on the right and easy to miss. This is perhaps the best part of the ride. It's just over a mile on a smooth, but narrow trail with killer views, and it seems tailor-made for mountain biking. The intersection of Mamane and Waiohuli is marked by a large lava pit crater. This was an eruption vent, where lava gurgled down the mountain.

Stop and poke around for a minute. Also, it makes an ideal shelter if it starts raining.

The short trail segment from the Mamane/Waiohuli intersection to Waipoli Road is the steepest, and you may want to walk the bike over part of it.

Once on Waipoli Road, the free ride is over. It's 2 miles, mostly flat but with a little uphill, to the paved part of Waipoli Road. Raise the seat and take it slow. Once on the pavement, the 1½-lane road is a delightful, extremely winding downhill joyride. Keep the speed down, and watch for cars on this sparsely driven road. All told, you rode almost 16 miles and lost nearly 7,000 feet!

Once on Skyline (marked by a gate) you'll hate what you see. The first mile is a pretty ugly surface of loose lava rocks, and you'll be forgiven if you want to walk your bike on parts of it. It's an easy walk, and the views are awesome. After a mile the road gets smoother, though it's always on a loose surface, so don't get too crazy. Avoid locking your front tire, or it will wash out. The road continues to improve the lower you get, and the riding gets more fun since you're a bit less worried about your traction. A gate at 3½ miles into the trail is easy to ride around.

*Map labels:*

Summit 10,023'
Science City
21
Gate
Skyline Road (Closed 4WD Road)
7,800'
9,000'
8,000'
Gate
8,000'
Kahua Rd
Waiakoa Trail (7.2)
Waipoli Rd
Boundary (.4)
6,800'
5,600'
Gate
Waiohuli (1.4)
Mamane (1.1)
7,200'
Redwood (1.7)
Foot Trails
Unpaved Roads
Contour Lines = 40 ft
Tie
Parking (6,160')
Polipoli Trail (.6)—Lengths are in miles
5,300'
Plum Trail (1.7)
Haleakala Ridge Trail (1.6)
5,900'
0   1 MILE
© 2008 Wizard Publications, Inc.

Some Tips

You'll probably want to lower your seat *a lot* for the downhill part for more comfort, stability and a lower center of gravity. It also allows you to use your legs more to keep some weight off your 'okole on the bumpy parts. Rent a bike with front shocks. Rear shocks, too (for about $45), if your tush is tender.

Some may not like the narrow Mamane section. They (and those who miss it) can continue on Skyline where it will wrap around to Waipoli. Add 2 miles of pedaling if you do it this way.

This adventure will take most of the day, if you include the shuttling. A good time frame is to pick up the car in Kahului and pick up the bikes at around 9 a.m. (we use Haleakala Bike 575–9575 in Ha'iku because they are a good shop and conveniently located for this). Then head to Waipoli to leave the car.

If you feel guilty about all that downhill riding, you can always take the Waiakoa Trail after Mamane for a 1,200-foot climb before rejoining Waipoli Road. (But you're probably not feeling *that* guilty.)

If you've never mountain biked before, yes, you probably can do this. We've taken a novice and she loved it, but she rode *nice and slow* and walked when she felt uncomfortable. Wear long pants and a jacket, and bring a tire patch kit. Sure, the riding surface is harder than the traditional downhill ride, but you go at your own pace, which is a big deal for safety.

HIKE TO THE HEART OF AN ERUPTION

Here's another example of uncertainty of outcome. You're either going to love this hike or hate it badly.

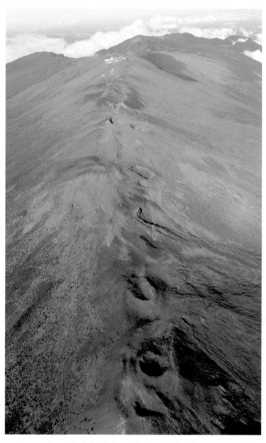

The spine of Haleakala with its chain of craters makes a glorious mountain bike ride. All downhill without the crowds.

Maui's last eruption was around 1790, and the vent where most of the lava came from, called Kalua o Lapa, can actually be visited. The problem is that, although there is obvious trail most of the way, at some places the trail is very vague and it'll seem like you're trekking through raw lava. Though the lava near the vent isn't nearly as difficult to walk through as the lava near the highway, it's still a difficult surface to trek through.

Rather than make a traditional map of the hike, we are including a marked aerial photo to use in navigating your way. Use it to orient yourself relative to hills, various patches of vegetation in the lava field and the vent itself.

See map on page 133. At the end of Makena Alanui Road, park near the La Pérouse Monument and walk back ²⁄₁₀ mile to a telephone marked 24A. Fifty

Since part of this hike requires navigating through the lava field, use this photo to orient yourself relative to hills and vegetation patches.

feet before the pole, squeeze through the trees on the mauka side of the road and emerge in a lava field after only 15 feet. Pass through a break in a short rock wall and follow the vague path up the lava flow. Head toward a sign at the top of this climb and continue on the actual lava trail.

The trail is made up of smaller pieces of lava. Your destination, the lava vent, is easily discernable as a charred-looking hill with a deep gash down the center. It's simply the most recent of many similar vents that are studded along the spine of Haleakala, marking the final stage of a dying volcano.

About ⅓ of the way up you come to a fork in the trail; stay on the main one to the right. At another junction, with a quasi-rock wall, take the left fork. At this point, if you turn around you'll notice that this is a four-way junction, with another trail coming up that you didn't see. When you return, make sure you take the correct one. (The aerial photo will help clarify this.) Looking back at the sea in the early morning, the normal trade winds should be roughing up the waters in front of and to the left of Kaho-'olawe, leaving the little sliver of Molokini in the calm. As the morning progresses, the choppy water will work its way toward Molokini.

Where a 100-foot-long rock wall ends, you should see a trail off to your right; take it. You're heading toward the forest. Once at the forest the difficulty begins. You want to skirt the edge of the forest, veering constantly to your right until you see the vent in front of you. Trail segments are very vague in spots and strong in others. Then you'll come to a series of ribbons of smooth pahoehoe lava meandering through the harsh a'a lava like natural sidewalks. The pahoehoe starts and stops abruptly, and it's up to you to discover as many segments of it as possible as you make your way through the lava field toward the vent above you. Some people wear gloves here to help balance in the lava field. The lava here is hell on shoes. Hiking shoes or boots are *strongly* recommended, as sneakers will get chewed up in no time.

At the base of the hill is a large lava tube with its ceiling caved in. Don't get too close to the edge. This tube was the volcano's aorta, where most of the vent's lava blood flowed to feed the rest of the flow. If you want to get to the top, you'll have to climb directly up through the cone. Start in the center until you reach the loose crumbling rocks that cover the inside of the vent. Then stay to the right and carefully maneuver up the back wall. Suddenly you're exposed to the strong winds that have been piling up along the bottom of the island, often venting off right here.

The view from the top is striking; just don't get knocked over. Notice the colors of the spatters of lava on top that blobbed out of the vent back in 1790. Just behind the cone is a road in the lava that a horseback riding company uses to bring riders to the vent. (They don't get to see the bottom of the vent the way you did.) The lava flow is conservation area owned by the state, not private property, and you're allowed to be there. The horseback company controls the forest around you, not the lava flow you're walking through.

The ranch is adamant about keeping trespassers off their land. The road may look like a better way to return, but you'll have to get back to your car the way you came. At this point you'll be amazed at how much better you walk through the lava; your feet have learned what to do.

Hazards include sharp lava that may shred your shoes, or your 'okole if you fall on it. Winds rock 'n' roll after the early morning burns off, so do this hike early. Navigation can be difficult. The trails are easy to follow *most* of the time, but there are many times when they are extremely vague, and the state doesn't want you veering from the trail, no matter how vague it is. The lava is surprisingly hard on shoes. We've hiked through hundreds of miles of lava on the Big Island but never had our shoes worn as quickly as we did here. All told you're hiking less than 3 miles, but it may seem like more. Your altitude gain to the top of the vent is about 500 feet, gentle most of the way.

DAY TRIP TO MOLOKA'I'S KALAUPAPA

Moloka'i's formerly notorious Kalaupapa leprosy settlement (see page 146 for more) is an isolated peninsula on the island's spectacular north side. Surrounded by sea cliffs thousands of feet high, the views from here, not to mention the incredible history, are available as day trips from Maui. The most popular way is Moloka'i Mule Rides (567–6088), which takes you down a 1,700-foot cliff to the settlement below. Book in advance. It's $165, which includes lunch and the tour below.

If you're already on Moloka'i, you can walk the trail yourself. Once at the bottom, Damien Tours (567–6171) takes you on a historical 4-hour tour of the settlement. It's $40 but doesn't include lunch. (Supplies here are hard to come by and they only get barge service *once a year*.)

Paragon Air (244–3356) has a package from Maui that includes flight, aerial tour of the sea cliffs, lunch and the ground tour for $285. A bit pricey. No one under 16 allowed. They almost *never* answer their phone, so book online.

TAKE YOUR OWN BOAT TO MOLOKINI

There are lots of charter boats you can take to Molokini. But what if you want to do things your own way? Only one company, located in South Maui, rents single-hull power boats, Sea Escape (879–3721), at 1979 South Kihei Rd. They'll meet you at the Kihei Boat Ramp and set you adrift. Take it virtually any place you want. And with speeds of up to 35 MPH, you can go to a lot of places. The catch? Price. They charge $99 per hour (4 hour min.) on the 21-foot boat, $119 per hour (5 hour min.) on the much nicer 26-foot boat, and $139 per hour (5 hour min.) for their power cat. Fuel is extra. Now, that's

a *big* chunk of money. But if you have 4 to 6 people, it's not quite as painful when you split it. Seeing the area this way is a real hoot, but nobody ever said hoots were cheap. For liability reasons they prefer that you've at least driven a power boat before. On calm days we like to explore the bottom of the island. They have water skis, fishing poles, porta-potties, etc., available for extra. We've even taken SCUBA tanks down south and dived absolutely pristine areas. Whatever you do, make sure that when you're captain, you practice giving meaningless orders with an arrogant snarl. *Swab the decks, batten down the hatches, bring me a flagon of grog, matey, or ye'll walk the plank for sure. Arrrgh.*

HIKE IN A LAVA TUBE

Maui Cave Adventures (248–7308) has an interesting tour. Their land has access to Ka'eleku Cave, a lava tube from Hana's past. The cave has some nice formations. This isn't like mainland mineral caves. Lava tubes aren't as colorful. But

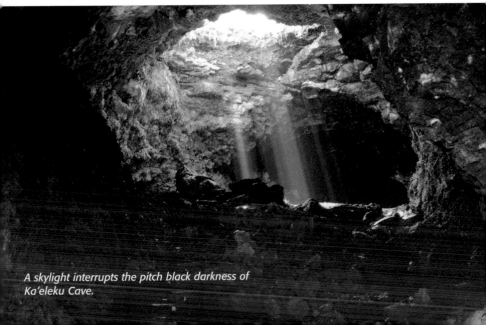

A skylight interrupts the pitch black darkness of Ka'eleku Cave.

it's a fascinating journey through a volcanic pipeline.

They have $12 self-guided tours with signs discussing various *ologies* and now have much better flashlights than in the past. They've marked various formations with signs explaining what you're seeing.

By the way, if you ever wanted to see what utter blackness looks like, the kind where you can't tell whether your eyes are open or closed, have everyone turn off their lights. That's darkness like you've never seen.

COME SAIL AWAY

You want to sail your own boat, but only one thing stops you—*you don't know how to sail!* Well, here's your chance. Several companies have small sailboats like Hobie Cats that are easy to learn. Only one sail to mess with, like a glorified windsurfer. After only a single lesson, most people are ready to sail off into the sunset. (Well, maybe not *that* far.) Sailing is gobs of fun. The clean sound of the boat cutting through the water is oh, so memorable, and it's amazing how much more arrogant your swagger will be when you become a *real* sailor.

In South Maui, Maui Ocean Activities at the Grand Wailea (875–1234) rents Hobie Cats for $55 an hour or $130 for 3 hours. Lessons are an extra $69 for an hour. They will put an instructor with you to teach and observe you (to make sure you're not an idiot), then let you sail off.

At press time nobody was renting sailboats in West Maui.

TRY A NIGHT OR SCOOTER DIVE

Some people say SCUBA diving is no longer considered an adventure *in and of itself.* Too mainstream, too common. Hmm, fair enough. But these dives are another matter entirely. Night dives are inherently exciting and unpredictable, as your eye follows the powerful light, wondering what it will reveal. You don't see anything that's beyond your beam, and that adds to the fun. You may come across parrotfish wrapped in their natural transparent sleeping bags, moray eels out free swimming, lobsters (known here as bugs) trying to avoid being tomorrow night's special, needlefish strangely attracted to your light, Spanish dancers shaking their maracas, perhaps even a manta ray. You never know what a night dive will bring. Maybe little, maybe the motherload, but a whole different crew works the reef's night shift. The same reef you may have seen yesterday suddenly seems so much more mysterious and thrilling in your night light.

See the SCUBA section for recommended dive companies. Most (though not all) do night dives. Examples are Maui Dreams (874–5332), which does 1-tank shore dives for $69. Ed Robinson (879–3584) has 2-tank boat night dives for $150. Maui Dive Shop (879–3388), does 2-tank night dives to Molokini and another South Maui spot twice a week for $130 or a night *shipwreck* dive in West Maui for $140.

Scooter Dives aren't your usual cerebral exploration. These dives are an unabashed thrill ride, like an underwater roller coaster. Forget finding exotic fish or colorful reefs. Here, the object is to cruise like you belong here. It wasn't until my first scooter dive that I realized that humans can be incredibly graceful in the water. Usually we look clumsy and awkward. But scooters allow you to maneuver like a sea lion. They are amazingly precise and easy to learn. After just a few minutes' practice, it's easy to skim the bottom, do loops and corkscrews, and soar like an underwater eagle. In short, they're a blast!

Cruising in style.

Keep in mind that having a scooter doesn't eliminate the laws of biology. You're still not supposed to rise faster than a foot a second. And the scooter makes depth changes so effortless and subtle, you'll often find yourself with some pretty ferocious mask squeeze if you're not careful. Here's where the breathing tip mentioned on page 223 really pays off. Because you're almost always exhaling, it provides a safety cushion for the depth changes. But be cautious and aware of what you're doing. If you're doing a loop, don't do it too shallow where the relative differences in depth are more pronounced. Also, you don't burn much air, but should still ask for an 80 tank. And make sure your BC is nice and snug. Things tend to come loose more easily with the increased speed.

Prodiver Maui (875-4004) at the Fairmont Kea Lani uses scooters that allow an hour-long dive. They will also take you to 5 Caves/5 Graves, a cool spot. Maui Dreams (874-5332) also does scooter dives for $89. Island Scuba (667-4608) in West Maui at the Marriott, Beach Activities of Maui (662-8207) at the Sheraton and Pacific Dive (667-

5331) also do this. 5-Star has several resort locations. They like to stop often and explore the reef by fin, which isn't as much fun as a nonstop ride. Tell them if you don't want to stop. They also have a shore dive package that includes a day, night and a scooter dive for $199. Otherwise, expect to pay around $100.

HALEAKALA CRATER GRAND LOOP

One of most incredible hikes on the island. It takes you down into glorious Haleakala Crater, across the floor, then back up via another trail. The views are unspeakably good, and the colors are amazingly varied. All told, it's a 13-mile hike. Though you start at 9,800 feet and eventually drop to 6,600 feet, you'll only climb back up 1,400 feet to the 8,000 foot level. Granted, climbing 1,400 feet isn't a picnic, but it's much easier than recapturing the 3,200 feet you lost coming down. See map on page 120.

Doing this hike necessitates leaving a vehicle at the Halemau'u Trailhead between the 14 and 15 mile marker and then starting at the Sliding Sands Trailhead past the 20 mile marker. You can either leave your car at Halemau'u and try to get a ride up, or rent an extra cheap-o car for the day. The latter is a sure thing, whereas getting a ride isn't.

Park at the Visitor Center and start at the Sliding Sands Trailhead around the corner. It's downhill virtually the entire way—until you pay the piper during the last 2½ miles. More on that later. On the way down, you may want to take the side trip to Ka Ku'u o ka 'O'o. The crater reveals its character only as you continue changing elevations and angles. After the trail levels, descends, then levels out again, you'll take the spur trail (there's a horse hitch at the intersection) to the left, heading north. Looking at the map, you'll want to veer right, then left at the next intersections to visit Kawilinau, formerly the Bottomless Pit. (The map makes this simpler.) See page 124 for more on this pit. Turn left and about 100 yards past the pit is an area called Pele's Paint Pot. Minerals in the rock created this colorful rock canvas.

If you have a few extra calories you need to burn, you can take a side (unmaintained) trail up a ridge near here which overlooks the Dinosaur spine and the grandness of the crater itself.

After the Silversword Loop, our old friend green will start to return as the vegetation increases while you get closer to the mountain and the Ko'olau Gap. Stop and rest at Holua Cabin if you wish, envying the lucky buggers who literally won the lottery for the right to stay there.

In another mile, it will be time to pay your dues. In terms of elevation, you've had it pretty easy for these last 10 miles. Now it's time to sweat. Fortunately, the trail switchbacks are only moderately steep. One of the switchbacks wanders over to the other side of the mountain, giving you a magnificent view (clouds permitting) of the Ko'olau Gap. Make sure to stop many times on the way up to enjoy the incredible views.

A Few Basics

Bring *gobs* of water with you. You lose water at a ferocious clip at this altitude. Since the only real climbing is at the end,

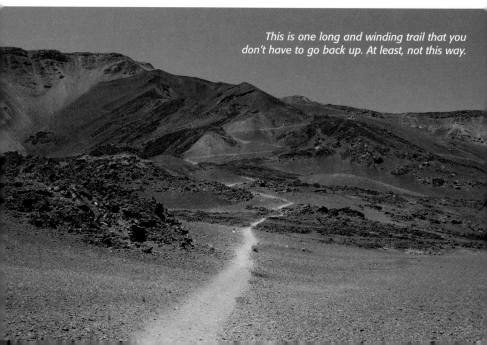

This is one long and winding trail that you don't have to go back up. At least, not this way.

it's no big a deal to drag more water than you *think* you'll need, *suck 'em up* all day, and pour out the excess before starting the climb. Also, bring a hat and sunblock. You fry fast up here. Rain is possible, especially at the end as you're climbing back up. A light rain jacket is a good idea, especially in the winter. Dress warm for the top and cool for the bottom. You never know what kind of weather you'll encounter on this hike. Hiking sticks can help with all the elevation changes, but the surface will be pretty brutal on the tips.

KAYAK TO AN UNNAMED BEACH

Until this publication, Keawanaku was unnamed and virtually unknown. We discovered this beach during a hike (described on page 201) and quickly realized that it would be a great beach to kayak to. Put in at La Pérouse Bay in Makena, and Keawanaku is less than 2 miles to the south.

The key to this adventure is to start *early.* When the winds kick up in the late morning and early afternoon, it becomes one of the windiest places on the island. Fortunately, mornings are usually fairly calm, and once the winds start, they *usually* help you *somewhat* on the way back, with an along the shore then offshore alignment. We put this in ADVENTURES because the winds need to be respected and anticipated. If you don't start early—heck, even if you *do*—they could cause problems for you. In fact, some kayak companies won't rent to you if you mention that you're doing this paddle. See KAYAKING on page 205 for more on renting a kayak.

SWIMMING WITH SHARKS

Have you ever visited a large aquarium and wished you could observe the fish and sharks from the *other* side of

Two kayakers discover Keawanaku, a hidden oasis in a sea of harsh lava.

the glass? Here's your chance and the experience is ridiculously cool.

Three times a week Maui Ocean Center in Ma'alaea allows two pairs of divers to spend around 40 minutes swimming with sharks, stingrays, puffer fish and all the other species in their three-quarter million gallon exhibit. And while the draw might be the 20 or so sharks in the tank, it's surprising that after a short amount of time many people start to forget that they're supposed to be afraid of sharks and find themselves oddly at home. Actually, we found it one of the most relaxing dives we've ever done, and during our dive the spotted eagle ray was the star. She loved to be touched and fed clams in their shells. We never realized how incredibly *loud* rays are when they crunch clam shells. In fact, you might not realize just how noisy the open ocean is until you've dived in this quiet tank. And with no current, surge or long swimming, you may be amazed at how little air you draw from your 50-cubic foot tank.

It's hard to believe that swimming with sharks can be so relaxing. But on this dive, it is.

There's nothing about this dive we didn't like—except the price. It's almost **$200** per person and *doesn't* include SCUBA gear which you'll have to rent elsewhere. (They say the price is steep because their insurance rates are so high.)

Don't think of this as a death-defying shark encounter. The sharks don't seem very interested in feeding on divers. Think of this as the best chance you'll ever have to spend quality bonding time with sea creatures. In the open ocean these animals avoid you. But in this tank, you're one of the gang. The adventure here is to discover just how wondrous these animals really are, when you're given the chance to observe them close up for so long.

You need to be a certified SCUBA diver and since they take so few people, call the Maui Ocean Center (270–7075) well in advance.

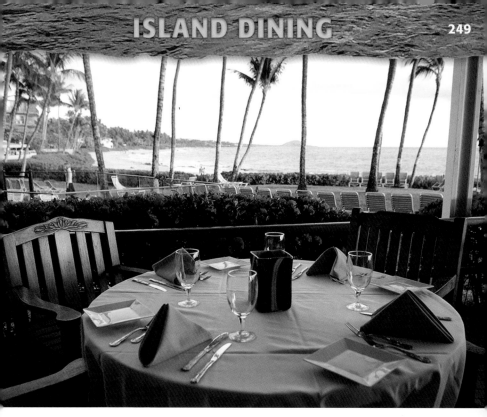

Yes, this table will do just fine, thank you.

By their very nature, restaurant reviews are the most subjective part of any guidebook. Nothing strains the credibility of a guidebook more. No matter what we say, if you eat at enough restaurants here, you will eventually have a dining experience directly in conflict with what this book leads you to believe. All it takes is one person to wreck what is usually a good meal. Many of us have had the experience when a friend referred us to a restaurant using reverent terms indicating that they were about to experience dining ecstasy. And, of course, when you go there, the food is awful and the waiter is a jerk. There are many variables involved in getting a good or bad meal. Is the chef new? Was the place sold last month? Was the waitress just released from prison for mauling a customer? We truly hope that our reviews match your experience. If they don't, *please* let us know. (It alerts us to both problems *and* jewels to check.)

This ISLAND DINING chapter was pretty overwhelming for us. A huge number of choices made it difficult to select which ones to include. (And hey, we can only *eat* so much!) Restaurants come and go, but if there's a place that you *really* loved (and don't forget the ones you *really* hated), please drop us a line at the address or e-mail on page 4.

Unlike some travel writers who announce themselves to restaurants (to cop a free meal, if the truth be told), we always review *anonymously* and only expose ourselves after a meal (not literally, of course) *by phone* if we need additional information. By their reviews, many guidebooks lead you to believe that every meal you eat in Hawai'i will be a feast, the best food in the free world. Frankly, that's not our style. Like anywhere else, there's ample opportunity to have lousy food served with a rotten ambiance by uncaring waiters. In the interest of space, we've left out *some* of the dives. We did, however, leave in enough of these turkeys just to demonstrate that we know we live in the real world. Restaurants that stand out from the others in some way are highlighted with **ONO** our ONO symbol.

For each restaurant, we list the price *per person* you can expect to pay. It ranges from the least expensive entrées alone to the most expensive plus a beverage and usually appetizers. You can spend more if you try, but this is a good guideline. *The price excludes alcoholic beverages since this component of a meal can be so variable.* Obviously, everyone's ordering pattern is different, but we thought that it would be easier to compare various restaurants using dollar amounts than if we used different numbers of dollar signs or drawings of forks or whatever to differentiate prices between various restaurants. All restaurants take credit cards unless otherwise noted. When we mention that prices are reasonable, please take it in context. We mean reasonable *for Maui.* (We *know* you pay less back home.) Food in Hawai'i is expensive, even if it's grown here. (You probably pay less for our fruit on the mainland than *we* do here.)

When we give directions to a restaurant, *mauka side* of highway means "toward the mountain" (or away from the ocean). The shopping centers we mention are on the maps to that area. And remember when making reservations that the area code is 808.

The definition of **local food** is tricky. Basically, local food combines Hawaiian, American, Japanese, Chinese, Filipino and several other types and is (not surprisingly) eaten mainly by locals.

Pacific Rim is sort of a fusion of American and various countries around the Pacific, including Asian and Hawaiian. It's a fine (and subjective) line between American and Pacific Rim. We don't have a separate **Seafood** section because nearly every restaurant on Maui serves fish.

Lu'aus, those giant outdoor Hawaiian parties, are described at the end.

When a restaurant requires **resort wear**, that means collared shirts for men (though nice shorts are *usually* OK) and dressy sportswear or dresses for women.

Some restaurants have the annoying and presumptuous habit of including the tip in the bill automatically. Be on the alert for it or you may double-tip. And what if you get horrible service and don't *want* to tip? Then you're left in the awkward position of making them remove it.

Dining at the resorts is expensive, but you probably aren't being gouged as much as you think because their costs are exorbitant. One resort GM we know confided that they had over $7 million in revenue for their food and beverage department one year, but only made $100,000 in profit. (And this was the first year they had ever made *any* profit on food.)

Below are descriptions of various island foods. Not all are Hawaiian, but this might be of assistance if you encounter unfamiliar dishes.

ISLAND FISH & SEAFOOD

Ahi–Tuna; raw in sashimi or poke, also seared, blackened, baked or grilled; good in fish sandwiches. Try painting ahi steaks with mayonnaise, which *completely* burns off when BBQ'd but seals in the moisture. You end up tasting only the moist ocean steak. Most plentiful April through September.

Lobster–Hawaiian spiny lobster is quite good; also called "bugs" by lobster hunters. Keahole Lobster is simply Maine lobster flown to the Big Island where it's revived in cold water.

Mahimahi–Deep ocean fish also known as a dolphinfish; served at lu'aus; very common in restaurants. Sometimes tastes fishy (especially if frozen), which can be offset in the preparation.

Marlin–Tasty when smoked, otherwise can be tough; the Pacific Blue Marlin is available almost year round.

Monchong–Excellent tasting deepwater fish, available year round. Usually served marinated and grilled.

Onaga–Also known as a ruby snapper; excellent eating in many preparations.

Ono–(Wahoo) *Awesome* eating fish and can be prepared many ways; most plentiful May through October. Ono is also the Hawaiian word for delicious.

Opah–(Moonfish) Excellent eating in many different preparations; generally available April through August.

'Opakapaka–(Crimson snapper) Great tasting fish generally cooked several ways. Common Oct.–Feb.

'Opihi–Limpets found on ocean rocks. Eaten raw mixed with salt. Texture is similar to clams or mussels.

Poke–Fresh raw fish or octopus (tako) mixed with seaweed (limu), sesame seed and other seasonings and oil.

Shutome–Swordfish; dense meat that can be cooked several ways. Most plentiful March through July.

LU'AU FOODS

Chicken lu'au–Chicken cooked in coconut milk and taro leaves.

Haupia–Coconut custard.

Kalua pig–Pig cooked in an underground oven called an imu (hot rocks go *inside* the beast), shredded and mixed with Hawaiian sea salt. Outstanding!

Laulau–Pork, beef or fish wrapped in taro and ti leaves and steamed. (You don't eat the ti leaf wrapping.)

Lomi salmon–Chilled salad consisting of raw salted salmon, tomatoes and two kinds of onions.

Poi–Steamed taro root pounded into a paste. It's a starch that will take on the taste of other foods mixed with it. Best eaten with kalua pig or fish. Visitors are encouraged to try it so they can badmouth it with authority.

OTHER ISLAND FOODS

Apple bananas–A smaller, denser, smoother texture than regular (Williams) bananas.

Barbecue sticks–Teriyaki-marinated pork, chicken or beef pieces barbecued and served on bamboo sticks.

Bento–Japanese box lunch.

Breadfruit–Melon-sized starchy fruit; served baked, deep fried, steamed, or boiled. Definitely an acquired taste.

Crackseed–Chinese-style, spicy preserved fruits and seeds. Li Hing Mui is one of the most popular flavors.

Guava–Tart fruit whose inside is full of seeds, so it is rarely eaten raw. Usually prepared with lots of sugar, so it's used primarily for juice, jelly or jam.

Hawaiian supersweet corn–The finest corn you ever had, even raw. We'll lie, cheat, steal or maim to get it fresh.

Huli huli chicken–Hawaiian BBQ style.

Ka'u oranges–Grown on the Big Island. Usually, the uglier the orange, the better it tastes.

Kim chee–A Korean relish consisting of pickled cabbage, onions, radishes, garlic and chilies.

Kulolo–Steamed taro pudding.

Liliko'i–Passion fruit.

Loco moco–Rice, meat patty, egg and gravy. *Never* served as health food.

Lychee–A reddish, woody peel that is discarded for the sweet, white fruit inside. Be careful of the pit. Small seed (or chicken-tongue) lychees are so good, they should be illegal.

Macadamia nut–A large, round nut grown primarily on the Big Island.

Malasada–Portuguese doughnut that is dipped in sugar.

Manapua–Steamed or baked bun filled with meat.

Mango–Bright orange fruit with yellow pink skin. Distinct, tasty flavor.

Manju–Cookie filled with a sweet center.

Maui onions–Grown in Kula; sweet, some people eat them like apples.

Musubi–Cold steamed rice, often with sliced Spam rolled in black seaweed.

Papaya–Melon-like, pear-shaped fruit with yellow skin best eaten chilled. Good at breakfast.

Pipi Kaula–Hawaiian-style beef jerky. Excellent when dipped in poi. (Even if you don't like poi, this combo works.)

Plate lunch–An island favorite as an inexpensive, filling lunch. Consists of "two-scoop rice," a scoop of macaroni salad and some type of meat, either beef, chicken or fish. Also called a Box Lunch. Great for take-out.

Portuguese sausage–Pork sausage, highly seasoned with red pepper.

Pupu–Appetizer, finger foods or snack.

Saimin–Thin Chinese noodles cooked in a Japanese-style chicken, pork or fish broth. Word is peculiar to Hawai'i. Local Japanese say the dish comes from China. Local Chinese say it comes from Japan.

Shave ice–A block of ice is "shaved" into a ball with flavored syrup poured over the top. Best served with ice cream on the bottom. Very delicious.

Smoothie–Usually papaya, mango, frozen passion fruit and frozen banana, but almost any fruit can be used to make this milkshake-like drink. Add milk for creaminess.

Taro chips–Sliced and deep-fried taro; resembles potato chips.

WEST MAUI AMERICAN

Beachwalk Market & Pantry
100 Nohea Kai Dr. • 667–1200

ONO Why would we give an ONO to a place that serves $11 burgers and Pizza Hut pizza? Because it's on Ka'anapali Beach, and you can take your food and plop down in the sand (or use their tables off the beach). Selection is pretty good with packaged salads, sandwiches and fruits, plus some grilled items. Pizza Hut never tasted so good until you've eaten it on the beach. At the pool next to the beachside path at the Marriott Ka'anapali. The Hyatt also has a similar set-up called **Pavilion**, but it's not as conveniently located, and the Westin's version, **Seadog**, is terrible. Beachwalk is $7–$12 for breakfast, $9–$17 for lunch and dinner.

Bubba Gump Shrimp Co.
889 Front St. • 661–3111

ONO Remember the movie *Forrest Gump*, when Bubba describes all the ways you can fix shrimp? Well, the owners of this small chain apparently didn't see it because most of the recipes mentioned in the movie aren't on the menu. But that's OK because this is a fairly easy place to like. The whole restaurant is based on the movie, and the dishes are named after its characters. Very friendly service (so friendly the waiter may come and sit at your table as he takes your order)—fun, loud and over the water. (Waves actually splash under the window tables, if you're lucky enough to get one.) The friendly service can seem a bit unresponsive until you realize that the license plates on the table that say, "Stop Forrest Stop," are meant as a signal to the waiter that you want him. (Beats the heck out of the old eye-contact method.) The food is mostly fairly good (certainly not great) with lots of shrimp dishes (obviously!), fish, some steak, burgers and salads. The peel-and-eat shrimpers' net catch makes a good appetizer, and they have some very good fresh fish. Their Medal Margarita is smokin' good, and the portion is hefty. We only have two complaints: They won't take reservations (and long waits are not uncommon), and they obviously want to turn tables over fast. This location serves over *800* meals a night (and 400 at lunch), raking in over $9 million a year. When we eat here, *we* set the pace by finding a nice way to tell them we're not in a hurry. Overall, a fun atmosphere and acceptable food make a good experience. We've certainly seen them drop the ball, but they're good about fixing things. In Lahaina between Lahainaluna and Papalaua. $10–$25 for lunch and dinner. If you've been to the Bubba Gump in Kona, note that this one is better.

Cheeseburger in Paradise
811 Front St. • 661-4855
A legendary place in Lahaina, it's fun to try at least once. Sharing a name with a song by Jimmy Buffet (who promptly sued them when he discovered the restaurant), the decor has plenty of *eye candy* to keep your eyes busy during your stay. Only *some* of the food is reasonably good. (Ironically, the cheeseburgers are their weakest offering, but the fries are *excellent*.) Try the chili cheese fries (hold the onions) for an appetizer. The Polynesian coconut shrimp are tasty but come with only six shrimp along with a large mound of their delicious fries. Their cocktails tend to be fruity and tasty. We've gotten quite a few e-mails from readers about this place, and they're oddly split between those who love it and go back repeatedly and those who balk at the rather ordinary burgers and the busy atmosphere, and, as wishy-washy as it sounds, we agree with both views. (This location serves over $7 million worth of food per year.) Often packed, with lines as long as *1½ hours* (which is ridiculous), service and the overall experience, surprisingly, seems *better* when they are busy (they get into a rhythm) and diminishes with the crowds. **$6–$11** for breakfast, **$9–$18** for lunch and dinner. Vegetarian burgers available. In Lahaina right on the water on Front Street and Lahainaluna. No reservations. If you're wondering where the ONO is, well we moved it to **Cool Cat**. *Certainly* not as good an atmosphere, but way better burgers. They also have a location at Shops at Wailea in South Maui called **Cheeseburger Island Style** (874–8990), but it lacks the energy of the Lahaina location. This Wailea location, however, is good for breakfast. Big portions and tasty food. Consider the excellent superspuds.

Coffee Store
5095 Napilihau St. • 669-4170
An acceptable, though not compelling, place to go for your morning coffee. Decent (though too-often old) baked goods and an agreeable coffee selection. Not the most compelling coffee joint in West Maui.

In Napili Plaza near 29 mile marker on Hwy 30. Also in Azeka Mauka in Kihei and Ka'ahumanu Mall in Kahului. **$3–$6.**

Cool Cat Café
658 Front St. • 667–0908

ono A '50s-themed restaurant, they make a great burger here; much better than Cheeseburger in Paradise for around the same price. Fresh fixin's, toasted buns and tasty variations. Try their onion rings for a side. Your food takes awhile, but it's worth the wait, so chill out daddy-o. They also have lots of sandwiches to choose from. Desserts include malts, shakes (made the old-fashioned way, thick and tasty), root beer floats and brownie sundaes. **$9–$15** for lunch and dinner. On the top floor of the Wharf Cinema overlooking Banyan Tree Park.

David Paul's Lahaina Grill
127 Lahainaluna Rd. • 667–5117

ono One of the nicest restaurants in West Maui. Food, service and setting are all rock solid. There's no view here, but the tasteful decor is complemented by outstanding food. This chef *really* knows flavors, such as the tequila shrimp and firecracker rice. Unbelievable flavor combinations. Duck, steak, lamb, fresh fish. We haven't had a bad meal here yet. Prices are *very* high, but if you're looking to splurge, you'll be pleased with the results. The kind of place that doesn't seem to change over the years. **$30–$55.** Reservations recommended. Near Front Street in Lahaina.

Dollie's Pub & Café
4310 Lwr. Honoapiilani • 669–0266

A bar with food. Average pizza and beer with sandwiches and some pasta. They're often too generous with the vast amount of pizza cheese; consider asking them to tone it down. Service is a bit scant. Wish we could say more, but the price isn't too bad. (Well, I guess their bottled beer selection is pretty good.) **$8–$15** for lunch and dinner. In Kahana Manor Shops just south of Hoohui Street. (See bottom of map on page 53.)

Foodland Deli
Old Lahaina Center • 661–0975

OK, so it's merely a grocery store deli. But you can grab some fairly tasty sandwiches for relatively little money. **$4–$7** and you're on your way. In Lahaina off Front Street and Papalaua.

Gazebo
5315 Lwr. Honoapiilani • 669–5621

ono Gazebo benefits greatly from its location. Eating near the shore with wicked ocean, Napili Bay and Moloka'i views for...*relatively* little money (for this area, at least) makes the food and service seem better. They've got a good selection of omelettes, and their signature mac nut pancakes are pretty good. Lunch is burgers, sandwiches and salads. Both are served simultaneously from 7:30–2 p.m., which is handy. They only have 15 tables and fill up quick (they don't take reservations), so either arrive well before they open or you'll have to wait, perhaps a *long* time. **$7–$12** for breakfast, **$9–$13** for lunch. South of Kapalua. Park at Napili Shores toward the back and walk through the resort.

Hard Rock Café
900 Front St. • 667–7400

Similar to the Hard Rock Cafés on the mainland but with tasty views of the ocean and Lana'i. Rock 'n' roll memorabilia (especially guitars) line the walls as music fills the air and music videos provide the eye candy. (The music is sometimes too loud—outdoor tables are quieter but have less ambiance.) Burgers, salads, sandwiches, steak and some pastas and fajitas. Most portions are large. Desserts are large and delicious. Frankly it's not the kind of place we go to for dinner, but we'll go there for pupus and a beer. **$10–$25** for lunch and dinner. In Lahaina Center on Front and Papalaua streets, Lahaina.

Hecock's on the Ocean
505 Front St. • 661–8810

We like this place for breakfast because of the relaxing location overlooking the ocean and Lana'i, and the view premium isn't that high. Lunch, too, is a pretty good value. But dinner? Forget it. Too expensive. Don't get us wrong. The food's not that great. But you ain't *paying* for great food. You're paying for a great location, reasonable price and merely *acceptable* food. And if they only sold breakfast, we'd probably give them an ONO. Lunch is burgers, sandwiches and fish and chips, dinner is steak and seafood. **$7–$10** for breakfast, **$8–$12** for lunch, **$25–$35** for dinner. At 505 Front St. Shopping Center off Shaw Ave. in Lahaina.

Honolua Store
502 Office Rd. • 669–6128

(ono) Ever wonder where employees in an ultra-expensive resort area eat? Well, for many, it's right here. They get an ONO because of the price alone. Inexpensive food is as scarce in Kapalua as RV parks. Simple, cheap breakfasts. Lunch is burgers, fish and chips, and sandwiches. And the food's not bad at all. Service can be pretty blank and uncaring, but that's OK. It's the only place in the area where two can eat for $10–$15. In Kapalua on Office Rd. near the Ritz. (Quite a contrast.) **$4–$7** for breakfast, **$5–$8** for lunch.

Hula Grill
2435 Ka'anapali Pkwy. • 667–6636

(ono) It's with nervous trepidation that we give them an ONO. Food can be good. It can also be awful. For instance, their chicken should be banned from the island. But many other items can be excellent. Their lobster and scallop pot stickers, when they have 'em, are outrageous as are their desserts. Love the shrimp and goat cheese quesadilla. The ambiance is *very* nice—next to Ka'anapali Beach with great water views and killer sunsets. Sandwiches, burgers and lots of salads for lunch, steak, seafood and pasta for dinner. In Whalers Village in Ka'anapali. **$10–15** for lunch, **$25–$35** for dinner.

Jonny's Burger Joint
2395 Honoapiilani Hwy. • 661–4500

A bar with burgers. The 6- & 9-ounce hand-packed patties come single or double, so if you're preparing to swim to Moloka'i, you can load up with a $13 *18-ounce* burger. When a lion takes down a wildebeest, it doesn't get that much protein! Veggie and fish burgers also available. Quality overall is fair. **$7–$15** for lunch and dinner (and they're open later than most restaurants). Below Giovanni's at Hwy 30 & Ka'anapali Pkwy.

Kahuna Kabobs
126 Lahainaluna Rd. • 661–9999

(ono) A good alternative to other high-priced food in West Maui. Kabobs and burgers are their specialty. Try the fish kabobs. For around $9 you'll get your fill of fish, rice and veggies. Give a little to the wild cats that sometimes visit from next door. They even have tofu kabobs for the vegetarian kittens. Hidden away in a courtyard in Lahaina Marketplace at Front Street and Lahainaluna, kitty-corner from Cheeseburger in Paradise. **$7–$13** for lunch and dinner.

Kimo's
845 Front St. • 661–4811

ono Dreamy location along the water's edge for lunch. Dinner is upstairs and slightly away from the water. (Some of the otherwise excellent dinner views are cut off by the roofline.) Lunch items are hit or miss, but mostly pretty good. Good burgers (need better fries, though). Their Hula Pie for dessert is worth the accolades. At dinner you can eat downstairs (which at night is designated as the bar) where some cheaper items are available. Otherwise, dinner is steak and seafood, usually with good results. Kimo's has a good atmosphere and usually good food. **$9–$15** for lunch. **$20–$35** for dinner (except the cheaper burgers). Good place for a sunset cocktail. In Lahaina between Lahainaluna and Papalaua. Reservations recommended for dinner.

Lahaina Coolers
180 Dickenson St. • 661–7082

An acceptable place for a meal and a cocktail. (They have some nicely concocted tropical drinks.) Food's not bad. Burgers, sandwiches, fish tacos, pasta and salad for lunch. Mostly steak with some chicken and fish and pizza for dinner. None of the entrées has us fantasizing about coming back, and the ingredients taste a bit cheap. But we won't steer you away, either. **$9–$12** for breakfast, **$10–$15** for lunch, **$11–$28** for dinner. On Dickenson near Wainee Street.

Lahaina Store Grille & Oyster Bar
744 Front St. • 661–9090

ono Besides great food, they sell a mighty fine view here. But their second floor seating has only half the view of the rooftop (dinner only). Lunch is seafood and burgers. Unless you're a certified oyster freak, avoid the disappointing oyster bar. Try the shish ka-bobs or fish and chips (avoid the kalua pork sandwich) and check out the belt-driven fans above you. The dinner menu offers a classier surf and turf fare. If you're sitting on the rooftop, ask for the back left corner where the views stretch from the mountains to the sea. (Go early, before sunset.) Presentation is very important here, but it's sometimes at the expense of flavor. Lunch is **$13–$30** or more, and dinner is **$26–$40**. Upstairs on the mauka side of Front Street between the Pioneer Inn and Lahaina Marketplace.

Leilani's on the Beach
2435 Ka'anapali Pkwy. • 661–4495

ono Two totally different menus and two totally different experiences. Downstairs, the **Beachside Grill** menu is a bargain considering the location and setting vs. the price. Stir fry chicken cashew or BBQ ribs are **$17** or less at the beachside setting. (Killer Hula Pie dessert.) You can order this menu at lunch or dinner. For the regular dinner menu upstairs, it's mostly steak, seafood and ribs for **$18–$28**. *Usually* good service and fairly good food, but with a *tasty* view, hence the ONO. In Ka'anapali at Whalers Village. Often busy, reservations recommended, though they *do* reserve some space for walk-ins.

Mama's Ribs 'n Rotisserie
Napili Plaza • 665–6262

Ribs and rotisserie chicken are their thing, and it's mostly take-out. (Just a few outdoor tables.) Solidly average best describes it, except for tastier whole chicken (which, at $15, tastes curiously similar to Costco's $6 chickens). Plate combo meals with so-so sides of beans, slaw, etc. also available. Despite the name, you're *not* treated like family here (unless blank indifference is the usual atmosphere at home). In Napili Plaza off Hwy 30's 29 mile marker. **$6–$20** for lunch and dinner. Closed Sun. No credit cards.

Maui Brewing Co.
4405 Honoapiilani Hwy. • 669–3474
Previously called Fish and Game, the name change brought little to the party. The beer can leave an unsavory aftertaste as can the menu prices. Sure, the presentation is nice, but $24 for ribs that taste like they came from a grocery store deli just doesn't cut it. Lunch is a bit more reasonable. It's one of Hawai'i's few microbreweries, so we're pulling for them. **$10–$20** for lunch, **$20–$40** for dinner. In the Kahana Gateway Center.

Moose McGillycuddy's
844 Front St. • 667–7758
This is a hopping place at night. Dinner is mostly steak (cow, not moose) and some seafood and is popular with singles looking for…well, what singles are *always* looking for. Entertainment and dancing at night. Lunch consists mostly of burgers. However, avoid having breakfast here unless you have *a lot* of time. Because if it takes 10 minutes for them to acknowledge your existence, 20 minutes to get a table and 25 minutes to get your food, you've donated almost an hour of your morning to the Moose before you even get a chance to eat. And for some reason, people are less willing to wait for breakfast than lunch or dinner. As for the food… we're talking biscuits and gravy even a starving moose wouldn't touch. **$5–$12** for breakfast, **$8–$15** for lunch, **$15–$35** for dinner. On Front Street in Lahaina. Also in Kihei (891–8600) at 2511 S. Kihei Road.

Pineapple Grill
200 Kapalua Dr. • 669–9600
ONO An unexpectedly good find at a golf course restaurant. The atmosphere is sort of upscale Hawaiian and the large selection of steak and seafood is coupled with a pretty vast and well-chosen wine selection. (Though their sommelier might not be as helpful as you'd like.) Torches outside make up for the lack of view at night. Items have an Asian twist, such as the excellent Asian braised short rib or the sake-soy grilled mahi mahi. Presentation is flawless, though service might be a tad lacking. **$12–$20** for lunch, **$30–$55** for dinner. Reservations recommended. At the Bay Golf Course.

Pioneer Inn Grill & Bar
658 Wharf St. • 661–3636
ONO A good place to go for breakfast, especially if you're taking a boat trip from adjacent Lahaina Harbor, and they open at 7 a.m. Service is fast and efficient. The big kahuna pancakes are giant, plate-covering items that are pretty impossible to finish off. (And hard to syrup without making a mess.) Lunch and dinner (same menu) are steak, stir fry, seafood scampi, fish, burgers and sandwiches. At the Pioneer Inn. **$7–$13** for breakfast, **$10–$25** for lunch and dinner.

Plantation House
2000 Plantation Club Dr. • 669–6299
ONO Tongue-wagging views all the way down the golf course to the ocean and Moloka'i, along with a rich, spacious feel, create an effective ambiance. Breakfast has several types of benedict (which have slipped) and a few other choices. The small lunch menu has ½-pound burgers, lots of salads (including one that's $18!) and maybe fish. Dinner is mostly steak and seafood. Quality is hit or miss; unusual for a restaurant of this caliber. Consider the calamari appetizer. Service can be nervous and rushed and almost cost them their ONO. **$8–$15** for breakfast (served until 3

p.m.), $10–$20 for lunch, $25–$40 for dinner. Hard to find. Take Hwy 30 north, 1 mile past the Kapalua exit, turn right at the Plantation Golf Course, then left to the clubhouse. Reservations required for dinner; collared shirt and no slippers.

Rusty Harpoon
2435 Ka'anapali Pkwy. • 661–3123

Not a bad place for a sunset cocktail and appetizer in a festive, slightly sports bar atmosphere overlooking the ocean and Lana'i at Whalers Village in Ka'anapali. Lots of appetizers to choose from. If you go to the entrées, it can get pretty expensive and includes steak, seafood and ribs. Overall food quality is acceptable, not stellar. **$11–$16** for breakfast, **$25–$50** for dinner, but you can spend less if you stick with the appetizers.

Ruth's Chris Steak House
900 Front St. • 661–8815

ONO Part of a chain, they are unabashed red meat pushers, and they do it very well. Steak and lobster with an emphasis on steak. Yes, it's expensive. Even an optional baked potato is $8. Is any potato worth $8? Probably not. But if you get one, it'll probably be the best darned potato you've ever had. (Lest you think this is just another overpriced Maui eatery, we called some Ruth's Chris restaurants on the mainland, and the prices were the same.) They cook the steaks at 1,800°, and the results are tender and juicy and served on a *500°* plate to *keep* it hot. If you want lobster, get only that. The steak and lobster entrée has a really small tail. Their chocolate sin cake is as dense as lead and just as deadly. Wine list feels particularly overpriced. In Lahaina across the street from the ocean on Front Street in Lahaina Center, and in South Maui in Wailea at the Shops of Wailea. **$25–$50** or more if you get the steak and lobster.

Son'z Maui at Swan Court
200 Nohea Kai Dr. • 667–4506

ONO They call it a fusion of European and Hawaiian cuisine, so what the heck, we put them under American. Although owned by the same folks that run Sarento's and Nick's in Wailea, the service is much more toned down to the point of being sporadic. Atmosphere and food, however garner them an ONO. You're overlooking a beautiful pond and waterfall at the Hyatt Ka'anapali with resident swans. The steak and seafood is good, but believe it or not, their best item is a Kobe beef *meatloaf*. (Strange, but impossibly delicious. If Mama had made it like that, I'd have eaten it more often.) The wait staff has some autonomy, so ask them if you want to deviate from the the menu. **$35–$55**. Reservations recommended.

Soup Nutz & Java Jazz
3350 Lwr. Honoapiilani • 667–0787

ONO The ambiance is really hard to describe. Call it assorted kookiness. Nearly all the artwork was created by the owner who occasionally plays guitar during dinner. But the food is good. Small menus for all meals, but the taste works. Sandwiches, salads and burgers (which are marinated and unusual) for lunch. Steak, pasta, fish and lobster for dinner. Sounds like a bigger menu than it is. But Hawaiian lobster (when available) for $28 is a good deal. **$8–$12** for breakfast, **$10–$13** for lunch, **$20–$30** for dinner (with a cheaper pasta). In Honokowai Marketplace, south part of Lower Honoapiilani Road. They open at 6 a.m. and have lots of coffee drinks.

Swiss Café
640 Front St. • 661–6776

We're still looking for what makes this café Swiss. It's basically an Internet café/sandwich shop with some pizza (so we put them under American). And if you don't see anyone working there when you walk in, your server is most likely one of the people on the Internet. The sandwiches are pretty good. Cold sandwiches, such as roast beef or turkey, hot sandwiches, such as Italian Boboli or turkey broccoli melt, and veggie sandwiches. The pizzas are cheap tasting and don't meet the standard the sandwiches do. Breakfast is mostly bagels, donuts or a simple egg combo plate. **$6–$10** for lunch and early dinner. **$2–$6** for breakfast. In Lahaina between Dickenson and Prison streets, across from the Banyan Tree Park.

Whalers Village Food Court
2435 Ka'anapali Pkwy.

(ONO) We certainly didn't give them an ONO because of the food. Five stalls with average food court options. Our happiness stems from the fact that the court offers some of the few cheap meals in Ka'anapali, and food always tastes better when you've just walked in off the beach. Even McDonald's tastes good when there's sand stuck to your feet. In Whalers Village Shopping Center next to Ka'anapali Beach.

WEST MAUI CHINESE

China Boat
4474 Honoapiilani Rd. • 669–5089

(ONO) The food quality is good enough to merit an ONO, but the service needs to improve. They are not attentive enough, so the ONO is marginal. Tell them to spice up your food, and they will *fully* comply. **$8–$15** for lunch, **$12–$25** for dinner. Full bar. Instead of Chinese music, you're more likely to hear Pavarotti. From Honoapiilani Hwy (30) turn onto the road at Kahana Gateway Shopping Center, then turn right on Lower Honoapiilani Road. Across from Kahana Reef. See map on page 53.

China Bowl
2580 Kekaa Dr. • 661–0660

Chinese food is surprisingly rare in West Maui. This place is one of only two, and the same family owns both. We could tell by the decidedly unChinese music (usually Jazz) playing inside. Lunch is a good bet here with nicely priced specials and big portions. We like the orange chicken. Items are fresh but sometimes drowning in sauce. Staff is warm and inviting, which makes this an easy place to recommend if you're craving Chinese comfort food. **$8–$13** for lunch, **$9–$20** for dinner. In Fairway Shops in Ka'anapali.

WEST MAUI FRENCH

Chez Paul
821B Olowalu Rd. • 661–3843

(ONO) This small and quaint restaurant is out in remote Olowalu. (In fact, this pretty much *is* the town.) So how is it they have survived this seemingly poor location since the '60s? Good food that's beautifully presented and good service at their 20 small tables. Though portions are small, the quality of their French entrées is outrageous. Check your credit card limit before you arrive, because you can either spend *a lot* or *a fortune*. **$35–$60** *perhaps*, but the American Sturgeon caviar hors d'oeuvre by itself is *$95*. Are you getting the picture? At the 15 mile marker on Hwy 30. Reservations strongly recommended, resort wear required.

Gerard's
174 Lahainaluna Rd. • 661–8939

People are going to be shocked and angry that we didn't gie Gerard's an ONO. We admit, the food's good. But it's just too overpriced. This section has lots of expensive restaurants, many providing an atmosphere you can't get back home. Gerard's, on the other hand, doesn't have anything you probably can't find in a reasonably sized city on the mainland, and it's *very* expensive. Lamb, pork, beef, veal, fish and chicken. There is no view, and the atmosphere at the courtyard and lanai tables is accompanied by traffic noise. Service is attentive, but we're appalled by the prices. Even dessert. I mean, $9.50 for two scoops of ice cream and chocolate sauce or for a *tiny* crème brûlée is ridiculous. If you're overlooking a gorgeous beach, *maybe*. But here? Only your wallet pain threshold can decide. We feel it's about a third overpriced, but maybe we're just savages. $35–$60 for dinner. In Lahaina at the Plantation Inn.

WEST MAUI ITALIAN

BJ's Chicago Pizzeria
730 Front St. • 661–0700

ONO This is probably the best pizza in West Maui at this time. Good views overlooking the harbor if you get a table on the ocean side. Chicago-style, deep-dish pizzas have super-thick crusts that are surprisingly light. They also have some pastas and sandwiches. Pizzas take a while and when they come, your first comment to the waiter is, "I didn't order it with tomatoes." They know. All pizzas come with very light sauce and stewed tomatoes. (They don't usually tell you.) They'll serve it without the tomatoes and with more substantial sauce (which is better) if you request it. Nice selection of beers and some wines. $12–$25 for lunch and dinner. In Lahaina on Front Street.

Longhi's
888 Front St. • 667–2288

Longhi's is an institution in Lahaina. Opened in 1976, the upscale Italian/seafood menu has historically been excellent and used to be a favorite with many locals and visitors. They *can* do wonderful things with lobster, shrimp and fresh fish. But the food is uneven, and e-mails from readers confirm our own observations. Parking is via the free valet. Extensive wine list. Dinner is expensive (and everything is à la carte) at $25–$75 per person (the latter price if you order the massive 3-pound lobster), $10–$25 for lunch, $10–$20 for breakfast. On Front Street at Papalaua. Reservations recommended. We could have put them in either the American or Italian category (they call it Mediterranean).

Penne Pasta Café
180 Dickenson St. • 661–6633

ONO Ah, so you *can* eat in Lahaina without paying a fortune. The food quality/price ratio is high here. Pasta, sandwiches and salads with a little pizza. (The latter has an ultra-thin crust and makes a good appetizer for two.) Portions are more than fair, and the flavors work. That'll do it for us *every* time. On Dickenson near Wainee. $7–$12 for lunch and dinner.

Pizza Paradiso
3500 Lwr. Honoapiilani • 667–2929

The hype is pretty big at Pizza Paradiso. Signs and ads proclaim they were voted "best pizza on Maui" and reviews from a guidebook saying theirs was the "best pizza I ever had." After repeatedly eating here, we can't help but wonder—were they eating in the same place? In fairness, the crust is fairly good and unusual: spongy but effective. But the pizza is lifeless and tasteless, as well as overpriced. It's on par with a really good frozen pizza, but does that impress you? Even if two people order by the slice, four slices and two sodas for $22 is *steep*. They have a pretty good Greek salad here.

Desserts are either the delicious but expensive home-made tiramisu or something less remarkable. **$5–$15**. At Honokowai Marketplace (between 25 and 26 mile marker on Hwy 30).

Vinny's Pizza
840 Wainee St. • 661–6773
Away from the main Front Street area of Lahaina in Lahaina Square, they have NY-style pizza and sandwiches. The sliced meatball sandwich is pretty good. Pizza has a very thin and limp crust, and it leans a bit toward the greasy. They'll deliver as far north as Ka'anapali. Overall, a decent value. A slice is $3. **$6–$10**.

WEST MAUI JAPANESE

Kobe Steak House
136 Dickenson St. • 667–5555
 This is a teppan-yaki restaurant. That's where you and seven other people gather around a grill as a talented, knife-wielding chef prepares your food in front of you. This restaurant seems to encourage the chefs to exuberantly engage the guests. The results can be fun. The food is mostly steak, seafood and veggies. Although the food isn't great, it's fairly good and, combined with the lively atmosphere and joking style of some of the chefs, it's a place we like to return to on occasion. Sushi bar also available. Prices are **$15–$45** for dinner. Big spread, we know. But it depends on what you want. Reservations required. In Lahaina between Luakini and Wainee.

WEST MAUI LOCAL

Aloha Mixed Plate
1285 Front St. • 661–3322
 A particularly great place for lunch. Good and varied local style food, meaning it may be a bit fattier than mainland tastes, but most visitors seem to like it. Items like kalua pig sandwich, lomi lomi salmon and chow funn noodles. If these sound a little too alien, don't worry. There's something for pretty much everyone. Prices are reasonable for what you get, and portions are large for most (though not all) items. Service is usually friendly but understaffed. They have an outdoor deck and beachside tables. (No alcohol allowed at the beachside tables due to Maui's goofy liquor laws.) They sometimes let the hedge grow high enough to block the surf, and flies can be a problem at times. But the food and price, along with the winning location, work well. **$6–$12** for lunch and dinner. North of downtown Lahaina near the Mala Ramp.

Honokowai Okazuya Deli
3600 Lwr. Honoapiilani • 665–0512
 How refreshing! A place in northern West Maui that serves good food but doesn't feel the need to soak you. Ambiance is…well, none, actually. Best to get it to go. The owner is a former executive chef at Mama's Fish House and the Kea Lani, so they know how to cook here. But instead of opening another highbrow (and high-cost) restaurant, they've channeled their energies toward the lower-end market. The menu is diverse enough to eat here repeatedly. Teriyaki steak, spaghetti and sausage, fresh fish, kung pao chicken, steamed tofu—the menu is all over the place, and we weren't sure how to classify them. We like to take food over to nearby Honokowai Beach Park if it's not too windy. (There are a few stools inside, but it's hot.) This place doesn't change much from year to year and we're glad. **$8–$15** for lunch and dinner. North of

Ka'anapali on Lower Honoapiilani Rd. just north of Honokowai Beach in the AAAAA Rent-A-Space Mall. No credit cards. Closed Sundays.

No Ka Oi Deli
222 Papalaua St. • 667–2244

ⓞⓝⓞ Huge sandwiches and salads served with a big smile at a great price. What more can you ask for? The prices are a welcome relief from the sticker shock that goes on just a block away on Front St. Sandwiches are basic but built on a grand scale, and the ingredients are fresh. Eat at the outdoor tables or take it away to a beach. On Wainee St. and Papalaua in Anchor Square. Only open 10 a.m. to 2 p.m. Open Monday through Friday. **$5–$8**. Cash only.

WEST MAUI MEXICAN

Cilantro
170 Papalaua Ave. • 667–5444

ⓞⓝⓞ The menu is a bit overwhelming because the items are not exactly standard. Take your time because the food's excellent and flavorful. Consider the taco al pastor—slow-cooked adobo pork with grilled pineapple salsa. And the nachos del sol are a great appetizer. Don't overlook the salsa bar to the right. Prices are not bad for the quality. Atmosphere is basic and simple. **$5–$13** for lunch and dinner. In the Old Lahaina Center.

Compadres
1221 Honoapiilani Hwy. • 661–7189

Pretty good food, though a tad pricey. Good chips and salsa. Ten different kinds of enchiladas. Usually reasonable specials Tuesdays with ample portion sizes. Tasty (though expensive) margaritas. Decent tequila selection. Try the Banana Chingalinga dessert—big enough for two. We waffled on giving

them an ⓞⓝⓞ, but the price hurt 'em. $20+ Mexican food entrées are hard to justify. In Lahaina Cannery Mall. Most items are **$9** at breakfast, **$10–$25** for lunch, **$15–$30** for dinner. The cheaper lunch menu also takes into account their take-out window with its cheaper prices. They advertise "best restaurant under $20," so whoever writes their ads apparently hasn't seen all those items on the menu over $20.

WEST MAUI PACIFIC RIM

Mala
1307 Front St. • 667–9394

ⓞⓝⓞ Dine right next to the water in an uncrowded part of Lahaina. Boat-lovers will enjoy the close proximity to the moored boats offshore backed by Lana'i and the nearby Mala Pier. They seem to really know how to tie entrées with sauces and are adept at picking side items. The core menu includes wok-fried moi (a local fish), gourmet mac and cheese and even a Kobe beef cheeseburger. Even the chips and salsa have a twist. That's not guacamole on the side, it's mashed edamame (boiled soy beans). Evening specials get more exotic and more expensive. **$8–$18** for lunch, **$10–$50** for dinner. On the north end of Front St. behind Lahaina Cannery Mall.

Pacific 'O 505 Front St. • 667–4341
'O 505 Front St. • 661–8422

ⓞⓝⓞ Lots of hype about this restaurant. Presided over by the acclaimed chef *James McDonald* (don't ask about the black sheep member of his chef family, *Ronald*), Pacific 'O is considered the "in" place to eat. So, does it live up to the hype? For the most part, yes. Great food, awesome beachside location and good service. That's what it's all about, right? Mostly fish with some steak sounds pretty typical. What's unusual is the way things are cooked. Lots of imaginative creations often with an Asian twist. Mac nut-crusted mahi mahi with a Thai peanut sauce or pork chops and scallops in oyster garlic sauce with arugula pesto. Even the few beef selections are marked with their distinctive touch. The outdoor tables can be a heavenly place to watch the sunset. Great wine and spirit list. For dessert, we like the lumpia. Though we're not big on dessert cocktails, consider heeding their suggestion to add a chocolate martini to this one. Wow! Lunch is simpler items such as fish and chips and burgers. It's **$12–$18** for lunch, **$30–$45** or more. Reservations recommended. In Lahaina at the 505 Front Street Shopping Center.

Next door is their sister restaurant, **I'O**. Same executive chef, though the flavors lean more toward European. Not quite as good a location or ambiance as Pacific 'O and it's not as popular, but the food's great here, too. **$30–$45**.

Roy's Kahana Bar & Grill
4405 Honoapiilani Hwy. • 669–6999
303 Piikea Ave. • 891–1120

ONO Roy's is a local chain, and they serve wonderful and often smartly conceived food. The menu changes nightly and runs from fish to pastas to steak, all served with an Asian/ island twist. Their fish is *always* a winner. We've never had a bad meal here, though it can get a little loud and rushed. Their baked chocolate soufflé is deadly but takes a while, so order while you're still eating. **$30–$45** for dinner. In Kahana Gateway before Hwy 30's 28 mile marker. Reservations recommended. The second number listed is in Kihei at the Pi'ilani Village Shopping Center.

Sea House
5900 Lwr. Honoapiilani • 669–1500

ONO Spectacular location right next to the beach at Napili Bay. Try to reserve a window table. They thoughtfully leave sun screens down during the brightest part of the late afternoon, then raise them for sunsets, which are awesome from here. *Yeah, but what about the food?* Well, it's good, too. Dinner is fresh fish (which they *occasionally* overcook), lobster, filet mignon or chicken. Quality is usually very good and service is fair. Lunch is sandwiches (such as crab on Hawaiian sweetbread) and some sushi and salads. **$6–$12** for breakfast, **$10–$15** for lunch, **$25–$45** for dinner. On Lower Honoapiilani Road at Napili Kai Beach Resort. The south parking lot is small and fills up, so consider the northern lot. Both require you to grope through the resort to the restaurant.

Tropica at the Westin
2365 Ka'anapali Pkwy. • 667–2525

ONO The restaurants at Whalers Village on Ka'anapali Beach tend to get crowded fast. This one, just down the beach path at the Westin, fills up later. And with a great beachside location and good food, it's easy to recommend. It ain't cheap, but they're comparable to their neighbors. For dinner, it's mostly seafood and steak and they really do the seafood well. (Absolutely *deadly* seafood bouillabaisse.) Most of the tables are excellent (except for the back ones), and there's live music most nights. This is a great place for a sunset cocktail. The wine list, however, is small and embarrassing. The chocolate heaven dessert is a cake with a soft center and pomegranate syrup. **$30–$45** for dinner. Reservations recommended At the Westin Ka'anapali; see map on page 51.

WEST MAUI THAI

Thai Chef
880 Front St., Suite A12 • 667–2814

 A friendly, family-owned Thai restaurant that has eluded us in the past. Tucked away in the Old Lahaina Center near Front St., the menu is similar to Maui Thai in Kihei, only cheaper. The service is warm and the curries warmer, just as we like them. Seating is limited and large tables are often shared, making it a social occasion. Drinking is BYOB with no corkage fee. $8–$20 for lunch and dinner. Closed on weekends.

WEST MAUI TREATS

The Bakery
991D Limahana Pl. • 667–9062

Hidden away in an industrial area, their baked goods are pretty good, reasonably priced (for Lahaina) and popular with locals. Strudel, croissants, bagels, macaroons, fresh bread, etc. Most items are quite tasty, though sometimes they seem old. They also have deli sandwiches, pizza and stuffed croissants. From Hwy 30 between Papalaua and Kenui, take Hinau mauka (toward the mountain) and turn right at the end. It'll be on the right side and isn't much to look at. $2–$6.

Cold Stone Creamery
900 Front St. • 667–2744

 See review on page 273. Just as yummy ice cream. In Lahaina near Papalaua. $5–$7.

Pretzelmaker
1221 Honoapiilani Hwy. • 661–5060

 Kind of goofy to put them under TREATS, we know. It's the same as the stores you see in malls across the mainland. The reason we single them out is that this one also has surprisingly good shave ice—worth stopping for. They also have tasty pretzeldogs and pretzelwraps. (Oh, yeah, they sell pretzels, too.) $3–$6. In Lahaina Cannery, Front Street and Kapunakea (north of where the Lahaina map ends).

SOUTH MAUI AMERICAN

Alexander's Fish, Chicken & Ribs
1913 S. Kihei Rd. • 874–0788

Fairly reasonable prices, but the portions are on the small side. For most items you get a choice of fried or broiled. Otherwise, everything else (including the mixed veggies) is fried. Their combos of two (fish, chicken, shrimp, ribs or veggies) are probably their best deal. The food is tasty but a bit greasy. Service is green and confused. (Hey, everyone needs a first job.) Order at the counter, then wait for your number and eat at the outside tables. On the mauka side of South Kihei Road across the street from the fake whale at Kalama Park. $7–$11 for lunch and dinner.

Big Wave Café
1215 S. Kihei Rd. • 891–8688

A well-chosen dinner menu of fish, steak, ribs and meat loaf. Lunch has a smaller menu of sandwiches, burgers and salads. Service can be clipped. In fact, we've experienced incredibly snotty service here. The food's usually good, though. They make a mean and unusual root beer float. It can be loud inside; consider the outdoor tables. $6–$12 for breakfast, $8–$12 for lunch, $10–$26 for dinner. In Azeka Mauka Shopping Center.

Blue Moon Café
362 Huku Lii Pl. • 874–8600

A large menu of fairly good (not great) sandwiches, salads, some fish and local-style entrées, including kalua pork and teriyaki chicken. The flavors are there, but the ingredients don't seem to be of a very high quality. If they used better ingredients, we'd give 'em an ONO. It can be fairly loud inside. Service is friendly but can be slow. Their "heavenly espresso nut sundae" is awesome. The small and pricey sundae uses their incredibly effective espresso sauce (a little goes a long way) with killer results. In north Kihei at Kihei Gateway Plaza on Ohukai near Hwy 31. **$5–$10** for breakfast, **$8–$12** for lunch, **$12–$23** for dinner.

Buzz's Wharf
Ma'alaea Harbor • 244–5426
Great views of the boats coming in and out of Ma'alaea Harbor. Food is usually fairly good with definite exceptions. The prawns are great—they seem to use an excellent grade and prepare them in the shell with tasty results. Other items are hit or miss. Burgers, fish and teri chicken for lunch, steak and seafood for dinner. Overall, it's a good place to try after your boat trip, though it's pricey. At Ma'alaea Harbor off Hwy 30 south of the 6 mile marker. **$10–$25** for lunch, **$20–$40** for dinner.

Carl's Jr.
Look, we don't normally review fast food restaurants, but we wanted to tell you that you can avoid the one in Ma'alaea without fear. A must-miss.

Dina's Sand Witch
145 N. Kihei Rd. • 879–3262
ONO Part sandwich shop, part pub. A good selection of sandwiches, ¼-pound hot dogs, and saimin (which is good). Healthy portions and good ingredients. (Avoid the burrito, though.) The walls are literally wallpa-

pered with money. Over the past 20+ years customers have given them currency, mostly ones, with their signatures and comments. Thousands of them cover the walls, creating a unique ambiance. **$6–$9** for lunch and dinner. Just north of Kihei town on the ocean side of Hwy 310 next to the Sugar Beach Resort.

Ferraro's at the Four Seasons
3900 Wailea Alanui Dr. • 874–8000
Not a bad place to overpay if you're looking for a good view, and service and price are less of a consideration. While it's true that $12 gelato can *never* be justified, the dreamy location overlooking Wailea Beach at lunch is simply wonderful. Food is pretty good *$20* burgers (though a bit greasy), Thai beef rice noodle salad (avoid), sandwiches, sashimi, salads and panini. Dinner is upscale Italian-style steak, seafood and pasta. Tables are outdoors, and those closest to the beach are most recommended. **$17–$28** at lunch, **$40–$55** for dinner. Reservations required.

Hawaiian Moons
2411 S. Kihei Rd. • 875–4356
A health food store with some so-so wraps, hot bar and smoothies. Pretty good baked goods. On S. Kihei Road. **$5–$8**.

Kihei Caffe
1945 S. Kihei Rd. • 879–2230
ONO Some tasty food if you can overlook their shortcomings. Breakfast is best (they open at 5 a.m. on weekdays) with good omelettes, breakfast burritos, biscuits and gravy (though they're a little salty), some truly kickin' raspberry twisties and the best turnovers in South Maui, plus coffee drinks. Some of the outdoor tables are almost penned in, making it popular with parents trying to corral

their keiki. (Kids seem to like the teddy bear or whale pancakes.) Lunch is mostly sandwiches, burgers and salads. Kihei Caffe makes mostly good food, but we wouldn't mind if it was a bit cleaner. The price certainly is reasonable. Get there early or expect a wait. Across from Kalama Park. **$7–$12** for breakfast and lunch. Cash only.

Life's a Beach
1913E S. Kihei Rd. • 891–8010
Average burgers, chicken sandwich, burritos, fish and chips. A local watering hole. Good 4–7 p.m. happy hour with cheap mai tais and beer. **$7–$13** for lunch and dinner. Across from Kalama Park.

Ma'alaea Grill
300 Ma'alaea Rd. • 243–2206
ONO We hope the name doesn't change again before you read this. The building has housed many culinary attempts in the past, but the dust may have settled on this one. It's slightly upscale but you can't tell by the prices. The seafood is excellent, especially the jumbo sea scallops. Also tempting is their onion soup topped with puff pasty and their flashy martini menu. We didn't like their kiawe grilled meats—way too smoky. Lunch is even more affordable with salads, burgers (also on the kiawe grill) and fish. In the Ma'alaea Harbor Village. **$10–$18** for lunch and **$18–$35** for dinner.

Ma'alaea Waterfront
50 Hauoli St. • 244–9028
ONO The food here is superb and the flavor combinations well-conceived. They have many different kinds of fish prepared nine different ways: Cajun spice, broiled with Hawaiian salsa, baked in parchment paper, stuffed with Alaskan king crab, etc. They use good quality fish. (Some restaurants sometimes mask bad fish with overpowering sauces, but not here.) Their crab cake appetizers, when they have them, are great. Service can be good, but sometimes clumsy, and the parking situation is terrible. Just a few spots; you'll probably have to park out on the street and walk to the place. But the food makes it worth it. The outdoor tables have beautiful views, but the indoor tables don't take much advantage of the location. Extraordinary wine list with over 150 wines. Avoid the punishment booth behind the hostess stand. Take Hwy 30 to Ma'alaea, then turn on Hau'oli Road. See page 127 for more. **$20–$50** for dinner. Reservations recommended.

Makena Grill
ONO Just a simple roadside stand across from Secret Cove in the southern part of South Maui on Makena Alanui Road. Though service might be a tad snippy, the fish tacos are excellent. They also have chicken kabobs, teri beef and whatever they feel like making that day. Pricey but tasty. They sometimes close for extended periods. **$7–$10**.

Peggy Sue's
1279 S. Kihei Rd. • 875–8944
ONO Small but effective 1950s style diner serving generous-sized burgers (a second 6-oz patty is $2 extra), ribs, salads, hot dogs and some sandwiches, such as steak, chicken and fish. Their burgers are very good, though the baked fries could use some seasoning. Portions are fairly generous for the price, and they have a good keiki (kid) selection with PB&J and grilled cheese sandwiches. Service can be slow because they are often busy, especially at lunch, and the waitresses seem overworked. (This has been going on for

years.) Getting a table can be hard at peak eating times. Real milkshakes are tasty (love the peanut butter), and the jukebox playing old 45s adds to the flavor. One problem: It can get *real* smoky inside if both doors are closed. Just remind them to open the back door, and the kitchen hood will be able to keep up, and the smoke clears out fast. In Azeka Mauka Shopping Center near Lipoa. $9–$18 for lunch and dinner.

Prince Court
5400 Makena Alanui Dr. • 874–1111
ono Located at the Maui Prince Hotel, they have a **Sunday champagne brunch** that is legendary. It's pricey (around $48), but the food is awesome and the variety stunning. Choose from the many breakfast items, the omelette station or try Chinese food or roast beef or sushi or...well, it keeps going. The desserts are exceptionally evil. It books up most of the time, so reserve as early as possible. They also have a Friday seafood and prime rib buffet for $48. Other nights are off-the-menu, such as steak, seafood, venison (deer) and lamb. Quality is usually top-notch. The ocean views are pretty good and the atmosphere relaxing. $25–$50. South of Wailea off Makena Alanui Road. Reservations recommended, resort wear required.

Pupu Lounge Seafood & Grill
1945 S. Kihei Rd. • 875–4111
ono This is a good place to go when you're looking for heavy appetizers (pupus) and a cocktail. They have regular entrées, too. But if you grab the pupu platter for two and maybe some coconut shrimp (which is close to perfect) and top it off with a tropical drink, you'll probably leave with a smile. (Love their "Got pupu?" shirts.) Their South Seas bamboo

atmosphere helps keep things calming. Across from Kalama Park. $10–$15 for lunch, $17–$30 for dinner.

South Shore Tiki Lounge
1913 S. Kihei Rd. • 874–6444
ono Good *home-made* sausage sandwiches for around $7, and the condiment bar has lots of goodies to put on top of them. Other items, such as the burgers, pizzas and sandwiches, aren't as compelling (and we wish their lava dogs were hotter). Overall, it's a good value, all served in a tiki bar atmosphere. Open till 2 a.m. $5–$12 for lunch and dinner. In Kihei Kalama Village.

Sports Page
2411 S. Kihei Rd. • 879–0602
A smokeless (public smoking is banned on Hawai'i) sports bar with decent $\frac{1}{2}$-pound burgers and sandwiches for $8 or $9 (but pitiful salads). Good pupu (appetizer) selection and (not surprisingly) a big beer selection. $8–$15 for lunch and dinner. At Kama'ole Beach Center.

Stella Blues
1279 S. Kihei Rd. • 874–3779
Readers have told us for years that Stella's is excellent and it's a definite local favorite. We come back often, but frankly, we don't get it. The food here looks and sounds good, but too often flavors are muted to the point of being bland. Take the delicious-sounding French toast as an example. How are they able to combine vanilla, cinnamon, eggs and bread to produce something so utterly tasteless? (Years of practice?) Lunch is probably your best bet if you *want* to like this place with a large selection of sandwiches and several vegetarian items. All sandwiches (pretty good Reuben) come with chips, and it's an extra $1.50 for fries or

pasta with feta and tomatoes (which is good). Dinner is mostly comfort food with half-chickens, pork chops, meatloaf and some pizza and pasta. **$7–$12** for breakfast, **$8–$15** for lunch, **$13–$25** for dinner. In Azeka Mauka Shopping Center.

Tommy Bahama's Tropical Café
3750 Wailea Alanui Dr. • 875–9983
If you've ever shopped at a Tommy Bahama clothing store, this is the same concept. If you don't mind overpaying for good quality in an islandy, tropical, tasteful atmosphere, this is the place. How else can you describe tasty ribs that cost almost $40? Or $20 lunch appetizers or salads? Lunch is lots of expensive salads, sandwiches and tropical drinks that taste good but leave you miffed over the price. Desserts are scrumptious. Dinner adds steak, fish and chicken. It's **$18–$30** for lunch, **$35–$55** for dinner. In the Shops of Wailea.

Volcano Bar
3850 Wailea Alanui Dr. • 875–1234
At the pool at the Grand Wailea, it's a good place to enjoy a cocktail and light food for a sunset in the winter. (Their 5 p.m. closing is too early.) Yeah, they have the usual resort $12.50 hot dogs (all beef, but at that price it should be ground up filet mignon) and $15 sandwiches, but you can grab something to drink and head to the beach for a relaxing late afternoon.

Waterfront Deli
3750 Wailea Alanui Dr. • 891–2039
Finding cheap food in Wailea is about as easy as finding Mongolian food in El Paso. While it ain't exactly cheap, they got $7 sandwiches, $3 pizza slices and $6 Caesar salads. In the Shops at Wailea. **$6–$12.**

SOUTH MAUI GREEK

Greek Bistro
2511 S. Kihei Rd. • 879–9330
ONO Sometimes called **Ziziki's** or **The Bistro**. Whatever its name, the food's good. Lamb, kabobs, spanakopita and other Greek items prepared with successful results. Their rack of lamb is incredibly flavorful. The tiny wine list features Greek wines, and their bartending skills overall are sadly lacking. If you don't get their baklava for dessert, you're completely insane. It's *sooooo* good. **$20–$32** for dinner. On S. Kihei Road near Dolphin Plaza.

Pita Paradise
1913M S. Kihei Rd. • 875–7679
ONO We've never seen people who can do so much with pitas. Here they're freshly made and topped (not actually filled—it's more like a wrap) with all manner of ingredients. Chicken, veggies, fish, meatballs and greens in clever combinations. Kabobs, too. Their ziziki bread makes a good appetizer. At dinner they lean more toward pasta, kabobs and seafood (which comes from the owner's own fishing boat). A quaint dinner here can be interrupted by noises from either of the two nearby bars. Try the baklava ice cream cake for dessert, and nothing will bother you. **$7–$15** for lunch, **$9–$25** for dinner. In Kihei Kalama Village.

SOUTH MAUI IRISH

Mulligan's on the Blue
100 Kaukahi St. • 874–1131
ONO Irish food such as Gaelic steak, fish and chips, corned beef and shepherd's pie (but no Irish stew) served in a campy, Irish pub atmosphere sometimes accompanied by Irish or other local live music most nights. (Saturday is

Celtic night.) Most of the food items are pretty good. (Awesome apple pie.) Indoor and outdoor tables. Service can be slow. **$10–$15** for lunch, **$10–$25** for dinner. At the Wailea Blue Golf Course.

SOUTH MAUI ITALIAN

Antonio's
1215 S. Kihei Rd. • 875–8800

 Southern (Sicilian) style Italian, nice ambiance, spotlessly clean. The food is great here. Many varieties of pasta, lots of veggie items, good lasagna, and the veal osso buco is delicious, as are the raviolis. The flavor combinations here are wonderful, though service *can be* snotty at times. The home-made tiramisu is a good way to end it. Decent wine list. In Longs Center on South Kihei Road. **$12–$25** for dinner.

Bada Bing
1945 S. Kihei Rd. • 875–0188

If you've ever seen Bada Bing on the television show, *Sopranos*…it *ain't* like that. This place pays homage in their decor to Frank Sinatra, mob movies and all things Hollywood Italian. It used to be one of our favorites, but something's gone terribly wrong. In the old days, service was only bad during Lakers games, but they've expanded it now to all hours. They have 10-inch pizzas for $10 and pretty good grilled chicken pesto. Avoid the picatta and the lasagna. Service and food *can be* good, but don't count on it. They disappoint more often than not, giving new meaning to the term, *fuhgeddaboutit.* Pretty good mai tais, and they have a $10 wine list. **$7–$12** for lunch, **$10–$20** for dinner. In Kihei Kalama Village.

Capische?
555 Kaukahi St. • 879–2224

Located in Wailea's most forgotten resort, Diamond

Hawai'i, they have a romantic atmosphere at the upstairs tables with elevated distant views of West Maui (and rooftops). Flavors are well-conceived with items such as cioppino (a seafood stew that is absolutely epic here), Italian herb-crusted opakapaka and shrimp Carbonara. Appetizers are very expensive and can really jack up the price of the meal. Wine list is excellent. Dessert features a 5-liquor tiramisu that's unusual and pretty boozy but a nice way to top off a meal. **$35–$60** for dinner.

Gian Don's
1445 S. Kihei Rd. • 874–4041

It was called Marco's, and the menu seems exactly the same. Boy, is *this* place overpriced! No view, and it's loud (but beautiful) inside; outdoor tables are quieter. Burgers are $10, chicken alfredo is $21. The food seems strangely tasteless. At breakfast, a simple cheese and mushroom omelette is $9, and the coffee is dreadful. Hmm. Hard to get happy about this one. On S. Kihei Rd. south of Lipoa. **$7–$13** at breakfast, **$12–$32** for lunch and dinner.

Matteo's Pizzeria
100 Wailea Ike Dr. • 874–1234

Their motto is "Italian Soul in the Heart of Wailea." Well, if Don Corleone ate here, he'd make them an offer they couldn't refuse. Like a cafeteria, you order and pay before you sit and only the busboy visits your table unless you tell them you're ordering drinks. Salty and over-pureed artichoke dip, mediocre pizza and a Bolognese sauce that took us back to junior high all point to a cheap experience. The open-air seating is nice and prices aren't high for Wailea, but you still don't get what you pay for. **$10–$20** for lunch and dinner. Near the Shops of Wailea.

Shaka Pizza
1770 S. Kihei Rd. • 874–0331

OK, here's the deal. It's **deliver** or eat in.

The hot sandwiches are actually *better* when they're delivered. (Being wrapped up improves the bread.) Pizza, on the other hand, is actually best if ordered by the slice. (The reheating helps the crust.) We know these are weird observations, but that's how it is. Their regular pizza has extremely thin and fairly tasty crust, but unremarkable sauce and toppings. It's so thin that you'll be surprised at how much pizza surface area you can dispose of, so don't worry that their only size is the 18-inch. They also have thicker Sicilian-style pizza and gourmet pizzas, such as spinach, clam and garlic, and white pies that are fine, but not great. Cheese-steaks and other sandwiches also available, and overall the sandwiches are their best asset, though pricey. A 14-inch sandwich is almost $13! **$4–$14.** By-the-slice pizza reasonably priced. In Kihei at Kupana St.

SOUTH MAUI JAPANESE

Sansei Seafood & Sushi
1881 S. Kihei Rd. • 879–0004

ONO Sushi, as well as non-Japanese food, such as seafood pasta, lobster, beef and duck served in a soothing atmosphere. The quality is good. Some items are pretty darned pricey, but you'll like the taste. **$25–$50** or more for dinner. Thur.–Sat. they have karaoke and half-priced sushi after 10 p.m. In Kihei Town Center near Foodland across from Kalama Park.

SOUTH MAUI KOREAN

Isana
515 S. Kihei Rd. • 874–5700

A traditional Korean restaurant complete with tabletop grills. If you order off the BBQ menu, plates of raw, seasoned meat are served along with small portions of spicy vegetables. (Because of this, you'll want to

get appetizers unless you're hankering for mostly protein.) They set up the grill and you do the cooking. Don't be afraid to crank it up, or you'll be there awhile. Portions are huge and may feed two, but they require two BBQ entrées to justify the grill. The sushi is pretty good, if a bit pricey. Try it for half price after 10 p.m. Wed.–Sat. Lunch and dinner are **$20–$35.** On S. Kihei Rd. between Ohukai and Kaonoulu.

SOUTH MAUI LOCAL

Da Kitchen
2439 S. Kihei Rd. • 875–7782

ONO Good selection of local items, such as loco moco, teriyaki chicken, chicken katsu. The saimin could use a little work, but the teri chicken sandwich is good. If you're presently wanted by the CHOLESTEROL POLICE, don't come here—they may raid the place. But if you're looking for generous portions of not-so-healthy local food at cheap prices, you could do a lot worse than Da Kitchen. **$4–$9** for lunch and dinner. In Rainbow Mall under Café O'Lei.

SOUTH MAUI MEXICAN

Enrique's Cocina Mexicana
2395 S. Kihei Rd. • 875–2910

ONO The sort of hole-in-the-wall that you pass by and ask yourself, *Hmm, I wonder if it's OK to eat here?* The answer is yes. The menu is surprisingly broad with items like shrimp tequila, chicken barbacoa and fish tacos in addition to standard Mexican items. Combo plates are around $7 and are a good value. Overall, the food's good for the money. Eat at one of the cheap, outdoor tables or take it to go. At the back of Dolphin Plaza. They serve breakfast, but open at 9 a.m. Otherwise it's **$7–$13** for lunch and dinner.

Fred's Mexican Café
2511 S. Kihei Rd. • 891–8600

ono I know. With a name like *Fred's* you're expecting *scrupulous* authenticity. Actually Fred was a regular at Moose's on the mainland and suggested they name a chain after him. Wadayano, they did. The food is good for the money, but we've noticed that you're best off sticking with red meat items. Decor is a mixture of crystal chandeliers and car hoods studded with light bulbs. Most items are under $12. Fajitas, tacos and massive burritos. (Too much lettuce, though.) The house margaritas aren't very good, but you'll like the top shelf. (Ask them not to load it up with too much ice.) The bar gets crazy on taco Tuesdays and the wait can be over 2 hours. All in all, it's a good value for the money. **$9–$15** for lunch and dinner. On mauka side of S. Kihei Rd. across from Kama'ole II Beach.

Jawz Tacos
1279 S. Kihei Rd. • 874–8226

Seems like they tried to be like Maui Taco…and failed. The food's too pricey and not very good. Unlike Maui Taco, however, they *do* serve alcohol. **$7–$15**. In Azeka Mauka Shopping Center.

Maui Taco
2411 S. Kihei Rd. • 879–5005
Also in:
Kahului: Q. Ka'ahumanu Ctr. • 871–7726
Napili: 5095 Napilihau St. • 665–0222
Lahaina: 840 Wainee St. • 661–8883

ono This small, local chain is a good place to go for tacos and burritos. Nothing fancy, but it's not overly expensive (though it's not cheap). They have a good selection, and the portions are large. Their various locations are pretty different. The Kihei location (Kama'ole Beach Center) is their best, followed by Kahului (Queen Ka'ahumanu Center), then Napili (Napili Plaza), followed by the disappointing Lahaina location (Lahaina Square). Sometimes their food is warm instead of hot, and don't forget the condiments bar if you find you need more seasoning. **$5–$10**. BYOB.

SOUTH MAUI PACIFIC RIM

Five Palms
2960 S. Kihei Rd. • 879–2607

ono They have one of the tastiest views of any restaurant. As soon as we walked in the first time, we knew we wanted to use their view for our dining section photo (page 249). It's right on the water and looks down Keawakapu Beach. They close off the upwind windows and open the downwind windows, allowing it to feel open-air without the normal afternoon winds messing things up. They also have outdoor tables. There are few bad tables in this place. The food is steak, seafood and lobster for dinner. In all the years we've been reviewing them, they *still* have the same problem about half the time: food being served warm rather than hot. And spending $43 for a lobster tail and scant vegetables, then receiving it at nearly room temperature is hard to swallow. But the food is tasty. The crab cakes are an awesome appetizer, and we also recommend the crab-crusted fish or the lamb. Sure, it's overpriced. But the setting is so good we're crossing our fingers and are trying to forgive some of their shortcomings like the *slooow* bar service. **$8–$18** for breakfast (which features $11 pancakes), **$11–$22** for lunch, **$30–$55** for dinner. In the Mana Kai Resort.

Humuhumunukunukuapua'a
3850 Wailea Alanui Dr. • 875–1234
Often called simply Humu (for obvious reasons), this is a truly memorable place to eat and *was* one of our favorites on the island. But it has slipped badly lately, bad enough

to lose the ONO and our affection. Exceptional ambiance: You're surrounded by and actually *over* a huge fishpond. Some of the fish and lobster swimming around are actually the main course. (But don't tell them.) Waterfalls and thatched roofs add to the exotic Polynesian feel. It's very expensive steak, lobster and seafood. But the food and especially the service are now lacking. We're really hoping they pick it up so we can recommend them again. In the Grand Wailea Resort; allow an extra 10 minutes to walk through the fabulous grounds, or save time parking at Wailea Beach access lot. **$30–$60** for dinner.

Nick's Fishmarket
4100 Wailea Alanui Dr. • 879–7224

(ONO) One of the finest restaurants in South Maui. Exceptional seafood in an elegant setting. The menu changes often, but we've never had or even *heard* of a bad meal here. Try the calamari for an appetizer. Their Hawaiian lobster is fantastic. So is everything else. Consider the chocolate "decadense" for dessert. World-class wine list. The service is unbelievable. Order a drink and see if it takes more than a minute. (And their drinks are *well*-concocted.) It's the closest thing we've seen to saying, "Tea, EarlGrey, hot." (You either get that one or you don't.) It's like a contest to see how excellent they can make the service, but the tag team approach seems to confuse some diners. Though attentive, they *don't* come around every five minutes, when your mouth is full, asking, "How is everything?" They just keep a watchful eye on you. We've never seen a water glass go empty. So what's the catch? *Exactly what you think.* Nick's isn't cheap. But if you want steak and seafood and need a good pampering, Nick's is the place to go. **$30–$50** for dinner. In the Kea Lani Resort in Wailea. Reservations recommended. Resort wear required.

Sarento's on the Beach
2980 S. Kihei Rd. • 875–7555

(ONO) We're kind of uncomfortable with this review. We get lots of very helpful e-mails from readers about restaurants, and Sarento's generates an astonishing number of bad e-mails. Poor food is *sometimes* a reader complaint, but we've only had one bad experience here. It's the service that irritates some. Personally, we like it, but the tag team approach confuses some diners. You get lots of attention from various staff, so if you want to be left alone you might not like it here. The location is right on Keawakapu Beach, one of the most intimate beach locations on the island. Fresh fish, steak, osso bucco (veal shank) and pasta. It's hard to classify the style, sort of a Pacific Rim/Italian/local. **$35–$65** for dinner. The wine list is vast with a number of bottles costing more than $1,000. (Sorry, but that's just insane to spend $25 *per sip* of wine.) At the Maui Oceanfront Inn. Reservations recommended.

SeaWatch
100 Wailea Golf Club Dr. • 875–8080

Located at the Wailea Gold Golf Course, the views of Molokini and Kaho'olawe from the outside tables are excellent, and it's a good place for a late breakfast as it and lunch are both served from 8 a.m. to 3 p.m. The kalua pork and Swiss is pretty good (though it's not the same kalua pork you get at lu'aus), and most of the sandwiches work pretty well. Service is good. **$7–$15** for breakfast, **$9–$18** for lunch, or a pretty pricey **$25–$40** for dinner.

Spago
3900 Wailea Alanui Dr. • 879–2999

(ONO) Lots of hype about this place, but guess what? They live up to it. This is Wolfgang Puck's Maui restaurant. (Though the wait staff told us they've only seen him twice.) The dishes are simply unbelievable. The spicy ahi tuna poke in sesame-miso cones is unlike anything we've ever had. Sesame-crusted fish are *ohhh* so good. Love the pan-seared scallops with Chinese garlic-pepper sauce. Actually, everything we've had is good. Portions are pretty small, and you can drop a lot of money quick here. But their nice ocean view and world-class cooking make it a treat. **$35–$65** and up. (The menu changes slightly each night and sometimes has items for $100.) In Four Seasons, Wailea. Reservations recommended.

SOUTH MAUI THAI

Maui Thai
2439 S. Kihei Rd. • 874–5605

⊙∩⊙ Although the ambiance is unremarkable, they unquestionably have the best curry in South Maui, especially the red. Lots of vegetarian items. If you ask for it hot, they won't save you from yourself. The pad Thai is not as recommended, however. And the Thai tea is way too sweet. No separate lunch menu, so it'll be pricey at lunch. **$13–$25** for lunch and dinner. In the Rainbow Mall.

Thailand Cuisine
1819 S. Kihei Rd. • 875–0839
Also in:
Kahului: 70 E. Ka'ahumanu • 873–0225

⊙∩⊙ Over 100 items to choose from (including *lots* of vegetarian items), and the entrées we've tried are quite good. The atmosphere is relaxing with Thai music filling the air. Their curries are flavorful, and they'll make them fatally hot if you desire. Prices are hard to predict. Dishes are $9 and up, and it depends on how many you order if you share. Figure **$10–$25** for lunch and dinner. In Kukui Mall. Their Kahului location isn't as nice.

SOUTH MAUI TREATS

Cinnamon Roll Fair
2453 S. Kihei Rd. • 879–5177

This is a good place to get warm, gooey cinnamon rolls (they're good about putting more goo on top if you want) for about **$3**. Also muffins, cookies and coffee drinks. They also have deli sandwiches at lunch. At Kama'ole Shopping Center, Kihei downstairs from Denny's. Cash only; opens at 6 a.m.

Cold Stone Creamery
225 Piikea Ave. • 875–8811

⊙∩⊙ Part of a growing national chain. The name refers to the frozen slab of granite they use to mix whatever your little heart desires into their home-made ice cream—mixes like candy bars, berries, brownies, etc. Outrageous dipped waffle cup liners. Price is steep. You can easily spend **$6** for a medium cup, but that's for a *ton* of ice cream. Near Safeway in Pi'ilani Village Shopping Center off Hwy 31.

Hula Cookies & Ice Cream
300 Ma'alaea Rd. • 243–2271

⊙∩⊙ Fresh baked cookies are the specialty, and they do them pretty well. Occasionally, they're not fresh, despite the claims. But most of the time, they're wonderful. They also have so-so ice cream, which is magically transformed when it's in their killer home-made ice cream sandwich. **$2–$5**. In Ma'alaea town at the only shopping center.

Sweet Spot
1819 S. Kihei Rd. • 879–8611

Mediocre shave ice and and unremarkable ice cream. Stick with the soft serve if your sweet tooth is calling and you're near the Kukui Mall. **$3–$6**.

SOUTH MAUI VIETNAMESE

Vietnamese Cuisine
1280 S. Kihei Rd. • 875–2088

ONO We really like the food here. Flavors will appeal to most people. The build-your-own Vietnamese burritos are great. And you *have* to try the rice-in-a-clay-pot. Stir it up first and look for the slightly burned parts. They're the best! Noodle dishes, rice dishes, stir fry dishes, plus steak. Lots of vegetarian items, too. **$10–$20** for lunch and dinner. In Kihei in the Azeka Makai on ocean side of Hwy north of Lipoa.

CENTRAL MAUI AMERICAN

Anthony's
90 Hana Hwy. • 579–8340

ONO An excellent place for a morning stop on your way to Hana. (They open at 5:30 a.m. but don't serve breakfast until 6 a.m.) A nice coffee selection, and a *phenomenal* choice of teas coupled with baked goods (like the coffee cake) and eggs and such means there's something for almost everyone. And the price is pretty reasonable. They also have free Wi-Fi. Most meals are around $5. The place is a bit disheveled inside, but it's nice to have good food on Maui without getting hammered. **$3–$7** for breakfast and lunch. (The latter is mostly sandwiches.) In Pa'ia on Hana Hwy, mauka side of the road.

Café Mambo
30 Baldwin Ave. • 579–8021

Pretty unremarkable sandwiches (which are also available as take-out picnic lunches), soups, salads, burgers and fajitas. They're outshined by other Pa'ia restaurants. **$5–$10** for breakfast, **$7–$15** for lunch, **$10–$20** for dinner.

Café Marc Aurel
28 N. Market St. • 244–0852

Boasting a "Bohemian Ambiance" (make sure you drop the terms, *groovy, dig, psychedelic or far out*) and a love of fine wine, coffee and cheese. They have the usually café fare here, such as bagels, salads and deli sandwiches made with good ingredients. Live entertainment most nights from various genres. If it weren't for the service we might have given them an ONO. But it can be so thin that if you want something with your meal, be sure to ask for it when you order, or you might not get another chance. Overall, a good place to relax and feed your senses. Open 7 a.m. to 10 a.m. for breakfast open again at 4 p.m. to close for dinner. **$4–$8** for breakfast, **$4–$14** for dinner. On Market St. just off Main. Closed Sun.

Charley's
142 Hana Hwy. • 579–9453

Good breakfast menu with the usual items, plus breakfast burritos, tacos and veggie entrées. Their highly touted eggs benedict is pretty mediocre. Lunch is good burgers, sandwiches, some fish and stir fry. Dinner is mostly Italian. Pasta, pizza and ribs. Prices are high, but portions are generous. Overall, good food, lousy service, which costs them their ONO. Known locally as an occasional hangout for celebrities who have homes on the north shore of Haleakala, but the staff gets starstruck and service gets even worse. So does Charley himself do the cooking? Hope not. Charley was a dog. He lives on as the restaurant's logo. **$7–$14** for breakfast, **$9–$15** for lunch, **$12–$25** for dinner. On Hwy 36 in Pa'ia.

Down to Earth
305 Dairy Rd. • 877–2661

ONO A health food store, café, deli and bakery. It's ironic that health food stores often have such bad food, but this one is an exception. Limited selection but outstanding quality. The hot bar sells food by the pound, including veggie lasagna, enchiladas, potatoes with herbs, steamed veggies, black bean soup, teriyaki tofu, etc. A few of the items are left without seasoning, which you can sprinkle on yourself. Also consider the veggie wraps. Every item lists all the ingredients. The bakery is excellent, and the goods aren't dry as is often the case in health food stores. (Try the mac nut bar.) Good salad bar. This place hasn't changed in years. There are some easy-to-miss tables upstairs. In Kahului across from Maui Marketplace. (The store itself is also very nice.) **$3–$8.**

Jacques North Shore
120 Hana Hwy. • 579–8844
Seafood, linguini, roast duck, steak, sushi, and salads in an industrial Polynesian atmosphere. The food is very good, varied and easy to like. The menu is more upscale than the surroundings. (By the way, flies can be a problem at times.) **$13–$27** for dinner. On mauka side at 120 Hana Hwy in Pa'ia east of Baldwin.

Mama's Fish House
799 Poho Pl. • 579–8488
This is where we come when we want to treat ourselves, so let's cut to the chase: diabolically satisfying food and an extremely pleasing ambiance. They are right next to a beach and tide-pool; the only things between you and the sand are picturesque palm trees. If you opt for lunch or an early dinner, you may see windsurfers plying the waters offshore. We like early dinners best. It's usually less crowded, and the views are as tasty as the food. Ask for a covered outdoor table—much preferred to the more crowded indoor tables. You know as soon as you

walk up the gecko walkway and through the banyan tree root archway (which got that shape when it crushed a building) that this will be special. The mostly seafood recipes are very imaginative and change daily, so it doesn't make much sense to mention specific ones. But we've never had a bad meal here. They even give credit on the menu to the fishing boat or fisherman that caught each particular fish. Polish it off with a Polynesian Black Pearl dessert and a chocolate martini. The only negatives are that it is a poorly kept secret (so expect company and maybe a difficult time getting a reservation), service that has slipped to acceptable from the formerly stellar and the price is *darned* expensive. **$45–$65** *or more* for dinner, you can shave $10 for lunch. But you won't mind paying top dollar if you get a top-quality experience, and you probably will. Northeast of Pa'ia on Hwy 36 just past the 8 mile marker. Reservations strongly recommended, and you may have to call them later to *confirm* them.

Maui Coffee Roasters
444 Hana Hwy. • 877–2877
An excellent place for coffee and a muffin in the morning. They also have breakfast sandwiches, eggs Benedict and various bagels. They get their baked goods elsewhere, and the results are flavorful. Lots of coffee flavors and coffee drinks, and it's the only place we can think of that sells coffee for around a buck. The coffees taste freshly roasted; not surprising since they do their own roasting next door. Lunch is tasty sandwiches and wraps at a good price. In Kahului on Hana Hwy near Dairy Road next to Marco's. **$2–$7.**

Pa'ia Fish Market
100 Hana Hwy. • 579–8030
One of the better Pa'ia eateries. They have a very

nice selection of fish, chicken, tacos, salads, sashimi, pasta, fajitas and burgers. The fish and chips are excellent, and they seem to use a very good grade of fish. Tables but no table service—order and pick up. Beer and wine available. An easy place to recommend and pretty popular, so you may have to wait during busy hours. $9–$17 for lunch and dinner. On the corner of Hana Hwy (36) and Baldwin Avenue in Pa'ia.

CENTRAL MAUI CHINESE

Dragon Dragon
70 E. Ka'ahumanu Ave. • 893–1628
A simple Chinese restaurant with great dishes and a passable dim sum menu. You should never judge a dish by its price, but the $10 shark's fin soup made us a bit curious as to the ingredients. (In China it can cost up to $175.) Everything else seems reasonable and the stir-fried eggplant is great. Not many spicy dishes but they're flexible. $9–$30 for lunch and dinner. In the Maui Mall across for IHOP.

CENTRAL MAUI ITALIAN

Flatbread Company
89 Hana Hwy. • 579–8989
ONO Located on the highway in Pa'ia, they probably have the best pizza on the island in a not-too-serious atmosphere. Check out their unusual homemade woodburning pizza oven. The pizza is amazingly thin, and you may find yourself clearing more pizza surface area than you anticipate. Their selection goes from fairly traditional to uniquely their own, and they try to use organic ingredients. It's a pretty kid-friendly place and it can get loud and hot inside, but it's an easy restaurant to like. $10–20 for lunch and dinner.

Marco's Grill & Deli
444 Hana Hwy. • 877–4446
An Italian restaurant set in a loud '50s-style diner. Pizza, pasta, sandwiches and salads are all heavily overpriced ($9 for a grilled cheese). The portions don't match the prices and flavors are bland. Gian Don's in Kihei has a strikingly similar menu (it was once Marco's South Side Grill) and a much more relaxing atmosphere. If you insist on eating this food, you're better off doing it in Kihei. $7–$13 for breakfast and $12–$30 for lunch and dinner. On the corner of Dairy Road and Hana Highway in Kahului.

Pizza in Paradise
60 E. Wakea Ave. • 871–8188
ONO Formerly called Two Fat Guys from Boston Pizza (who sold it because their "crane business was too good"), the pizza isn't the best you'll find on Maui, but it's a really good value for the money. The price is reasonable, and the portions are generous (by-the-slice is a very good deal). Two people can get a couple of slices and a Coke for around $12, which is a pretty good price for Maui. The oven baked subs are pretty good. $4–$12. In Kahului between Puunene (Hwy 311) and Hukilike Street. Closed Sundays.

CENTRAL MAUI JAPANESE

Wow Wee Maui Kava Bar & Grill
333 Dairy Rd. • 871–1414
ONO First of all, it's not really Japanese. It's really more American with burgers and sandwiches. But they *also* have a sushi bar which, frankly, is the only reason we gave them an ONO. (Its separate phone number is 871–5050.) The sushi's fresh, reasonably priced and has some surprisingly good flavors. *Excellent* edamame (boiled soy-

beans). At the Dairy Road Center near Alamaha. $6–$15.

Unisan
2102 Vinyard St. • 244–4500
The generous portions of sushi might satisfy most appetites, but the scant service may leave you hungry. Burgers, noodles and plate lunches make up the rest of the menu. Dinner brings more choices such as steak and seafood at reasonable prices. (Surf and turf is $25.) Nightly entertainment sometimes requires a cover charge. Call and ask first. $7–$15 for lunch and $9–$30 for dinner. At Vineyard and Church Street in Wailuku.

CENTRAL MAUI LOCAL

Ba-Le
270 Dairy Rd. • 877–2400
ONO You can forget classifying this place. They call themselves a French Sandwich and Bakery, but serve mostly Asian dishes, huge portions, flavorful results, very cheaply. Vietnamese plate lunches, French sandwiches, local entrées—and you'll probably spend about $5. In the Kau Kau Food Court in Maui Marketplace in Kahului. $3–$7.

Cary & Eddie's Hideaway
500 N. Puunene Ave. • 873–6555
Imagine a lu'au without all the song and dance. Their daily Hawaiian buffet includes most items you would find at a traditional lu'au: kalua pork and cabbage, lau lau, lomi lomi salmon and, of course, poi. The lunch buffet and Sunday brunch are $11, and the dinner buffet adds ribs, chicken and seafood for $21. The best seats are in the back with a view of Kahului Harbor and 'Iao Valley. In Hawai'i we say, "Don't eat till you're full, eat till you're tired." And this is a place to do it. Behind First Hawaiian Bank at Puunene and Kaahumanu in Kahului.

Tasty Crust
1770 Mill St. • 244–0845
ONO Let's start by saying the place is kind of dumpy. And it's not as…kempt as we'd like. But if you're looking for very cheap and very hearty, this is the place. Their pancakes are known island-wide. Light, soft and large with a good texture, they even serve peanut butter with them, if you want. (I know how it sounds, but you'd be surprised how well the flavor combination works.) Portions are large, but the plate is too small to negotiate the syrup transfer. (That's pancake tech-talk.) They also have limited omelettes, loco moco (a local-style cholesterol lover's best friend, described on page 252) and eggs. In the traditional local way, Spam or vienna sausage available with breakfast. (Locals *love* Spam.) Lunch is saimin, pork chops, spare ribs and burgers. This place is a long-time local restaurant that lasts because they serve large portions at a good price, and they do what they do well. *That's* why we gave them an ONO. $3–$6 for breakfast, $5–$9 for lunch and dinner (add some pricier steaks at night). No credit cards. In Wailuku, from 32 go right on Central to the end. Turn right on Mill. Opens at 6 a.m.

CENTRAL MAUI MEXICAN

Amigo's
333 Dairy Rd. • 872–9525
ONO More of a festive atmospere than many other Mexican restaurants, the portions are big, the combinations tasty. The burritos are especially grande and satisfying. Along with daily specials they occasionallly have lengua tacos. (If Spanish isn't your native *tongue*, eat it first then look it up.) $5–$12 for lunch and dinner. Near Wow Wee Maui on Dairy. Like Las Piñatas, they have beer available.

Las Piñatas
395 Dairy Rd. • 877–8707

ONO This is the place to go for a quick bite, but you still want to sit down and eat reasonable quality, relatively inexpensive Mexican food in acceptable surroundings. (If that sounds less than glowing, it's because *you aren't paying* for a glow at this place.) Burritos are large and most are around $5–$7. Chicken enchiladas are pretty tasty. Mostly Mexican beers. In Kahului between Hana Hwy and Maui Marketplace next to Kinko's. And yes, they do have lots of piñatas hanging from the ceiling. $5–$10 for lunch and dinner.

Mañana Garage
33 Lono Ave. • 873–0220

ONO It's technically not Mexican; it's Latin with dishes from Central America and Cuba. The decor is a whimsical garage look. (The napkin holders used to be hose clamps but they kept losing them—apparently too many customers must have had radiator hose leaks.) With items like BBQ duck and sweet potato quesadilla, chili adobe-pulled pork, chicken hazelnut empañadas and fish chimichangas, this is a good place for flavor-lovers and those looking for an unusual menu. Their chips come from home-made corn tortillas—very fresh. $11–$16 for lunch, $20–$30 for dinner. Near Ka'ahumanu Avenue in Kahului.

Milagros
3 Baldwin Ave. • 579–8755

ONO The food alone qualifies them for an ONO, but what really impressed us was their reverence for tequila and margaritas, which they call *Da Kine Ritas*. You won't find Jose Cuervo here. The bar is raised a bit higher than that, and you will be more involved in how your *rita* is concocted. Oh, yeah. And for the food, lunch is the best value with large portions under $10. At dinner try the fajitas; they're sweet, smoky and delicious. Their ahi taquitos are equally amazing. Most seating is outside, making it a perfect place for observing the diverse population of Pa'ia. At the stoplight on the Hwy in Pa'ia. $6–$10 for breakfast, $8–$12 for lunch, $14–$25 for dinner.

CENTRAL MAUI THAI

Saeng's
2119 Vineyard St. • 244–1567

ONO At Saeng's *hot* means *hot,* and they'll hurt you if you ask them nicely. Too often Thai restaurants try to save you from yourself if you tell them to turn up the heat. Not here. Most items are under $10. We like the pad Thai. The Pad Ped sauce is good with anything, such as their slipper lobster tails which are small but tasty. You can't go wrong with the curries, either. Most of the seating is open air, so bring something warm for the cold Wailuku nights. (You Green Bay residents can stop laughing now.) On Vineyard between High St. and Church St. $6–$14 for lunch and dinner.

CENTRAL MAUI TREATS

Aloha Island Shave Ice
77 Hana Hwy. • 579–8747

ONO Their shave ice is a finer grain than any we've seen on Maui, and they chill the syrup to prevent icing on the bottom. That syrup is *real* sweet and they use a lot of it, so you may want to have them go easy on it. As you enter Pa'ia on the ocean side. $3–$5. Closed Mondays.

Home Maid Bakery
1005 Lower Main St. • 244–7015

Large selection of baked goods, some breads and tasty hot malasadas (a Portuguese donut) all served with icy service—like you're in line for prison food. If you don't need a warm hug to start the day, you may like the baked goods here. On Lower (east) Main between Hookahi and Waena in Wailuku. **$2–$5**.

Maui Bake Shop
2092 W. Vineyard St. • 242–0064

ONO Tasty baked goods, some small pizzas, soups, prepared salads and sandwiches. Try the raspberry lunette. They have some real cute baked items for keiki, and they're cheap. On Vineyard and N. Church in Wailuku. **$3–$6**. Closed Sun. and Mon.

Maui Specialty Chocolates
180 E. Wakea Ave. • 871–1222

Pretty good chocolates for the price made on the premises. You can get an assorted 8-ounce box for under **$9**. On Wakea Avenue at Hukilike Street, Kahului.

Moana Bakery & Café
71 Baldwin Ave. • 579–9999

ONO Expensive but very good baked goods from their French pastry chef. The chocolate eclairs (when they have them) and the chocolate macs will send you into orbit. They also have a good lunch with wraps, sandwiches (made from their breads) and some salads. Dinner is pasta, fresh fish, lamb, steak and sashimi. **$7–$13** for breakfast (they open at 8 a.m.), **$9–$15** for lunch, **$12–$33** for dinner. Live music some nights. In Pa'ia. Overall, pricey but good.

Stillwell's Bakery & Café
1740 Ka'ahumanu Ave. • 243–2243

Lots of sandwiches made on their own bread, but be specific about what you

want. There are no condiments on the tables. Also some salads and soups. Baked goods are what they do best. Try the crème brûlée or the chocolate eclairs. **$5–$9** for entrées, **$2–$4** for baked goods. If you're there around Christmas check out their home-made gingerbread houses; everything's edible. On Hwy 32 on the right side just before you enter Wailuku.

CENTRAL MAUI VIETNAMESE

A Saigon Café
1792 Main St. • 243–9560

ONO One of the more exciting restaurants on Maui, their food is outstanding. The menu is vast and contains an enviable array of foods, many from other Asian countries. Their garden delight summer rolls are a *great* way to start it off. The shrimp pops (ground shrimp pasted on a stick of sugar cane, steamed and grilled) are also a novel appetizer. Consider the garden party shrimp (with or without a shell), tofu with curry and lemongrass, Vietnamese burritos…it all works. Service is very competent and accommodating. **$8–$20** for lunch and dinner. It's tricky to find. Coming down Hwy 32 into Wailuku (as if you're going toward the Iao Needle), turn right onto Central, quick right onto Nani, right onto Kaniela, then it will be on your left side at Kaniela and Main. At press time there was no sign out front because the owner, who has the signs, is "waiting for the right day to put them up" and has been "too busy." This is a popular place with locals; reservations recommended.

UPCOUNTRY DINING

Rather than create separate categories with only one entry, we're lumping all of Upcountry in one section and labeling them.

Café 808
4566 Lower Kula Rd. • 878–6874
Local—In Kula, they have items such as teri beef, loco moco, curry stew, saimin, kalbi shortribs, chicken katsu and burgers in an atmosphere that's a cross between a worn cafeteria and a garage that could probably use a bit more TLC. Quality is not bad, not great. Consider the burgers and the wraps (which are pretty good). **$5–$10** for breakfast, lunch and dinner. Off the lower highway (37). At ⁸⁄₁₀ mile past the 11 mile marker, go mauka (up the mountain) at Lower Kula Road, drive ²⁄₃ mile up, and it'll be on your right side.

Casanova
1188 Makawao Ave. • 572–0220
Italian—Dinners are their weakest point here. Some portions (especially the pathetic salads) are too small and the raviolis are simply horrible. Their thin 12-inch pizzas make good appetizers if you can split them with others. (It's their best offering.) Breakfast and lunch are served in their deli. Egg sandwiches, coffee drinks and baked goods for breakfast, tasty sliced pizza and sandwiches for lunch. **$4–$10** for breakfast and lunch, **$13–$30** for dinner. In Makawao. Live music Wednesday–Saturday.

Colleen's Pizza & Bakeshop
810 Haiku Rd. • 575–9211
American—Located in Ha'iku on Ha'iku Road at the Haiku Marketplace, the baked goods are very tasty. Definitely worth the stop. A bit less sweet than most bakeries. Breakfasts are good. Their Hangover Cure breakfast is a great deal and lives up to its name. Lunches offer sandwiches, burgers and wraps. The pizza, however, is marginal. Served only at night, it has decent crust, but the toppings are bland and pizzas are too cheesy. (But they sure do stay hot a long time. The Earth's core cools faster than their pizzas.) **$6–$12** for breakfast, **$7–$15** for lunch, **$12–$25** for dinner which includes steak, pasta and salads.

Grandma's Coffee House
153 Kula Hwy. • 878–2140
ᴏɴᴏ American—If you're coming 'round the mountain from Kaupo after the long Hana Hwy drive, this is one of the first places you'll see upcountry on Hwy 37 between the 16 and 17 mile marker. Consider stopping if you're hurting for a decent coffee or some home-made sweets in a decidedly old fashioned atmosphere. Open 7 a.m. to 5 p.m. **$2–$5**.

Hali'imaile General Store
900 Hali'imaile Rd. • 572–2666
ᴏɴᴏ Pacific Rim—The location for this somewhat upscale restaurant is unexpected. You have nowhere, then you have Hali'imaile, which is 3 miles south of nowhere. The food is very good, if overpriced given the location, especially at dinner. Small lunch menu of salads, salmon tacos and ribs. Lunch during the week only, and they tend to rush you. Dinner brings items such as mac nut-crusted fish, ribeye steak and kalua pork enchiladas. ($14 for enchiladas is pretty pricey, huh?) Desserts are rich enough to make you sweat. We almost withheld our ᴏɴᴏ because dinner prices feel about 25% overpriced. Keep that in mind. Their ads mention the names of all the celebrities who have eaten there. Well, maybe overpaying for dinner doesn't bother Michael Jordan or Dustin Hoffman, but it irritates mere mortals like us. The back of the menu is a full page dedicated to the owner's accolades and accomplishments. **$12–$20** for

lunch, **$25–$40** for dinner. Between Baldwin Avenue and Haleakala Hwy. (37). See map on page 115.

Hana Hou Café
810 Haiku Rd. • 575–2661

ONO Local—Probably the best food in Haiku. It's local style with plate lunches, fish and chips (which is delicious), dry mein (one of their cheapest items, and it's hearty and good), burgers and salads. At dinner it gets more expensive when they add steak and seafood and a lu'au plate with items like kalua pig, lau lau, etc. You'll eat at their semi-outdoor tables. Not a high-end atmosphere, but the food's worth stopping for. **$8–$12** for lunch, up to **$20** at dinner. At the corner of Haiku Road and Kokomo at the Haiku Marketplace.

Komoda Store & Bakery
3674 Baldwin Ave. • 572–7261

ONO Treats—Who would expect that in this uninspiring, little semi-dumpy building would reside some of the best bakers on Maui? Their cream puffs are legendary around the island (more like eclairs). Stick donuts, malasadas (Portuguese donuts) chocolate croissants; we've liked almost everything we've tried here. (And we're quite diligent in reviewing them every time we're in the neighborhood.) They've been here since the island rose from the sea. (OK, OK, since 1916.) Service is friendly, and the price is very reasonable. As at most bakeries, before noon is best. On Baldwin Avenue in Makawao just off Makawao Avenue. **$2–$4**. Closed Sun. and Wed.

Kula Lodge
15200 Haleakala Hwy. • 878–1535

ONO American/Pacific Rim—An easy place to like. The views and ambiance are glorious. With sweeping views down the mountain, you can see South Maui, West Maui mountains and Kahului. An all-glass wall takes full advantage of the views. During spring and summer, some outdoor tables near an incredible stone and brick oven are available. They also use that oven for pizzas. The food is usually excellent. Steak and seafood. Prices are high, even for lunch, but it's a treat worth splurging for, at least once, for the view. Early dinners are best, and you can get some unbelievable sunsets from up here. Desserts can be rich and decadent but sometimes miss the mark. Breakfasts are expensive and can be busy if they fill up with bicyclists, but the food's good and the view with the sun behind you is unbeatable. **$9–$18** for breakfast, **$12–$20** for lunch, **$20–$35** for dinner. On Upper Highway (377) before 378.

Pauwela Café
375 W. Kuiaha Rd. • 575–9242

American—A hidden gem with dishes you wish your mom could make. The food's fresh and the ingredients are healthy, though portions could be a bit larger. Lunch includes sandwiches, burritos and salads. Breakfast has some unusual choices, such as Pain Perdu (which means *lost bread* in French—don't pronounce it like PANE, say it with a French swagger) soaked in orange vanilla custard and baked with fruit on top. Baked goods are made on premises with uneven results. (Good scones, though.) The eggs Benedict special on weekends is great, made on fresh baked cornbread. **$6–$12** for breakfast, **$8–$15** for lunch. Almost ½ mile past the 12 mile marker on Hwy 36 is West Kuiaha Road. Turn Mauka and in ½ mile you'll see the Pauwela Cannery.

Polli's Mexican Restaurant
1202 Makawao Ave. • 572–7808

Mexican—Fairly good selection of standard Mexican items, plus ribs and BBQ chicken. Service and the food have one thing in common: They're both lacking what you really want and the surroundings aren't too hot, either. Hmm, I guess that covers it. **$8–$16** for lunch, **$11–$21** for dinner. Located on Makawao Avenue in Makawao. Their motto is, "Come on in, or we'll both starve."

Serpico's
7 Aewa Pl. • 572–8498

ONO An Italian restaurant transplanted from New York. (There's even a guy named Mario in the kitchen.) It's a great place to stop on your way back from Haleakala. The pizzas are outstanding with thin, hand-tossed crust and light sauce. They also have ravioli, baked ziti and even shrimp parmigiana. Most entrées can feed two, especially their baseball-sized meatballs. If you don't leave room for their brownie sundae, you're missing out. **$6–$18** for lunch and dinner. BYOB. On Old Haleakala Hwy and Aewa Place in Pukalani. (See map on page 115.)

Stopwatch Bar & Grill
1127 Makawao Ave. • 572–1380

ONO American—In a town that prides itself on its cowboy heritage, it's surprisingly hard to get a decent burger in Makawao. That's why we gave an ONO to Stopwatch. The burgers are pretty decent (though they may cook them more than the medium-well they claim—consider telling them medium or med-rare). They also serve fish and chips, fresh fish, Thai stir fry, steak, and sandwiches. Not much healthy stuff; head down the road for that. **$8–$20** for lunch and dinner. Good views. Our biggest complaint applies to all Makawao restaurants. After prolonged rains, they are sometimes invaded by irritating gnats, which can make things miserable. On Makawao Avenue southwest of Baldwin Avenue.

ISLAND NIGHTLIFE

The sun has set and the scenery faded, but you don't want the day to end. If you're a night owl, you'll find that Maui probably has enough to keep you happy, but don't expect Las Vegas. This is still a relatively quiet island, especially in South Maui.

Nightlife is something that's ever-changing. Many restaurants are constantly bringing in new musicians and trying new things. We hate to pass the buck, but by definition, nightlife is something that changes all the time. Different establishments do different things, sometimes every week. No one covers this week's action as well as an insert in Thursday's *Maui News* newspaper called *Maui Scene*. Grab a copy to see what's shakin' this week. It includes special events, concerts, movies, stage plays, resort entertainment, galleries, and it has coupons.

For **movies**, the best theaters are in Kahului. (West and South Maui's theaters are small and unimpressive.) Call 249-2222 and 875-4910 for showings.

West Maui Nightlife
Lahaina is the center of West Maui nightlife. One of the most effective ways to feel out the nightlife in Lahaina is to walk along Front Street and see what strikes your fancy. One popular spot to be is **Moose McGillycuddy's** (667–7758) at 844 Front Street, which is usually a pretty happenin' place with music every night. Especially popular with the 21–25-year-old crowd.

In **Ka'anapali**, watching the cliff diver mentioned on page 50 is a good way to start off an evening. Several of the beachside path restaurants there often have live music. Most of the resorts also have goings-on.

South Maui Nightlife

Nightlife isn't as good in South Maui. The hub is the **Kihei Kalama Village**, locally know as **The Triangle**. Bars like **Life's a Beach**, **South Shore Tiki Lounge** and **Lulu's** are hopping most nights of the week. **Kahale** (875–7711) is a watering hole in the Triangle with surprisingly bad live music. **Mulligan's on the Blue** (874–1131) at the Wailea Old Blue Golf Course mauka of the Fairmont Kea Lani Resort has live music every night and often sports one of the most festive atmospheres you'll find, especially when the Celtic band is playing on Saturday nights. The **Fred's/ Moose McGillycuddy's** (891–8600) at 2511 S. Kihei Road is a lively place for the younger crowd Their *Taco Tuesday* has cheap tacos and boozy margaritas. Lastly, Maui's best musician is **Willie K**. This guy's a master guitar player and vocalist and rocks out like none other. Hopefully you'll spot him playing somewhere.

Nightlife Elsewhere

In **Hana**, find a bright light and watch the geckos eat night bugs—you crazy party animal, you. Actually, the **Hotel Hana Maui** (248–8211) often has some pretty good local musicians at their restaurant.

Upcountry isn't a nightlife mecca either. Might want to wander around Makawao and see what's shakin'. **Casanovas** (572–0220) has a dance floor and lively music on weekends. Sometimes **Stopwatch** (572–1380) has live performers.

In **Pa'ia**, **Charley's** (579–8085) has music on the weekends with occasional drop-ins from local celebs like Willie Nelson.

In **Kahului**, the **Maui Arts & Cultural Center** is on Kahului Beach Road. Call 242–7469 to see what's happening there. Their Castle Theatre is a great place for a movie or play. The two rows of balconies provide excellent vantages.

LU'AUS

We've all seen them in movies. People sit at a table with a mai tai in one hand and a plate of kalua pig in another. There's always a show where hula dancers bend and sway to the beat of the music, and sometimes a fire-knife dancer twirls a torch lit at both ends. To be honest, that's not far from the truth. Lu'aus can be a blast, and, if your time allows, they are highly recommended. The pig is baked in the ground all day, creating succulent results when prepared right. Shows are usually exciting and fast paced. Maui's lu'aus have all you can eat and drink (including alcohol) for a set fee. If the mai tais they are serving don't satisfy you, they have an open bar to fill your needs. Remember that piece of info when you pick up your first complimentary (and sometimes watery) mai tai. The bartender will season it for you or serve you whatever you want. Since they are usually held outdoors at night, you might want to consider spraying mosquito repellent on your legs before the show or wear slacks.

Lu'aus will usually cost you **$80– $110**, and the better ones are at the higher end. Book them in advance. If you want to know what lu'au foods are like, see page 251.

Different resorts hold their lu'aus on different nights. These change with the whims of the managers, so verify the days listed here before making plans. Here's how they stack up in order of preference.

One thing you need to know is that five of the lu'aus on the island are all put on by the same production company, **Tihati**. This means their shows are all similar so they can interchange personnel. Right down to the same MC jokes. The shows are less personal and more of a commodity. Expect competence but little enthusiasm.

West Maui Lu'uas

West Maui's **Old Lahaina Lu'au** (667–1998) is your best bet. We've reviewed virtually all the neighbor island lu'aus, and we can say that Old Lahaina has the most professional crew we've yet encountered. Competent, friendly and always up, they make you feel very welcome. The organization is quality top to bottom. The grounds, next to but not *on* the shore, have an assortment of thatched hales. Free drinks, served almost all night, come from their accommodating bar. The food is above average with some items that are hard to find elsewhere.

The show strives for a more authentic Hawaiian feel than the others, achieving good results most of the time. No lounge lizard MC singing *Tiny Bubbles* or *Hukilau,* no shiny foil shirts. Other things missing from the more typical shows, however, include fire-knife dancers (because that's Samoan, not Hawaiian) and the Maoris wandering through the audience threatening you. Also missing is the part where they haul people from your table up onstage to embarrass them. (Which, truth be told, can be a hoot to watch when done right.) All of these are omitted since they are considered unauthentic. We *really* miss the fire dancers and Maoris (they can be lots of fun to watch), but that's the price you pay for authenticity. Perhaps the stage could be a

bit higher so all 500 visitors can see better, but this is minor quibbling. They fill up most of the time, so book well in advance if you can. In Lahaina on Front Street across from Lahaina Cannery. $92.

Next in our preference for West Maui lu'aus would be the **Sheraton Maui** (877–4852). It's right on Ka'anapali Beach with Black Rock for a backdrop. It's a **Tihati** show with great food. We like how they grill their steaks on the lawn rather than pile up precooked meat. Seating is spacious and the servers attentive. There's an open bar throughout the night, but avoid the mai tais. You could water you lawn with them and never give the worms a buzz. $83 on Mondays, Wednesdays and Fridays.

The **Hyatt Lu'au** (667–4420) in Ka'anapali. It's a Tihati production but one of their bigger venues with a bigger, less cramped stage. (But the same Tihati show.) The food's OK, nothing special. It's located next to the beach, but you can't see the ocean from your table. Actually, our biggest complaint is that they make you stand in line for up to half an hour in the hot sun before bringing you in. As with most lu'aus, you might want to pass on the watered-down mai tais and consider the free open bar, if you're libation-inclined. $86 or $119 for reserved seating.

Our last choice in West Maui is the **Royal Lahaina Resort** (661–9119). The show is upbeat and better than most. Although the performers obviously care about their performance, we can't say that about the rest of the experience. You're packed into a table-filled gravel pit like sardines. And the food is simply bad. (*Promise* us you won't eat the mac salad.) $88.

It's not your typical lu'au, so we put it at the end, but it's the classiest of the bunch. **Feast at Lele** (667–5353). No pig ceremony, no waiting in lines. Each party has a private table. This is an aptly named feast with an absolutely killer location:

right next to a beach in Lahaina with slightly tiered tables, so everyone gets a view. The food is *incredible* with dishes from Hawai'i, Tonga, Tahiti and Samoa. (Anyone who can serve us squash and have us begging for more gets our respect.) The service is well-paced, and the accompanying hula show makes good use of their location for several dramatic moments. They also have exceptionally sneaky mai tais—you don't taste the rum...but it's there! So what's the catch? The price. It's a wallet-choking $110, and you often have to book *well* in advance. If you can stomach the cost, it's highly recommended. They seat 150 max.

South Maui Lu'uas

In South Maui the best lu'au is **Honua'ula** (875–7710) at the Wailea Marriott. We like this lu'au for its nontraditional and highly entertaining show. The producer used to work for **'Ulalena** and uses some similar cirque-type elements here. They have a fantastic fireknife dancer as well. Equally impressive is the view of the ocean and Kaho'olawe at sunset. The buffet isn't of the highest quality, but it'll do. What hurts this lu'au the most is its size. With a capacity of 500 people, the service is below average when compared to smaller shows. Monday, Thursday, Friday and Saturday for $94.

The **Maui Prince** (and presumably discontinued by the time you read this **Renaissance Lu'au**) is a Tihati show with poor service and mediocre food. Either check out the **Honua'ula** or drive to a West Maui lu'au.

DINNER SHOWS

Lahaina has several night-time attractions that you should consider. One's a traditional dinner show. Two are sort of a dinner show...without the dinner.

The best is **Warren & Annabelle's** (667–6244), probably the most amazing show in all Hawai'i. Put simply, our jaws never stop dropping the whole time. After the first time we saw it, we were so impressed we told everyone we knew on Maui, "You gotta go see this." Most said, "Oh, I don't really like magic shows." Doesn't matter. It's not the kind of magic show you're thinking of. It might sound corny, but the whole evening's magic. Every person we've ever sent to this show has come back a raving fool. (Now the island is populated with raving fools. We're sorry to be the ones responsible.) You enter the theater in a unique way. (We won't give it away.) Then you're in an incredibly beautiful parlor, elegant in every way. You spend some time inside having tasty (though pricey) pupus and absolutely killer desserts or cocktails while their resident ghost (Annabelle) plays at the piano. You call out a song, and she probably knows it. (Hey, wait a minute. If the ghost has been dead for 150 years, how come she knows the theme to *Cheers*?) Then it's into the cozy 78-seat magic theater for— we promise you—the most amazing show you'll ever see. No smoke and mirrors, no elaborate props. Don't think David Copperfield or anything like that. Just a close-up view of a very engaging (and hilarious) man doing the absolute impossible. And we mean that literally. In fact, the first time we saw the show, we were so blown away that we were convinced that some of the audience members had to be plants. After the 2-hour show, we told Warren our suspicions. One of us told him, "I've seen great magicians, but *nobody's* that good." He proceeded to do some of the same things for us. (We didn't tell him who we were that night— just viewers.) We don't want to give anything away, but we can tell you that Warren does things that have literally kept us awake at night. It's simply not possible, and we've come to the awkward conclusion that Warren is simply not of this world. We've seen lots of magicians and even taken one to see Warren. But none of us has ever seen anything like it, and we've since seen the show several times.

If you only see one show on Maui, this is it. $56 per person, plus whatever you eat and drink before the show. Book in advance. Though the act is "clean," it's age 21 and over.

The other magic show is **Kupanaha** (667-0128) at the Ka'anapali Beach Hotel. The magic is totally different from Warren and Annabelle's and not as impressive. It's mostly prop-driven and is often the same trick several different ways. (Somebody in a box, a curtain or panel goes up and when it comes down they're gone or have changed into someone else. Impressive at first, a bit repetitious as the night wears on.) Some tricks are excellent, but on some you're advised not to look *too* closely. Also, the magicians' attempts at humor are a bit spotty.

One way Kupanaha is different is that it's a real dinner show and the food is actually quite good, though they suffer from a common dinner show ailment— it's hard to serve everyone at once and have the food hot. (And some portions—like the tiny steak and two shrimp—could be increased.) Overall, the food is their strongest point and they are admirably efficient in serving it. Intermixed with dinner is hula and puppets (the latter seems a bit cheesy but harmless). Mai tais, beer and wine are included, but other drinks cost extra, and the bar closes when the show starts. (This is an early event, starting at 4:30 and ending at 7:30 p.m.) Overall, if you're looking to be wowed by magic, stick with Warren & Annabelle's. If you really have your heart set on a dinner show, Kupanaha isn't a bad show, and kids are allowed. $79–$89.

The last show, **'Ulalena** (661-9913), is the biggest, most elaborate show ever to take place on Maui. It's also known as **Maui Myth & Magic**, which is oddly named because it has nothing to do with magic. This 700-seat theater in Old Lahaina Center was specially created for musical shows. 'Ulalena is a Hawaiian opera about life in Hawai'i before and after western contact, and about the gods and their deeds. The theater is state of the art with booming sound and excellent lighting. The show is sung entirely in Hawaiian; there is no dialogue, but the English narration helps orient you a bit during the show. The music and percussion throughout are effective and the dancers are disciplined. The show was actually written by Canadians and, as a result, the story shows a pretty shallow view of Hawaiian life. The Hawaiians are shown to be happily toiling away in peace, harmony and innocence until the evil westerners arrive. (Actually, the 200 years preceding western contact were the bloodiest in Hawai'i's history.) And Captain Cook is portrayed as the Prince of Darkness, complete with black hat and mask, who literally walks on the backs of the trusting natives. (See page 17 for the real skinny on Cook, who they fail to mention was killed by the Hawaiians.) In this story, westerners bring only guns, sickness and sadness. But all this is mostly forgotten by some *very* creative scenes. Like the dazzling waterfall scene where the actress/ spirit dangles from the falls. And the last three scenes are so beautiful and uplifting, you can't help but leave smiling. 'Ulalena may not be the best show on Maui (we prefer Warren & Annabelle's), but it's fun and entertaining. Cost is $60, $70 or $100. They don't serve dinner, but you can get packages that include meals at nearby restaurants.

DINNER CRUISES

Not all the Hawaiian islands offer these, but Maui's often placid evening waters make dinner cruises a delight.

In West Maui the **Maui Princess** (667–6165) is a huge 120-foot yacht with over 100 passengers at dinner. $90 per person includes prime rib and chicken, open bar, live entertainment and dancing. While the brochure may show a cozy table for two, there are, in fact, four people seated at each table; just so you know. Tables are all on the open top deck: half along the railing, half in the middle. If the anemic mai tais are too tame for you, don't hesitate to take them to the bar and have them *seasoned* for you; it's all free. The crew is good, and, while you may expect glorified airline food for such a large crowd, the food is better than we expected. Even the desserts are good. The slow cruise during the sun's golden hour creates pretty views of Lahaina and Ka'anapali. After dinner there's dancing below decks. You don't feel as crowded on this boat (except during boarding) as you may think. The boat is very smooth, and they stay out from 5:30–8 p.m., leaving from Lahaina Harbor.

Pacific Whale Foundation (249–8811) has a dinner cruise for $90 for up to 80 people.

There are also lots of sunset **cocktail cruises**. Most include the open bar in the price. Out of Lahaina the smallish **Scotch Mist** (661–0386) does a good job on their 50-foot sailboat for $50. No bar, just champagne, beer, wine and snacks. Out of Ka'anapali Beach the **Teralani** (661–0365) has a 2½-hour $80 trip. From Ma'alaea **Pride of Maui** (242–0955) has a 2-hour trip. Heavy pupus and an open bar, but we've seen them run out of food in only 30 minutes. The crew's pretty unenthusiastic, and it seems overpriced at $70. **Pacific Whale** has a cocktail cruise for $50.

From Lahaina, the **Spirit of Lahaina** (662–4477) is a very mixed bag. In some respects it's everything a dinner cruise *shouldn't* be. The bright spot, however, is the crew. Unfortunately, they're saddled with a boat that's ill-equipped for this purpose and an organizational system that makes it worse. We've seen more passengers than seats, forcing them to cram too many people at the tables. Even when it's not too crowded, it's indoors and so loud that conversations are very difficult. Long waits, cold food, insanely slow service getting drinks at dinner and poor food (except the tasty steaks) make the experience similar to cattle being led to slaughter. But after dinner the crew, which exudes *tons* of aloha, takes you upstairs and puts on a show that includes audience participation, and they go a long way toward bringing smiles to the grumpy diners. It's $99 for the 2½-hour cruise with up to 140 people.

DINNER ON A BEACH

This is one of the more romantic treats you can give your honey. Just the two of you and your own personal chef on a beach or grassy perch overlooking the ocean. (It will make up for the time you forgot her birthday.) We've done it, and it's quite impressive. **Tableside Chefs** (875–8980) takes people to one of several locations in South or West Maui (we chose north Maluaka Beach) and serves 3-, 4- or 5-course meals for $325–$375 per couple in South Maui. Add $50 for West Maui. Arrange in advance to be sure they have an opening.

That's it...we're not leaving...ever!

Your selection of where to stay can be one of the more important decisions you'll make in planning your visit. To some, it's just a place to sleep and rather meaningless. To others, it's the difference between a good vacation and a bad one.

There are four main types of lodgings on the island: hotels, condominiums, bed and breakfasts, and single-family homes. The overwhelming majority of visitors stay in one of the first two types. Hotels offer more service but lack kitchens. Condos usually have full kitchens and more living area but usually lack daily maid service. Many condos have minimum stays—usually three to seven nights. This varies between different rental companies. If your group or family is large, you should strongly consider renting a house for privacy, roominess and plain

ol' value. There is a list of **rental agents** on page 291 who represent most of the condos and many of the vacation homes on the island.

CONDOS

When describing condos **(shown in purple)**, three-bedroom/two-bath units are described as 3/2, two-bedroom/one-bath units are described as 2/1, etc. Differentiation between half baths and full baths is not made. The price spread for rooms of a given size are due to different views, different locations within the resort and sometimes seasonal fluctuations. So when you see that a 2/2 unit rents for $190–$250, you should figure that $250 units have a better view or are closer to the water. The terms Ocean Front, Ocean View and Garden View are used rather capriciously in Hawai'i, so we often avoid them. Unless otherwise noted, all condos come with telephones, complete kitchens, coffee makers, lanais (verandas), cable TV, coin-op laundry facilities and ceiling fans and have cribs available upon request. None have a/c, maid service is not included unless otherwise noted and local calls are free. Cleaning and some *annoying* booking fees may be added to your costs, so read the fine print.

All condos are non-smoking. Some allow you to smoke on the lanai, some don't want you smoking any place on property. If you smoke, you will want to check the rules before you book.

The important thing to remember about renting condos is the fragmented nature of the market. Each unit usually has a different owner, they all use different rental agencies to manage them, and it changes all the time. (Spreadsheets, blinding headaches and blurred vision are all necessary to figure it out.) Therefore, when we review them, we may look at 10 units and get 10 winners. *You* may rent one and get a dump because the owner is using furniture from a landfill and carpet from the finish line at the Maui Marathon. An individual owner may opt not to participate in the community hot water, instead giving you a tiny, underpowered hot water heater, while all the other units bask in hot water. Or a resort may be scrupulously maintained, but an individual unit (yours) may have a recurring problem with marauding ants. The owner may use a different cleaning service, leaving you in a squalid mess. You truly never know what you're going to get. There's no way to take into account the individuality of units, so to a certain extent, you are playing the odds with many condos.

HOTELS

As for hotels (shown in green), unless otherwise noted, all *do* have a/c, tele-phones, small refrigerators, lanais, coin-op laundry facilities, cable TV and cribs available. None have room service unless we mention it. But if they *do* have room service, watch for built-in tips. It's easy to double tip, and you can bet that no one will point it out to you. Rooms are smaller than condos since they don't have kitchens and usually don't have a separate bedroom. If you're a smoker, call about their policies.

A FEW GROUND RULES

All prices given are RACK rates, meaning without any discounts. Tour packages and travel agents can sometimes get better rates. Many places offer discounts for stays of a week or more, and some will negotiate price with you. Some won't budge at all; others told us *no one* pays RACK rate. Also, be aware that these prices are subject to taxes of $11\frac{1}{2}\%$.

The gold bar indicates that the property is exceptionally well priced for what you get.

The gem means that this accommodation offers something *particularly* special, not *necessarily* related to the price.

A REAL GEM

WHERE ARE THE REST?

We ran into a *big problem* when we tried to do this section. What worked on the other islands—printing in-depth reviews of nearly every place to stay other than B&Bs—was *impossible* here. There are nearly 150 hotels and condo complexes on the island. Our book would have been as heavy as a phone book if we tried to print them all. We had two choices: Give the bare bones info on all of them or do detailed reviews on a small fraction. Neither choice seemed palatable.

So we came up with a third way: List minimal info on all, print detailed reviews on some, and post full reviews of the rest on our website, **www.wizardpub.com**. After all, most people use this section *before* they come to the islands. And with the Web (which has infinite space available), we could do more, such as post larger aerial photos of the resorts with specific buildings labeled when appropriate, offer constant updates when necessary, and put links to the various rental agents or hotels right in the review, allowing you to go to their sites and get more photos of the rooms. You should remember, however, that resorts post photos to lure you in, and some aren't above posting modified or overly flattering shots when they were new and sparkling. Our aerials don't lie and are designed to give you a feel for their ocean proximity (does oceanfront *really* mean oceanfront?), so you'll know what kind of view to expect from a given location within the resort. Resorts whose review is posted on our Web site are identified with Web Review.

Please remember that all these reviews are *relative to each other.* We'll repeat that later because it's so important. Even staying at a dump right on the ocean is still a *Golly!* experience. In other words, *Hey, you're on the ocean in Maui!* So if we sound whiny or picky in critiquing a resort, it's only because their next door neighbor might be such a better experience. It doesn't mean you'll be miserable, it just means that *compared to another resort,* you can do better.

Also be aware that we don't review long-term condos or apartments or resorts that are all or nearly all timeshare. Unfortunately, we also don't review **B&Bs**. Reviewing the B&Bs in depth just isn't practical, though we recognize how nice it is to stay in some. And while in our Kaua'i and Big Island books we were able to list a B&B service that could link you up with one, we haven't found anyone on Maui that we're comfortable recommending. (There are off-island services, but we're not comfortable recommending someone who's not on-island.) So we'll pass the buck and suggest that you use the Internet and hope for the best.

We're describing the resorts geographically from the top of West Maui to the bottom of South Maui with others, including Hana, at the end. All resorts (except Ma'alaea) are shown on the various maps. If you have trouble seeing some things on the aerial photos, go to the Web site where the photos are larger.

WHERE SHOULD I STAY?

Resorts are concentrated in a dozen regions on Maui. Each has its pluses and minuses.

Kapalua resorts are few and in the extreme far north of West Maui. Weather is poorer here than any other resort area, featuring strong winds much of the time and more passing drizzly showers. It's a long drive to off-site attractions, but many people like the relative seclusion.

Napili accommodations are mostly mid-'60s buildings and are clustered around wonderful Napili Bay.

The area from **Kahana** down to (but not including) Honokowai, includes the strip of condos and hotels that line the shoreline, most built in the '70s. Some are good values. The biggest problem is that, with few exceptions, most have no beach or the water may have seaweed. We don't want to overstate the seaweed problem. (In fact, the water quality has been improving lately.) It comes and goes. It's just that you may not find the crystal clear water available in other parts of the island, and we don't want you to be surprised when you find yourself swimming around.

Resorts in **Honokowai** are in a different category than the ones directly north of here. The condos have hotel services and hotel prices. The sandy beach here is the northern part of Keka'a Beach, not the beach traditionally known as Ka'anapali. It's cleaner (not much seaweed) than the beach patches north of here, but the nearshore waters are a bit rocky. The beach is not anywhere near the caliber of Ka'anapali Beach. There's a grocery store nearby for condo users.

The resorts on **Ka'anapali Beach** are all about living on this fantastic beach. Water is usually clean and clear and the beachside path along much of the beach makes for great walking.

When visiting West Maui, people usually speak of staying in **Lahaina**. The irony is that relatively few people actually *stay* in Lahaina because there are limited choices available. Nearly all West Maui accommodations are north of Lahaina, in Ka'anapali, Honokowai, Kahana, Napili and Kapalua. **Ma'alaea** is an unusual place to stay and describe on page 299.

We separate **north Kihei** from south Kihei for a simple reason. The ocean and beaches in part of north Kihei suffer from the quality problems we mention on page 158. South of Cove Park, however, Kihei's beaches are lovely. Also,

the extreme northern part of Kihei (Sugar Beach area) often has wind, dust and possibly seaweed on the beach (mentioned in the reviews). We're not trying to portray north Kihei properties as bad places. In fact, some are wonderful places to stay. But remember, our job is to review accommodations *relative to each other*.

The beaches in **south Kihei** are usually clean and clear. Enjoy the water.

Many people consider **Wailea** the most desirable place to stay on Maui. Gorgeous beach after gorgeous beach along with almost perfect weather make it a vacationer's paradise. The only downside is the price. If you look around for packages, however, paradise can be had even if your last name isn't Gates.

There are really only two reasons to stay in **Kahului**: cheap rooms and closeness to the airport. Few would come here to lounge around the pool. Both large hotels are on Ka'ahumanu Ave.

It's surprising that a place as glorious as **Hana** has fewer than 200 rooms available. And that includes private homes for rent. There are only two sizable resorts. We list some other options in addition to those resorts.

Rental Agents

AA Oceanfront Condo Rentals	(800) 488–6004 or (808) 879–7288
Ali'i Resorts	(866) 284–2544 or (808) 879–6284
Bello Realty	(800) 541–3060 or (808) 879–3328
Chase 'n Rainbows	(800) 367–6092 or (808) 667–7088
Classic Resorts	(800) 642–6284 or (808) 661–3339
Condominium Rentals Hawai'i	(800) 367–5242 or (808) 879–2778
Destination Resorts Hawai'i	(800) 367–5246 or (808) 879–1595
Hana Maui Travel Co.	(800) 548–0478 or (808) 248–7742
Kumulani Vacations	(800) 367–2954 or (808) 879–9272
Leisure Properties	(800) 888–6284 or (808) 879–6770
Ma'alaea Bay Rentals	(800) 367–6084 or (808) 244–5627
Maui Beachfront Rentals	(888) 661–7200 or (808) 661–3500
Maui Condominium & Home (ResortQuest)	(800) 822–4409 or (808) 879–5445
Maui Lodging.com	(800) 487–6002 or (808) 669–0089
Paradise Vacations	(800) 927–7672 or (808) 874–7672
Whaler's Realty	(800) 676–4112 or (808) 661–3484

(Continued on next page...)

See all Web Reviews at: www.wizardpub.com

See all Web Reviews at: www.wizardpub.com

See all Web reviews at: **www.wizardpub.com**

KAPALUA

Villas at Kapalua
(800) 545–0018 or (808) 669–8088
500 Office Rd.

This property is divided into three separate areas called; Golf, Ridge and Bay. The units are priced based on view—not area. The Bay has the best ocean views; the Ridge can have some decent ocean views or partial ocean view units. Fairway view or partial ocean view units can be found in both the Ridge and the Golf villas. All of the units have been or are planned to be completely upgraded to luxury (they call them "gold") standards, including new bathrooms, kitchens with granite counters and high-end appliances, and new furnishings. They are consistent in the look and feel of the decor, which is very nice.

Golf villas have 186 units, 3 pools, and are older and smaller than Ridge villas which have 161 units and 2 pools. Bay villas hug the shoreline (or at least some of the units do) and also have 3 pools. Floor plans are extremely variable. All upgraded villas have a/c, washer/dryer and daily maid service. There is a *mandatory* resort fee of $19 per day, which pays for things like: hi-speed and Wi-Fi Internet access, self-parking, local calls and some long distance (including the mainland and some foreign countries), rooms safes, tennis, shuttle service in Kapalua and discounts on golf. They also offer some nice services like grocery shopping (for an extra fee, of course).

All the villas are comfortable in size and start at 1,137–1,345 sq. ft. for a 1/2 and 1,774–2,160 sq. ft for a 2/2 unit. Prices ain't cheap at $329–$579 for a 1/2 and $499–$779 for a 2/2 villa. At press time you could still get some "deals" on a 1/2 that has not yet been upgraded for about $279 and a 2/2 for $389.

NAPILI

Hale Napili
(800) 245–2266 or (808) 669–6184
65 Hui Dr.

18 units, daily maid service, BBQ, free Wi-Fi, free room safes and free laundry room. A dreamy location on Napili Beach with clean, comfortable rooms, and an extremely warm staff make you feel like visiting ohana (family). As with many Napili resorts, most visitors are long-time repeats and

A REAL GEM

See all Web reviews at: **www.wizardpub.com**

they can book out a year in advance. Layouts and furnishings are amazingly variable, but most are quite nice and most face the ocean. Some of the studios have pull-down Murphy beds, and all have dishwashers. It was built in 1965 and is certainly not plush, but Hale Napili is an easy place to like— and an easy place to return to. Studios (386–593 sq. ft.) are $160–$215. 1/1s (484–572 sq. ft.) are $260.

KAHANA

Kahana Village
(800) 824–3065 or (808) 669–5111
4531 Lwr. Honoapiilani Rd.

42 units, pool, spa, maid service midweek, BBQ, free room safes, washer/dryer

A REAL GEM

in the units. Wonderfully spacious rooms, high-grade appliances and a great oceanfront location. The proximity to the ocean is stellar. Units have lots of glass and an open feel, but are still private if you want. The ground floors are massive 1,600 sq. ft. 3/2s with sunken tubs, wet bars, nice kitchens, and the additional bedrooms are equally large. The shoreline from the oceanfront units seems delectably close. The oceanview building with units 37–42 would probably be classified as ocean*front* at most resorts, which makes it a particularly good bargain. Upstairs units are 1,200 sq. ft., 2/2 townhouse-type units with the second bedroom as a loft-type—not quite as desirable as the lower units. All units

have nice, large lanais. They have three categories: standard, deluxe and luxury, the latter completely upgraded. Since the overall quality at the property is very high, you will probably be just as happy in a standard unit for less money. And here's a real treat. They have *free long distance* phone calls (even if you're calling Mongolia) and free hi-speed Internet access in every room. Kahana Village is a good value for the price. 2/2s (1,200 sq. ft.) are $260–$400, 3/2s (1,700 sq. ft.) are $385–$595. The reason for the price spread is due to the individual unit's quality rating. 5-night minimum and a $25 "booking fee."

HONOKOWAI

Maui Kai
(800) 367–5635 or (808) 667–3500
106 Ka'anapali Shores Pl.

80 units, pool, spa, BBQ, central air conditioning, free hi-speed Internet access,

SOLID GOLD VALUE

free room safes, daily maid service. Though the building is old (1969) and the exterior relatively unimpressive, this one's a winner and the best priced in this area. They are impossibly close to the ocean—around 25 feet!— so rooms look almost straight down into the water. Their sandy beach is narrow but gets wider next door. The pool obviously wouldn't fit on the ocean side, so it's tucked away on the mountain side and has

See all Web reviews at: **www.wizardpub.com**

no view, but there's a computer for you to use, free Wi-Fi and a kitchen at the pool to cook your meals. Units vary *a lot,* but we didn't see any we wouldn't want to stay in. Some of the studio units have pull-down wall beds, which are preferable. Once you're out of bed, just pop it up and you have the whole room. Corner units offer particularly tasty views. Free morning coffee and cappuccino in the lobby. All in all, it's an excellent deal. Studios, which they call Jr. Suites (500–550 sq. ft.), are $189–$239, 1/1s (750–850 sq. ft.) are $245–$323, 2/2s (1,175 sq. ft.) are $484. 3-night minimum.

KA'ANAPALI

Hyatt Regency Maui
(800) 233–1234 or (808) 661–1234
200 Nohea Kai Dr.

Napili Tower   Atrium Tower   Lahaina Tower

806 rooms, 2 pools, spa, 4 restaurants, 6 tennis courts, 24-hour room service, coin-op laundry, 10 conference rooms, business center, Wi-Fi, PlayStations, 24-hour fitness center and day spa, numerous shops, lu'au nightly, valet parking, empty refrigerator, child care program. Wow, where do we start? This is the biggest resort on Maui, consisting of three 8- and 9-story buildings among 40 acres of spacious and exotic grounds. The two outstanding pools are large with waterfalls, and one has a fast 150-foot waterslide (you must be at least 4-foot tall) and a swinging bridge. Little ones can enjoy a shorter waterslide, a sand-lined lagoon and a synchronized fountain. Between the two is a poolside

A REAL GEM

bar filled with the roar of the artificial waterfalls. The lobby is next to the huge atrium, which, in the mornings, is filled with the sound of wild birds there to steal some food.

They have tours of the wildlife strewn about the grounds (like warm weather penguins, swans and parrots), and there's a nice oceanside state-of-the-art fitness center and day spa with all the bone-melting fixin's. (They'll even treat your child at the spa and offer them services such as the M & M manicure—a different color for every nail.) They charge $20 ($15 for kids) for the guided rooftop astronomy demonstrations with their 16-inch scope and you get a *Milky Way* or *Starburst* afterwards. There are 4 restaurants, including the Cascades Grille & Sushi Bar and the Son'z at the Swan Court. Both have dreamy atmospheres, though they're not cheap. Downstairs near the pool is the cheaper food court-style eatings called the Pavilion. Feel free to wear your bathing suit there. Watch for the thieving birds who'll rob you blind if you turn your back.

The Hyatt has a lu'au (the oceanfront rooms in the Lahaina Tower are exposed to the sound until 8–8:30 p.m.). We only have two dings with this resort. One is the *mandatory* $15 resort fee that covers things such as local calls, room safe, fitness center, daily coffee, etc. Valet is an additional $12. The other ding is that their part of Ka'anapali Beach *occasionally* gets seaweed blooms, especially in front of the Napili Wing. And there's more reef in the nearshore waters, so you can't frolic in the shallow waters without reef shoes, or you may tear up your feet. They have ocean activity booths where you can rent water toys such as boogie boards and snorkel gear at normal resort prices (meaning expensive—boogie boards are $8 *per hour*). Cabana chairs are $40 per day.

See all Web reviews at: www.wizardpub.com

Hyatt's keiki program (called Camp Hyatt) is $65 or $80 per day, plus they'll watch your little one at night for $12 per hour. They haven't left out adults with treats to pamper such as massages by the ocean and dinners under the stars for $478 per couple. You can even rent your own thatched hut by the ocean for $125 per day and they'll bring you just about anything for a price, of course.

In all, the Hyatt does a very good job, and the staff is very warm and professional. The place radiates the dreamy warmth that you want from a fantasy resort. It's especially pretty at night. Rooms are nicely furnished and are a respectable 451 sq. ft. costing $400–$755. Regency rooms (marginally nicer but more amenities— namely free continental breakfast in a private lounge—not worth the upgrade) are $605–$820. Suites (554–2,500 sq. ft.) are $950–$5,500.

The Whaler
(800) 922–7866 or (808) 661–4861
2481 Ka'anapali Pkwy.

360 units, pool, spa, BBQ, air conditioning, sauna, elevator, fitness center, salon spa, 24-hour business center, free hi-speed Internet access, free Wi-Fi in some common areas, daily maid service. This 1975-built property consists of two 12-story towers on delicious Ka'anapali Beach. The services for a condo resort are admirable. The daily maid will even do your dishes if you want. The resort is well-run and friendly. Staff is excellent, many

of them long term. However, this property lost its REAL GEM rating in this edition because the rooms didn't have the polish you'd expect at this price. Though rooms still have a great layout with a bedroom and common room sharing the view, many rooms have a very dated decor. We debated which ocean views were best, but lean toward north-facing views because Moloka'i looks better than Lana'i from your lanai. Oceanfront has the best views, of course, but the extra $160 or more is pretty painful. Regardless, consider the 1/2s instead of the 1/1s. Extra full bathrooms are $20 more (a deal). You have signing privileges at many other Ka'anapali properties. It's $12 a day to park. $3 per day for a room safe. Studios are relatively spacious at 640 sq. ft. (and some have pull-down beds, offering more usable room for up to 3 people) at $270–$345. 1,114 sq. ft. 1/1s are $360–$435. At 1,118 sq. ft. the 1/2s are $305–$550, and 1,952 sq.ft. 2/2s are $400–$800.

LAHAINA

Puamana
(800) 676–4112 or (808) 661–3423
34 Puailima Pl.

230 units, 3 pools, tennis court, Wi-Fi in clubhouse, most have washer/dryer in unit, BBQ, children's playground, a/c. This is a huge, 28-acre gated community just outside Lahaina town, but a million miles away in terms of the tempo. Relaxed, soothing and lovely.

A REAL GEM

See all Web reviews at: www.wizardpub.com

Think of it as a tiny village on the outskirts of a busy town. Units are nicely furnished. The oceanfront units are highly coveted and worth the upgrade as they're less than 50 feet from the water. The beach is a walking beach, not good for swimming because it's reefy and cloudy. One of the pools is literally *touching* the ocean. Unlike most condos, each owner owns the *land*, as well, and variation between layouts is great. Units are large. 1/2s (800 sq. ft.) are $155–$300, 2/2s (1,250 sq. ft.) are $205–$405, 3/2s (1,600 sq. ft.) are $310–$500, 4/3s (2,600 sq. ft.) are $595–$715. They have an extra $6 per day "registration fee." (A small but nakedly unnecessary charge.) 7-night minimum.

MA'ALAEA

As mentioned on page 129, we don't particularly recommend staying in Ma'alaea unless you're simply looking for a place to lay your head at night. It's the windiest place to stay on Maui and possibly in the whole state. Dust from sugar operations, smell from the landfill upwind, and other reasons make it a questionable place to choose to stay. Many people come back year after year; others grumble of Ma'alaea's shortcomings. In this case we have to side with the grumblers. Price is the only thing that should lure you here, and prices range from $125–$285. Some pluses, however, include the central location (between West and South Maui), the awesome winds do tend to keep things cooler, they all have pretty nice views with three properties located on a sandy beach, and units here tend to be very well maintained. **Ma'alaea Bay Rentals** (800) 367–6084 or (808) 244–5627 has the most units here. Call them if you're set on staying in Ma'alaea. 5-night minimum. Some condos have washer/dryers in units and/or

hi-speed Internet access, If you need those things, ask for them. They handle units at **Makani a Kai**, **Hono Kai**, **Kana'i a Nalu** and **Ma'alaea Kai**.

We're choosing to devote the space we'd normally use to describe the nine resorts here to what we consider more viable accommodations elsewhere. That may anger some, but we only have so much space, and it doesn't make sense to use so much for Ma'alaea when you can do so much better at other locations. We will mention that your best bet is probably **Island Sands** (888) 997–2637 or (808) 244–0848 at 150 Hauoli St. A nice, clean, 84-unit building with rates for 1/1 units (670 sq. ft.) at $135–$198. 2/2 units (1,010–1,227 sq. ft.) are $190–$256. Summer is cheaper and windier. It's not on the sandy beach area, but it's a short walk. 4-night minimum.

The other condos in the area are mostly long term.

NORTH KIHEI

Kealia Condominium
(800) 265–0686 or (808) 879–0952
191 N. Kihei Rd.

50 units, pool, a/c, washer/dryer in units, hi-speed Internet access, lanais, elevator. An institutional-looking building, but it's clean. Most of the small units have been nicely upgraded, so ask for one. The 2/2 units are by the ocean and have good

See all Web reviews at: **www.wizardpub.com**

views. The studios face the street. Some of the 1/1s can only accommodate two people. In all, you can get more space for the money elsewhere. It's real windy and dusty here, too. Studios (420 sq. ft.) are $115–$130, 1/1s (which are a tight 556 sq. ft.) are $150–$190, 2/1s are $215–$250, and they also feel small at 730 sq. ft. 4-night minimum.

Koa Lagoon
(800) 367–8030 or (808) 879–3002
800 S. Kihei Rd.

42 units, pool, BBQ, a/c, washer/dryer in units, free hi-speed Internet access, elevator. What a steal! Though the building isn't overly impressive from the outside, the mid-'70s concrete walls hide an incredible find (and block the sound, as well). Exceptionally stunning oceanfront views, with West Maui as part of the backdrop. Rooms are impeccably clean, comfortable and large. Six floors; the upper ones have some palm tree crowns in the view. The beach isn't a good swimming beach, but it's pretty. This is one of the best deals in Kihei with one caveat: There is some seaweed in the water and on the beach. However, they scrape the beach each morning. You may want to avoid swimming here though, and you may have to step around some seaweed on the beach. Deluxe units cost an extra

SOLID GOLD VALUE

$10, but they're probably not worth it since the overall quality of the rooms is already so high. 1/1s (697 sq. ft.) are $130–$160, 2/2s (979 sq. ft.) are $160–$190.

SOUTH KIHEI

Kihei Surfside
(800) 822–4409 or (808) 879–5445
2936 S. Kihei Rd.

84 units, pool, BBQ, shuffleboard, hi-speed Internet access, lanais on all, washer/dryer only in 2/2s. A semi-circular building with nice views north up the coast, especially rooms ending with 01 or 02. Though built in 1974, it's clean, tidy, and they have nice extras such as a good front office, huge lawn area, putting green, games like croquet and horseshoes and video rentals. It's a short walk to Keawakapu Beach. Lanais are walled on the side for privacy. Three room layouts: 1/1 D units (500 sq. ft), 1/2 B & C units (650 sq. ft.) and 2/2 A units (950 sq. ft.). B & C units are the best deal. Rooms ending in 03–06 overlook the pool, which may be a bit noisy. Overall, it's a very nice place to stay because of the price and location, not the rooms themselves, which are acceptable but not remarkable. 1/1s are $195–$240, 1/2s are $225–$275, 2/2s are $285–$385. 4-night minimum.

See all Web reviews at: **www.wizardpub.com**

Maui Oceanfront Inn
(800) 263–3387 or (808) 879–7744
2980 S. Kihei Rd.

Keawakapu Beach

72 units, free Wi-Fi, a/c. It is truly inconceivable that a property can be built at the beach and yet make it feel like you are nowhere near the ocean. Yet this place manages to do both. In fact, almost all the rooms have no ocean views. The tiny rooms (200 sq. ft.) are incredibly cramped. Tiny bathrooms, tiny sinks; even the stairway to the second floor is small. The "suites" are simply two tiny rooms combined to make one puny suite. Rates are $159. Suites are $395. Hope you did better than this RACK rate.

WAILEA

Four Seasons Resort Maui
(800) 334–6284 or (808) 874–8000
3900 Wailea Alanui

380 rooms, 2 pools and a keiki pool, 2 spas, day spa, 24-hour fitness center, valet-only parking, child care program, 2 lighted tennis courts, Nintendo & PlayStation, Wi-Fi in rooms and resort-wide, 3 restaurants, 5 shops, 24-hour business center, 9 confer-

A REAL GEM

ence rooms, lanais, 24-hour room service, empty refrigerators, wedding coordinator. Oh, my, where do we start? We're fearful of sounding like drooling stooges for the Four Seasons, but this is our favorite resort in Wailea. When you walk in, you can actually feel the tension falling from your limbs. It soon becomes evident why. Here, they did everything right. The resort is immaculate and lovingly cared for. The smallest details seem to have been anticipated. The grounds are impeccable. No dead leaf or blade of grass in sight. The staff here is the most professional we've seen and seem genuinely concerned about your happiness. There are 1.6 employees for every room. (It's getting harder and harder to find those .6 employees.) While you're at the pool, they'll come by and spritz you with Evian water, offer chilled towels, fresh fruit, popsicles and even wet the beach sand with water so you don't toast your tootsies. The pool area doesn't feel as packed as some other Wailea resorts. Oh, yes, you have arrived, and you'll weep when you have to leave. The number of complimentary services is way too long to list, but includes *free* child care program that goes from 9 a.m. to 5 p.m. (you only pay for their lunch), free cabana chairs at the beach (other resorts charge up to $250 *per day* for that), free snorkel gear for an hour at the beach each day, free SCUBA lessons, free daily aerobics and yoga classes, free access to their indoor-out-

See all Web reviews at: **www.wizardpub.com**

door fitness room, free coffee in rooms (they even give you whole beans and let you grind 'em), rooms safes, etc. They even have a free game room with free video games, billiards, etc. It goes on and on. It's clear that they've made a decision to not nickel and dime their guests. We were a bit surprised that they charge $18 for valet-only parking (that used to be free), Internet access is extra and local calls are a buck. Laundry services are valet only.

Rooms are very large (650 sq. ft. including lanai), and the bathrooms are fit for a king—lots of marble, deep tub, separate shower and tons of wiggle room. Rooms are elegantly furnished in keeping with the rest of the resort. They were renovated in 2007 with very pleasing results. Housekeeping would make an operating room nurse proud. Dirt is simply not tolerated and is dispatched with extreme prejudice.

Their beach, Wailea Beach, is one of the best on the island, an absolute dream.

If you have kids, they'll ask for their names and spell them out in colored sponges in the bathroom, and they'll kid-proof the rooms.

The Four Seasons doesn't give many discounts, even to the numerous celebrities who visit, but their RACK RATES start lower than most of their competition in the area, and with all the freebies it's actually a good deal. Rates are $475–$990. Suites (1,000–3,700 sq. ft.) are $1,005–$12,800. The $475 mountain side rooms are actually a very good deal as the rates increase *a lot* with better views.

Maui Prince
(800) 321–6284 or (808) 874–1111
5400 Makena Alanui Dr.
310 rooms, pool and keiki pool, 2 spas, free fitness center, hi-speed Internet

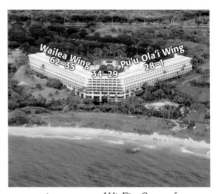

access in rooms, Wi-Fi, 2 conference rooms, free valet parking, child care program, day spa, VCRs upon request, 5 restaurants, laundry facilities, empty refrigerators, 6 tennis courts (4 lighted), room service, wedding coordinator. This is probably the most subdued resort in South Maui. It's not actually in Wailea, but rather on its own, farther south in Makena. In fact it's the last resort—literally—in South Maui. Maui Prince rarely has a crowded feel, even when it's full. That's partially because you're less likely to spend as much time at the resort than at some others in Wailea. The pool area is decidedly low key. You won't find waterslides and rope swings, but you won't find it too crowded either. Their beach, Maluaka beach, is a winner and shared with no other resort. There is a boat, the Kai Kanani, that leaves directly from the resort beach and heads to Molokini; very convenient. The snorkeling off the left side of the beach is excellent, and many boats bring paying passengers here. (It's one of their so-called *turtle towns*.)

No all-encompassing resort fee here. Though services aren't overly abundant, they do tend to lean toward providing most services free, like valet parking, daily coffee in the rooms, room safe,

See all Web reviews at: **www.wizardpub.com**

pool-side cabana chairs, 9-hole putting green, etc. (Local calls, however, are 75¢.) The child care program is $50 per day. Golfers get preferred rates and tee times at their golf courses.

Rooms are relatively simple and small-ish at 433–515 sq. ft. (The tapered building means that the higher you go, the smaller the rooms.) Bathrooms are small. The rooms looked much fresher on this visit with new linens and drapes.

They have a free shuttle that takes you to Wailea so you can participate in the restaurant selection there and walk the beachside path without feeling totally cut off. The resort is relaxing and fairly quiet. Nice place to arrange a relaxing massage by the ocean.

The staff is very warm here. The resort was sold at press time, so some changes may be in the works. Rates are $380–$555. Suites (941–1,694 sq. ft.) are $700–$1,500. They have lots of packages, so it's unlikely you'll pay that.

KAHULUI

Maui Seaside
(800) 560–5552 or (808) 877–3311
100 Ka'ahumanu Ave.

190 rooms, pool, fitness room. This local chain usually has clean and tidy rooms and grounds, and this one is no exception. The rooms, though clean, are looking dated, and we noticed a musty smell in them on this visit. Their RACK rates listed should be taken with a grain of salt. Nearly everyone gets discounted,

and they have lots of packages. Staff is friendly. Parking is free; no room safes. Local calls are 50¢. Rooms (168–378 sq. ft.) are $125–$135, poolside rooms are $170, kitchenettes (when available) are $180. Larger rooms are in the tower building, and its even-numbered rooms have better views.

ACCOMMODATIONS ELSEWHERE

Kula Lodge
(800) 233–1535 or (808) 878–1535
15200 Haleakala Hwy. (Route 377)
5 rooms, free coffee daily. Located up Haleakala at the 3,200 foot level, this is the place to stay if you're hankering to be close to Haleakala Crater, you want to stay where it's cool or just want to get away from it all. No phones, no TV, no Internet and maybe no cell phone reception. Rooms have gas stoves since the winter temps dip into the low 60s (summer gets into the *upper* 60s). Hey, that might not be chilly where you come from, but it's considered the Arctic to Maui residents. Rooms are simple and quaint if a bit overpriced at $125–$205. No laundry facilities on site. At the junction of 377 and 378.

HANA

Hotel Hana Maui
(800) 321–4262 or (808) 248–8211
5031 Hana Hwy.

See all Web reviews at: **www.wizardpub.com**

67 rooms, 2 pools, spa, room service, 2 tennis courts, day spa, valet parking,

A REAL GEM coffee maker with free coffee daily, free hi-speed Internet access in club room, restaurant. This resort has been though quite a lot. Built as a high end getaway for the well-to-do, in the late '90s it fell into disrepair. Two owners later it has reclaimed much of its former glory and now exudes an old-world feel. (But it was for sale again at press time, so it's hard to say where it's going.) It's impossible to stay here and not feel relaxed—unless you contemplate the bill that awaits you at the end.

Tranquil grounds, fairly large rooms ranging from 543–835 sq. ft., good staff and special touches are available like in-room massages, private spas in some of the rooms (for extra) and a concerted effort not to nickel and dime you. Free local calls, free room safes, free fitness room, free laundry facilities, some free items from the fridge and free valet parking (though you don't need it) and use of some of the day spa facilities (treatments are extra). They have a 3-hole putting green and have free bikes for use for 2-hours per day.

Rooms are comfortable, and many have nice ocean views. No TVs or alarm clocks and no a/c. (You can request a fan if you're hot, particularly at night.) This is Hana, and you're not supposed to *care* what's on TV or what time to get up.

Hotel Hana Maui is expensive, but it's the kind of place that will soothe your soul. It captures the essence of Hana's unique place in Hawai'i. Note that a few times a year they have "adult-only" months (usually May or September) and also run some room packages to take the sting of the rates. Rooms are $495–$875. Suites (942–1,475 sq. ft.) are $1,125–$1,675.

Hana Kai Maui Resort
(800) 346–2772 or (808) 248–8426
1533 Uakea Rd.

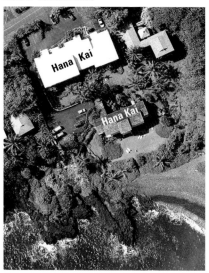

17 units, BBQ area with free Wi-Fi, coin-op laundry (when hotel is not using it). Not a real *ooh-aah* place but dependable, and they usually have vacancies. Pretty good Hana Bay views from most units. No phones except in deluxe ocean front unit. They do have a free phone for guests to use (your cell phone may not work). No TVs and sound carries a bit too efficiently. Studios are a decent deal. All rooms have complete kitchens. Studios (300–400 sq. ft.) $167–$225, with 1/1s (550 sq. ft.) $190–$349. 2-night minimum.

Other Places in Hana

Aside from those two resorts, **Hana Maui Travel Co.** (800) 548–0478 or (808) 248–7742 is probably the big-gest rental agency in Hana. They represent 15–20 private houses for rent. The homes

See all Web reviews at: www.wizardpub.com

we've seen could be cleaner, but some are okay deals. Although we've stayed at many of the houses, it's not practical for us to stay at them all. For what it's worth, our reader e-mails about them leans heavily toward the negative.

Some other accommodations in Hana include:

Aloha Cottages (808) 248–8420 at 83 Keawa Place is five cheap and very dreary units with a kitchen or kitchenette. Don't expect much here—no phone, no Internet and not much aloha. Some rooms have a TV. If you want to look at the rooms, you'll be asked to "look through the windows." We suggest you keep on looking—*elsewhere*. $65–$110.

Bamboo Inn (808) 248–7718 also on Uakea Road has 3 rooms with TVs and phones for $175–$240. They're fine and clean. Rates include continental breakfast. The all have Jacuzzi tubs—some on the decks.

Hana Bay Hale (800) 471–8082 or (808) 248–4999 at 4950 Uakea Road is a triplex with kitchenettes, TVs and BBQs. Across the street from the ocean with decent views through power lines. 1/1 is $175, 2/2 (full kitchen) is $275. You can do better. 1-night stays pay a cleaning fee.

Hana Hale Inn (808) 248–7641 on Uakea Road is 4 varied units with kitchens, Jacuzzi tubs, TVs and phones. Free hi-speed Internet is available in the lobby. The Royal Suite (1,800 sq. ft.) is the smashing upstairs unit of a duplex. Gobs of beautiful wood. Only ding is the hardwood carries sound well to other rooms. $260 for 2 bedroom. They also have a bungalow for $185, a small one bedroom suite for $160 and a treehouse cottage (not actually a treehouse, but nicely incorporated into the landscape) for $200.

All these units overlook a serene fishpond. Rates include continental breakfast. The units could be cleaner, and expect to share your units with some of nature's creatures.

Hana Maui Vacation Rental (800) 991–2422 or (808) 248–8087 at 4176 Hana Hwy. 3 clean, simple, very basic units with kitchen or kitchenette, TV but no phone. Grounds are homey. Good deal at $85–$95. No credit cards.

Hana Oceanfront Cottages (808) 248–7558 on Haneoo Road. 2 units with BBQ, kitchens, TV, Wi-Fi and phone. Lovely grounds and very nicely furnished units, if a tad pricey. But they do give you just about all you may need from coffee to sunscreen. A suite is $250 (1,000 sq. ft.) and a cottage $275 (600 sq. ft.), both across street from Hamoa Beach. No kids. Owners live on property. 3- or 4-night minimum.

Heavenly Hana Inn (808) 248–8442 at 4155 Hana Hwy. has 3 units, more like a B&B, all connect to common area. Exotically decorated, beautiful wood floors, very nice bathrooms, open serene grounds. Pretty pricey, and they charge $16 for breakfast. Two-night minimum, no kids allowed. Suites are $190–$260.

Joe's Place (808) 248–7033 at 4870 Uakea Road. It's $50 for a shared bath and kitchen, $60 for a private room. Fairly tidy. You get what you pay for here.

Na Pualani o Hana (808) 248–8935 on Kalo Road. 5 units with kitchens or a kitchenette, BBQ, TVs. The setting is nice, surrounded by lush grounds, but the rooms are pretty unkempt. Good deal if you have a group since many can stay. Studios $75, 2/2s $130.

Lastly, you might find individuals renting their homes using the Internet, though it's more of a crapshoot.

INDEX

Island Dining Index on page 248, Where to Stay Index on pages 292–294.

Island Dining Index on page 248, Where to Stay Index on pages 292–294.

INDEX

Island Dining Index on page 248, Where to Stay Index on pages 292–294.

Island Dining Index on page 248, Where to Stay Index on pages 292–294.

INDEX

Island Dining Index on page 248, Where to Stay Index on pages 292–294.

INDEX

311

Island Dining Index on page 248, Where to Stay Index on pages 292–294.